Welcome ...and congratulations!

Congratulations? For what? Well, studies show that the single most important factor in a divorce is starting off with the right information. The fact that you are reading my book shows you have a desire to know and participate that will lead you to successful solutions. You are definitely on the right path.

My life's work has been developing ways to help people take some control when going through a divorce—one of life's toughest passages. Divorce is hard enough without having to struggle against a legal system that tends to make things worse instead of better. If you follow my advice you won't have to go through that.

Divorce Helpline. After 30 years of producing materials to help people help themselves, the next step was to reinvent the practice of law. My goal was to develop a way for lawyers to help people in a way that would be effective and affordable; a practice that would solve problems, not cause them. So, in 1989, Sherman, Williams & Lober was formed and Divorce Helpline was born. Over time we grew and recently have become Sherman, Naraghi, Woodcock & Pipersky, with more talent and energy than ever to bring you the best and most effective service in California (or anywhere).

Many people can get through a divorce without any help outside the covers of my books—and well over a million people have done so. The books are as complete as I know how to make them without becoming cumbersome, but books can't replace years of experience. People with some resources to protect will find that doing their own divorce with the help of an experienced Divorce Helpline attorney can save money and bring peace of mind. This is just one more tool we have invented to help you help yourself. You get to choose what works best for you.

This is a book you can talk to. If you have questions to ask or problems to solve, or if you want a friendly, reliable attorney to act as your coach or "just do it" for you, call Divorce Helpline. Tell them Ed Sherman sent you.

Ed Sherman

PS - I invite you to get free tips from me by email. Go to **www.nolodivorce.com/tips** and sign up.

Doing your own divorce doesn't mean that you can't get help.

The important thing is that you keep control of your own case. We created Divorce Helpline to provide legal support and practical advice for people doing their own divorces. When you use Divorce Helpline you are still doing your own divorce because the control of your case and your life stays in your hands, where it belongs.

At Divorce Helpline we are expert at helping you solve problems, settle issues, negotiate agreements and get through your divorce in the best way possible. We do not take cases to court; instead we used discussion, negotiation, mediation, collaborative divorce and arbitration. Our highly experienced, top-quality attorneys have helped over 60,000 people since 1990, so we can almost certainly help you.

We are friendly, supportive, easy to talk to and easy to reach. Call and ask for more information about how Divorce Helpline can help you

Video Conference Available

Consult with us in a secure video connection or in a group conference for negotiation or mediation. There is no additional charge for this service.

All you need is a computer, broadband and a webcam.

Call for an appointment and easy setup instructions.

Tools to keep you out of court

www.nolodivorce.com

Get free email tips from the author
www.nolodivorce.com/tips

Start any case and finish it if no opposition in court
HOW TO DO YOUR OWN DIVORCE

This is the book you use to start any case. It is the **only** book you'll need if your spouse doesn't oppose you in court. Could be long gone, doesn't care, or you two can settle divorce issues peacfully. Explains the law, provides advice, and step-by-step instructions with a sample agreement and all the forms you'll need to complete a peaceful divorce.

For cases that aren't going smoothly (or might not)
MAKE ANY DIVORCE BETTER

This is the book you use to keep easy cases easy, or turn difficult cases into easier ones. Shows you specific steps you can take to reduce upset, insecurity, conflict, protect children. How to talk to your Ex, how to negotiate, how to organize your facts, documents and your thinking. This is the newer, better version of the famous, award-winning *Divorce Solutions*. CD with worksheets included.

For cases that seem headed for court
HOW TO SOLVE DIVORCE PROBLEMS—*In or Out of Court*

This great book by Ed Sherman shows you how to get the information you need from you Ex, how to defend against legal action or take your own case to court if you need to go there. Or, if you *want* an attorney to take over your case, how to choose and supervise one and know if your case is being handled competently, and how to fire an attorney who is not giving good service. Includes free Bonus CD full of forms and resources to help make your job easier.

Book 1 and Book 2
To use **Solve Divorce Problems** you also need **How to Do Your Own Divorce**. For cases in court, they work together. So for convience, in the text of both books we sometimes refer **DYOD** as as Book 1 and **SDP** as Book 2.

How to Do Your Own
DIVORCE
in California

31st Edition

A GUIDE FOR PETITIONERS
AND RESPONDENTS

By **Ed Sherman**
Divorce Specialist Attorney

Everything You Need for an Uncontested Divorce
of a marriage or a domestic partnership

Nolo Press
o c c i d e n t a l
501 Mission Street, Suite 2
Santa Cruz, CA 95060
(831) 466-9922

DATED MATERIAL
THIS BOOK WAS PRINTED IN
JANUARY 2008

Do not use an old edition of this book!
Out-of-date information can cause trouble

Laws and forms change often, usually in January and sometimes July. This book is printed at least once each year, sometimes twice, to give you the latest information. Using an old edition can be dangerous if the information or forms in it are wrong. **Make sure you are using the most current edition.** If the date above is over one year old, you are taking chances.

FREE UPDATE NOTICES
look for new laws, forms & fixes
at www.nolodivorce.com/alerts

30% OFF ON UPDATES

If you have an old copy of this book and want to update, tear off the cover and send it to us with $20.97 plus tax and shipping = $27.49 total. You can also get our great companion book, *How to Solve Divorce Problems* for 30% off, too—that's only $53.73 including tax and shipping for *both* books! If you bought your book from our site, just call up and say so, that's all.

© 1971–2008 by Charles E. Sherman
ISBN: 0-944508-66-9   ISBN13/EAN: 978-0-944508-66-4
Library of Congress Control Number: 2007943358

Design and graphics: Ed Sherman
Cover design: Ed Sherman, Ben & Shirley Thompson
Photo credits: Page 1 and 3: Todd Tsukushi
　　　　　　　　　Page 2: David Weintraub

TABLE OF CONTENTS

Part One — All About Divorce

Part 2—How to do your own Regular Dissolution

Part 3—Summary Procedures

Blank Forms — 175

Index

A combined index for *How to Do Your Own Divorce* and *How to Solve Divorce Problems* can be found online at **www.nolodivorce.com/index**

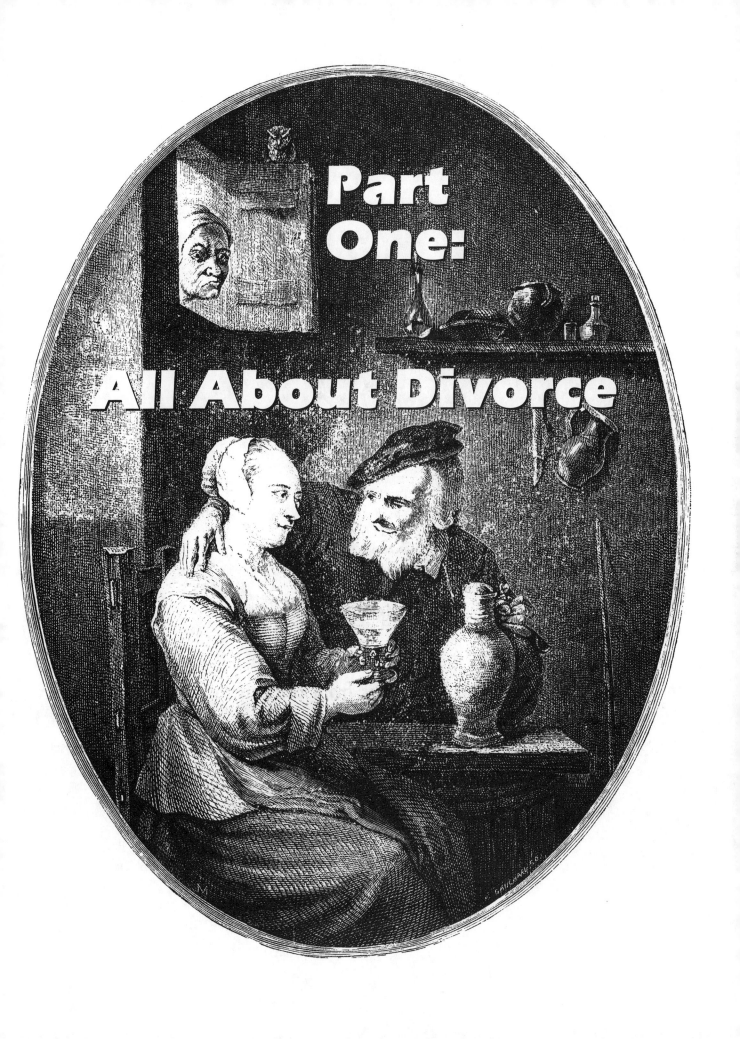

Part One:

All About Divorce

This book is dedicated
to all of my clients
and to my ex-wife
from whom I learned so much
about the subjects in these pages

•

Thanks to my partners at Divorce Helpline
who helped to improve this book

•

Free email tips from the author
www.nolodivorce.com/tips

1
DOING YOUR OWN DIVORCE

The first thing you need to know is that the word "divorce" is technically incorrect. Marriages and registered domestic partnerships in California are dissolved, so what you get is a dissolution, not a divorce. Still, we've never heard anyone say, "I'm going to dissolve you!" so we use both "divorce" and "dissolution" in this book, but you can call it anything you like outside of court.

Registered domestic partners. Starting January 1, 2005, California marriage and divorce laws apply equally to registered domestic partners. However, domestic partnership is new and acquires its rules almost entirely by reference to existing marital laws that use terms like *spouse, marriage, husband, wife,* and so on, without adaptation to suit domestic partners. Likewise, in this book we ask domestic partners to read with the understanding that marital terms apply to them, too, unless clearly stated otherwise.

Over 150,000 divorces are filed in California each year. When this book came out in 1971, less than 1% were done without an attorney. Today, with the help of this book and our Divorce Helpline service, nearly 60% are now done without lawyers. Californians are saving at least half a *billion* dollars every year in unnecessary legal fees.

1.1 Can you do your own divorce? Should you?

Yes! You can! Since this book was first published, millions of Californians just like you have done their divorces without retaining lawyers, so you can almost certainly do it too.

Yes! You *should* do your own divorce. Most people would be better off if they did not *retain* an attorney unless they have a very clear reason for doing so. The legal process—and the way attorneys work in it—tends to cause trouble, raise the level of conflict and greatly increase your expense. We will tell you when you should get help and how to get help from an attorney without *retaining* him/her to take over your case. If you can work things out with your spouse without going to court, this book is all you'll need.

What if things don't go smoothly? If you have trouble agreeing about things, *Make Any Divorce Better* gives you specific steps you can take to reduce conflict, solve problems, talk to your spouse, and negotiate a settlement. If your case is headed for court, you'll want Book 2, *How to Solve Divorce Problems* for how to use legal action or how to defend yourself if your Ex takes legal action.

1.2 What "do your own divorce" means

Too many people think doing their own divorce means filling out forms and maybe getting their spouse to sign an agreement. That's a big mistake. Divorce is not about filling out forms; it is about thinking things out, solving problems, and making sound decisions. Likewise, if your case needs a settlement agreement, having it typed and signed is not the point. The value of an agreement is in the depth and detail with which you think things through, discuss issues, and work things out between you.

A lot of people are reluctant to think things through and make decisions, and they will do almost *anything* to avoid talking things over in detail with their partners. This is completely understandable, given the nature of divorce, but it is something you need to do if you don't want to become a victim of divorce. If necessary, you can get help from an attorney-mediator to help you work out an agreement.

Doing your own divorce means that you do not *retain* an attorney—no one should unless they have a clear reason for doing so, but that doesn't mean you can't get advice and help from an attorney. Doing your own divorce means that you take responsibility for your case, your decisions, your life. You find out what the rules and legal standards are, how they apply to your case, maybe you call up Divorce Helpline for some advice, then you decide what you want, what's fair, how to deal with your spouse, what to do next. If your spouse is in the picture and cares what happens, it means having detailed discussions—perhaps with help—to reach a thoroughly negotiated agreement.

At Divorce Helpline, we help over 3,500 people each year and from them we have learned why people become victims of the legal system. People often feel they can't deal with their divorces, their partners, themselves. They feel overwhelmed, so they want someone else to take over and just do it, make it go away. The attorney says, "I'll take your case; I'll take care of everything; I'll get it done for you." It sounds good, but it isn't true. In the end, even if you retain an attorney, you will be gathering the information, making the decisions and, very likely, negotiating the terms yourself. Most people do.

1.3   What it means to "retain" an attorney—and a better idea

It is okay to use an attorney, but most people should never *retain* one in their divorce unless there is a clear reason for doing so. Here's why.

When you *retain* an attorney, the attorney takes professional responsibility to act in your behalf— to represent you. You are *literally* handing over your power and authority to act.

Standards of professional conduct require any attorney who represents you—even one with a good attitude—to act in ways that will complicate your case and make it worse instead of better. Attorneys tend to take cases to court quickly, even when that is likely to cause upset and make settlement more difficult.

An attorney who represents you must go to great lengths to protect himself against later malpractice claims by his own client—you. This means doing things for the attorney's benefit instead of yours. California's leading family law authority advises attorneys to either get clients to waive the attorney's responsibility or else "do the absolute maximum" in every case. Doing the maximum may or may not help you but it will certainly raise the level of conflict and it will cost plenty.

Never forget that when you *retain* an attorney, the more trouble you have, the more money the attorney makes. That's hardly an incentive to keep things simple.

Our system of justice is known as "the adversary system." It began in the middle ages when trial by combat meant that whoever survived was right, and that approach to justice forms the basis of our legal system today. The attorney works in our system as a combatant, but that is not what you want for solving family and personal problems. Law schools do not require courses in counseling or communications. They teach aggressive and defensive strategy and how to get the advantage in every case. Lawyers are taught to look for problems, not solutions.

It would be nice if you could get help from an experienced attorney with a good attitude who does not want to be retained, but few attorneys will take an interest in your case unless you retain them. That's why we created Divorce Helpline, operated by Sherman, Naraghi, Woodcock & Pipersky. This is the only law firm we know of that works exclusively on divorce settlement. Instead of "taking" your case, we serve as your guide and assistant. When you use Divorce Helpline, you are still doing your own divorce because the responsibility and control of the case stays in your hands. We guide you, help resolve problems, handle the red tape and paperwork, but your case doesn't get out of control because *you* are in charge.

1.4 Advantages to doing your own divorce

Getting a good divorce

Studies show that active participation in your divorce is the single most important factor in getting a good divorce. "Good divorce" means such things as better compliance with agreements and orders after the divorce, less post-divorce conflict, less post-divorce litigation, more good will, and better co-parenting.

People who take an active role generally do much better emotionally and legally than those who try to avoid the work and responsibility for solving their divorce problems. This doesn't mean you shouldn't get help from an attorney—it means you should be actively involved, become informed about the rules and make your own decisions. Put yourself in charge of your case; run your own life.

It's much cheaper

Perhaps the most obvious advantage to doing your own divorce, even with the help of Divorce Helpline, is the savings in cost. When an attorney takes your case, the initial retainer could be anywhere from $750 to $5,000, but the retainer is only the beginning. The total cost will typically be a *minimum* of $2,000 to $5,000 *for each party* for even the simplest cases, and many attorneys admit that few of their cases *stay* simple! An informal survey in 1987 revealed that the average cost of a represented divorce in LA, Orange County and other urban areas is about $18,000 *for each party.* A contested case can cost hundreds of thousands *on each side!*

Keeping it simple

Most people start off with a case that is either fairly simple or one that could probably become simple if it is handled right. Such cases don't usually stay simple after an attorney is retained. Divorces tend to be fairly sensitive and it doesn't take much to stir them up, but lawyers have a way of making almost anything more complicated, more stirred up, worse instead of better. This is because of the way they are trained and the way the system works.

When one spouse or partner gets an attorney, the other is likely to get one too, and then the fun really begins. Two attorneys start off costing just double, but pretty soon they are writing letters, filing motions and doing standard attorney-type things, just like they were taught. Now we have a contested case, more fees and charges, and a couple of very upset spouses.

In the end, you will still have to negotiate your settlement with your spouse. Over 90% of all cases settle without trial, but when attorneys are retained, settlement usually comes after the parties are emotionally depleted and their bank accounts exhausted. Why go through all that?

The moral of this story is this: don't *retain* an attorney. If you do it entirely by yourself, or with the help of Divorce Helpline, there's a much better chance of keeping a simple case simple and of reaching a settlement much earlier.

1.5 How to start a divorce—Petitioners and Respondents

The Petitioner and the Respondent. Every divorce starts with a Petition. The Petitioner is the person who first files papers and gets the case started. The Respondent is the other party. A Response need not be filed, but it is a good idea, otherwise the inactive person has little say about when or how the divorce is completed, unless there is already a written agreement. In general, the more both parties participate, the better. After a Response is filed, the divorce can only be completed by written agreement or court trial. Agreement is better.

Equality. Once a Response is filed, Respondent has equal standing and there is no legal difference between the parties or their rights. Respondent can take any legal step in our books, just as Petitioner can. Where instructions indicate "Petitioner," Respondent can substitute "Respondent" and take the same action.

The Petition. To get your case started, you file a Petition and serve it on your spouse or partner. The only thing you need to know before you do this is that you want to start a divorce. The issues can all be sorted out and resolved later. On the other hand, it wouldn't hurt to read through Part One before you start.

Advantages to serving the Petition:
- Starts the clock ticking on waiting periods.
- Automatic restraining orders take effect.
- Helps establish the date of separation.
- Has psychological value for Petitioner and tells Respondent a divorce is really going to happen.

Possible downside: serving papers can stir up conflict if you don't properly prepare the Respondent.

Start smoothly. Unless your partner is an abuser/controller, you will probably want to start things off as nicely as possible. An abrupt start will probably increase conflict and an upset spouse is more likely to run to an attorney who will probably make your case more complicated. So, take some time to prepare your spouse and let him/her get used to the idea that a divorce is about to get under way. If you aren't comfortable discussing things in person, use mail or email. Let your spouse know you are committed to working out a settlement that you can both agree to and live with. Unless you are under time pressure, don't serve your Summons and Petition until your partner seems ready to receive the papers calmly.

The Response. A Response *should* be filed within 30 days of receiving the Summons and Petition, but *can* be filed any time before Petitioner declares the Respondent's default (chapter 17). Filing a Response is not an aggressive act. In fact, it is usually a good idea for Respondent to take part in the action, especially if you have kids or property or debts to be divided. It is easy to do. The only disadvantages are Respondent's filing fee of about $320(see chapter 7.3), and the possibility that you might have to file a questionnaire about your case in order to avoid a case conference hearing (see page 98).

There are numerous advantage to filing a Response. If there's no Response, Respondent has little control over when and how the divorce is completed so the Respondent feels insecure. By filing, Respondent joins the case on an equal standing with Petitioner, so Respondent feels more a part of the process, more in the loop, more confident. Experience and studies show that the more Respondent participates, the better the divorce outcome is likely to be.

1.6 Three ways to get it done

After you file your Petition, there are only three ways you can make your way to the Judgment of Dissolution: 1) by default, 2) by contest, or 3) by written agreement.

The default divorce

In a default case, Respondent is served with the Petition but does nothing. No Response is filed, so the case is completed by default, without participation by Respondent. Default should be used only if you have little property or debts, no children, and no need for spousal or partner support, or in cases where Respondent is long gone or refuses to participate. If Respondent is around and cares what happens, it is better if a Response is filed.

The contested divorce

If a Response is filed, you can complete your divorce only by written agreement or by taking the case to court and having a judge decide issues that you can't settle. Until there is an agreement, your case is *technically* considered to be contested. Whether or not there is a battle and a lot of legal activity depends on how you go about solving problems and reaching agreement. If you have problems reaching agreement, read *Make Any Divorce Better*. If you end up in a court battle, get Book 2, *How to Solve Divorce Problems*.

Divorce by settlement agreement

When the problems are all solved and you finally reach an agreement, one of the parties files a stipulation (chapter 12.7) and steps out. The case is now uncontested and sails through. If your spouse is in the picture and you have children, significant property or debts, or you need to arrange spousal support, then you should make *every* effort to reach a written agreement on all issues. Look what you gain:

- You can be certain exactly what the orders in the Judgment will be.
- You can complete your case by mail and almost certainly won't have to go to court;
- Both parties participate and the Respondent can feel confident about letting the divorce go through without contest or representation because the terms of the judgment are all settled;
- It invariably leads to better relations with your ex-spouse or partner. Where there are children, this is extremely important; and,
- You are far more likely to get compliance with terms of the divorce after the judgment.

These advantages are so important that you should struggle long and hard to get an agreement. Chapter 6 discusses written agreements in detail. Book 2 tells you how to talk to your spouse, solve problems in or out of court, with or without legal action, and negotiate a settlement.

1.7 Solving divorce problems

To agree or not to agree, that is the question. This is the point that divides easy cases from difficult ones. Inability to agree is almost never a matter of law—it is about the personalities of the parties or their lawyers. The main reason for a difficult divorce is that at least one person is terribly upset—angry, frightened, distrustful—and this is something that can usually be fixed with patience and understanding (see Book 2). However, if one spouse is a controller/abuser, the divorce can become

MAP – How to get there from here

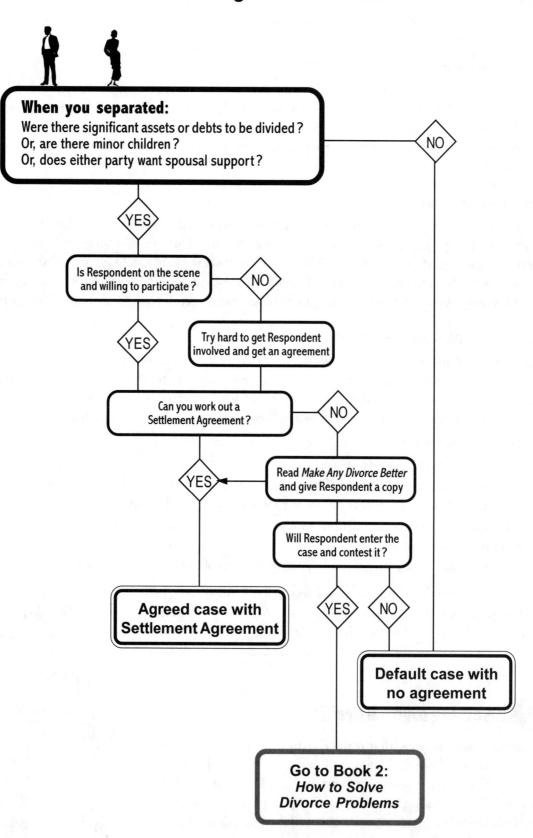

When you separated:
Were there significant assets or debts to be divided?
Or, are there minor children?
Or, does either party want spousal support?

NO

YES

Is Respondent on the scene and willing to participate?

NO

Try hard to get Respondent involved and get an agreement

YES

Can you work out a Settlement Agreement?

NO

Read *Make Any Divorce Better* and give Respondent a copy

YES

Will Respondent enter the case and contest it?

YES

NO

Agreed case with Settlement Agreement

Default case with no agreement

Go to Book 2:
How to Solve Divorce Problems

just another way to continue the control/abuse, and the solution could be much more difficult.

If your case might turn into a fight, remember this: it is one thing to get an order against someone, but it is very much another thing to enforce that order. Especially in cases with children, a dissolution is a change in your relationship but not the end of it. You still have to deal with each other in the future because of the kids. Therefore, in more ways than one, it pays to work things out if you can do so fairly and honorably.

If you can't agree on basic issues peacefully, wait a while to see if things settle down. Read my book, *Make Any Divorce Better* andlearn specific things you can do to reduce insecurity, upset and conflict and how to negotiate an agreement. I suggest that you send a copy of *Make Any Divorce Better* to your spouse, then try to discuss some of the ideas in it. This can get you talking about practical, constructive things. Your spouse may misunderstand what a divorce is really about and how things work. Informed people are usually less frightened or emotional, easier to talk to. Call Divorce Helpline because they are expert at helping people solve problems and reach agreement. Ask your spouse to call, too. For cases that seem headed to court, get Book 2, *How to Solve Divorce Problems,* which shows you how to handle a case in court so you can either do it yourself or know how to supervise an attorney.

Mediation. If you are unable to work out an agreement on your own, you should try mediation, preferably with a family law attorney-mediator who will work with both parties to help you communicate, solve problems, break through impasse and settle things fairly. Mediation is not just for friendly divorces. Angry, conflicted couples are especially in need of mediation and stand to gain the most, particularly if they have children. Mediation can be very effective, even in cases with high conflict, when conducted by a good family law attorney-mediator like those at Divorce Helpline. Unlike many mediators, if the parties can't even agree to try mediation, they are willing to contact the other side and try to arrange a meeting. We work by phone throughout California or at our offices in Santa Cruz, Sacramento, San Jose, San Francisco, Walnut Creek, San Diego, Los Angeles, Encino and Irvine. They can even do telephone mediation, which can be surprisingly effective and a lifesaver if parties can't meet at one location in person.

1.8 When you should get some help

In some situations, you can get a lot of good from a little advice. In *any* case, you can get peace of mind from knowing you are doing things right. A few hundred dollars for advice may not seem unreasonable when weighed against the value of your property, debts, possible tax savings, all future support payments, and the importance of a good parenting plan. You can often save more than you spend.

If you have any one of the situations listed below in your case, you have good reason to get some expert advice. Weigh the cost of getting advice against what you stand to lose if you don't.

SITUATIONS THAT CALL FOR PROFESSIONAL ADVICE
Property
- The division of assets and debts is not equal.
- Home or real estate is being kept to sell later.
- A major asset is being divided or sold—avoiding capital gains problems.

- You aren't sure how to value some assets.
- Stock options: valuation, division, relationship to child and spousal (partner) support.
- Separate and community money was invested (mixed together) in a major asset.
- Pension from employment during marriage—how to value; how to divide without penalty.
- Your estate is valuable so it's worth taking extra care, getting good advice about it.
- One or both parties are self-employed owners of a business or professional practice.

Debts

- Lots of debts; how to protect yourself from debts of your spouse.
- Either party might declare bankruptcy.
- Joint credit card or other accounts not closed.

Your spouse (solutions for these problems are discussed in Make Any Divorce Better and Book 2)

- You can't agree about important issues.
- You can't get information from your spouse about assets, debts, or income.
- You suspect your spouse might be hiding assets.
- Your spouse is threatening you, the children or the marital property.

Children

- Disagreement over parenting arrangements.
- One parent doesn't want the other to move.
- Either parent earns over $30,000—consider saving on taxes by arranging for family support instead of child support.
- Special needs or health problems.

Spousal or partner support

- Marriage of 5 years or more.
- More than 20% difference in incomes.
- One spouse is not self-supporting.
- One spouse put the other through school or training.
- Preschool children.
- Special needs or health problems.

Personal

- With a good income and busy schedule, you would be better off if someone else did the paperwork.
- You want to be sure you're doing the right thing and know things are being done right.
- You don't understand your situation or what to do about it.
- You want help and suggestions for how to negotiate with your spouse.

1.9 Who can help? How much will it cost?

Friends and relatives are the least reliable sources of advice. Accept all the moral support you can get, but when they give you advice, just smile and say "Thank you," but do not take it seriously. Also be wary of "common knowledge." If you didn't get it from this book or a family law specialist attorney in California, *don't trust it!* Just because you like or trust someone doesn't make them right.

Legal Document Assistants (paralegals)

Non-attorneys who offer legal forms services directly to the public are called Legal Document Assistants (LDAs) and must register unless working under the supervision of an attorney or non-profit organization. In theory, you tell an LDA what you want to say on which forms, then they type them up and handle the secretarial work. In practice, they provide more guidance. Rates are anywhere from $200 to $800 for doing divorce paperwork. We introduced this innovation in legal service in 1972 and it has since changed the face of the legal map.

No particular education or training is required to be an LDA, but the California Association of Legal Document Assistants (CALDA), offers its members training and promotes high standards in education, ethics and business practices. We are a Sustaining Member of CALDA. There are many CALDA members in our Directory at the back of this book, or you can find one near you at their website: **www.calda.org**.

LDAs can't give you reliable legal advice, nor should you have one prepare your settlement agreement unless they are using Nolo's DealMaker software or closely following the example in this book. Just as when hiring a lawyer or mechanic, be careful who you hire. Ask how long he/she has been in business and check references. If you know exactly what you want and have no legal questions and no problems, an experienced and reliable LDA is a good way to get your paperwork done.

For a list of divorce services near you, look in the back of this book or go to www.nolodivorce.com/dir

Court Facilitators

Every county has a Family Law Facilitator's office where you can get free assistance, at least with support issues: determining the correct amount, understanding rules and forms, establishing a child support order and enforcing it. In many counties, that's all they do, while in other counties they will help you with other aspects of your case. Most offer self-help seminars. We hear that the quality of service ranges from poor to excellent, mostly depending on the availability of additional funding. Demand far exceeds supply, so it takes a fair amount of time and persistence to actually get in and get help. If you have time to spare—or no better option—you should go see what help you can get. The more prepared you are, the more effective their help will be. Don't forget to take all your notes and paperwork with you when you go in. For contact information, call your clerk's office or go to **www.nolodivorce.com/links**.

Lawyers

Lawyers who *specialize* in divorce know a lot that could help you, but, because of the way the system works and the way lawyers work, they will almost certainly create unnecessary conflict and expense if you retain one. Unfortunately, getting information and advice from attorneys without retaining them can be tricky, because they don't really want to help you help yourself; they want to be retained to do it all.

Attorneys will frequently do the first interview for a fairly small fee, but too often they spend that time convincing you that you need them to handle your case. Hourly rates can run from $100 to $450, but $175–350 per hour is normal. Most attorneys require a retainer—$1,200 to $5,000 is typical—but the amount doesn't matter because the final bill can be *much* higher. Few attorneys will give you a definite maximum figure for the whole job. You are doing *very* well if you end up spending less than $2,500 *per spouse* on the *simplest* case. The average in LA and Orange counties when both spouses are represented is *well* over $18,000 *per spouse!*

Limited representation. A small but growing number of lawyers are offering representation limited to specific tasks or portions of your case while you keep overall responsibility. For example, only to draft your agreement, or only to appear in court if you are asked to show up there for some reason, or just to file and appear on one motion. We've heard that some county bar associations actively discourage attorneys from offering this sort of service, but, nonetheless, it *is* becoming more common. If you need a bit of service from a family law attorney, ask if they offer "limited representation" or "unbundling," the two names by which this is known. Or, call Divorce Helpline: we've been doing this sort of thing since 1990.

Collaborative divorce. Increasingly popular, in this approach, spouses and their attorneys pledge in writing not go to court or threaten to go to court; rather, they will use negotiation and mediation to reach a settlement. If there's no settlement, the spouses will have to get different attorneys to take the case into litigation. Ideally, the collaborative team will include some other professionals, such as a divorce coach, family counselor, child specialist, accountant, or financial planner. Collaborative divorce has a good track record and, even with all the professional services you get, it will still cost less than a court battle.

Divorce Helpline

Divorce Helpline was created to change the way attorneys practice in divorce cases and to provide expert support for people who are doing their own. Divorce Helpline is operated by the law offices of Sherman, Naraghi, Woodcock & Pipersky. We will not litigate (go to court) because we don't believe in it. Instead, our expert family law attorneys work exclusively as your guide and assistant, helping you plan, solve problems, and reach a fair settlement. We offer advice, mediation, arbitration and collaborative law, working by telephone throughout California, or at our offices in Santa Cruz, Sacramento, San Jose, San Francisco, Walnut Creek, San Diego, Los Angeles, Encino and Irvine. Divorce Helpline attorneys are trained in mediation and communication, and are good at solving problems. We'll answer your questions but can do a better job for you when we do the *whole* case—the paperwork and the settlement agreement— as well as giving you advice. That way we have *all* the information, not just the small bit you are asking about. When we do the whole case we often find problems to solve and ways to save money that people don't know to ask about. Our methods have proven to be highly successful and very affordable.

You can learn more about Divorce Helpline, including our rates and services, at **www.divorcehelp.com**, or call 800-359-7004 for a free explanation of how we work and how we can help you.

1.10 Looking ahead

As mentioned in chapter 1.5 above, you can file your Petition and serve it at any time, assuming you have arranged for a smooth start by preparing your spouse or partner to receive it. You can then take some time to make decisions and work out the details about your property, support, and kids. We discuss the basic rules of these subjects in chapters 3 through 5, then in chapter 6 we show you how everything can be wrapped up in a settlement agreement once you get things worked out.

While you are reading through the next few chapters, at some point you should jump ahead to the Judgment (chapter 18) and take a look at the Judgment and the various attachments to the Judgment that are relevant to your case. Read the language so you understand the kinds of orders that are used in Judgments so you can understand where all this information you are reading about will end up. Then you'll have a better idea of where you are going while reading about how to get there.

2

BASIC INFORMATION ABOUT DIVORCE

2.1   Dissolution, nullity, and legal separation

There are three ways a court can end a marriage or registered domestic partnership: dissolution, nullity, and legal separation. In any of these procedures, the court can make orders on property, debts, child custody, child support, and spousal or partner support.

A nullity (formerly called annulment) declares that the marriage or partnership never existed, while a dissolution says that the relationship will cease to exist at the end of the dissolution. Both have the effect of restoring the parties to single status, but the nullity permits you to remarry immediately after the hearing, while with a dissolution you sometimes have to wait a bit. Since the grounds for nullity are more complicated than for a dissolution, and since courts tend to be more strict in nullity cases, we recommend that you do not try to do your own nullity. This book does not show you how to get one. If you want a nullity, see an attorney or call Divorce Helpline.

A legal separation makes orders about children, support and property, but the parties remain legally joined while living apart. This is useful to couples who can't divorce for religious or moral reasons but also can't continue to live together. There are a few situations where a legal separation is a better choice— where sizeable Social Security benefits, Veterans' benefits, retirement, or other benefits may be lost if there is a dissolution, or where a long-term spouse with an illness or disability *might* be able to stay on the employed spouse's health insurance—call the plan to see if they allow this. The companion CD that comes with this book has an article about legal separation in the Reading Room section and the Kit section has instructions for how to get one using the forms in the back of this book.

A dissolution (divorce) will usually serve your purposes as well or better than either of the other methods. That's what the rest of this book is about.

2.2   Regular vs. Summary Dissolution

The traditional way to get a divorce we will call a *Regular* Dissolution. There are also simpler procedures called *Summary* Dissolution for married couples and *Termination* for domestic partners. Not everyone is eligible, and of those who are eligible, not everyone will want to do it that way. The regular method has advantages even for those who are qualified to use the simpler methods.

Summary Dissolution for married couples must be filed before the fifth wedding anniversary, and they *must* have prepared and signed a property agreement dividing marital assets and allocating their debts. Both must give up all rights to spousal support. When you sign the Petition, you and your spouse will be swearing that:

1. Both spouses have read and understood the Summary Dissolution Booklet (you get this at the Clerk's office, along with the necessary forms for your case);
2. One spouse has lived in California for at least six months and in the county in which you file for at least three months immediately before you file your Petition;

3. There are no minor children and the wife is not pregnant;

4. Neither spouse has *any* interest in real estate *anywhere*, not including a lease of a residence occupied by either party if it terminates within one year after the petition is filed and there's no option to buy;

5. There is less than $4,000 in community debts, not counting car loans;

6. There is less than $32,000 in community property, not counting cars; and,

7. Neither spouse owns over $32,000 separately, not counting cars.

Still interested? If you meet these requirements you can use the Summary procedure. For six months after you file the Petition, there is a waiting period during which time either spouse can back out simply by filing a form. If revoked, either spouse can file a Regular Dissolution, but some time will have been lost. If not revoked, then after the waiting period, either spouse can file a simple form requesting the final Judgment. Unless and until the final Judgment has been requested and entered, there is *no* divorce.

How to get a Summary Dissolution is discussed further in chapter 22.

Notice of Termination of Domestic Partnership is almost exactly parallel to the Summary Dissolution procedure above, so read those requirements to see if you qualify. The only differences are that the mandatory booklet and Notice of Termination form are obtained from the Secretary of State and the Notice of Termination is filed with that office, and there is no residency requirement *if* your partnership was created in California—in that case, you can file even if both partners no longer live here. How to do the Termination of Domestic Partnership is discussed further in chapter 23.

Comments

A simple procedure is a good idea, but there is some risk. This is because either spouse (or partner) can revoke the proceeding at any time before the relationship is dissolved. For *at least* six months, maybe more, your dissolution is at risk. Divorce often involves personal drama and emotional turmoil—a time when otherwise reasonable people can play bad games. Are you absolutely certain that your spouse won't spoil the process for the next six months or so? Finally, if your five-year deadline is near, it would be a big mistake to rush things just to get filed in time.

Advice

Even if you *are* eligible for the simpler procedure, don't do it unless you can start in plenty of time to make important decisions, get the property agreement worked out and the papers filed without feeling under pressure to meet the deadline. Divorce is too important to rush, and mistakes may come back to haunt you later. And, do not do the simpler procedure unless you can be certain your agreements with your spouse are firm and mutual. If there is even a small chance that during the next six or more months one spouse might become temperamental, uncertain, or unstable enough to revoke the procedure, then you would both be better off filing a Regular Dissolution to begin with. It's a bit more trouble but it is a lot more stable and certain. It costs the same for filing fees.

2.3 Grounds for dissolution

The primary ground for dissolution in California is "irreconcilable differences." In a Regular Dissolution you are also allowed to use "incurable insanity," which refers to people who are medically, scientifically crazy. Your spouse may seem weird to you, or even dangerous, but that may not be enough to be found legally insane. The insanity case is too complicated for you to present without an attorney, but if you are disturbed because your spouse is "different," then you can definitely go ahead and use the grounds of irreconcilable differences. In practice, anyone who wants a divorce has irreconcilable differences. You have irreconcilable differences when there is any reason at all for not continuing the marriage *and* if you are sure there can be no reconciliation. You don't need to actually state a reason—just the fact that one of the spouses wants a divorce is enough. Almost all divorces are granted on these grounds.

2.4   Residency requirements

For married couples, California has jurisdiction over their marriage and the power to dissolve it only if at least one spouse has lived in California long enough: either you or your spouse must have lived in California for at least six months, and in the county where you file your papers for at least three months, just prior to filing the Petition. Being away temporarily, as on a business trip or vacation, does not count against your residency time. **Domestic partners** who registered in California have no residency requirement because they consented to the court's jurisdiction when they signed the registration form. Partnerships created elsewhere can be dissolved only if the same residency requirements as for married couples are met. **After you file your Petition** there is no more requirement for residency, so you can move anywhere you wish. However, if you have children, you can't take them out of the state without the written consent of your spouse (see chapter 2.7), and, while most cases can be completed by mail, there is a small chance that you *might* have to return for a hearing (see chapter 20.1).

2.5   Serving papers—giving notice to your spouse

In our system, any lawsuit is a struggle between two contestants conducted before an impartial authority, the judge. It seems obvious (doesn't it?) that you can't have a fair contest if the other side doesn't know one is going on. The essence of notice is that your spouse or partner is given or sent a Summons and a copy of your Petition and can therefore be presumed to know what the suit is about, what you want, and when and where the contest is to be held. The court cannot act in your case unless you properly notify your spouse or partner of the lawsuit.

Chapter 12 shows how this is done. The notice requirement is especially important in cases that go by default, which is what happens when your spouse or partner gets notice and doesn't file a Response. Your spouse or partner has seen the Petition, so not showing up is like saying that you can have your way. Subject to the judge's approval, that is what you will get.

2.6   Jurisdiction and the power of the court to act

Your marriage or partnership might come under the court's power (jurisdiction) for reasons discussed in chapter 2.4 above, but that does not mean it necessarily has authority over your spouse or partner personally. To make an *enforceable* order against a *person*, the court must have power (personal jurisdiction) over that person. This can get complicated, but what it comes down to is this: if you want the Respondent to pay money (support, debts), transfer property, or do or not do any other act, the court's power to make that kind of order will be most clear if your spouse is either served in person *inside* the State of California (chapter 12.4), or your spouse signs the Appearance and Waiver form (chapter 12.7). If neither of those methods of giving notice is possible, the enforcement of personal orders depends on whether or not your spouse had sufficient "minimum contacts" with California. If you can't serve your spouse as described, get advice. Possibly your local Facilitator's office will help you or you can call Divorce Helpline for advice.

Automatic restraining orders

Some basic restraining orders are built into the Summons and become automatically effective in every case when the Summons is served. Both parties are ordered by the court not to: (1) remove a child of the parties from the state without prior written permission of the other parent or order of the court; (2) transfer, sell or encumber (borrow against) *any* property except in the usual course of business or for necessities; (3) cancel, transfer or borrow against any insurance (including life, health, auto, disability) held for the benefit of either the other spouse or a minor child; (4) notify the other party at least five days in advance of any extraordinary expenses, not including attorney fees or court costs for this case.

These orders remain in effect until the date you get your Judgment. If you have use for even one of these orders in your case, get the Summons served on your spouse as quickly as possible. The restraining orders may not be enforceable if you can't serve your spouse personally inside the state (see 2.6). If you want any order to last beyond the date of the Judgment, you have to ask for it at the time of the hearing, give a good reason why the order you want is necessary, and write the order into your Judgment.

Nonautomatic restraining orders are also available, but they must be requested by special motion. Most significant of these are orders prohibiting your spouse from abusing, harassing or otherwise disturbing you or the children, and orders that your spouse must move out and stay away from the family residence. It is also possible to get quick, temporary orders for support, custody, or visitation. If you need any of these orders, see Book 2, *How to Solve Divorce Problems,* or call Divorce Helpline.

Enforcement of orders. Whoever violates a court order is guilty of contempt of court, a civil offense that is punishable by a threatening lecture from the judge and ma-a-aybe time in jail or a fine, depending on the seriousness of the offense. You will need Book 2 to take your spouse or partner to court for contempt.

Police: It is a felony/misdemeanor crime if either parent violates the order against taking a child from the state without written permission from the other parent. Violation of the other orders is a misdemeanor. If your spouse violates a restraining order, call the police first, then the D.A.'s office. Make sure you have a copy of the restraining order to show them, otherwise not much will happen.

If your spouse or partner abuses you physically or harasses you, call the police immediately—but *don't* call them unless you are willing to follow through and have your spouse prosecuted criminally. If you have good reason to believe that your spouse may abuse or harass you in the future, don't wait for something bad to happen—go to court immediately for a restraining order. Restraining orders are about 85–90% effective, but practical things you can do to help yourself are very important. Get in touch with a domestic abuse support group in your community. The law requires police agencies to keep a list of domestic abuse services in your area. Call the police with jurisdiction over your residence, work or school for a referral.

2.8 Mandatory disclosure of all marital information

Spouses and partners in a dissolution or legal separation are *required* to exchange court forms that disclose complete information about all their property and debts, as well as details of their income and expenses. Until the divorce is completely settled, you are required to keep each other updated immediately, in writing, of any new information. Disclosure forms are required to be exchanged by both parties before a written agreement is made for support or division of property and before the court can enter a Judgment of dissolution. The disclosure law is an extension of the duties spouses and partners owe each other, described in chapters 3.2 and 3.3. It is intended to ensure a full exchange of information between spouses and partners. How to do disclosure is discussed in chapter 14.

A side effect of disclosure law is that lawyers get to do lots of extra work in every divorce. If you want to keep your case simple and inexpensive, it is more important than ever that you do not *retain* an attorney and that you try very hard to settle differences on your own or with a mediator. You can probably do better by managing your own case. Read this book and use Divorce Helpline if you want help.

2.9 When is it over? How final is your judgment?

If you enter into a complete settlement agreement, the minute you sign it you have settled everything by contract. Your agreement will actually become your judgment and all you have left is the red tape it takes to get it. You are, for most practical purposes, done. When your Judgment is entered, your divorce is legally complete and you can remarry. *However....*

How final is your judgment? To be final, your judgment must have been obtained fairly and be based on complete and accurate disclosure. Traditionally, laws favor the finality of judgments in the belief that society is best served by having things over and done with for good and forever. Exceptions were few and limited until 1993, when lawmakers decided to make sure no spouse enters into a divorce agreement or suffers a judgment taken under unfair conditions. A divorce judgment can now be attacked and some or all of its orders can be set aside under the following circumstances:

• within two years of Entry of Judgment in case of duress (unfair pressure or force).
• within one year of Entry of Judgment in uncontested or agreed cases where there was some mistake of law or fact by one or both of the parties.
• within one year of the time a party discovers, or should have discovered, an actual fraud, where the party was kept in ignorance or otherwise fraudulently prevented from full participation.
• any time within one year of the time a party discovers, or should have discovered, perjury in the Declarations of Disclosure or Income and Expense Statements.
• any time within one year of the time a party discovers, or should have discovered, the failure to comply with disclosure requirements.

In all cases, the facts alleged must have materially affected the outcome and the party seeking relief must be benefited if relief is granted.

In summary, any divorce agreement or judgment is potentially subject to attack for an indefinite period of time due to high standards of care between spouses and partners, disclosure requirements, and the new rules extending the time for setting aside all or part of a divorce judgment. The greater risk is borne by a spouse or partner who managed community affairs because that person is presumably in possession of more information that can be hidden, overlooked or forgotten.

These new rules are meant to ensure disclosure of all information between spouses, but they also increase the opportunities for litigation and provide new weapons for revenge. These laws concern property and, to a lesser degree, support, but upset over any matters—child custody, for example—could easily find an outlet in property issues. What to do? How to make a judgment or an agreement stick?

How to make your judgment final. Attacks against the judgment are limited more by practical considerations than legal ones. It costs a lot of money and more in emotional determination to conduct a legal battle. This means your risk increases with the value of your estate *and* the amount of upset between the parties.

If you want to get on with your life and not have your divorce become a career, it is more important than ever to work for a fair resolution of all issues, emotional and financial, that satisfies both sides. Be open, fair and temperate in all dealings with your spouse; listen more than you speak; don't argue. If necessary, use mediation and even counseling or therapy. Be *very* careful and thorough with your disclosure declarations. Make sure you have a high-quality settlement agreement. If you have enough income or property to make a legal attack worthwhile, it is *not* a good idea to write your own or have a paralegal do it. A good agreement is one that has been thoroughly discussed, worked out in great detail, and is very carefully drafted. All facts have been disclosed and the parties have given each other open access to every document and record. If you do these things, you can go a long way toward making sure the divorce is really over when it's over.

2.10 Taxes

Almost every aspect of divorce can *possibly* have important tax consequences. Depending on your property and income, you might be able to save a lot of money by looking carefully into your tax situation and maybe getting expert tax advice, especially before making a settlement agreement, arranging support, or dividing or selling a major asset.

Domestic partners have significant differences from married couples in this area. Federal law does not recognize domestic partnership, so partners can file only as single or head of household, depending on whether they have dependents that will be recognized under federal tax law. California law requires partners to use the same filing status as is used on their federal income tax returns. For both federal and state returns, earned income may not be treated as community property for income tax purposes.

Married couples. If you don't want to file a joint return, you should know that Married Filing Separately may cost you more. To file as a single person for any year, your Judgment must be entered no later than December 31 of that year, and that means your Petition must be filed *and* served on your spouse before June 30. If you are desperate, you can get a Legal Separation first (no waiting period) and get your divorce later. As all issues are settled in the Legal Separation, the divorce case will be relatively simple, but you do have to pay a new filing fee and do another round of paperwork.

Some common tax issues will be raised elsewhere, more to call your attention to basic tax issues than to give detailed tax advice. Tax rules are too complicated and they change too frequently to be covered here in detail. Fortunately, there are some excellent pamphlets that tell you much of what you should know and they are absolutely free at your local IRS office. After that, if you want tax advice, see a tax accountant.

• IRS publication 504, Divorced or Separated Individuals. If you only get one, get this one.

- IRS publication 523, Selling Your Home.
- IRS publication 596, Earned Income Credit.
- IRS publication 503, Child and Dependent Care Expenses.
- IRS publication 594, The IRS Collection Process.

2.11 Attorney fees

In the past, people representing themselves couldn't get attorney fees because they had no attorney. However, the appellate court in Los Angeles decided in October 2002 that while you can't be reimbursed for your own time, you *can* be awarded the cost for attorneys who help you represent yourself. Asking a judge to award attorney fees is part of a *contested* case, so unless you make it part of your settlement agreement (chapter 6), we won't be dealing with it in this book. However, if your case fails to settle and you end up in court, you will be working in Book 2, *How to Solve Divorce Problems,* where it will then be appropriate to ask for an award to cover the cost of any attorney assistance.

2.12 Common questions and answers

a) **How much will it cost to do my own dissolution?** It now costs about $320 to file your papers in most counties. If Respondent files papers, there will also be a Response fee of a similar amount (see chapter 7.3). Add a few dollars for photocopies and postage, and that's it for costs. If you hire a lawyer, all of these charges will be added to the legal fee, so you will be paying them either way. People who are very, very poor can file an application to have the fees waived (see chapter 7.2).

b) **How long will it take?** A few months, at least. You can turn in the papers for getting your Judgment 31 days after notice is served on your spouse. As soon as your Judgment is entered, all orders are effective immediately *but* your marriage or partnership is not finally dissolved until at least six months after notice was served on your spouse (or, in the case of a Summary Dissolution, six months after the Petition was filed). However, if you are in no hurry, you can take up to five years (longer in some cases) to request the Judgment and finish your divorce.

c) **What if we've already divided our community property?** It is still community property and it stays that way until it is formally divided by a court. Even if it has already been divided by agreement of the parties and already transferred, both parties own it as tenants in common until changed by court order. Same for debts.

d) **What if we reconcile?** Reconciliation is a state of mind that goes beyond dating or occasionally sleeping together. But, what do you do about the dissolution if you are certain you no longer want a divorce? If no Response has been filed and no Judgment has been obtained, the case can be dismissed if Petitioner alone can file a Dismissal form. If there's been a Response, both parties have to sign. You can get a Dismissal form with instructions in the Kit section of the companion CD that comes with this book. However, if an order for support has been entered, you will need help to get the case dismissed.

e) When can I remarry? You can't remarry (or repartner) until after the Judgment has been entered and the date specified on it for termination of your marriage has passed—at least six months after the date the Summons was served. It is quite all right to wait longer.

f) What about those quick, cheap divorces from the Dominican Republic? Divorces from a foreign country are generally valid in the U.S. if they are valid in the country that granted the divorce. However, in cases where neither of the parties actually goes there to establish residency, such divorces will almost certainly be invalid in any U.S. court and any orders regarding your property, children and support will not be enforceable. Unless acting on the advice of a reliable attorney, don't waste your money on a phony piece of paper from a mail-order Dominican divorce scam.

g) Divorcing aliens. Resident aliens who are divorced after less than two years of marriage are in danger of losing their resident status and they and their dependent children may be in danger of deportation. There will, however, be no prejudice to status if the divorce was caused by child or spouse abuse. If there's a recent green card in your case, you should definitely consult an immigration attorney.

h) Divorce after legal separation. If you get a legal separation Judgment and later want to be divorced, you have to start from scratch and file a new case. However, it should be smooth and easy, just paperwork, as all issues will already have been decided in the legal separation.

3

DIVIDING PROPERTY AND DEBTS

In every divorce, you have to divide your community estate—the property and debts of the marriage or partnership—if there is any. Debts are a form of property (the negative form) so, when you see the word "property" below, always remember to think of your debts in the same terms.

- If you have *very* little or no property, just read 3.1–3.4, and 3.8.
- If you have *some* property, read it all!

3.1 Income, debts and your date of separation

Income, accumulations and debts of either party that are acquired *after* the date of separation are their own separate property, whether or not a divorce action has been filed. An exception would be retirement benefits or any other forms of delayed compensation that are community property to the extent earned during marriage or partnership even if paid out after separation or divorce.

Debts are a negative form of property so, along with any other property you may have, all unpaid debts must be characterized as either separate or community property; then, by agreement or court order, they must be either confirmed as the separate property of one party or assigned for payment by one party.

You are responsible for all *community* debts incurred by either party between the dates of marriage or partnership and separation. Debts from before marriage are the separate property and responsibility of whoever incurred them. Loans for the education and training of a spouse or partner are treated as the separate property of that person. In general, neither you nor your share of the community estate are liable for your spouse's debts after separation, *except* that you can be liable for debts incurred for the "common necessaries of life" for your spouse or the children—food, clothing, shelter, medicine—*unless* you have a written waiver of support or have settled the matter in court. So move right along; file your Petition and establish your claimed date of separation, even if nothing else is understood or settled yet.

You are responsible after separation for accounts that are in both of your names, or in the name of one party with a merchant who extended credit knowing you were married or partnered and who has no reason to know of your separation. It is very important for you to actually *close* all credit card accounts and accounts that were in use during your marriage—it is not enough to simply have your name removed. Open new accounts and get new credit cards in your separate names. Give written notice to all creditors that either party might have dealt with during the marriage—tell them that you are separated and will no longer be responsible for your partner's debts. Be sure to tell your spouse well in advance when you close accounts or take other steps that could have an effect on his/her life.

You will *always* be liable for any debt for which you were originally liable when it was incurred. This means that orders of the court and agreements between parties about who must pay which debts are *only* effective between the parties and do *not* affect the people you owe. If a debt incurred during marriage is assigned by court order to your partner and he/she fails to pay it, *you* still owe the money. The creditor can come after you or repossess the property or both. Your spouse may be in contempt of court or breach of contract, for all the good that does you.

If one spouse is worried that the other will not actually pay off debts as agreed—a very reasonable concern—try to get them all paid out of community funds *before* the CP is divided. Or have each spouse get a new loan *after* separation to pay off their share of the community debts. If nothing else works, make paying debts a matter of spousal or partner support so that all or part of the support will be paid directly to creditors—but get help if you do this because it could be tricky to draft.

Bankruptcy. If you are burdened by debts, read Nolo's book about bankruptcy or get advice through Divorce Helpline. If one spouse is considering a bankruptcy that includes community debts, the other spouse will be affected so therefore should be notified and given an opportunity to join. In general, it is better to complete your divorce settlement *before* filing for bankruptcy **Note:** Debts and property obligations incurred pursuant to dissolution or legal separation can't be discharged in bankruptcy, but the other spouse must respond quickly if notified of bankruptcy. Support claims have very high priority.

Date of Separation affects the character of both income and liability for debts, yet this is an ambiguous date, both emotionally and legally. In most cases, it won't particularly matter whether separation was one time or another. But, if the date of separation has significant financial consequences and there is a contest over the date, the date of separation is whenever you can prove that one spouse intended to make a complete, final break (not just a temporary separation), with *simultaneous* conduct furthering that intent. Living physically apart is indispensable, which generally requires a separate residence. It is possible to "live apart" in the same house, but this must be shown by clear, unambiguous conduct. Living physically apart does not, by itself, determine the matter because one can live apart without intending a final break. Courts consider evidence of all conduct and circumstances.

Let's suppose the wife earned a large commission on April 1. And say that on January 15 she had said, "I'm leaving you for good and this isn't like the other times I said it; this time I really mean it," and the couple stopped sleeping together from that time on, but it took until April 15 for her to actually move out. The husband thinks the date of separation was April 15 so therefore the commission is community property and he should get half. The wife thinks the separation was on January 15 and her earnings thereafter are entirely her own. Here's another case. Does the wife have to pay half of a loan the husband took out two months before she moved out when six months ago he had announced (again) his intention of divorcing her and she believed him so she started sleeping with another guy? It's often hard to say exactly when the separation actually took place. In the examples, any lawyer would be happy to argue either side, assuming the couple can't work it out. This is when you need to weigh the cost of fighting against the amount at stake. We think you should mediate before you litigate.

3.2 Management of property and the duty spouses owe each other

Management and control of property. Spouses and partners have equal rights to manage and control their community property. When doing so, each party owes the highest duty of good faith and fair dealing to the other, including openness, honesty, and full access to whatever books and records happen to exist. Disclosure duties and penalties for breach are discussed in the next sections.

Either party can sell community *personal* property (other than furnishings or clothing of other family members) without having the written consent of the other, but any such transfer must be for fair and reasonable value. Neither spouse may mortgage or give away community property without the written consent of the other spouse, with the exception of a gift between spouses or by both spouses to a third party. A non-consenting spouse can void an improper transaction if action is taken within one year of transfer of personal property or three years in the case of real property.

Businesses. A person operating a community property business (or in which the community has an interest) has primary control and may act alone in all transactions but must give prior written notice to the other spouse if all or substantially all of the personal property used in the operation of the business is being sold, leased, mortgaged, or otherwise disposed of.

Duty spouses owe each other. When dealing with community property, spouses owe each other a very high standard of care, the highest good faith and fair dealing. This duty continues beyond separation and lasts until all property has been legally divided. Even after the divorce, if any property was hidden or just simply overlooked, the spouse's high duty of care continues with respect to that undivided property.

3.3 Duty to disclose all information

The standard of care that one spouse owes the other also includes a high degree of openness and disclosure:
- to provide each other with full access to whatever books and records happen to exist on community transactions or transactions with third persons that involve community property,
- to account for and hold as trustee for the other spouse any benefit or profit derived from investment or use of community property, and
- to give, *on request*, full and true disclosure of virtually everything, including all material facts and information regarding the existence, character and value of all assets and debts that are or may be community property.

Mandatory disclosure. The duty to disclose *requires* that disclosure forms be exchanged in every dissolution or legal separation, as discussed in chapter 14. A spouse *must* also disclose any investment opportunity that results from any activities of either spouse during the marriage. This investment disclosure must be done in writing in time for the other spouse to decide whether to participate. Absent disclosure, any gain from such an investment would be held as tenants in common and subject to the continuing jurisdiction of the court to divide later. So, be very careful about investments after separation; make sure they are either disclosed or obviously clear of involvement with activities of either spouse during the marriage.

Remedies. A spouse who fails in the fiduciary duties of care and disclosure may be liable for 100% of the value of any undisclosed or transferred asset, or—what may amount to much more—50% of the value *plus* attorney fees and court costs for the legal action on the breach.

Set aside. If material information is withheld, misrepresented or even simply overlooked, a disadvantaged spouse can set aside all or part of an agreement or judgment. Thus, the settlement of your divorce is potentially open to attack for a very long time. To make sure your case is really over when it's over, read and heed chapters 2.9 and 14 very carefully.

3.4 Cases where there is no community property

Do not conclude that you have no community property or debts without carefully going over the Schedule of Assets and Debts in chapter 14.3. Use it as a check list to make sure you have thought of everything, especially pension plans, retirement benefits, intellectual properties (writing, painting, music, software, etc.) or other kinds of property that are easily overlooked. Read 3.6(b) below about retirement benefits, and also read 3.1, above, about income and debts.

Caution! Do *not* assume there is no community property just because you have already divided it between you if the assets have significant value or if there is property with title (autos, real estate, pension or retirement accounts, etc.). Such assets, even though divided informally, are still community property and *must* be divided properly in your Judgment to become the separate property of either spouse.

If you truly have *very* little or no community property, you may not want the court to get involved with it at all. In your Petition, simply tell the court that there is no significant property to be divided and the court will do nothing. There will be no inquiry into your property and no orders about it.

3.5 Cases where there is some property

If the community estate is valuable or contains titled property, pensions, or debts of significant value, then you need to have things divided properly before you can complete your dissolution.

Before you make an agreement or take your case to court, make sure you understand your estate and know *all* that it contains. Read sections 3.1 and 3.6 and work through the Schedule of Assets and Debts in chapter 14.3 to make sure you have thought of everything. You have to do a complete inventory in every case to satisfy disclosure requirements. Be careful and complete; a court can reopen old cases to divide overlooked community property assets or debts that were not previously divided by Judgment. Hidden or overlooked property is owned after the divorce as tenants in common until it gets divided, however long that takes. Coming back to court will cost both sides a lot of time, trouble and money, so get all your property listed and divided correctly now.

If you think your spouse may have hidden assets, either see an attorney or get Book 2, *How to Solve Divorce Problems,* chapters 8 and 17, and learn how to get information, including how to force your spouse to give information under penalty of perjury.

In a dissolution, all separate and community property must be itemized, characterized, valued, and divided.

- **Itemize.** Make a list of *all* of your property using the Schedule of Assets and Debts (chapter 14.3).
- **Characterize.** Define each item as either "community" or "separate." See chapter 3.6.
- **Value.** Determine the fair market value of each item or group of items of community property.
- **Divide.** Property can be divided by the parties or by a judge. You can divide your property any way you think fair but a judge *must* follow the law and divide equally. If you want an *unequal* division of CP worth more than $5,000, this can *only* be done by written agreement (chapter 6), but be very careful because when spouses are not represented, undue influence in the signing can be presumed if one spouse gets significant advantage over the other. This does not apply where the agreement is the result of mediation and more than six months have passed. So, if you expect a significantly unequal division of CP, best to call Divorce Helpline for advice and assistance.

Date of valuation. The date property is valued can make a big difference; say, in rising or falling markets. If the spouses cannot agree, the law says the date of valuation is as close as practical to the time of trial. But you don't want a trial, therefore you need to agree to a date of valuation that seems fair to both of you, like the date of separation or the day you sign your settlement agreement (Chapter 6).

Basic principles. When thinking about dividing your property, keep in mind that getting the last cent might not be your best or highest goal. On the other hand, you have a responsibility to your own future and a right to your fair share. Consider the children (if any), your relative earning abilities, your general situation, fairness and other such things. Consider what will be best for everyone.

How to proceed. If you have community property but no written agreement when you file your Petition, you have two choices. First, and usually best, simply state in the Petition that property will divided by agreement. This shows your peaceful intentions. If you fail to get an agreement, simply file an amended Petition listing all property and serve it again. It doesn't cost more. If you have trouble agreeing, get my book *Make Any Divorce Better* and learn specific steps that will reduce conflict, solve problems and settle disagreements, including ten clever ways to divide property without going to court. Or call Divorce Helpline. The second way to do a Petition is to list all property and debts, then, if there is still no agreement by the time of the hearing, your community property will be divided *equally* by a judge. Neither spouse will be entirely in control of exactly how the property gets divided, although the judge will be strongly influenced by the suggestions of the Petitioner.

Promises to pay. If there will be a note or any other promise to pay in the future as part of your divorce settlement, make sure such promises are *correctly* secured by a lien on real property or some other form of security, if at all possible.

If the court awards you property that is in the possession of your spouse, you still have to figure out how to get it. If this might be a problem, be sure to read 2.6 about the power of the court to make orders against your spouse and get advice if the court may not have jurisdiction.

Property law can get extremely intricate, but the section below will give you some basic rules. If you have a lot of property, think about getting professional advice or letting Divorce Helpline supervise your case. How much is "a lot" is up to you and depends in part on how concerned you are about whatever you happen to have. A professional can tell you how to locate, value, divide, and transfer property and, especially, how to protect your interests.

3.6 Understanding your estate

a. Community and separate property

Only community property needs to be divided since separate property already belongs to one spouse or the other. However, to prevent disagreement in the future, you should list any items you want to have clearly understood as separate. The list is made in a settlement agreement, on your Petition, or in a Property Declaration attached to your Petition. If listed with the Petition, by not filing a Response your spouse concedes that your list is accurate.

Separate Property (SP) belongs just to one spouse and not the community. Separate property is a) property that was acquired before the marriage; or b) property that at *any* time was given specifically to one spouse by gift or inheritance. After the separation, the earnings, accumulations, and debts of each spouse are generally separate. Community property that has been informally divided by the spouses does not become separate—both spouses still own it equally until it is officially divided by the court.

Community Property (CP) is anything earned or acquired by either spouse during the marriage that is not separate property. This includes debts incurred by either spouse up to the time of separation. Don't forget accumulated vacation pay, pension funds, employee stock options, tax refunds, and equity in insurance policies that may have accumulated during marriage. Any part of an intellectual property (writing, painting, music, software, etc.) that was created during the marriage will be CP. Personal injury awards are usually SP but characterizing Workers Compensation awards is tricky. Rules in this area are complicated and evolving, so get legal advice if there are injury awards in your case.

Because spouses are like partners, community property belongs to both spouses equally no matter who actually earned it. Each spouse is entitled to an equal share on dissolution. In a written settlement agreement, spouses can agree to divide their property any way that seems fair to them but, if divided by a judge, community property will be awarded so that each spouse receives an equal share. The judge does not have to equally divide CP valued at less than $5,000; for good cause, all or any part can be awarded to one spouse.

The term **"quasi-community"** property appears in the Petition and property forms. It refers to property acquired in another state, before residency in California, which would be community property if it had been acquired in California. It is treated the same as community property, but must be identified separately on your forms.

Jointly owned property. Title documents are commonly used for things such as cars, real estate, bank accounts, stocks, and so on. Any property acquired by spouses during the marriage in any form of co-ownership (both names on the title document) is *presumed* to be community property. However, spouses can make valid agreements that change the character of property or there might be a right of reimbursement (more on this below). One spouse acting alone can take all the money out of a joint bank account (unless the account is set up to require two signatures) or sever jointly-owned titles to other kinds of personal property (unless there is a written agreement otherwise). This means that any property in jointly owned accounts is at risk until you serve the Summons with its automatic restraining orders.

There are three kinds of joint title for real estate. Each has its own advantages:

1) Husband and Wife as Joint Tenants. Each owns an undivided half of all the property. Creditors of either spouse can reach it all. The property will pass automatically on death to the survivor without tax or probate, a result you may not want any longer. This right of survivorship is not affected by your separation or by a will. It can only be terminated by a new title, a Judgment or a *correct* unilateral termination; then your interest will pass according to your will. Should you do this? Maybe—but that also means you have lost *your* right of survivorship and will not take all if your spouse happens to be the one to go first.

2) Husband and Wife as their Community Property. This is like joint tenancy, except there is no right of survivorship. Each spouse's share passes on death according to their will, so it has to go through probate. However, this form of ownership has valuable tax advantages not available to joint tenants, and a spouse's share cannot be taken to pay a *separate* debt of the other spouse.

3) Husband and Wife as Tenants in Common. Each owns an undivided portion as his or her separate property. The shares need not be equal. No right of survivorship. Creditors of one spouse can't reach the share of the other spouse.

Mixed-up property. The general rules about property are fairly clear, but if you mixed separate and community property together, you may have a situation that is easy to argue about and difficult to unravel. Here are some guidelines.

Changing the character of property (transmutation). Sometimes spouses have an agreement or an "understanding" that would change separate into community property or the other way around. Unless it is in writing, such an agreement is *not* valid if made after January 1, 1985. After that date, a *written* agreement is required to change the character of property. Oral agreements or understandings made before January 1, 1985 will be given effect *if* they can be proved. However, even if the character of property was not effectively changed, there may be a right to reimbursement.

Tracing. In order to sort out community from separate property, you *must* be able to trace it—that is, show very clearly where certain money came from and how it was spent. This sometimes requires expert evaluation and assistance. If you have questions about whether or not assets in your case can be traced, you should consult a local attorney or call Divorce Helpline.

Return of SP used to benefit a community asset—*Reimbursement I.* If, after 1983, a spouse used separate property to buy or improve a community asset, that spouse will be entitled to a reimbursement if it can be traced (see above). There will be no presumption that it was a gift, unless this was written down. The reimbursement includes down payments and any payments that reduce the principal of a loan used for the purchase or improvement of community property, but does *not* include payments on interest, insurance, taxes, or maintenance. No interest will be paid nor adjustments made for changes in the value of money. The amount reimbursed is limited to the amount paid and also to the net value of the property at the time of the divorce hearing. Separate property spent on living expenses or vacations is not reimbursed, nor is separate property spent to benefit the other spouse's separate property.

Before January 1, 1984, separate property spent on a community asset was considered a gift to the community unless a written agreement or an "understanding" existed that it would be paid back some day. There is a large collection of cases about how to establish an oral "understanding." Very messy and expensive to litigate.

Return of CP funds spent on education, support, debts—*Reimbursement II.*

(1) The community may be entitled to reimbursement, with interest, for community contributions to the education or training of a spouse that substantially increased that spouse's earning ability. This does not include ordinary living expenses. This rule is most likely to be applied when a divorce takes place shortly after completion of training, before the community has had a chance to benefit from the increased earnings.

(2) The community is entitled to be reimbursed for payments for support obligations from a prior marriage, but only to the extent the person who owed the support had separate resources available that were not used.

(3) Reimbursement is possible where, after separation, separate funds are used to pay community debts or improve or preserve a community asset. But if one spouse acting alone decides to make the improvement, reimbursement is limited to the actual increase in market value.

(4) **Big gifts.** Uh-oh! SP that was used to buy a "substantial" gift for a spouse is entitled to reimbursement unless there was a written statement of intent to "transmute" SP to CP. Who do you know that sends statements with gifts? "Substantial" is subjective and related to the size of the estate.

Apportionment—*Community funds used to benefit a separate asset:* If community funds were used to help pay for or improve a separate asset, the community has an interest in it. For example, if the wife had her own home before the marriage, and during the marriage the couple used community income to make payments or improvements, then the community has an interest in wife's separate house. If you have this situation, you will need expert help to figure the exact amount of the community interest.

If your estate is tangled, complicated, or in any way difficult for you to understand or deal with, call the Divorce Helpline and we will help you untangle it.

b. Pensions and retirement funds

Pensions are an important and often valuable property that absolutely *must* be dealt with as part of your dissolution. Only a technically correct written agreement can effectively divide a future pension benefit. If you have retirement benefits earned during marriage, read this section very carefully.

When you think "pension plan," also think about Individual Retirement Accounts (IRAs), Tax Sheltered Annuities (TSAs), Keoghs, IRS 401(k) and 403(b) plans, and Employee Stock Option plans (ESOPs). Retirement benefits are derived from employment—a kind of deferred compensation—so if either spouse participated in one or more retirement plans or funds during the marriage, then at least part of such plans' benefits is community property.

Each spouse gets half. On dissolution, each spouse is entitled to half of the portion of any retirement plan or delayed compensation fund that was earned during the marriage.

Must be dealt with properly. If either spouse (or an employer) made contributions to or participated in any kind of pension plan during the marriage, the community has an interest in it —and that interest absolutely *must* be dealt with *formally* as part of your dissolution, even if one spouse is keeping it. It is *not* okay to divide it verbally or ignore it, even if you think it isn't worth much. Casual treatment could come back to haunt you. In many cases, an ordinary settlement agreement is inadequate to divide or establish an interest in a pension plan.

May be worth more than you think. If your marriage was very short, or employment meager and irregular, there may not be enough community interest in a pension fund to worry about. But if regular contributions to a retirement plan were made during the marriage, you may have a valuable right that is worth protecting.

Must be valued correctly. To decide what to do with a pension plan, you need to know what the community interest is worth. You also need the correct value to fill out your Disclosure Declaration (chapter 14). If a spouse fails in his/her disclosure obligation by reporting "unknown" or an incorrect pension value, a judge *must* set aside the settlement agreement or judgment if the other spouse discovers later that the pension was worth more than they thought. You *must* disclose the correct value.

Periodic summary statements that report plan value might be misleading and might not reflect the true value or the community interest:

- If your plan is a tax-deferred savings account, the value is probably the figure shown on the summary statement.
- For plans where you have to wait for a certain age or number of years of employment to begin receiving payments, then the correct value is probably *not* the same as the figure on the summary statement. It is often *much* more, but it takes an expert to say how much. You *must* have your plan appraised by a professional pension actuary. This costs from $150 to $300, but it is money well-spent! If you need an appraisal of a pension plan, call Divorce Helpline.

Military and Federal Pensions. Military retired pay and federal civil service annuities are community property, but military disability pay can*not* be reached, nor can you reach military retirement that was waived in order to receive disability benefits. Spouses of marriages that last through ten years or more of military service gain big advantages in the enforcement of pension awards. Former spouses of marriages that saw at least twenty years of active military service are entitled to commissary and PX benefits.

Don't rush the date of divorce if you are approaching a 10 or 20 year deadline. **Note:** a spouse retiring from the military can be bound to a written agreement to designate a former spouse as beneficiary under a Survivor Benefit Plan (SBP) *if* the agreement is incorporated, ratified or approved in a dissolution Judgment, and if the Secretary concerned receives a request from the former spouse along with the agreement and court order. If you have this issue in your case, call Divorce Helpline.

Social Security is not community property and not subject to division by a court. It is a federal program with its own rules, so contact the Social Security Administration to get information about your rights after a divorce. **Note:** benefits accrue to spouses of a marriage that lasted at least ten years. So, if you are near the ten-year deadline, don't rush into a Judgment that could conveniently be postponed.

How to divide a pension plan. Before you do anything else, call the employer's personnel department and get a copy of the Pension Plan Booklet. It is full of information needed by you or anyone helping you. Next, unless the term of your pension plan or marriage has been very short, you need an *expert* appraisal of the current value of the community interest in the plan. This is the only way to be sure of its true value. Finally, choose one of the following three methods to divide it:

1) **The waiver** can be used if the community interest is truly worth very little. The non-employee spouse simply gives up, in a settlement agreement, all interest in the employee's pension fund.

2) **The trade-off** (present day buy-out) is a clean and easy way to divide a pension fund; courts like it and it has no immediate tax consequences. By this method, one spouse trades his or her interest in the employee spouse's pension plan for something else of equal value, such as a larger share of the family home, or a promissory note. Be careful—insist that any note be secured, preferably with a Trust Deed on real property.

Note that the employee-spouse trades hard dollars in the present for something that *might* be collected if he or she stays employed long enough and lives long enough to collect. The employee-spouse will pay taxes on that future income while the other spouse pays no taxes on the trade. However, the employee-spouse may need the entire pension to live on after retirement; so it is better to pay now rather than have less to live on later. Or maybe the community interest is relatively low and easy to pay for now, just to get things wrapped up cleanly.

3) **The payoff** (division into two accounts) awards present ownership of a share of *future* pension rights (when they come due) to the non-employee spouse. Transfers following a payoff *must* be done in strict accordance with IRS rules or you might suffer an *immediate* tax liability.

This method has no serious disadvantages, except it costs several hundred dollars for the QDRO; the non-employee spouse may have to wait for his/her share; and the employee-spouse will have a smaller pension check to live on. It is most appropriate in long marriages where the pension is the only or largest asset. Sometimes the employee-spouse will use it to reduce or eliminate spousal support payments.

To make sure the plan follows your agreement and does not improperly pay funds to the employee spouse, you *must* file a Joinder to join the pension plan to your case. Do it immediately. You also need a special order called a QDRO, which is like an official title or "pink slip" to a share of the pension fund, 401(k), or annuity. This must be done *before* the marriage is dissolved or the non-employee spouse could lose rights. For example, if the employee spouse dies after a divorce Judgment but without a QDRO, the non-employee spouse would very likely lose everything.

Two different plans require two Joinders and two QDROs. One plan with multiple parts may require more than one QDRO. Joinders and QDROs are too complicated to cover here. Call Divorce Helpline to see if there is some way to get what you want *safely* without having to prepare a Joinder or QDRO.

QDRO orders are difficult to draft and any mistake could be very expensive, so we *strongly* recommend that you call the Divorce Helpline or an attorney with a lot of pension fund experience. Don't take a chance; get expert advice. It will be worth it.

Death benefits. Divorce automatically removes a spouse as beneficiary under some plans but not others, so the employee-spouse should notify the plan of the divorce and name a new beneficiary. The non-employee spouse may want to be continued under the plan, but it is usually better to value this part of the plan separately and replace it with an annuity or life insurance of equal value and cover the cost in the settlement agreement, perhaps with a small increase in spousal support.

Be careful when deciding what to do with a pension—there are often tax consequences and penalties if pensions or 401(k)s are not correctly divided or if withdrawals are made before retirement age. Don't touch a pension fund without making sure your changes won't end up costing you. If you want advice about how to deal with a pension or help deciding what's best for you, call Divorce Helpline. Our attorneys will help you achieve a fair division of your pension funds the best and safest way. We can arrange a valuation for you and do the paperwork necessary to make your plans work correctly.

c. The family home and other real estate

If you and your spouse own a home or other real property in any form of joint title, or if any real property was paid for or improved with funds earned during the marriage, then the community has an interest in it. You must now value the community interest and decide how to divide it.

What is the community interest worth? The amount one actually owns in property, the "equity," is the difference between what you can get for it on the current market less any amounts due on it. Deduct the cost of sale *only* if it is going to be sold immediately. The best way to find out the current market value of your property is to consult a professional real estate appraiser—call around for prices. You can get free estimates from local real estate agents, but this may not be as reliable. Once you know the market value, deduct amounts owed to get your equity. If, and only if, the house is to be sold right away, you also deduct an agent's commission and costs of sale of about 7–8%. Next, deduct any traceable separate property contributions that need to be reimbursed (see 3.6(a), above). The amount left over is what the community interest is worth.

To keep or not to keep. In thinking about who, if anyone, will keep the family home, you will naturally consider the children, your emotional ties to the home and neighborhood, and the ghosts of the past. But you also have to carefully consider it as a business deal—even if you get it, does it make economic sense to keep it? Can you afford all the payments, taxes, insurance and regular maintenance costs? Be sure to get advice about tax consequences of any decision you might make before you decide.

Dividing the family home. Some of the more common ways you can divide the community interest in a family home are:

- sell it and divide the community property interest; or
- transfer it entirely to one spouse in exchange for something worth half the community interest— other property; interest in a pension fund; a *secured* note for an amount to be paid monthly or on a specific future date, or upon some specified event, such as when the youngest child reaches a certain age, or when the house is sold, or the spouse remarries or moves; or any specific time or event that you can agree to; or
- change title to tenants-in-common (separate ownership) with each spouse holding a stated percentage, and agree to let the custodial parent and kids live in the home until some time or event (as above); or

- the spouse that keeps it refinances the property to buy out the share of the other spouse (the preparation of documents and transfer of funds will be handled by the title company).

Child on board? Where there is a child (especially a disabled child) living in a long-established family home, a judge *may* decline to force a sale *if* a sale would cause economic, emotional, or social detriment to the child. But, first, the judge must find that the in-spouse can afford to pay for mortgages, insurance, maintenance, taxes, and so on. If so, the judge will consider all circumstances and then *may* defer the sale, *unless* the economic detriment to the nonresident spouse would outweigh the other considerations. This kind of order, regarded as additional child support, *might* last until the youngest child reaches majority, but, rather than defer the sale for a long time (if at all), most judges would look for some logical earlier date—for example, when the affected child would normally change from one school to another. Unless otherwise agreed by the parties, such an order can be modified or terminated any time on a showing of changed circumstances. Remarriage of the resident spouse strongly suggests that continued deferral is no longer fair. Once popular, these orders are uncommon now because high property values have made them economically unfeasible in most cases. To get such an order over the objection of the out-spouse, there would have to be evidence of a special reason why a child should not be moved, something strong enough to outweigh the financial burden to the nonresident spouse.

Transferring real property. The best way to transfer title is by drawing up a deed and possibly a note (promise to pay money). Any note should *definitely* be secured by a Deed of Trust (a mortgage on the property) to simplify matters in case of nonpayment. To transfer real property from joint ownership by both spouses into sole ownership of one spouse is simple: just get a blank "interspousal transfer deed" and fill it out. Method 2: if your Judgment orders a change in title for property in California, the Judgment itself can be used to transfer title if you take a certified copy of it to the County Recorder for the county where the property is located and have it recorded.

Deeds must be signed before a Notary and recorded at the Recorder's office in the county where the property is located. There will be a small fee for recordation and maybe a small transfer tax. Any transfer of real property requires a Preliminary Change of Ownership (PCO) statement which is available at your County Recorder's office. This form will let the County Assessor know not to reassess your property to a higher rate. Notes must be properly drawn and should be secured by a Deed of Trust. If you need help making up your deeds and notes, you may be able to get assistance from a title company (escrow), a bank, or a local attorney. Call around to see what they charge.

Note. Transfers of property do not remove a spouse's name from any mortgages that were originally on the property—both are still liable. This *could* create a credit problem, so you might want see if you can get the property refinanced in the sole name of the spouse who is keeping it.

Real property *must* be disposed of in any settlement agreement or listed with your other property as shown in chapter 15. If it is still not transferred by the time of the hearing, or settled by written agreement of the spouses, the judge will divide it along with all the other listed property.

 **Taxes**

Remember, federal tax laws do not recognize domestic partnership but state laws do. Domestic partners should probably see a tax accountant to clarify potential confusion.

Transfers of property between spouses as part of a divorce settlement are not taxable, but sales to third parties are. Always get expert tax advice before dividing or selling a major asset as there could be significant tax consequences. Read the tax pamphlets described in chapter 2.10. Be very careful how you divide retirement funds or you might face a tax or a penalty.

Family home and other major assets. A spouse who keeps the home or any other major asset also keeps the *potential* liability for capital gains taxes and sales commissions whenever the property is sold. Tax consequences should be understood by both spouses and negotiated as part of any agreement.

Under 1997 tax laws, you can no longer avoid tax on gains from the sale of a residence by rolling the funds into the purchase of another home. Instead, *anyone* can now exclude capital gains from the sale of their primary residence ($250,000 for single people and $500,000 for joint filers), and you can do it as often as once every two years. When one spouse takes possession of the house *as part of a court order,* the out-spouse can claim the house as principal residence during the period of exclusion, so hurry up with that order! If the home was acquired as part of a divorce, the new owner can claim the period that the other spouse owned the home. There is also an exclusion amount for sales forced by health reasons or change of place of employment.

 Wills, insurance beneficiaries, and nonprobate transfers

Wills. A dissolution *automatically* revokes bequests to a former spouse and children or relatives of the former spouse who are not also related by blood to the testator. It also removes such persons as executor under any will made before the dissolution. If you want your former spouse or his or her relatives to be included in your will or one of them to be executor of your estate, you will have to make a new will after the dissolution.

Insurance beneficiaries. A dissolution does *not* remove a spouse as beneficiary of insurance policies on the life of the other spouse. This is something you should cover in your settlement agreement. Be sure to contact your insurance carrier if you want to change your beneficiary.

Nonprobate transfers invalidated. A nonprobate transfer is any instrument other than a will that transfers property on death of the transferor. Any nonprobate transfer of property made before or during the marriage will fail if the recipient is no longer the transferor's spouse due to dissolution or annulment. Any such documents should be reviewed at this time.

4
CHILDREN: CUSTODY AND VISITATION

The parenting plan may be the most important matter you deal with in your divorce and it can sometimes be the most difficult. "Parenting plan" refers to all your arrangements for the children and how the parents will share responsibility for their care and upbringing.

What is in the child's best interest? This is the question asked by the law, by judges, and by concerned parents. It is the question you and your spouse or partner should ask. One thing that is clearly best for children, a huge gift that can be difficult to give, is for parents to resolve their personal issues so that bad feelings are reduced to a minimum and cooperative parenting becomes possible. This is *vitally* important.

Studies show that harm to children is more closely related to conflict *after* divorce. Everyone has conflict before and during a divorce, but if you want to protect your children, get finished with conflict and resolve it, at least within yourself, as quickly as possible. Remember that children need *both* parents and parents need all the help, good will and cooperation they can get from each other to raise a child.

Which children? Divorce courts are concerned with *minor* children born to *both* parents or legally adopted. If the wife (or a partner) is pregnant, that child *must* be listed in the Petition as "one unborn."

Whose child is it? Any child born to a married woman is presumed to be her husband's. If they were cohabiting on the date of conception, and the husband was not medically impotent or sterile, the presumption is just short of conclusive. We must presume, for now, that these rules also apply to same-sex registered domestic partners. For more, see Nolo's *Legal Essentials for California Couples*. If there is or might be a dispute as to paternity, you had better contact an attorney or call Divorce Helpline for advice.

Which court? If a child has not lived in California for six consecutive months before the Petition was filed, it is *possible* for a parent to claim that some other state or country has superior jurisdiction over the children. Temporary absences (vacations) do not affect the six month period. If you can't satisfy this time requirement, and if your Petition is in fact attacked, consult an attorney immediately.

Parenting programs. At least seven counties (Humboldt, Marin, Placer, San Luis Obispo, Santa Barbara, Santa Cruz, Tuolumne) require parents to attend a short but useful program about children before you can get a Judgment. When you file your Petition, the clerk will give you details about the program and local requirements. There's also the informational form FL-314 with information the state wants you to know about custody. It's in the CD. Take a look and consider sending a copy to the other parent.

Modification. All orders concerning minor children—custody, visitation, and support—are subject to modification at any time. This means either parent can go back to court and seek a change by showing that there has been some important change in circumstances since the last order and that a change in the order is necessary to protect the best interests of the child.

Parental agreement. If you have trouble working out a parenting plan, both parents should read my book *Make Any Divorce Better* for specific steps that will help you reduce upset, solve problems, negotiate, and reach agreement. Consider seeing a counselor or mediator, or call Divorce Helpline for advice. If your case seems headed to court, get Book 2, *How to Solve Divorce Problems* to learn how to handle a case in court or supervise an attorney. On the other hand, if your spouse is gone or not interested in the children, you can probably get any reasonable orders you want. Make up something that will work and that will encourage stable parental contact if and when your spouse becomes interested in the children again.

If parents can't agree about their parenting plan, it must be decided in court. But, before going to court on any custody matter, parents are *required* to meet with a court-appointed mediator. If you have already worked with a private mediator, the court mediator will decide if you satisfied the requirement. Mediation is confidential, but counties vary as to whether the court mediator will make a recommendation to the court if parents can't reach an agreement.

Severe conflict. In extreme cases, the court can appoint an attorney to represent children and/or order parents into counseling or substance abuse treatment for up to six months in an effort to reduce conflict and improve parenting. The spouses will bear the cost in a reasonable proportion determined by the court.

Moving before Judgment. Once the Summons is served and until the Judgment is entered, restraining orders are in effect (see chapter 2.7) and neither parent can take a child out of the state without the prior written consent of the other parent. When you get your Judgment, the court can be asked to extend the restraining order or to make a new order regarding moves. We recommend that your settlement agreement or Judgment require either parent to notify the other parent in writing at least 60 days ahead of any change in a child's residence that will last more than 30 days.

Moving after Judgment. If the custodial parent wants to move away, he/she should consider the impact on visitation with the other parent. In general, absent bad faith, a custodial parent is free to move anywhere, but the other parent can require a hearing to determine (a) if the move is made in bad faith, say, to impair visitation, and (b) if the move will cause such detriment to the child that a change in custody is required for the child's welfare. The result depends very heavily on the judge's discretion, so best to avoid the expense and trauma of a court hearing with uncertain outcome. If a parent wants to move, try to negotiate or mediate new co-parenting arrangements that meet the needs of both parents and the child.

Child snatching. It is a felony to take or keep a child with intent to defeat a custody or visitation right. If this happens to you, report it to the police and go see your D.A. immediately. However, it is a defense if there is a reasonable belief that the child will suffer immediate physical or emotional harm. A pattern of domestic violence, not necessarily in the child's presence, is evidence of danger to the child. If you have reason to fear a child might be abducted (taken) see a family law attorney or call Divorce Helpline.

Smoked children. Courts are receptive to the idea that a parent should not smoke in the same house with a child present. Weight of scientific evidence that secondhand smoke has an adverse effect on health, especially for children, is nearly overwhelming and therefore difficult for judges to ignore. If demanded by one parent, not smoking could *possibly* be made a condition of custody or visitation.

4.1 Custody

The traditional terms, "custody and visitation," are losing favor because they encourage parents to think of the issue as something to win or lose rather than a child to be cared for. One parent ends up feeling that he or she has "lost" custody and somehow lost the child. This thinking needs to be changed. All you are trying to do is settle child care arrangements (parenting schedules) when parents no longer live together. We call this "the parenting plan" or "parenting arrangements." You should always call it that, too, even though the law still speaks of custody and visitation.

Custody Terms Defined: Here's what the law means by its terms:

1. **"Joint custody"** means *both* joint physical and joint legal custody.

2. **"Joint legal custody"** means that both parents share the right and responsibility of making decisions relating to the child's health, education, and welfare.

3. **"Joint physical custody"** means each parent will have significant periods of physical custody arranged to assure the child has frequent and continuing contact with both parents. It need not be 50/50; even 70/30 would be okay.

4. **"Sole physical custody"** means the child will live with and be under the supervision of one parent. A parent with sole custody *may* have an advantage when it comes to moving away over the objection of the other parent. "Primary physical custody" is often used instead—it has a similar legal meaning but doesn't have the harsh implication that only one parent has the child. The other parent can think of himself or herself as having less time rather than no custody.

5. **"Sole legal custody"** means that one parent has the right to make decisions relating to the child's health, education, and welfare.

Ideally, you will use these terms only in court, and outside of court you will continue to remember that the child still has and still needs two parents and you will think of each other that way. You both need all the help you can get raising the child. Remember, too, that parents who feel cut off and left out are less likely to make support payments in full and on time.

Nonsexist laws. There is no *legal* preference for one form of custody over another, nor any *legal* preference for mothers over fathers. In court contests, the best interest of the child is the prime consideration, but the judge may have personal opinions as to what's best. In custody contests, the judge can require a family study before making a decision, and all other things being equal, for the sake of stability, the judge will often decide to keep the child in whichever home he or she has been living since separation. When the child is old enough to make intelligent choices, the judge will give some weight to the desires of the child. However, most children don't want to be put in the position of having to choose.

Details, details. In most cases, it is very useful for you to work out your parenting plan in as much detail as possible. Parents in agreement can arrange things any way they like from day to day, but if disagreements come up in the future, you will always have the specific terms of your agreement to fall back on as to who does what and when. Section 4.3 has two sample parenting plans you can use as a guide; one is very simple, the other is highly detailed.

Joint custody. There has been a growing trend for parents to request joint custody (both physical and legal) as a way to encourage the maximum involvement of both parents. Most judges now wisely require a plan for joint custody to be spelled out in some detail so that in the future each parent will know what is expected and when. Parents can freely arrange things any way they like, but when agreement is lacking, the plan must be followed. For purposes of determining school district or welfare eligibility, your agreement or order can specify one parent as the primary caretaker and the primary home of the child. By law, an order for joint *physical* custody *must* specify the parenting time of each parent with enough detail that a judge can determine clearly if one parent is being deprived of custody by the other. If your request for joint custody is denied, the judge must state the reason in the decision *if* you request this in writing within *ten* days of the order. It's best to do this at the hearing.

Joint legal and primary physical custody. This may have become the most popular parenting order today, and for good reason. It is used where one or both of the parents is not comfortable with full joint custody, yet it does not isolate the out-parent as much as an order for sole custody and visitation. What you do is award joint *legal* custody to both parents with primary physical custody to one parent, along with a highly detailed parenting plan showing the times the child is with each parent. This arrangement is clean, clear, definite, and judges are comfortable with it. The child has the stability of living primarily in one place most of the time, yet both parents are legally equal, thus minimizing the sense of loss to the parent with less child care time. An order for joint legal custody *must* specify any circumstances where consent of *both* parents is required. In all other situations, either parent alone can make decisions about the child's health, education and welfare.

Primary custody with rights of visitation. The old standard order grants sole custody, both physical and legal, to one parent with detailed visitation rights to the other parent. The parent with sole custody has the major responsibility of caring for and raising the child, and that parent has the last word on all matters concerning the child's upbringing. The drawback is that it tends to make one parent feel more or less cut off and at a real disadvantage in maintaining a relationship with the child.

Domestic abuse and alcoholism. When custody is an issue, a judge *must* consider abuse or threats of abuse by either parent to any family member, mate or someone they dated, and continual or habitual use of alcohol or drugs. No form of custody—sole, joint physical or joint legal—will be awarded to a person the judge finds has committed domestic abuse in that family. The presumption can be overcome only by a preponderance of evidence. The judge can require independent proof of allegations made by one parent against the other, and a stiff penalty plus attorney fees can be awarded for a false accusation of child abuse.

If, after reading this chapter and the possible custody orders in chapter 18.4, you find you still have questions about the parenting plan and its terms or if you want help setting it up, you may want to discuss your case with a family law attorney, or you can call us at the Divorce Helpline. If you and your spouse are having difficulty communicating or working out terms for custody and visitation, then I strongly recommend that you both read *Make Any Divorce Better*. It that doesn't solve all problems, consider getting help from a counselor or mediator. Find out how to use your court mediation service; it is often a superb bargain. Custody fights are to be avoided at any cost as they are hugely expensive and *always* destructive—especially to your children.

Visitation

A good parenting plan will keep the best interests of the child uppermost and help the parents to create as open and flexible an atmosphere as possible to permit a good relationship between the child and both parents. Both parents and the child will have a degree of certainty and stability.

In the past, the parent who did not get custody was often awarded "rights of reasonable visitation." This means that the other parent is entitled to visit at reasonable times and places, upon reasonable notice, and with the consent of the parent with custody. It is left to the parents to work out exactly what this means in terms of where and when visitation takes place. This can be very good if the couple is truly cooperative, but you can see how this vague order could foster uncertainty and disagreement between parents. Nowadays, some judges grant "reasonable visitation" orders only if given a good reason for doing so, and some won't accept "reasonable visitation" orders at all, insisting on more detail. If you enter into a settlement agreement, you can probably do as you wish. However, in almost all cases, it is much better to have very detailed parenting orders that set out specific days and hours for visiting, including overnights.

Day by day, parents can agree to any schedule they like, but whenever they can't agree, the specific terms of the visitation schedule will settle the issue and eliminate argument and further conflict. The next section has samples of parenting plans that you can use as a guide for thinking about your own. When you compose your plan, use simple words, be very clear and be specific. Avoid terms that are subject to more than one interpretation. If you want help with your parenting plan, call Divorce Helpline.

Virtual visitation means staying in touch with your children via video calls, email, instant messaging, and cell phones. Relatively inexpensive, video calls allow you to hear and see each other, share documents, help with homework, play games, bring friends or grandparents into the visit, and so on. It is not a substitute for quality time spent together, but rather an extremely valuable supplement. Virtual visitation benefits all parties, as it allows the custodial parent to stay in touch with the child during extended summer or holiday visits with the non-custodial parent, and the child never has to feel cut off from either parent at any time. For more information, a tale of personal experience, tips on how to do it, and suggestions for how to word virtual visitation in your settlement agreement, look in the Reading Room folder on our companion CD. Other resources can be found at **www.internetvisitation.org**.

Visiting for non-parents. You can include in your agreement periods of visitation for a stepparent, grandparent or any other person with an interest in the welfare of the child. Absent agreement, a judge has discretion to award visiting rights to grandparents whenever it would serve the best interests of the child. Grandparents can join in any action between the parents or bring their own action for visitation. Grandparent visitation time can be allocated between the parents for the purpose of calculating support. It is also possible to order support to a grandparent to cover the expenses of care and visitation.

Problem cases. The relationship between parent and child is so protected that courts rarely order no visitation at all. If you show good cause, you can get an order to conduct visitation only under supervision, but to get an order preventing any visiting at all you must have a very strong case showing that even supervised visits will most likely be very dangerous or detrimental to the child. If you need a court order that prevents all visiting, see an attorney.

If your spouse has a history of harassing you, word your agreement or orders so you exchange the child in a public place, or even so that you never have to see your ex-spouse at all, possibly by arranging exchanges through a third person or agency.

Any parent who keeps or conceals a child to frustrate custody or visitation orders is guilty of a crime. The parent with custody is not entitled to forbid an arranged visitation for any reason other than the well-being of the child. If the visiting spouse arrives in a drugged or drunken state, for example, it would be reasonable to prevent the visit on that occasion. However, visiting cannot be refused because of a disagreement, ill will between the parents, or even because of a complete failure to provide support. Likewise, support cannot be suspended because visitation has been frustrated. In extreme cases, however, deliberate and persistent interference with visitation and the parental relationship has led to reduction or termination of support or a switch of custody to the other parent. Concealment of the child has been upheld in some cases as a defense to collecting unpaid support.

The law provides for additional support as compensation to help cover costs for periods when the visiting parent fails to assume caretaker responsibility. Conversely, a parent prevented from exercising visitation rights is entitled to compensation for expenses incurred.

Once you have your custody and visitation order, it is hoped that all will go smoothly. If not, and if you can't work things out peacefully and finally, you should try counseling or mediation.

Two parenting plans and some other ideas

Use these parenting plans and forms as a guide in making your own agreements and orders. You can (should) change them to fit your own ideas and circumstances or you can combine ideas from all of them. Other plans and good ideas can be found in some of the books listed at the end of this section.

How much detail? In general, more detail is better. Parents can vary from a detailed plan at any time by agreement, but if there's a problem, you just drag out the agreed plan and you know who is supposed to be where and when; end of argument. On the other hand, a very detailed plan might be harder to negotiate—especially if emotions are raw—and parents under detailed plans can sometimes become inflexible. The need for flexibility is always important, as parents must be prepared to accommodate the child's changing needs over time as well as the changing circumstances of the parents.

Carefully study the terms for visitation found in Judgment attachments listed below so you can see the kinds of terms attorneys have thought up for parenting plans to cover every kind of situation. Next, study the sample plans below to see a range of possibilities for customizing your own plan. Almost anything parents agree to, within reason, will be acceptable to a judge.

Future moves. What happens when the custodial parent wants to move away usually can't be worked out until it is about to happen. It is best negotiated at the time based on circumstances existing then. Moves that tend to reduce the other parent's contact with the children are generally disfavored by judges but may be allowed if in the child's best interest.

JUDGMENT ATTACHMENTS

You can draft your own parenting plan, as illustrated in the samples below, or you can attach forms to your Judgment to spell out custody and visitation. These forms are found on the CD in the forms folder. Take a close look at FL-341, FL-341(C), FL-341(D), and FL-341(E) to see the kinds of parenting terms devised by attorneys to cover almost anything that might come up in any kind of case.

SAMPLE PARENTING PLAN A

This plan represents the bare minimum for very cooperative parents. It's just a sketch of intentions with lots of details left to be worked out day by day. It may be easier to write down now but it won't help settle disagreements that may come up later about who is to do what and when. It's good for joint custody, but don't use this one unless you are secure with the relationship you have with your co-parent.

A. The parties agree to joint legal custody of their minor child. Primary physical custody of the child shall be with Wife. Husband shall have the child as follows:

1) for long weekend school holidays;

2) for half of the summer school vacations;

3) for the Easter school vacation in odd-numbered years;

4) for Thanksgiving school vacations in even numbered years;

5) for half of the Winter Break school vacation;

6) for such other time as the parties shall agree.

B. At all other times, the child shall be with Wife.

C. Each party shall give the other two week's advance notice if the party is planning to take the child from the State of California for a period exceeding (one week/ten days/one month).

(Alternately, you could specify "the county of residence" rather than the state).

D. Both parties shall participate in making medical decisions concerning the child and each party shall promptly inform the other of any medical emergencies that may arise.

SAMPLE PARENTING PLAN B

This plan is relatively detailed so don't just copy it—think about it carefully and tailor the terms to fit your family and your particular circumstances.

1. (Mother/Father) shall be designated as the "Primary Custodial Parent." The Primary Custodial Parent shall have the primary physical responsibility for the children except for (Mother's/Father's) parenting time set forth below.

2. Basic Parenting Plan:

    a. Weekends: Alternate weekends, commencing _____, from Friday at 6 p.m. until Sunday at 7 p.m. The weekend shall be extended to 7 p.m. on Monday if the Monday is a holiday when the children are scheduled to be with (Mother/Father).

    b. Weekdays: Every (other) Wednesday, commencing _____, from 4 p.m. to 9 p.m.

    c. Spring School Vacation: During the children's spring vacation from school, (Father's/Mother's) parenting time shall be from 6:00 p.m. Friday to 6 p.m. Wednesday if his/her regular weekend is before the vacation, or shall be from 6 p.m. on Wednesday to 7:00 p.m. Sunday if his/her regular weekend is after the vacation.

    d. Summer School Vacation: Six weeks during the children's school vacation time during the summer with starting and ending times to be agreed upon by the parties. During these six weeks, the children will spend alternate weekends with (Mother/Father) from Friday at 6 p.m. until Sunday at 7 p.m. The weekend shall be extended to 7 p.m. on Monday if the Monday is a holiday when the children are scheduled to be with (him/her).

    e. Holiday Schedule:

    Thanksgiving: In odd-numbered years, from 6 p.m. on the Wednesday before Thanksgiving until 6 p.m. on the following Sunday.

    Winter:

    In odd-numbered years, from noon on December 26 until 6 p.m. on the day before school resumes in January.

    In even-numbered years, from 6 p.m. on the last school day before the Christmas school vacation until noon on December 26.

    or

    Seven consecutive days, including any regularly scheduled weekend time, during the children's Christmas holiday from school. The starting and ending times shall be agreed upon by the parties.

    Other Holidays: As agreed by the parties.

3. Each parent shall be responsible for picking up the children at the beginning of his or her parenting time.

4. Either parent may designate any competent adult to pick up the children and to be with the children when they are picked up.

5. Each parent shall give at least 24 hours advance notice to the other parent if he or she must change the schedule. The parent requesting the change shall be responsible for any additional child care costs that result from the change.

6. Both parents will cooperate in finding alternate child care for those periods when regular child care is not available, and the cost of said child care shall be included when the parties establish how the cost of child care is to be shared.

7. Neither parent may remove, or cause to be removed, the minor children from the state of California without 30 days prior written notice to the other parent. This provision applies to vacations and trips outside of the state of California.

8. Neither parent may change his or her residence or the residence of the minor children without 60 days prior written notice to the other parent.

RECOMMENDED READING

Here are some of our favorite books. An expanded list can be found on the companion CD in the Reading Room folder.

- *Mom's House, Dad's House*, Isolina Ricci (Macmillan, 1980). This famous old standard is full of good stuff. It has, among other things, a more detailed joint physical parenting plan, one in which Dad has more parenting time than in Plan B.

- *Second Chances*, Wallerstein & Blakely (Ticknor & Fields, 1990).

- *Helping Your Child Succeed After Divorce*, Florence Bienenfeld (Hunter House, 1987).

- *Surviving the Breakup*, Judith Wallerstein & Joan Kelly (Basic Books, 1980).

- *101 Ways To Be A Long Distance Super-Dad*, George Newman (Blossom Valley Press).

- *Helping Your Children With Divorce*, Edward Teyber, Ph.D.

- *How to Resolve Custody and Get on With Your Life*, Robert Adler (1988).

5

CHILD SUPPORT AND SPOUSAL SUPPORT

Child and spousal or partner support are discussed separately because they have different rules and priorities. But first, here are some points that apply to both kinds of support.

Support priorities. Child support has priority over spousal/partner support. Spousal support will be considered only after children have been adequately provided for and will be based on the finances of the parties after child support has been accommodated.

Earning ability. Support is normally based on actual current income, but if a court finds that a spouse has voluntarily reduced income when employment at a higher level is available, then support can be based on that spouse's *ability* to earn. Occasional overtime and bonuses can be included in earnings if likely to continue in the future, but excessive overtime beyond a reasonable work schedule should not be included.

New mate income. For *spousal* support, you can't consider income or expenses of a *payor's* new mate to figure the amount of support, but if the *recipient* has a live-in mate it can be presumed there is a decreased need for support at least to the extent expenses are reduced. For *child* support, new-mate income can be considered *only* if the parent intentionally quit work or remains unemployed or underemployed and relies on the new mate's income to do so, and if including it will not cause a hardship to any other child that the payor *or* the new mate supports. *For tax purposes only:* support is based on *actual* taxes paid, so if a party files taxes jointly with a new mate, the new mate's income and deductions have to be included in order to figure the correct amount of taxes attributable to the payor.

Mandatory wage assignment. Whenever there is an order for child or spousal support, there *must* also be an order assigning wages of the paying spouse. More about this in section 5.5, below.

Jurisdiction. Don't forget! To make an enforceable order for the payment of money, the court needs "personal jurisdiction" over the person ordered. Do you have this in your case? See chapter 2.6.

Insurance. The automatic restraining orders (chapter 2.7) forbid either spouse from canceling or transferring life or health insurance policies held for the benefit of the other spouse or a minor child. Violation is a misdemeanor. On filing of a dissolution, a notice can be sent to insurance providers requiring them to continue named beneficiaries until the Judgment and requiring notice of any lapse of payment or change of beneficiaries. Later, a copy of the Judgment can be sent to put the insurance provider on notice of orders that affect or protect beneficiaries.

Life insurance on the life of the payor should be considered to protect the recipients. This is especially important where the supported spouse keeps the home and the home mortgage as, if the payor dies, the supported spouse will get stuck with the mortgage and no support.

Family support and tax savings. Where the spouses' incomes differ significantly and child support will be paid, the family can save on taxes by ordering the payment of "family support," which is entirely deductible, whereas child support is not. Tax savings must be shared with the children, but all profit at the expense of the IRS. If you want a family support order, get help because it takes expert advice and drafting to make it work, but it will probably be worth it. Call Divorce Helpline for more information.

California's mandatory guideline. California has a statewide guideline for *child* support based on the actual after-tax income of the parents and the amount of time each has physical custody of the child(ren). The guideline is mandatory, meaning a judge *must* order the guideline amount unless the parties have a written agreement or unless certain exceptions can be proved (see below).

Bottom line. What people want to know first is the bottom line: "How much?" The short answer is that the guideline formula is so complicated that you'll want to get a computer calculation of the correct amount for your case. In fact, you pretty much have to because even if you agree to an amount you have to show that you knew the correct guideline amount before you made the agreement. To help you get what you need, we created CalSupport, very inexpensive professional-quality software that is easy to understand and easy to use (see sections 5.3 and 5.4 below).

Details

Duration. A child is entitled to support until the child reaches 19 or reaches 18 and is not a full-time high school student, or dies, or marries, or becomes self-supporting, whichever occurs first. If the parents agree in writing, support can be ordered to age 21 or through college or training. Support for a disabled minor or adult child who is unable to work can be extended so long as the disability lasts. Child support usually starts when ordered, but it is *possible* to have it made retroactive to the date the Petition was filed. Child support does not end automatically when the recipient dies, but a written agreement or Judgment can state that child support ends on death of the recipient if the payor takes custody of the children.

Additional support: insurance. In addition to basic guideline support, health insurance for children *must* be made a part of a support order **if** it is available at a *reasonable* cost to either parent (usually part of employment benefits or through membership in some group); if not available, the order must require it to be obtained if ever it becomes available at reasonable cost in the future. Group health insurance is generally presumed to be reasonable in cost. A health insurer cannot refuse to cover a child because it doesn't live with the insured parent, lives outside the coverage area, is not claimed as a dependent on the insured's tax return, or was born out of wedlock. If you have an uncooperative spouse, the court can order the employer directly to enroll the children in the health plan. The court can also award a sum of money to cover the cost of life insurance on the paying spouse to benefit the dependent spouse or children.

Additional support: shared expenses. In *addition* to guideline support, both parents are responsible for certain child care expenses which *must* be shared equally unless the parties agree or a court orders them shared in proportion to net incomes. The two *required* add-ons are (1) child-care expenses to enable either parent to work, and (2) uninsured health care expenses. The two *discretionary* add-ons are (1) educational or special needs of a child, and (2) travel expenses for a visiting parent.

Uninsured health care expenses. Every child support order must include an order that the parents will share reasonable uninsured health care costs for the child, either equally or in proportion to their net incomes. Amounts actually paid are presumed reasonable unless evidence is presented to show otherwise. A form stating the parents' rights and duties must be attached to any Judgment containing this order.

Exceptions to the guideline. The judge cannot depart from guideline amounts unless evidence is introduced in court to show one or more of the following special circumstances:
- sale of the family residence is being deferred to benefit the children and the fair rental value of the residence exceeds the mortgage, taxes and insurance;

- extraordinarily high income would result in an excessively high award;
- special circumstances that would cause the application of the guideline amount to be unjust or inappropriate;
- necessary job-related expenses beyond the normally allowed deductions;
- financial hardship due to expenses from extraordinary health expenses or uninsured catastrophic loss or care of a live-in child by another relationship.

Evidence of any of these circumstances can be raised with the court, but because the judge has discretion to consider the total circumstances and the best interests of the children, you can't be certain of the result.

Low income adjustment. If the payor's *net* monthly income is below $1,000 a judge has discretion to reduce child support, but by no more than the percentage by which the payor's net monthly income is less than $1,000. If an adjustment is made, the judge must state on the record the reasons that justify it.

Taxes, exemptions and credits. Be sure to read the tax information pamphlets (chapter 2.10). To be claimed, a child *must* have a Social Security number. The child support exemption is a valuable deduction that can be claimed by the *custodial* parent. However, the *non*-custodial parent can get it if the custodial parent signs IRS form 8332—each year—releasing the right to claim the exemption, and a copy of that form is filed with the tax return of the non-custodial parent. Because the high-earner saves more on taxes, it is usually best if the high-earner takes the exemption and pays part of the tax savings to the low-earner to cover any extra taxes. Don't forget, the person taking the exemption also gets the valuable child tax credit. Finally, parents may be eligible to take child-care expense deductions and a dependent care tax credit. For more detailed advice, call Divorce Helpline.

Agreed child support. Parents can agree to any reasonable amount of support, but an amount different from the support guidelines requires a written agreement (chapter 6) or the Stipulation to Establish Child Support (chapter 18).

Low or zero child support. It is generally not easy to get an order for very low or zero child support, but it can usually be done when child care is substantially equal. Even then, it requires a carefully drafted settlement agreement and depends on continued good will between the parents, because a motion to modify can be made at any time when an order is below the guideline. If you want support ordered that is more than a little bit below your guideline amount, we suggest you have Divorce Helpline prepare your settlement agreement and see your paperwork through to Judgment.

Both parents are obligated to support their child. A parent cannot escape this obligation by voluntarily reducing income. Petitioners with children *must* include an order for child support in the Judgment in *every* case, even if the other parent is unemployed, unemployable or long gone. Either parent can receive child support. It can even be ordered to a low-earning noncustodial parent to help care for the child during visitation.

Child support is based on the *current* wealth of both parents, so a significant change in income can mean different support. If the payor enjoys a life-style that far exceeds that of the custodial parent, child support must reflect the richer life-style, even if this produces some unintended benefits for the custodial parent.

Child support can't be withheld even if visitation is being frustrated and visitation can't be refused even if child support is not being paid. This is the law, but exceptions have been made in extreme cases. Where the child was hidden, a court reduced the amount of child support; several courts have discharged unpaid support arrearages for periods when a child has been concealed from the other parent; and, in one case, deliberate and persistent interference with visitation and the parental relationship led to termination of the support obligation.

Modification. Child support orders and agreements can be modified at any time to accommodate changes, such as incomes, cost of living, needs, or other changes. A sudden increase or *unavoidable* decrease in income would be a reason to request modification of child support, as would the end of a major obligation. The parties can agree (stipulate) to a changed amount or it can be done by motion in court. The court order is what determines how much is owed—informal agreements don't count. Don't fail to do it right!

Once a year, either party to a support order can serve FL-396, a request for a completed Income and Expense Declaration, on the other party without going through the court. This will help you decide if a motion for modification is in order. The form is available in Book 2 or at the Clerk's office.

Welfare cases. If child support is ordered for a parent receiving welfare for the children, the support *must* be paid through the Department of Child Support Services (DCSS). Contact their office in your county.

5.2 Spousal or partner support

If you want spousal or partner support, it must be requested in the Petition or Response. Parties can agree to any amount, duration and terms, but if decided in court the judge must follow the law.

Spousal support is not favored where the marriage is very short or where there are no children and both spouses can take care of themselves. For medium and longer marriages, the trend is to try to equalize the standards of living for the spouses after divorce. A wife can be ordered to support her husband if she earns more because the law is gender-neutral.

How much? There are guidelines for spousal support, more or less standard through the state, but, unlike child support guidelines, these are not mandatory. In fact, by law, each case *must* be decided on its own merits. In the majority of counties, the guideline is 40% of the supporting spouse's net income after deducting child support, less 50% of the supported spouse's *net* income not allocated for child support. Some counties reduce spousal support slightly if there is child support. In any case, a judge will typically start with the guideline figure but, by law, *must* consider the following factors before deciding:

> **Family Code §4320:**
> In ordering spousal support under this part, the court shall consider all of the following circumstances:
> (a) The extent to which the earning capacity of each party is sufficient to maintain the standard of living established during the marriage, taking into account all of the following:
>   (1) The marketable skills of the supported party; the job market for those skills; the time and expenses required for the supported party to acquire the appropriate education or training to develop those skills; and the possible need for retraining or education to acquire other, more marketable skills or employment.
>   (2) The extent to which the supported party's present or future earning capacity is impaired by periods of unemployment ... incurred during the marriage to permit the supported party to devote time to domestic duties.
> (b) The extent to which the supported party contributed to the attainment of an education, training, a career position, or a license by the supporting party.
> (c) The ability to pay of the supporting party, taking into account the supporting party's earning capacity, earned and unearned income, assets, and standard of living.
> (d) The needs of each party based on the standard of living established during the marriage.
> (e) The obligations and assets, including the separate property, of each party.

(f) The duration of the marriage.

(g) The ability of the supported party to engage in gainful employment without unduly interfering with the interests of dependent children in the custody of the party.

(h) The age and health of the parties, including, but not limited to, consideration of emotional distress resulting from domestic violence perpetrated against the supported party by the supporting party where the court finds documented evidence of a history of domestic violence, as defined in Section 6211, against the supported party by the supporting party.

(i) The immediate and specific tax consequences to each party.

(j) The balance of the hardships to each party.

(k) The goal that the supported party shall be self-supporting within a reasonable period of time. Except in the case of a marriage of long duration as described in Section 4336, a "reasonable period of time" for purposes of this section generally shall be one-half the length of the marriage. However, nothing in this section is intended to limit the court's discretion to order support for a greater or lesser length of time, based on any of the other factors listed in this section, Section 4336, and the circumstances of the parties.

(l) Any other factors the court determines are just and equitable.

How long is a long marriage? Section 4336, referred to above, presumes a marriage or partnership of 10 years or more to be of long duration, but under some circumstances a shorter marriage can also be considered to be of long duration, and a longer marriage with periods of separation could fail the test.

How long does spousal support last? The parties can set any term by agreement but, when decided by a judge, the duration will be related to the length of the marriage and the circumstances of the spouses. Cohabitation before marriage will *not* be considered. A rule of thumb is half the length of the marriage, as cited in the statute above, but note that this does not apply to long marriages. Unless agreed otherwise in writing, spousal support is not terminated by cohabitation with another party, but it automatically ends on remarriage of the recipient or the death of either spouse. To get support beyond the life of the payor, make life insurance part of the support agreement.

Impact of domestic violence. Under clause (h) in the statute above, if domestic violence by the payor against the recipient is proven, it can affect the amount or duration of support. If the recipient was convicted of violence against the payor in the five years prior to the divorce or *at any time afterward*, there is a presumption that there should be no award for spousal support (Family Code § 4325).

Zero support vs. termination of support right. Spousal support can stay steady, go down over time, or be set at zero. But there is a *big* difference between zero support and terminating all right to it. So long as the court keeps jurisdiction over spousal support, a spouse can come back to court later to ask for a modification of the original order. Even if support was ordered to end on a certain date, if a motion is made before that date a judge can extend the term on a showing of need.

Jurisdiction. Courts should *not* retain jurisdiction over spousal support where the marriage was short and the spouses are in good health and self-supporting. For "long" marriages, the court *must* retain jurisdiction indefinitely unless the parties have agreed otherwise in a technically correct writing. What's long? A marriage of ten years or more is long by legal definition, but shorter marriages can be considered long, depending on circumstances. In fact, a judge *might* be willing to retain jurisdiction—for a while—over spousal support in marriages of only four or six years.

In a written agreement, spouses can specify that the support amount cannot be modified, or that the time cannot be extended, or both. In fact, a written agreement is almost the only way you can be completely certain that spousal support will stay fixed at a certain amount or end on a certain date or condition.

Termination. To end forever all right to spousal support—that is, to terminate the jurisdiction of the court to make orders on the subject in the future—it must be waived in open court or in a written agreement. For long marriages (even some medium ones) a waiver or a written termination will not be approved if it isn't made clear that both spouses know that a judge *would* retain jurisdiction if asked to and that both spouses are capable of supporting themselves.

Right to continue health insurance. If one spouse is covered under other's health insurance *at the time of the dissolution*, COBRA (a Federal act) gives that spouse the right under almost all plans to continue coverage for up to three years after the Judgment at similar rates, at their own expense. To exercise this right, within 60 days of judgment you *must* deliver a written notice of the divorce to the Plan Administrator and tell them you want to continue under COBRA. The cost may seem to go way up after the employer's contribution is no longer applied, so here's what you do. Way ahead of the judgment, call the plan or the employer's personnel department and find out what the coverage is and your cost under COBRA after the divorce. Then call other plans and shop around for a better deal. However, if you have a preexisting illness, you will probably need to stay with the old plan. **Domestic partners** are not covered by this federal law unless their particular plan happens to have a COBRA look-alike written into it.

Creativity. Spousal support has inspired a great deal of creativity; in fact, there are books much larger than this one devoted to nothing else. We cover the basics here, but if spousal support is a difficult issue in your case, call Divorce Helpline to explore options and get advice based on their long years of experience in dealing with this thorny subject.

5.3 Support software to calculate guidelines

The guidelines are incredibly complicated, to the point that very few lawyers or judges actually understand them. At the same time, when parents make a support agreement, they are supposed to show the correct guideline amount and state whether the agreed amount is higher or lower. Increasingly, courts are requiring you to attach a computer printout to your paperwork. So what's a parent to do?

Lawyers have had software since at least 1984 to help them calculate guideline child and spousal support. Although support guidelines are intended to guide the parties, lawyers' software is designed for litigation, which is not the same thing at all. The legal software printouts are extremely difficult to understand, so when you *do* get your results, you will need a consultation to have it explained.

Lawyers typically charge $150–$250 for running the program and it often has to be done many times over as you negotiate your way through various proposals. Divorce Helpline attorneys will calculate the guidelines for you for $75, plus $25 for reruns. Many paralegals and mediators offer support calculation service as well. Every county has a Family Court Facilitator's office (chapter 1.9) and branch office of the Department of Child Support Services. Either one of these can help you with child support issues, among other things. Call to see what help you can get and what you must do to get it.

Your best option. To make the support guidelines more accessible and more useful, we developed CalSupport™ for Windows, a program designed for the public and professionals who serve the public. It is much easier to use and understand than the professional software for attorneys, yet it is very affordable and, better yet, it is designed to help you communicate and settle. That's what guidelines are for, right?

It costs only $34.95 to register CalSupport™ for Windows, yet it gives you the same results you would get from a lawyer entering the same data in a $500 program. It is approved by the California Judicial Council and accepted in all courts, but if you use CalSupport™, you aren't likely to end up in court because its built-in negotiation tools will help you settle.

When you use CalSupport™, you don't argue about how much support one person wants and how much the other wants to pay. Instead, you focus your discussion on the accuracy of data entered and let CalSupport™ tell you how much support is fair under California guidelines. That's the range you negotiate. You won't go to court because lawyer's bills could easily run from $10,000 to $25,000 for each side and the outcome would probably be near the guidelines anyway.

How to get it. A trial version of CalSupport™ for Windows is on the CD that comes with this book, and you can always download the latest version at **www.nolodivorce.com/CA**. CalSupport™ PRO, a professional version with extended features, is also available for $149 at **www.nolodivorce.com/PRO**.

5.4 Other ways to calculate support guidelines

The child support guideline figure is mandatory, so it is *essential* for you to know about it. The spousal support guideline is not mandatory (see section 5.2 above), but it is still extremely useful. Knowing the guideline figures for your case will help you decide what's fair and make your negotiation much easier. You will know that there is little to gain by dragging the matter into court because you'll probably end up near the guideline amount anyway. You might wonder if there are alternatives to computer calculation. In practical terms, not really, but here are two other possibilities.

• **Do without.** If you have children, more and more counties make it almost mandatory for you to have the computer printout for child support. However, you *might* be able to get through a divorce with children without calculating the guideline amount of support. Try going to court without a figure and ask the judge to award "the guideline amount" for child support. Some judges will calculate the figure at the hearing. If the judge asks *you* for the guideline amount, just ask for a continuance and come back for your hearing after you get the figures.

• **Do it by hand.** If you have math ability and time, you can hand-calculate child support using the instructions at the end of this chapter. If you want to see the entire child-support statute, look for Family Code Sections 4050 to 4076 at your county law library, or find the Family Code on the companion CD. When working by hand, figuring taxes will be a challenge, and if either parent has a live-in child by another relationship, the allowable deduction will be extremely difficult to figure. Finally, the only thing you will have to show your spouse or the judge will be some incomprehensible pages of figures.

5.5 Enforcement of support orders

Support may be ordered, but it is not always paid. In fact, only 17% of all recipients are paid in full and on time. This is why you should make *every* effort to settle the amount of support by agreement because you get better compliance later.

Mandatory wage assignment. Every order for child or spousal support *must* include an order assigning the wages of the paying spouse to the recipient spouse or an agency appointed by the court to collect support. If the order is served on the payor's employer, all or part of the support payments will automatically be deducted from wages by the employer. The wage assignment can be stayed by court order, but not easily. However, it is *entirely* up to the recipient *when* the wage assignment order is actually *served* (if ever) on the employer, so, as described in chapter 19, the parties can agree in writing that the order will not be served on the payor's employer so long as payments are current. Read chapter 19 for more information on the use of wage assignment orders.

Keep track! Both parents should keep careful records of support paid or received because if ever the issue of overdue support comes up, the person with the best records wins. To make your job easier, we created **Tracker** software to help you keep track of support payments, amounts overdue, and interest that is automatically added to amounts overdue. For more information, see **www.nolodivorce.com/CA**.

Teeth that really bite. Cash-hungry governments are putting more teeth than ever in enforcement laws. Here are some of the sharper ones:

> **Security deposits** can be agreed to or required by a judge in the amount of up to one year's support. You can also ask the payor to provide life or disability insurance to replace support in case of accident or death. Security is a very good idea where the payor is self-employed.

> **License and passport blocking.** Deadbeats face revocation of their drivers' license and business and professional licenses and passports can be revoked or renewal refused.

> **Intercept** tax refunds, unemployment and State Disability payments, or lottery winnings.

> **Credit rating affected** by nonpayment of child or spousal support can ruin the payor's credit rating. The Department of Child Support Services is *required* to report nonpayment of support to credit agencies and the agencies are required to include it in any report until cleared.

> **It is a Federal crime** to willfully fail to pay a past-due support debt from another state.

> **Contempt of court** if payor fails to make a good-faith effort to find employment.

> **Penalties** of up to 72% can be added to amounts past due and interest can be added, but you have to take legal action to get it.

> **Liens on real or personal property** belonging to the payor can be obtained.

> **Seek a work order.** Deadbeats can be required to submit a report to the court, every two weeks or some other reasonable period, listing places where he/she applied for work.

Help is available. All child support services except for criminal prosecution are handled by the Department of Child Support Services (DCSS) with offices in each county. They get involved with spousal support *only* if it is part of an order for child support. The Family Law Facilitator will also help people with support orders. Unless a parent is receiving welfare, you should probably contact your county Family Law Facilitator first. Some offices are more effective than others and most are understaffed, so think about getting your own attorney. However, establishing and collecting child support is primary function, so they should be experts on the subject. County attorneys do not actually represent you but they can still be useful. Contact information for these offices can be found on our companion CD under "Links" or at **www.nolodivorce.com/links**. Give them a call or, better yet, go see them.

Good record keeping is extremely important for both parties in case of future claim or disagreement. Keep records safe and keep them until the obligation for support is long over.

Register your Judgment if you move to another state. This is essential if you might ever want the right to enforce the support orders in your new state.

Don't put off collection too long. If you don't bother to enforce your unpaid support for many years, this *could* be interpreted as evidence of a waiver of the right to support, especially in the case of spousal support. This is not a hard rule, but it has happened before.

Family Code Section 4055
CS = K [HN – (H% x TN)]

CS = Guideline child support for the first child.
Calculate it in this order:

Figure TN = Total net monthly disposable income of *both* Mother and Father. Use the Income Information Form (Figure 16.2) to get net monthly disposable income on line 16. Figure it for both Mother and Father.
- Add the results for both parents together to get TN.
- Whoever has the highest net monthly disposable income (HN) is High Earner.

Figure H% = Timeshare for High Earner (see next page).
If there are different arrangements for different children, use the average that the high earner spends with each child. If there's no evidence of timeshare, court will use 0% or 100% depending upon who has custody.

Figure HN = High Earner's net monthly disposable income.

Figure K = Percentage of parents' *combined* net incomes (TN) that is allocated for children. Figure the K factor like this:
- If H% is less than or equal to 50%
  K = (1 + H%) times fraction below:
- If H% is greater than 50%
  K = (2 – H%) times fraction below.

disposable income			fraction		
$0	to	$800	.20	+	TN/16,000
801	to	6,666	.25		
6,667	to	10,000	.10	+	1000/TN
Over 10,000			.12	+	800/TN

Figure CS: Multiply H% by TN, subtract the result from HN and multiply by K. This is the Guideline figure for the first child.

Total Guideline Child Support:

If there is more than one child, multiply CS by:

2 children	1.6
3 children	2
4 children	2.3
5 children	2.5
6 children	2.625
7 children	2.75
8 children	2.813
9 children	2.844
10 children	2.86

If the result is positive, the high earner pays the low earner that figure. If the number is negative, the low earner pays.

NOTES & DEFINITIONS

1. **"Net disposable income"** is gross income reduced by actual amounts attributable to:
   - State and federal income tax actually payable (not necessarily the amount withheld from the paycheck). Unless the parties agree otherwise, this shall not include the tax effects of spousal support. **Note:** this step requires you to calculate the probable tax bill for both parties—one of the major reasons hand calculation is difficult and imprecise.
   - FICA. For people not subject to FICA, any amount actually used to secure retirement or disability benefits, not to exceed the equivalent FICA amount.
   - Deductions for mandatory union dues and retirement benefits that are required as a condition of employment.
   - Deductions for health insurance for the parent and any children the parent has an obligation to support and deductions for state disability insurance.
   - Any child or spousal support actually being paid pursuant to a court order to benefit any person not a subject of the current calculation, or any child support actually being paid without a court order for a natural or adopted child not residing in the party's home and not a subject of the current calculation. No deduction under this section is allowed unless it can be proved.
   - Hardship deductions: 1) minimum basic living expenses of minor children, natural or adopted, of other relationships who actually live with the parent; 2) extraordinary health expenses for which the party is obligated; 3) uninsured catastrophic losses. These deductions are discretionary with the court upon a showing of evidence.

2. **Authorized add-ons.** These are 1) child care costs related to employment or necessary education or training for employment skills; and 2) uninsured health care costs for the children.
Discretionary add-ons: 1) costs related to educational or other special needs of the children; and 2) travel expenses for visitation. **Sharing:** Add-ons are generally shared equally but a judge can order or parties agree that it be in proportion to their net incomes.

3. A hardship deduction for basic living expenses for a live-in child of another relationship can be taken from gross income by judge's order or agreement of parties. The amount may not be more than the prorated amount ordered for each child under the current order. If this is a factor in your case, you have yet another reason for getting a computer calculation that applies all formulas and takes all factors into account.

4. Low income adjustment. If the payor's net monthly disposable income (HN) is less than $1,000, it is presumed that the guideline child support (CS) will be reduced by an amount that may not exceed the percentage by which HN is less than $1,000. The maximum adjustment, therefore, is: CS x (1,000 - HN)/1,000. This presumption can be rebutted by evidence showing the adjustment would be unjust and inappropriate.

Estimating Timeshare

Timeshare is the percentage of time the parent has primary physical control. There are no state rules for how to figure it, so you can calculate timeshare any way the parties can agree on.

Credit for time in school or day care. You should negotiate how to credit time the child spends in school or day care, but a judge would decide based on factors like who is on call for emergencies, who arranges and pays for it, who drops off and picks up the child, and participation in school and extracurricular activities. If you both do these things, share the time in proportion.

Some counties have voluntary guidelines in their Local Rules of Court (ask the Clerk's Office or at the county law library). As an example, here's the guide that Santa Clara County judges use when parties disagree about how to figure timeshare:

Definitions:

Weekend	=	6 pm Friday to 6 pm Sunday
Extended weekend	=	Close of school Friday to opening of school Monday
Evening	=	After school to after dinner
Overnight	=	Close of school midweek to opening of school next day
Alternate holidays	=	New Year's, President's Day, Easter, Memorial Day, Mother's Day or Father's Day, July 4, Thanksgiving (2 days), Christmas, child's birthday
Summer vacation	=	12 weeks (84 days) mid-June to September 1
School vacation	=	Summer, 2 weeks at Christmas, 1 week Spring, 2 days Thanksgiving, plus seven other days. (school holidays vary from one district to another).

Parenting arrangement	Days	%
1 weekend per month	24	7
1 extended weekend per month	36	10
1 weekend per month plus one evening per week	50	14
Alternate weekends	52	14
Alternate weekends plus 2 weeks in summer	67	18
Alternate weekends and holidays plus 2 weeks of summer	73	20
Alternate weekends plus 1 evening per week	78	21
Alternate extended weekends	78	21
Alternate weekends plus 1 overnight per week	78	21
Alternate weekends and holidays plus 4 weeks of summer	86	24
Alternate weekends and holidays plus half of summer	100	27
Alternate extended weekends plus 1 evening per week	104	29
Alternate weekends and holidays plus 1 evening per week plus 4 weeks of summer	112	31
Alternate weekends and one evening per week, and half of school vacations	135	37
Three days per week	156	43

6
SETTLEMENT AGREEMENTS

This chapter explains why an agreement is the best thing you can do in most cases and how to make your own written settlement agreement (**SA**) either with the simple sample printed in this book or with the more sophisticated capabilities of Nolo's DealMaker software (see inside front cover).

Here's why you should work hard to get a well-drafted SA if an agreement is even remotely possible:

- With an agreement, you won't have to go to court. Without one, you almost certainly will.
- Essentially, your SA becomes your Judgment and you will be ordered to comply with its terms, thus you get to decide everything ahead of time and have total control over the Judgment. Without a settlement agreement, you are more limited and a stranger (the judge) who doesn't know you or your family decides everything after spending very little time getting to know the facts.
- With a settlement agreement, you can get far more depth, detail, flexibility and protection.
- If your community property is worth more than $5,000, a settlement agreement is the only way you can arrange an unequal division, if this is what the spouses agree is fair.
- Once you sign, your divorce is mostly finished except for red tape and paperwork.
- Divorces that are settled by good agreements usually work out better afterward—spouses are more likely to comply with terms, have better post-divorce relationships, better co-parenting, faster healing, and it just feels better.

Money and more. Often, a lot of money can be gained or lost depending on how things are handled in your SA, especially if significant assets, debts or support are involved. Careful planning, problem-solving and drafting can save thousands or tens of thousands of dollars.

A settlement agreement can be tailored to suit your specific situation: protection from a spouse's debts, dealing with the family home, avoiding taxes and penalties. For spousal support, you can be creative about fixing dates, amounts and various conditions so that you never have to come back to court again. Your parenting plan can be designed to calm the concerns of both parents about their future relationship with the child and each other.

Write your own? Get help?

How much is good help worth? The settlement agreement is virtually your entire divorce. Stop to think if it is worth it to get professional help or if you should do it yourself. Add up the value of all your property and debts then add all future support payments. Compare that figure to a couple of thousand for professional help and a settlement agreement that is done right. If expert help isn't worth it, or you still want to go it alone, consider drafting your own settlement agreement by following the sample agreement below, or the more sophisticated and powerful capabilities of Nolo's **DealMaker** software.

Who can help? To go beyond the simple sample agreement, below, get the more sophisticated agreement produced by **DealMaker** software (see inside front cover), or have it done by a family law specialist like those at Divorce Helpline. Do *not* let a non-attorney draft your settlement agreement unless you have little property and they follow the agreement in this book or use **DealMaker** to produce your agreement. Do not use anyone else's agreement as a guide as it may be from a different state or a different time, and it will certainly be for different people. Get one professionally tailored to your needs and today's laws.

The three befores. If you get help, be sure to get your information and advice *before* you state your position to your spouse, *before* you draft your settlement agreement, and *before* you sign anything.

Getting your agreement

If you need help with negotiating and otherwise working things out, read my book *Make Any Divorce Better,* or call Divorce Helpline. We can help with suggestions, problem solving and negotiating techniques or mediate disagreement if there's an impasse.

Settlement agreement highlights

Timing. You need to file your Petition (chapter 10) before you finalize an agreement because you *must* complete disclosure (chapter 14) before signing an agreement, which is done *after* the Petition is filed. Also, agreements take time to work out and you don't want to rush something so important. File your Petition, do the disclosure, then forget about it while you negotiate your agreement.

Thorough discussion and complete agreement. Because set-aside rules are relatively relaxed for divorce cases (see chapter 2.9), you want above all to avoid a situation where either spouse has second thoughts in the months after the agreement is signed. This means you want more than just a signature on the contract— you want a true meeting of the minds on all points, and that means a contract that has been thoroughly thought out and negotiated in depth and detail *by the spouses, personally.*

Never sign a settlement agreement without disclosure! You can't make a sound agreement unless both parties have complete financial information. In fact, unless both parties fulfill disclosure requirements, (1) you might not be allowed to complete your divorce, and (2) your Judgment might be vulnerable to attack in the future. How to do disclosure is described in chapter 14. The law requires both spouses to serve each other with preliminary *and* final disclosures before or at the time of entering into any written agreement regarding property or support. Using form FL-144 (chapter 14), the spouses can mutually agree to waive the Final Disclosure, but this is not recommended in cases with significant property because you *want* the other party's sworn disclosure on the record before you sign anything.

Secure promises to pay. A debt between spouses to settle their divorce case should be secured whenever possible, preferably by a trust deed (mortgage) on real property, if there is any.

Death of either spouse will terminate spousal support unless stated otherwise in your settlement agreement.

Voluntary changes. If you later agree to alter your arrangements for custody, visitation or support, be sure to do it in writing and then get your judgment modified. Informal understandings won't affect your written order and obligations under that old judgment are binding until changed.

Modification. If circumstances change, either party can make a motion to change the orders for child support or custody. Spousal support can be modified *unless* your agreement states in legally correct language that it can't be modified either as to amount or duration or both.

Reconciliation. A settlement agreement is not canceled if you reconcile later. To terminate a written agreement, you will have to change or revoke it in writing.

Taxes. Many aspects of a settlement agreement can have tax consequences, so be sure to read the tax information booklets (chapter 2.10) or get expert advice. You may be able to save quite a bit on taxes by customizing your agreement.

Signing. When the settlement agreement is being signed you should also have prepared all other documents that need a signature: interspousal transfer deeds, notes, auto pink slips, and so on.

Notarize. It's a good idea to notarize both signatures to your settlement agreement in any case and some counties require it. If you file the Request for Default form (chapter 17), you *must* have Respondent's signature notarized. Butte County wants the parties to have two different notaries.

Welfare. If a party is receiving welfare, the District Attorney's office will need to sign an approval on any SA or Judgment with provisions for child support. They will need proof of the payor's income.

Warning!

Think carefully before signing an agreement for less than your fair share of property and support. Buying peace is not always a bad idea, but think carefully first so you don't end up sorry later that you mad that decision. Don't give away valuable rights because you feel guilty, or to make your soon-to-be ex-spouse like you better. It is very difficult and expensive to try to break an agreement.

> ## A sample settlement agreement
> (also available on the companion CD for editing)

A *simple* settlement agreement (SA) is included here to show you what one looks like and for you to use as a guide. **Caution!** This agreement is most suitable for simple cases—a few household goods, vehicles, a few debts—but nothing big or complicated. For a more sophisticated agreement, get Nolo's DealMaker software (**www.nolodivorce.com/CA**) or call Divorce Helpline (800) 359-7004 for assistance.

Things not covered. Here are some situations where we suggest professional advice or help with drafting:
- Zero child support in joint custody cases
- Family support (instead of child support, to maximize tax savings)
- Child support beyond age 18 for college or technical training
- Security for payment of debts or amounts to be paid later
- Spousal support—stepping up or down; making the amount or duration depend on a condition; or termination of support in cases where t here is a long marriage (see chapter 5.2)
- Sale of a major asset to take place after SA signed—protection of respective interests until sale and allocation of expenses while you own it
- Tax consequences of sale of a major item—maximizing tax savings, minimizing tax liability
- Equalization payments to balance unequal division of property
- Future interest in a pension plan, to be distributed upon reaching retirement age
- Self-employment, solely owned business, sideline business—valuation and division
- Intellectual property—ownership and future value of music, writings, art, software, inventions, etc.

When. Settlement agreements are filed with your Judgment. In most counties, it is attached to the Judgment; in LA and San Bernardino, the SA is filed separately as Exhibit 1 in evidence. See chapter 18.2.

Details. You will need the original and three copies of the agreement, typed on one side only. When signing, both spouses should also initial each page at the bottom and initial any alterations or corrections.

Doing your own. If you write your own settlement agreement, use the parts below that apply to you. Change wording to suit your needs; disregard what doesn't fit, but *don't* leave out paragraphs X to XV. Use clear and specific wording because vague terms with more than one possible meaning cannot be enforced. Your settlement agreement will, in effect, become your judgment, so it *must* be right. If you have trouble understanding the agreement, or wording it to fit your own case, get help.

SETTLEMENT AGREEMENT

I, _____, Husband, and I, _____, Wife, agree as follows:

I. GENERALLY: We make this agreement with reference to the following facts:

A. MARRIAGE: We are now husband and wife. We were married on the __ day of _____, 20__, and separated on the __ day of _____, 20__.

B. CHILDREN: There are (no minor children/the following minor children of the parties):
(list full name, age and birth date of each minor child of the marriage)

C. IRRECONCILABLE DIFFERENCES: Unhappy and irreconcilable differences have arisen between us which have caused the irremediable breakdown of our marriage.

D. DISCLOSURE: We each acknowledge receipt of Final Declarations of Disclosure from the other.

E. We now intend, by this agreement, to make a final and complete settlement of all of our rights and obligations concerning child custody, child support, spousal support, and division of property.

II. SEPARATION: We agree to live separately and apart, and, except for the duties and obligations imposed and assumed under this agreement, each shall be free from interference and control of the other as fully as if he or she were single.

III. PARENTING PLAN: **(choose one)**:

A. Joint custody: Husband and Wife shall jointly share the legal and physical custody and care of our minor children. Our parenting relationship shall be guided by the following terms and conditions: **(put down your parenting plan in as much detail as possible)**.

B. Joint legal custody with primary physical custody: Husband and Wife shall jointly share the legal custody of the minor children of the parties, and **(Husband/Wife)** shall have the primary physical custody of said children. Our parenting relationship shall be guided by the following plan: **(put down your parenting plan in as much detail as possible; see 4.3)**.

C. Sole custody and visitation: (Husband/Wife) shall have the sole legal and physical custody of the minor children of the parties, subject to the right of **(Wife/Husband/other)** to visit said children as follows: **(write the parenting plan in as much detail as possible; see chapter 4.3)**.

Optional: Each parent shall give the other parent at least 60 days prior written notice before making any change in a child's residence that will last longer than 30 days. **More options:** consider other provisions such as a) visits with grandparents; b) a successor to visitation rights in case of death of visiting parent; c) written notice to other spouse in case of changes in health, education, well-being, educational progress; d) agree to provide documents to allow spouse to inquire directly with doctors, hospitals, school personnel. **Still more options:** That the children will keep the father's surname and not take on the mother's maiden name or name of any new spouse, at least until the child is old enough to make that decision. Some spouses want an agreement about the children's religious upbringing and education.

IV. BASIS OF AGREED SUPPORT: The support established by this agreement is based on the following facts:

A. Before separation, our gross combined family income was $____ per month, and our average expenses were $____ per month.

B. At the time of this agreement, Husband's gross monthly income is $____ and average monthly expenses are $____. Wife's gross monthly income is $____ and average monthly expenses are $____.

C. **(If there are children)** Under our agreed parenting plan, the children will be in the physical care of the Wife __% of the time and in the physical care of the Husband __% of the time.

D. The mandatory Wage Assignment Order for support will be issued.

(Optional): E. AGREEMENT NOT TO SERVE WAGE ASSIGNMENT ORDER: We understand that a Wage Assignment Order (WAO) must be issued by the court whenever support is ordered, but so long as support payments are no more than ___ days in arrears, (Wife/Husband) agrees not to serve the WAO on (Husband's/Wife's) employer. Until the WAO is served, support payments will be made directly to (Husband/Wife) and both parties will keep a record of all payments made and received for the duration of the support obligation.

V. SUPPORT OF CHILDREN: Pursuant to California Family Code §4065, the parties make the following declarations: (1) We are fully informed of our rights concerning child support; (2) The child support award is agreed to without coercion or duress; (3) The agreement is in the best interests of the children involved; and (4) The needs of the children will be adequately met by the stipulated amount. **(Do not alter foregoing language.)** We are aware that the guideline amount for our case is $____ **(chapter 5.4)** and acknowledge that this agreement (does/does not) follow the guideline. **If not on welfare, add:** The right to support has not been assigned to the county under Section 11477 of the Welfare and Institutions Code and no public assistance application is pending.

As and for child support, _____ shall pay to_____ a total of $____ per month, payable in advance on the __day of each month, beginning on the __day of _____, 20__. Support shall be apportioned for each child as follows: **(Use guideline apportionment shown in the child support order, chapter 18.4, or substitute your own. This is not done if you have different time share with different kids).** Support shall continue for each child until said child dies, marries, becomes self-supporting, reaches 19, or reaches 18 and is not a full-time high school student, whichever occurs first.

HEALTH INSURANCE. (Husband/Wife) shall obtain and maintain an insurance policy providing major medical, dental and vision coverage for each child for the duration of the support obligation. The child's reasonable health costs that are not covered by any policy of health insurance shall be (paid by Husband/Wife) (shared equally) (paid __% by Husband and __% by Wife).

CHILD CARE. As additional child support, _____ shall pay to _____ for child care a total of $__ per month, payable in advance on the __ day of each month, commencing on _____, 20__, and continuing as long as child care is necessary and actually being paid.

Life insurance option: During the term of the support obligation for each child, (Husband / Wife / both equally/other) shall carry and maintain a policy of life insurance in the amount of $_____, and shall name as sole irrevocable beneficiaries (Wife / Husband / said minor children), and shall not borrow, assign or otherwise encumber said policy.

Note on tax status: To file as Head of Household, during the tax year you must have actually paid more than half the cost of maintaining a home for you and a party you are entitled to claim as a dependent. To cover time when a supported child is away at school, you can include this clause: When (child) is living at school, college or other post-high school training, the principal abode of (child) shall be with (Husband/ Wife) and said parent shall pay more than half the cost of (child's) support and maintaining a home for (child) during (child's) temporary absence at school.

Termination option: The child support obligation shall terminate upon the death of the recipient if the payor assumes full custody of the children.

Optional payment for college or training: Many parents prefer the flexibility of renegotiating this point when the child graduates high school to examine the child's level of commitment or the parent's ability to pay, but if you think the payor may be stingy later and you can get the agreement now, you might want to pin it down. Get advice on the pros and cons of making this kind of agreement now and how to word it.

VI. SUPPORT PAYMENTS TO SPOUSE: The parties agree that the following amount of spousal support (does/does not) completely meet the current needs of the recipient for support.

   (Use A or B)

   A . Waiver of Right to Support: In consideration of the other terms of this agreement, and whereas both spouses are fully self-supporting,   **(Choose one of the following):**

   ...there will be no order for spousal support at this time, but the court shall retain jurisdiction over spousal support.

   ...we each waive all right or claim which we may now have to receive support from the other. No court shall have jurisdiction to award spousal support at any time regardless of any circumstances that may arise. We understand that either of us could ask the court to retain jurisdiction over the subject of spousal support. **For marriages over 5 years, add:**   We are informed and aware that, if requested by either party, the court is required by law to reserve spousal support for long-term marriages of over ten years, and may be disposed to do so for marriages shorter than ten years. Even so, we each waive the right to receive spousal support now or at any time in the future.

   B. In consideration of the other terms of this settlement agreement, _____ agrees to pay to _____ the sum of $_____ per month, payable on the __ day of each month, beginning _____, 20__, and continuing until **(any or all of the following—some certain date, the death of the payer, death of the recipient, remarriage of the recipient, some specific condition— Note: unless specified here, no amount of cohabitation will equal remarriage, so be exceptionally clear if you intend otherwise)**, whichever occurs first.

Optional: Said (termination date/amount/date and amount) is absolute and no court shall have jurisdiction to modify the (termination date/amount) of spousal support at any time regardless of any circumstances that may arise. Spousal support may not be requested for any period after the termination date, nor will any court have jurisdiction to order spousal support to be paid for any period after the termination date, regardless of any circumstances that may arise and regardless of whether any motion to modify spousal support is filed before, on, or after said date.

More options: 1) amount decreases at set times; 2) amount adjusted automatically for increases in paying spouse's income; 3) court retains jurisdiction over spousal support, but no payments now; 4) a policy of life insurance required naming support recipient as sole irrevocable beneficiary (see life insurance option under child support, above), or specify that spouse and/or child to be named or retained as irrevocable beneficiary under some existing policies; 5) spouse to be dropped as beneficiary under a certain policy.

VII. CONFIRMATION OF SEPARATE PROPERTY:

   A. The following property was and is the separate property of Husband, and Wife confirms it to him and waives any claim to or interest in it: **list—describe clearly.**

   B. The following property was and is the separate property of Wife, and Husband confirms it to her and waives any claim to or interest in it: **list—describe clearly; for example, use vehicle license numbers and VIN, assessor's parcel numbers and legal description for real estate.**

VIII. DIVISION OF COMMUNITY PROPERTY AND DEBTS: The parties warrant and declare under penalty of perjury that the assets and liabilities divided in this agreement constitute all their community and quasi-community assets and liabilities. In the event that the division is unequal, the parties knowingly and intelligently waive an equal division of the community property.

   A. Husband is awarded and assigned the following assets as his share of the community property: **(list each item or groups of items. Give legal description of real estate including assessor's parcel number; license and VIN for vehicles).**

B. Wife is awarded and assigned the following assets as her share of the community property: **(list as instructed for Husband).**

C. Husband shall pay the following debts promptly when due and indemnify and hold Wife harmless therefrom: **(list—identify clearly, give value of each item).**

D. Wife shall pay the following debts promptly when due, and indemnify and hold Husband harmless therefrom: **(list—identify clearly, give value of each item).**

E. Husband and Wife each warrants to the other that, after the date of this agreement, no debt or obligation will be incurred for which the other may be liable, or that could be enforced against an asset held by the other. We agree that if any claim be brought seeking to hold one liable for the subsequent debts of the other, or an undisclosed obligation of the other, or for any act or omission of the other, then each will hold the other harmless, defend such claim, and indemnify the other for any liability on the obligation, attorneys' fees, and related costs.

F. If either party has any knowledge of any community asset other than those disclosed and listed in this agreement, warrantor will transfer or pay to warrantee, at the warrantee's election, one of the following: (a) If the asset is reasonably susceptible to division, a portion of the asset equal to the warrantee's interest in it, plus 10% per annum compounded annually from the effective date to the date of payment; or (b) The fair market value of the warrantee's interest in the asset on the effective date of this agreement, plus 10% per annum compounded annually from the effective date of this agreement.

G. If either party decides to claim any rights under bankruptcy laws, that party must notify the other of this intention in writing at least fourteen days before filing the petition, including the name, address and phone number of the attorney, if any, who represents the party in that petition and the court in which the petition will be filed. The party receiving notice will have five business days to elect to participate jointly with the notifying party in a consolidation proceeding and may choose to be represented by the same attorney, if any.

H. These provisions will not impair the availability of any other remedy arising from nondisclosure of community assets or debts.

Note about pension plans: Read chapter 3.6(b). If there is a community interest in a pension plan, it must be dealt with in your settlement agreement. If it is to be given entirely to the employee-spouse, list it in item A or B above. If the pension will be divided by the payoff method (see 3.6(b)), you shouldn't try to do the SA or the Judgment orders yourself. Call Divorce Helpline and get help.

Note about family home: spouses may agree to a) sell and divide the home now; or b) a buy-out by one spouse, maybe with a promissory note to the other (payments can be deferred to some future time or event); or c) joint ownership. Call Divorce Helpline for help if you plan to use method (c).

IX. TAXES:

A. Any tax refunds for the current fiscal year shall be distributed as follows: **(specify).**

B. Any tax deficiencies for the current year shall be paid as follows: **(specify).**

C. For any year in which support payments for said child are not over ___ days in arrears, the parent paying support may claim the tax exemption for **(names of children)** and the recipient will execute a waiver of the right to claim the exemption for that year. **(Note: before you do this, be sure to analyze the effect on the amount of support paid and the net income of both parties. CalSupport™ can give you this analysis.)**

X. RESERVATION OF JURISDICTION: The parties agree that the court shall have jurisdiction to make whatever orders may be necessary or desirable to carry out this agreement and to divide equally between the parties any community assets or liabilities omitted from division under this agreement.

XI. ADVICE OF COUNSEL: The parties recognize that the termination of the marriage, issues of child custody, visitation, child and spousal support, and division of marital property will be determined by this instrument. We recognize that we each have a right to seek advice from independent counsel of our own choosing and that we knowingly and with due regard for the importance of same have elected to proceed with this agreement.

XII. EXECUTION OF INSTRUMENTS: Each agrees to execute and deliver any documents, make all endorsements, and do all acts which are necessary or convenient to carry out the terms of this agreement.

XIII. PRESENTATION TO COURT:
   A) Los Angeles & San Bernardino: This agreement shall be presented to the court in any divorce proceeding between the parties, the original of this agreement will be placed in the court's case file, and the court shall be requested to accept the agreement and order the parties to comply with its provisions. It is the intention of the parties that all warranties and remedies provided in this agreement shall be preserved.
   B) All other counties: This agreement shall be presented to the court in any divorce proceeding between the parties, it shall be incorporated into the Judgment therein, the parties shall be ordered to comply with all its provisions, and all warranties and remedies provided in this agreement shall be preserved.

XIV. DISCLOSURES: Each party has made a full and honest disclosure to the other of all current finances and assets, and each enters into this agreement in reliance thereon. Each warrants to the other and declares under penalty of perjury that the assets and liabilities divided in this agreement constitute all of their community assets and liabilities.

XV. RESOLUTION OF DISPUTES
All disputes arising between us on any matter whatever will be resolved as follows:
   A. Mediation
   (1) If we are unable to resolve any dispute ourselves or with counseling, then we each agree to make a reasonable good-faith effort to resolve the matter in mediation. On the written request of either party, we will within thirty days submit our dispute to mediation with a mediator agreed upon by both of us. If we are unable to agree on a mediator, we will each choose one person to make a choice on our behalf, and those two persons together will appoint our mediator. We will participate in mediation in good faith and we will each be responsible for half the cost of mediation.
   Optional. Unless we agree otherwise, our mediator must be a California family law attorney who specializes in family law mediation.
   (2) We are each entitled to representation in mediation by an attorney of our choice. Each party will be responsible for his or her own attorney's fees.

   B. Arbitration
   (1) If mediation does not resolve all issues within a reasonable number of sessions, then on the written request of either of us, we will submit the matter to binding arbitration within ninety days. The arbitrator will be agreed upon by both of us, but must be a California family law attorney who specializes in mediation or arbitration, or a retired California family court judge. If we are unable to agree on an arbitrator, the matter will be decided by a panel of three arbitrators. We will each choose

one arbitrator, who need not have any particular professional background, and our two arbitrators together will appoint the third arbitrator who must be a California family law attorney or retired California family court judge.

(2) If we use a single arbitrator, we will each be responsible for half the cost of the arbitration. If we use a panel of three arbitrators, each of us will pay the fees of the arbitrator we appoint and we will each be responsible for half the fees of the third arbitrator and other costs of arbitration.

(3) We are each entitled to representation in arbitration by an attorney of our choice. Attorney fees will be borne by each party separately.

(4) The arbitrator(s) will have the power to interpret the terms of this agreement, decide questions of their own jurisdiction, and settle disputes arising between the parties regarding the arbitrability of claims and the interpretation of the agreement. The arbitrator(s) will not have the power to alter, modify or terminate any provision of this agreement. The arbitration will be conducted under the rules of California Code of Civil Procedure sections 1280 to 1294.2, as modified by the Nolo Supplementary Family Arbitration Rules, a copy of which is attached to this agreement as Exhibit A.

(5) **Arbitration is binding and final.** The decision of the arbitrator(s) will be binding and final, not subject to review in any court. We each understand that by agreeing to binding arbitration, we are choosing arbitration as the sole remedy for any dispute between us, and we each expressly give up our right to file a lawsuit or family-law proceeding in any court against one another, or to request a court to resolve any dispute between us, except to compel arbitration or enforce the decision of an arbitrator. We understand that this means we are giving up the right to trial by a court or by a jury. To whatever extent the law does not allow any issue between us to be decided by binding arbitration, we agree to submit such matters to nonbinding arbitration before submitting the issue to any court.

Optional. (6) If an action is required to enforce the use of binding arbitration required by this agreement, or the decision of an arbitrator, the costs and expenses of the prevailing party in such judicial proceeding, including, but not limited to, his or her reasonable attorney's fees, will be paid by the unsuccessful party.

XVI. BINDING EFFECT: This agreement, and each provision thereof, is expressly made binding upon heirs, assigns, executors, administrators, representatives, and successors in interest of each party.

Dated: _____   _____,Husband

Dated: _____   _____,Wife

ATTACHMENTS:
    Exhibit A: Nolo Supplementary Family Arbitration Rules

If the Department of Child Support Services (or some other court office) is providing support enforcement in your case, add this:

The Department of Child Support Services **(or other office)** for the County of_____ , State of California, approves the child support as agreed herein. This office claims jurisdiction only to approve the matter of support.

Dated:

_____   _____
        Type or print name   for the Department of Child Support Services

Note: Child support, some counties. If your settlement agreement has child support in it, some counties (Alameda, Imperial, Santa Barbara, Santa Cruz, Solano, Stanislaus, and possibly some others) want the Stipulation to Establish Child Support (chapter 18). A computer calculation of the guideline amount is also required in Alameda and Imperial counties.

Note. If your case involves any kind of support, you *must* file income and expense forms (chapter 16) unless you have a settlement agreement. Even if you do have a settlement agreement, many counties (Alameda, Contra Costa, Monterey, San Francisco, Santa Clara, Solano, probably many others) want to see the financial forms—call the clerk to see if they are required in your county. If they are, include them along with the other paperwork when you are ready to get your Judgment (chapter 20).

Mediation and arbitration

Sometimes it isn't completely over even when it's over, especially for parents. So, if any disagreement should arise after your divorce is completed, this clause will help you stay out of court, where no family should ever go. Clause XV of the SA says that any disputes between you in the future will be resolved by mediation (which has a high success rate) or binding arbitration as a last resort in case mediation does not resolve the matter in a reasonable time. While not pleasant, this is a much better way to resolve disputes than going to court. If you should ever need a family law mediator or arbitrator, call Divorce Helpline.

Choosing a mediator or arbitrator. For the kinds of disputes that come up after a settlement agreement is signed, it is usually not necessary to choose a mediator who is a family law attorney, especially where the primary issue is parenting, or where cost is an issue and you know of a non-attorney mediator with a good reputation and lots of experience. However, if you believe that the issues are more likely to be based on law rather than personalities, a lawyer-mediator is still a good choice. When it comes to the arbitrator, this person should definitely be a California family law attorney or a retired California family court judge, as knowledge and experience with the law is essential to conduct an arbitration correctly.

Nolo Supplementary Family Arbitration Rules *must* be attached to this agreement and marked Exhibit A, as stated in clause XV. A copy of the rules can be found at the end of the forms section in the back of this book or on the companion CD in the forms folder. Arbitration rules have been established by many organizations and states, including the California rules which are used in this agreement. However, these rules were created with business disputes in mind and do not provide for the kinds of temporary, preliminary or interim measures that are often necessary in family disputes, nor do they provide for post-judgment relief and modifications that are sometimes necessary in family disputes. To fill this gap, Nolo Supplementary Family Arbitration Rules are intended to supplement any set of arbitration rules a couple might adopt, in order to deal with situations not anticipated by arbitration rules currently available.

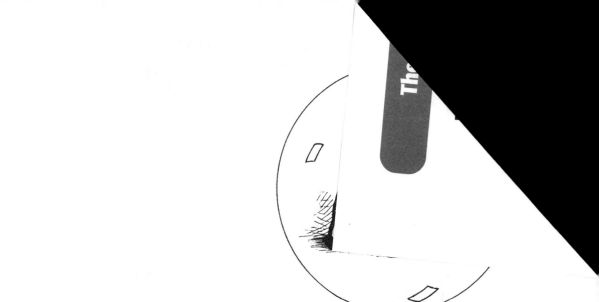

Part Two:
How to do your own
Regular Dissolution

The Chapters in Part Two

WE CAN DO IT FOR YOU

You probably have important things to do with your time, so, if your plate is already full, let us take this red-tape burden off your hands. You will feel better knowing that your paperwork will be done promptly and correctly by Divorce Helpline's staff of family law attorneys and documents experts.

DIVORCE HELPLINE   (800) 359-7004

DOING YOUR OWN FORMS

> This part of the book tells you exactly how to do your own *Regular* Dissolution. Chapter 2.2 describes Regular and Summary Dissolutions and tells you how to choose which one to use.

How hard is it? Get help?

Remember, filling out the forms is *not* what "do your own" divorce is about. The real work is in the process—thinking things through and making decisions, negotiating an agreement with your spouse.

That said, how hard it is to do your own paperwork depends on how much time, talent and determination you have and the complexity of your case. Even easy cases take time and careful thought. Don't expect to do these forms in one day or even a few days.

Millions of people have done divorces entirely by themselves, but not all have done it well. Doing the paperwork is not as easy as it was ten years ago. Like the law, paperwork has become increasingly complicated and dealing with the bureaucracy has become *much* more trying (to put it nicely).

Can you do your own paperwork? Yes, almost certainly—but it does take some effort. Your real question is, "What do I have to lose if I don't do it right?" Not much? Do it. A lot? Get help. If you can afford a few hundred dollars, your time might be better spent on your job, your children, and getting on with your life.

Look through this book to get an idea of how complex your case is and how it might feel to do it yourself. Then review chapter 1.9 (Who can help?) to decide if you want to get help and from whom. Even if you do get help, you will still be in charge, still "doing your own divorce," still better off.

When and how to start

Respondent. If you are the Respondent, your case has already been started, so go to chapter 11 and find out how to file your Response.

Petitioner. You need to plan carefully when and how you will deliver the message as how you do this will set the tone for the future. Typically, one spouse is ready to act long before the other has accepted the idea of a divorce—a primary cause of a lot of conflict. You don't want to frighten or anger your spouse into running to an attorney and taking the case into conflict. Take some time to prepare your spouse and let him/her get used to the idea that it's going to happen. However, if you are dealing with an abuser/controller, there's not much point to talking until you establish a position of power. There are a variety of ways to do that, from the beginning (see Book 2, chapters 3-4).

Softening the blow

Unless dealing with an abuser/controller, you probably want to tell your spouse ahead of time that papers are coming and there's lots of time to talk and work things out before a Response is necessary. Send a letter saying that you are filing papes in order to get the case on record but you very much want an agreement and you promise not to take the case further without giving 30 days written notice. If you prepared the Petition so it *requires* an agreement and you *can't* go forward without one (see chapter 10, item 5b), be sure to point this out. These steps let your spouse know there's no need to Respond in a hurry, that there's time to talk. Send Respondent a copy of this book. Good information really helps.

If your spouse responds you have only two ways to proceed: by agreement or by trial. You *really* don't want to go to trial, so work hard on getting an agreement. Get *Make Any Divorce Better* to learn how to reduce conflict and negotiate an agreement. Send a copy to your Ex. Or call Divorce Helpline for exper problem-solving assistance. Ask your spouse to call, too, so we can explain things to both of you.

How to use the forms

All dissolutions in California must be filed on forms designed by the Judicial Council. There is a complete set in the back of this book, and another set on the companion CD that you can fill out on a computer. The forms in this book include many that your case does not require—just use the ones you need as explained in the instructions below. Forms are also available at your county clerk's office for a small fee. In the following chapters, you will find a description of each form with detailed instructions on how to fill it out. But first, here are some general instructions that apply to all forms:

Generally

Get it together. Keep your papers safe, neat, organized, and all together in one place.

Typing? Complete your forms very carefully, either on a computer or with a typewriter. If typing, it you should use the larger size type (Pica), as some clerks will occasionally refuse forms with smaller type (Elite). If prepared on a computer, the type is already specified in the forms provided on our CD.

Color your world. Some counties used to require that certain documents be filed on colored paper, but effective January 1, 2007, new Court Rules 1.31(f), 1.35(f) and 2.103 superseded local rules and all court documents are now to be filed on white recycled paper, at least 20-pound weight. If a clerk returns a document and requests it on colored paper, you have two choices: either file it again with a note calling the clerk's attention to the above Rules of Court or you just do as the clerk asks—sometimes that's easier.

Picky, picky. We once heard that a clerk in Fresno refused to accept forms directly from this book because they are ever-so-slightly less than 8.5 x 11. If this rare pickiness happens to you, either try again with a different clerk or make copies of all blank forms you need and you'll end up with full-sized paper.

To tumble or not to tumble. It is now optional to copy two-sided forms tumbled (upside down on the back), just as you see them in this book. You don't have to do this, but judges seem to like it that way so, if you are printing out your own forms and if you feel like it, print the second sides upside down on the backs of the first pages. Like we said; this is optional.

Sign in blue. Not a legal requirement, but it's a *very* good idea to sign documents in blue ink so both you and the clerk can tell easily which copy is the original.

Captions

At the top of each form is a heading, called a caption. Slight variations have appeared over the years—moving the phone number, adding fax and email—so you'll have to adapt, but basically, it goes like this:

Figure 7.1 HOW TO FILL OUT THE CAPTION

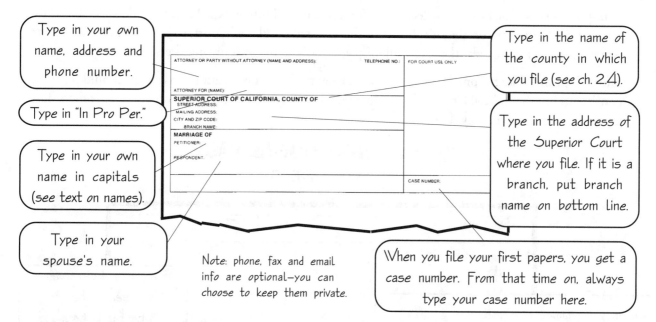

Type in your own name, address and phone number.

Type in "In Pro Per."

Type in your own name in capitals (see text on names).

Type in your spouse's name.

Note: phone, fax and email info are optional—you can choose to keep them private.

Type in the name of the county in which you file (see ch. 2.4).

Type in the address of the Superior Court where you file. If it is a branch, put branch name on bottom line.

When you file your first papers, you get a case number. From that time on, always type your case number here.

ATTORNEY OR PARTY WITHOUT ATTORNEY (NAME AND ADDRESS): TELEPHONE NO.: FOR COURT USE ONLY
ATTORNEY FOR (NAME):
SUPERIOR COURT OF CALIFORNIA, COUNTY OF
STREET ADDRESS:
MAILING ADDRESS:
CITY AND ZIP CODE:
BRANCH NAME:
MARRIAGE OF
PETITIONER:
RESPONDENT:
CASE NUMBER:

Petitioner/Respondent/In pro per

The Petitioner is the person who first files papers; the Respondent is the other person. The words "in pro per" appear in captions and other places. This is abbreviated legal Latin, meaning that you are appearing for yourself, without an attorney. In some states, they use the term "pro se," which means the same thing.

Names

While not required, it is a good idea to use full names, but be consistent: names should appear exactly the same way each time, including your signatures. The court won't know that John Smith, J.W. Smith, John W. Smith and J. Wilson Smith are the same person. It is better to type names in capitals. Use names in normal order—last names go last. Use the wife's married name, unless the form asks specifically for her maiden name, or unless she used her maiden name during the marriage.

Change of address

If your address changes at any time after you enter the case, it is *essential* that you file a formal change of address. A form for this can be found in the Kit section of the companion CD, with instructions.

Number of copies

You need the original and two copies: original to the court and copies for you and the other party, but make an extra copy or two in case the others get lost. It happens. Some counties want an extra copy of each form when you file in a branch office. You are required to use *recycled* paper, though how they'll check this is a mystery. When you copy a form with material on the back, you'll have two pages, so staple them together at the top left corner. If you copy or print forms on both sides of a single sheet, like the originals, make sure the text on the back is "tumbled," that is, upside down, just as on the original.

Additional pages

If you need more room to complete an item on a form, use the Additional Page. Identify each item that is being continued by typing "Continuation of Item Number __." For the Property Declaration (chapter 15) there is a special continuation form to use instead of this one. You can also use this form to make a declaration; for example, the Declaration of Compliance (chapter 20.2), located in the back after the Petition. Keep on blank Additional Page and make copies as needed.

Computer users: The form provided by the Judicial Council (on our CD) enters single-spaced text not lined up with numbers on the side, but their forms are like Rules of Court, so just use it as-is and don't worry about trying to make the text double-spaced or lined up with the numbers.

Short Captions, like the one below, are acceptable with the names in either order. You should try to be consistent, but the Judicial Council forms do it one way on some forms and the other way on others. Just go along with however they do it.

Figure 7.2 ADDITIONAL PAGE
Form MC-020

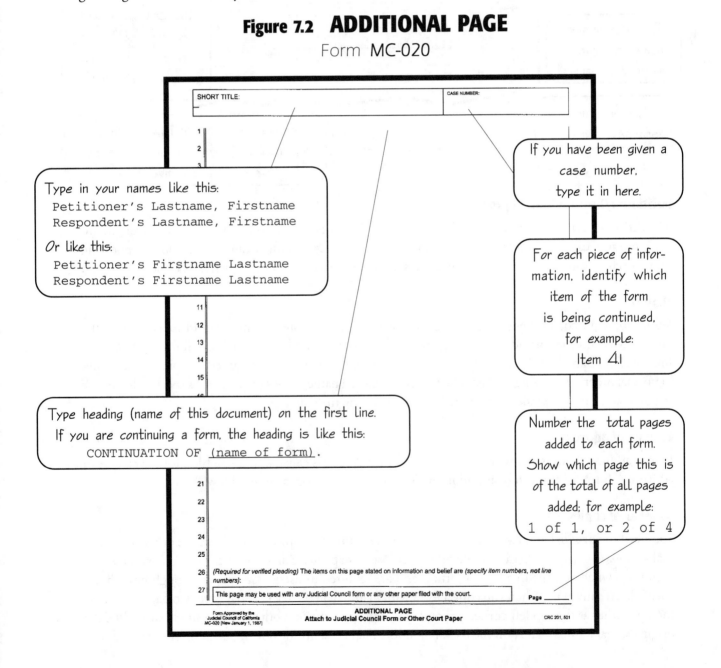

Privacy

Court documents are public so you do **not** want Social Security or financial account numbers on view for identity thieves. Therefore, on any document filed with the court that requires a Social Security or financial account number, use only the last four digits preceded by a code number associated with that item, for example: "R1 = ***–**–4321" could be your Social Security number, now identifed as "R1" in all documents, and "R6 = ******-7654" could be a Schwab account. Keep a private list of each code and the related full account number. If some day you are asked by the court to identify your information, you must file form MC-120, shown below. Do not file it unless asked. This form is on the CD. **Only documents filed in court.** Do **not** use codes on documents that are served on the other party—they have a right to the complete number. You only code information on documents filed with the court. **Settlement Agreements.** If you file a Settlement Agreement with the court, use your code number in place of all Social Security or financial account numbers in the copy that goes to the court.

Figure 7.3 CONFIDENTIAL REFERENCE LIST OF IDENTIFIERS
(Form MC-120)

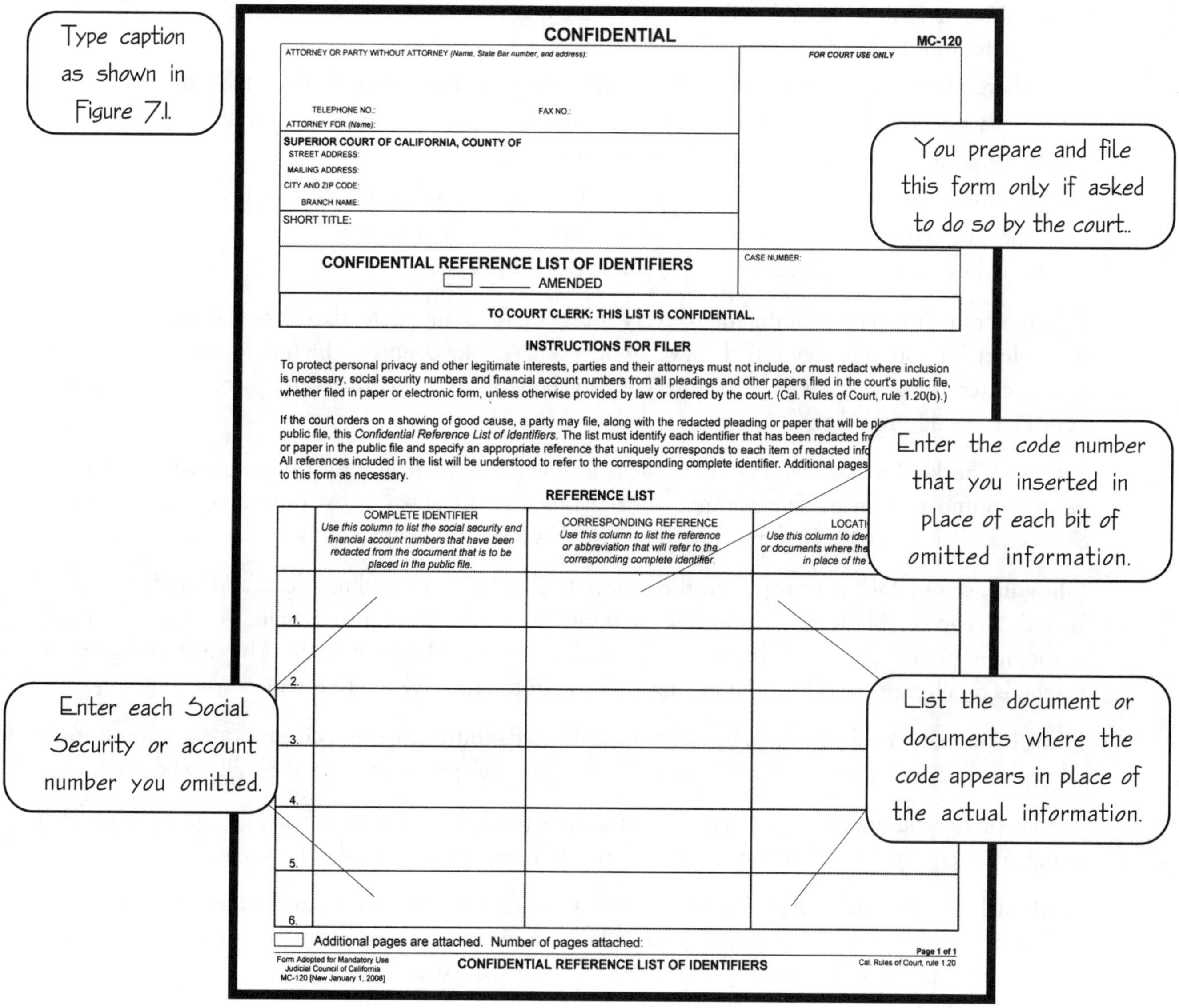

[Form illustration with annotation callouts:]

- Type caption as shown in Figure 7.1.
- You prepare and file this form only if asked to do so by the court.
- Enter the code number that you inserted in place of each bit of omitted information.
- Enter each Social Security or account number you omitted.
- List the document or documents where the code appears in place of the actual information.

7.3 How to file your papers

Domestic partners can file anywhere in California, but for married people, the county in which you file is determined by the residency requirement (chapter 2.4) and must be where one of the parties lives. Before you start, call the Clerk's office and ask some questions:

- How to find the Clerk's office and the desk where you file divorce papers?
- Is there a branch court where you can file papers that is nearer to you than the main office?
- Exactly how much are the filing fees for a dissolution; can filing fees be paid by personal check?
- Are there any printed instructions for people filing "in pro per?"
- Are local forms required in a dissolution? For filing in a branch court? For setting a hearing?
- Where can you buy local forms and Judicial Council family law forms?
- Are colored forms required for any part of a dissolution case?

You must punch two holes at the top of every sheet you file, using a standard 2 hole punch. The clerks won't do it for you, but they usually have a hole punch at the counter. The holes must be $2^1/2$ inches apart, centered, and $^5/8$ inch from the top. **Los Angeles County** wants an extra copy of the front page of your Petition. Humor them.

Privacy. Check all forms before you file them to make sure there are no complete account or Social Security numbers on them. The same goes for attachments, such as pay stubs or the settlement agreement. See section 7.2. The Case Registry form is excepted as it is not on public view.

Filing in person. Take your papers to the county Clerk's office, civil filings desk, and hand them over. Include all copies with the original so they can stamp them. If your county has branch courts, you can file at the main branch or at a branch where either party resides. Filing can be done by mail, but going in person is much more certain and immediate if it is not too inconvenient for you.

Filing by mail. If you file by mail, be sure to include a self–addressed, stamped envelope for the return of all copies. In busy counties it can take some time to get your papers through the mill, so be patient.

When you file your first papers, you pay your filing fee (see below). The clerk will give you a case number and, from that time on, all documents you file *must* have your case number on them.

Clerks will not give you legal advice because they are not attorneys and it would be illegal for them to do so, but, if they feel like it, they can help you a lot with information about the filing of papers and how matters are handled in their county. Don't be afraid to ask questions.

SASE envelope for free document review service

A clerk recently confided that less than 1% of divorce papers go through the first time, so yours will probably come back with a page of notes of things they want done differently. This is great! Think of it as a free document review service and carefully do whatever they ask. This is why, when you file papers, you need to include a self-adressed stamped envelope that is large enough and with enough postage to get all papers back. If you need your judgment by a particular date, say to remarry or by December 31 for tax purposes, you should allow several extra weeks for this inevitable and invaluable part of the process.

Clerk errors

Clerks make mistakes. Are you shocked? It doesn't happen every day, but now and then a clerk will send back papers that are correct or demand a fee that is not required. If this happens, the best thing would be to do whatever they ask. If you feel strongly about it, double check to make sure you followed our instructions exactly, then resubmit your papers and see if you get a different result. If you are in a hurry, take them in personally and try a different clerk or talk it over with the supervisor. However, unless you have a very important reason, it almost always works out better if you just do whatever they ask.

Non vexas amanuensis

If you run into an unpleasant clerk, stay polite no matter what. If necessary, try to get another clerk to help you, even if you have to come back. Never, never, never piss off a clerk, even if they deserve it. *Never.* There's nothing to be gained and it can come back to haunt you if you need a clerk's cooperation some other day. By the way, the header above is Latin (so beloved in the law) for "don't irritate the clerk."

Filing fees

Filing fees are paid when you file the first papers. It is now $320 in most counties, plus up to $50 more in Riverside, San Bernardino, and San Francisco for a court construction surcharge. Some counties will accept personal checks, otherwise fees should be paid with cash or a money order. About 30 counties also charge an additional fee to cover mandatory mediation services. Call the clerk's office to get the exact amount in your county.

A Response fee equal to the first filing fee (see above) is charged for anything filed by the Respondent. There is no charge for an Appearance & Waiver when filed by a member of the armed forces.

If filed by the Petitioner, there is no fee for filing a settlement agreement, a stipulation to the date of termination, stipulated postjudgment modification of child support, or stipulation to modify a settlement agreement. If a clerk tries to charge for any of these, refer them to Government Code § 70677(c).

Waiver of fees

If you are *very* poor, you may not have to pay filing fees. You don't have to be absolutely destitute, but not too far from it, either. Your application will be easy and you will probably be allowed to file for free if (1) you receive financial assistance (SSI, SSP, TANF/CalWORKS), food stamps, county relief, or general assistance), or (2) if your *gross* monthly income is less than the amounts shown in the table. In L.A., if you don't fit in category (1), you must attach a recent tax return or a

Number in family	Family income
1	$ 1,063.54
2	1,426.04
3	1,788.54
4	2,151.04
5	2,513.54
6	2,876.04
7	3,238.54
8	3,601.54
Each additional	362.50

letter from your employer on a company letterhead verifying monthly wages. If you don't fit the first two categories, but your income is not enough to pay for the common necessaries of life for yourself and the people you support and also pay court fees, then you have to prove your case by filling out detailed income and expense forms. Don't be afraid to try it, you have nothing to lose but time and trouble.

You will find a set of forms to apply for a waiver of court fees, with instructions, in the Kit section of the companion CD, or you can get a set for free from the Clerk's office.

7.4 Local forms and rules

Some counties require local forms in addition to the official set. Look for them at your county's Superior Court website. You can find links to court websites at **www.nolodivorce.com/links** or at **www.courtinfo.ca.gov/rules/localrules.htm** or call your Clerk's office, civil filings desk, and ask what local forms they use in an uncontested dissolution and get copies. Ask if they have special local requirements (colors of forms, preferred time and manner of filing documents, etc.). Ask if they have printed instructions for people filing "in pro per."

If you come across a form you can't figure out, just mail us two blank copies with a **stamped self-addressed envelope** and we will send instructions.

Branch courts. If you file your first papers in a branch instead of the main office, some counties want a Certificate or Declaration of Assignment (Alameda, Riverside, San Bernardino, San Mateo, Ventura; Los Angeles County wants one in every case, even if you file in the main office). We show the L.A. form as an example, but note that forms from other counties look different. They all want to know what court district you are filing in (get the correct name from the Clerk's office) and the reason, which is invariably because you or Respondent reside in that district. So, if you are asked, check a box or write "(Petitioner/Respondent) resides in said district at (give address)." The time for trial, if requested, would be about 15 minutes.

ADR information packet. Many counties now require a notice about Alternative Dispute Resolution (ADR) with the Petition and Response. This form explains the advantages of mediation, arbitration and possibly other alternatives to taking your case to court. Check local rules or your court clerk's office.

L.A. wants a Family Law Worksheet for every case filed in the Central District. Some counties require attendance at a program for parties with children and will probably require you to serve notice of the program on Respondent. Santa Barbara also wants an extra $50 with the filing fee to cover the cost of the program. They'll tell you what they want and give you papers for it when the Petition is filed.

The next time you are likely to meet a local form is when you request a hearing. These are described at the end of chapter 20.3 where they are more relevant.

Figure 7.4 CERTIFICATE OF ASSIGNMENT
(Los Angeles County)

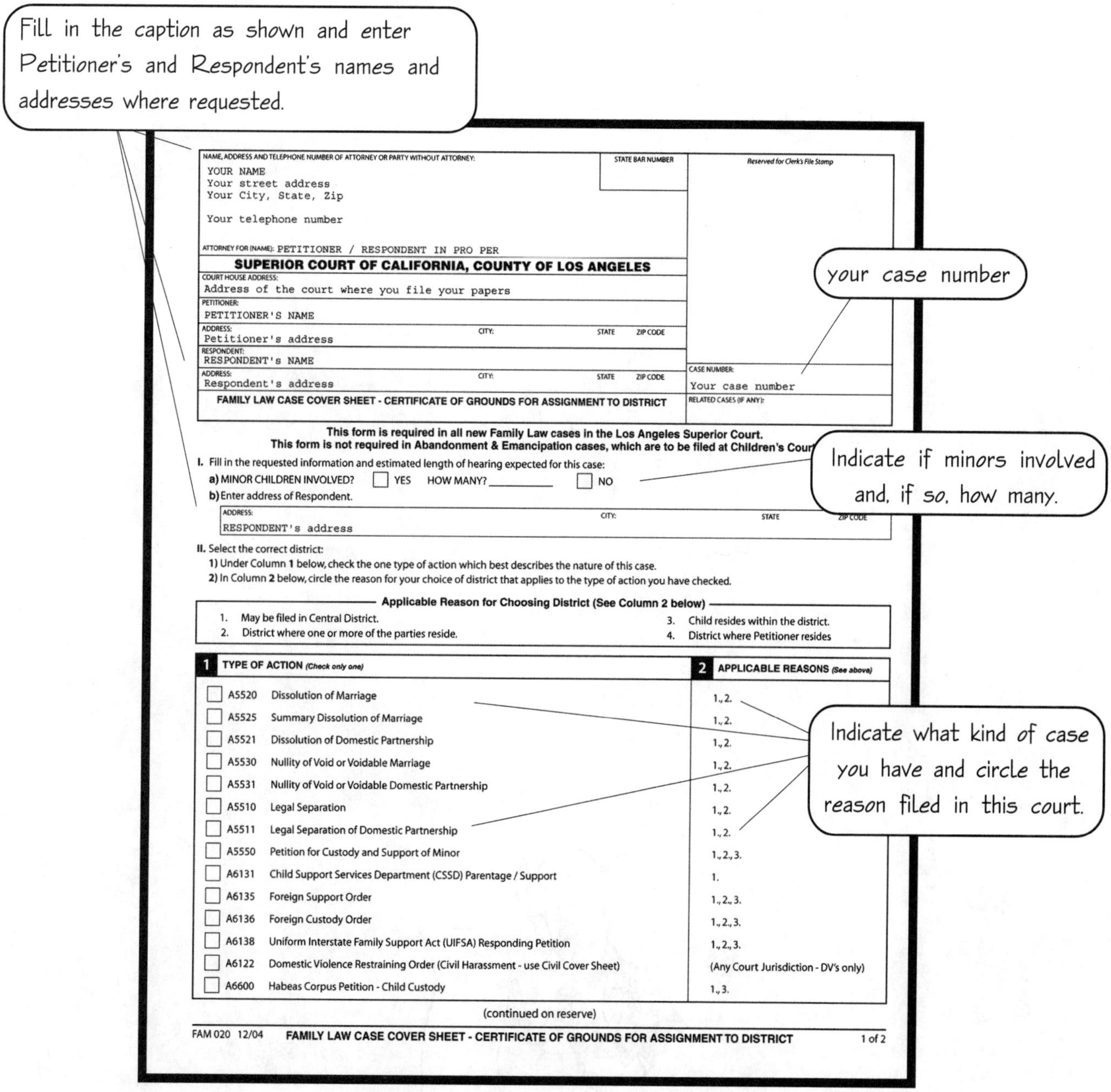

Fill in the caption as shown and enter Petitioner's and Respondent's names and addresses where requested.

your case number

Indicate if minors involved and, if so, how many.

Indicate what kind of case you have and circle the reason filed in this court.

Second page

Enter the name of the branch court where you file your papers at item III (3), then date and sign the form.

Note. You can download this form at **www.lasuperiorcourt.org/forms/** under the Family Law section.

CHECK LIST

The check list on the next page is your "How to Do It" guide; a step-by-step list that shows you what to do and when to do it, with references to the chapters where you will find detailed information about each step.

As you will see from the checklist on the next page, you only have to go through four steps to get your dissolution:

Step	Task	Chapters
One	File the Petition or Response	9–11
Two	Serve papers on your spouse	12–13
Three	Declarations of Disclosure	14
Four	Get your Judgment	15–21

Each step has a choice to make, a few forms to fill out, and a task to perform. You only need to use the chapters and the forms that apply to your own case. While doing the forms is not the easiest or most fun thing you will ever do, no case uses all the forms in this book, so don't be put off by the number and variety that you see on these pages.

Check each item as you progress

CHECK LIST

■ = a form to fill out   ▲ = a decision to make

1
- ☐ ■ SUMMONS (chapter 9)
- ☐ ■ PETITION (chapter 10) or RESPONSE (chapter 11) No Summons filed with Response
- ☐ ■ DECLARATION UNDER UCCJEA (if there are minor children of this marriage) (chapter 10)
- ☐ ■ Local form required in some counties when filing in a branch court. Ask the clerk—see chapter 7.4.
- ☐ **Optional:** Do Preliminary Disclosure documents now (Step 3 below; chapter 14) and serve them with the documents above.
- ☐ **Task:** File papers with Clerk (chapter 7.3). If you are *very* poor, read chapter 7.3 and consider applying for waiver of fees.

2
- ☐ ▲ **Decision:** Which method of service? Read chapter 12. Prepare additional forms if required by your method of service. **Option:** File the Response now or the A&W (chapter 12.7) and skip this step.

Personal Service	Acknowledgment	Certified Mail
(chapter 12.4) no other forms	■ ACKNOWLEDGMENT (chapter 12.5)	(Return receipt comes from the Post Office)

- ☐ ■ PROOF OF SERVICE (ch. 13) (Attach the *original* Summons and any forms required by your method of service, as above.)
- ☐ **Task:** Get papers served (chapter 12). Make sure Proof of Service is filled out correctly and signed by person serving papers.
- ☐ **Task:** File the Proof of Service with any attachments required by your method of service. But . . . .
   Note: Important! Some counties (like Santa Clara) want these papers and all the rest (Steps 2-4) filed at one time when you are ready to complete your case and get your Judgment. It is permitted and often convenient to do this in any county.

3
- ☐ ■ PRELIMINARY DECLARATION OF DISCLOSURE (chapter 14) Petitioner *must*, Resp. should. Served, not filed in court.
- ☐ ■ LIST OF ASSETS & DEBTS (chapter 14) Served, not filed in court.
- ☐ ■ INCOME & EXPENSE DECLARATIONS (chapter 16) Served, not filed in court.
- ☐ ■ DECLARATION RE SERVICE OF DISCLOSURE (Fig. 14.4) This is filed in court with Proof of Service (see chapter 14.2).
- ☐ **Task:** Have someone serve the Preliminary Declaration of Disclosure on Respondent, preferably within 60 days of service of Summons. That person then signs either a Proof of Service by Mail (Fig. 13.3) or Proof of Personal Service (Fig. 13.4).

4

CASES WITH A SETTLEMENT AGREEMENT (SA)	CASES WITH NO SETTLEMENT AGREEMENT
☐ ■ INCOME & EXPENSE FORMS (chapter 16) (Only a few counties want these if you have an SA) ☐ ■ FINAL DECLARATION OF DISCLOSURE (Fig. 14.1) ☐ ■ SCHEDULE OF ASSETS & DEBTS (14) Served, not filed. ☐ ■ DECLARATION OF SERVICE OF DISCL. (Fig. 14.3) ☐ ■ PROOF OF SERVICE (of disclosure) (Fig. 13.3 or 13.4)	☐ ■ PROPERTY DECLARATION (chapter 15) ☐ ■ INCOME & EXPENSE FORMS (chapter 16) Note: If there's no SA and no Response, Petitioner can waive the Final Declaration of Disclosure requirement, either in the Declaration for Uncontested Dissolution or at a hearing.
IF A RESPONSE WAS FILED	**IF NO RESPONSE WAS FILED**
☐ ■ APPEARANCE & WAIVER (A&W) (chapter 12.7) Signed by both parties. If Proof of Service of Summons not previously filed, be sure to return *original* Summons with your papers at this time.	■ REQUEST FOR DEFAULT (chapter 17) with a stamped envelope addressed to Respondent's last known address with court clerk's return address.

- ☐ ■ JUDGMENT (chapter 18) **Note:** If you have a settlement agreement, file it now, along with the Judgment.

Attach to Judgment if you have child OR spousal support	**If you have child support, also attach:**
■ WAGE ASSIGNMENT ORDER (Fig. 19.1 or 19.2) ■ REQUEST FOR HRG. RE WAGE ASSIGNMENT	■ NOTICE OF RIGHTS & RESPONSIBILITIES (ch. 18.4) ■ INFORMATION SHEET RE CHANGES OF SUPPORT ■ CHILD SUPPORT CASE REGISTRY (chapter 18.4)

- ☐ ■ NOTICE OF ENTRY OF JUDGMENT (chapter 21) and stamped envelopes addressed to each party, clerk's ret. address.
- ☐ ▲ **Decision:** Will you go to a hearing or mail in the Declaration for Default or Uncontested Dissolution? Read chapter 20.

Mailing the Declaration (chapter 20.1)	**Hearing** (chapter 20.3)
☐ ■ DECL. FOR UNCONTESTED DISSOLUTION (ch. 20.1) ☐ **Task:** Mail to Clerk together with other papers in Step 4. ☐ Include *original* Summons if not filed already.	**Task:** Get a date for your court hearing. ■ Local form required in some counties to request hearing **Task:** Go to the court hearing. Take all papers with you.

- ☐ **Task:** Mail spouse a copy of Judgment and Notice of Entry. However, if Judgment orders support or anything to be done in the future, serve a copy of the Judgment on your ex-spouse by personal service and file a Proof of Service with the court.

When you get the signed Judgment and the Notice of Entry back . . . . CELEBRATE !!

THE SUMMONS

What it is

The Summons is a message from the court to the Respondent. It states that a Petition has been filed that concerns the Respondent, and that if there is no written Response within 30 days, the court may go ahead and grant the Petitioner what has been asked for. A copy of the Summons has to be served on Respondent along with the Petition (see chapter 12).

Restraining orders

The back of the Summons contains restraining orders directed to *both* parties that go into effect immediately when the Summons is served. See chapter 2.7. Be sure to read them, and be careful that you live within those rules until the Judgment is entered. Don't forget and transfer funds or let the kids go visiting outside California without the required notice.

When you file your first papers (Step 1), the clerk should keep the original Summons. When you serve the first set of papers, you will include a *copy* of the Summons. However, if you happen to get the original Summons back, take very good care not to lose it, because you *must* return it when you file the Proof of Service of the Summons (chapter 13).

How to fill it out

Fill out the Summons as shown in Fig. 9.1. Prepare the original and make 3 copies.

Note: If you lose or misplace your original Summons, you are in for extra trouble because you will have to prepare and file a Declaration of Service of Lost Summons. If this misfortune happens to you, look in the Kit section of the companion CD for the Lost Summons form and instructions.

Figure 9.1 SUMMONS
Form FL-110

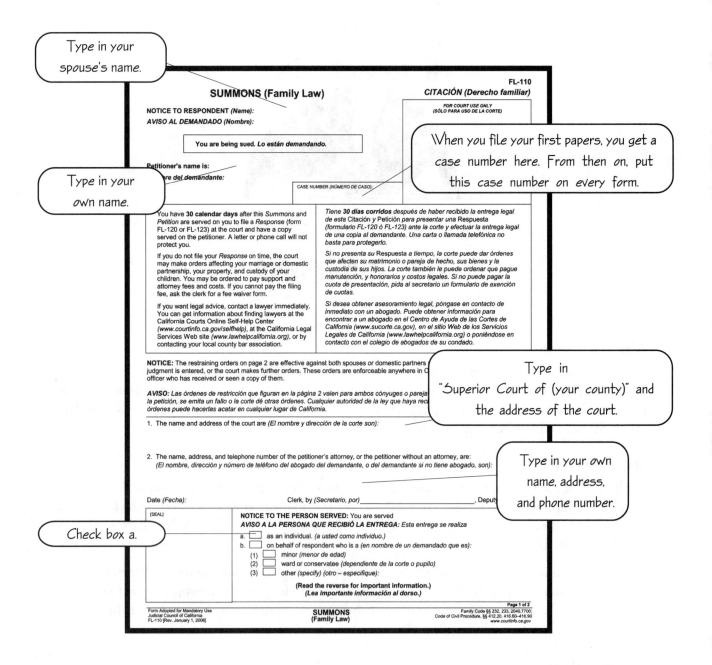

Type in your spouse's name.

Type in your own name.

When you file your first papers, you get a case number here. From then on, put this case number on every form.

Type in "Superior Court of (your county)" and the address of the court.

Type in your own name, address, and phone number.

Check box a.

THE PETITION

What it is

The Petition states basic information about your marriage or partnership and tells the court what you want done. When it is served on the Respondent (Step 2), it gives notice of what's happening in court. If Respondent sees the Petition and declines to respond, then the judge is free to assume that Respondent has no objection to letting the case go by default. See the introduction to chapter 7 for suggestions about how to defuse the effect of serving the Petition on Respondent.

How to fill it out

Prepare the original and make 3 copies. L.A. County wants an extra copy of the front of the Petition.

- **Married people:** Fill out FL-100 Petition as shown in Figs. 10.1 and 10.2.
- **Domestic partners:** Use FL-103 Petition, which is almost identical to FL-100 except for language referring to registered domestic partnership. Follow the instructions for FL-100 below.

NOTES FOR THE PETITION

If you need more space to complete any item, use an Additional Page form (chapter 7.1) with the heading "Continuation of Petition." For each item continued, type a sub-heading that reads "Attachment (number of the item being continued)," and complete your list. Staple the original and copies to the original and all copies of your Petition.

Item 2b. The date of your separation is the last day you were living together as husband and wife or partners. If there is any question in your mind about what date to use, read about the date of separation in chapter 3.1. If you still don't have an exact date, just get as close as you can. If you have separated several times, use the most recent date. Merely sleeping together does not affect separation or dissolution.

Item 7. This is where you tell the court and Respondent what you are asking for in your case. If you don't check it here, you can't get it in your Judgment.

Item 7e, Spousal support. If there will be some spousal support in your case, check box 7e and check a box to indicate who will be the recipient of the support, Petitioner or Respondent.

Item 7g, Terminate . . . spousal support to Respondent. Check this box to notify Respondent that you are going to ask the court to terminate all possibility of any spousal support, either now or in the future.

CASES WITH CHILDREN

Item 3b. The children you list here will include only those presently under 18 (or 18, enrolled full-time in high school and not self-supporting) who were born to or adopted by both you and your spouse. Don't include stepchildren who have not been formally adopted. If the wife is pregnant, include the unborn child by putting "one unborn" in the space provided for the name of child. However, if you want to challenge the paternity, call Divorce Helpline.

Figure 10.1 PETITION
Form FL-100 (page 1)

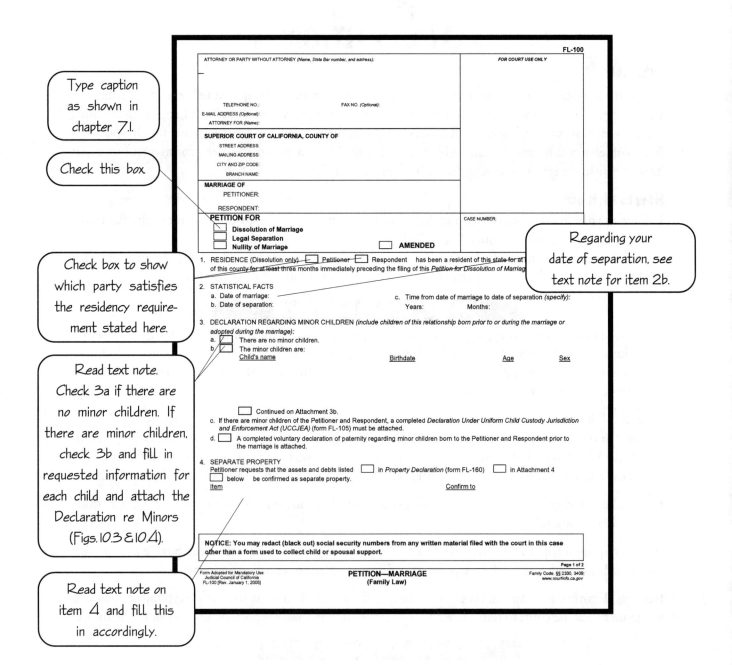

Type caption as shown in chapter 7.1.

Check this box.

Check box to show which party satisfies the residency requirement stated here.

Read text note. Check 3a if there are no minor children. If there are minor children, check 3b and fill in requested information for each child and attach the Declaration re Minors (Figs. 10.3 & 10.4).

Read text note on item 4 and fill this in accordingly.

Regarding your date of separation, see text note for item 2b.

FL-100

ATTORNEY OR PARTY WITHOUT ATTORNEY (Name, State Bar number, and address):

FOR COURT USE ONLY

TELEPHONE NO.:   FAX NO. (Optional):
E-MAIL ADDRESS (Optional):
ATTORNEY FOR (Name):

SUPERIOR COURT OF CALIFORNIA, COUNTY OF
  STREET ADDRESS:
  MAILING ADDRESS:
  CITY AND ZIP CODE:
  BRANCH NAME:

MARRIAGE OF
  PETITIONER:
  RESPONDENT:

PETITION FOR
  ☐ Dissolution of Marriage
  ☐ Legal Separation
  ☐ Nullity of Marriage   ☐ AMENDED

CASE NUMBER:

1. RESIDENCE (Dissolution only) ☐ Petitioner ☐ Respondent has been a resident of this state for at least six months and of this county for at least three months immediately preceding the filing of this Petition for Dissolution of Marriage.

2. STATISTICAL FACTS
  a. Date of marriage:
  b. Date of separation: c. Time from date of marriage to date of separation (specify):
                           Years: Months:

3. DECLARATION REGARDING MINOR CHILDREN (include children of this relationship born prior to or during the marriage or adopted during the marriage):
  a. ☐ There are no minor children.
  b. ☐ The minor children are:
    Child's name   Birthdate   Age   Sex

    ☐ Continued on Attachment 3b.
  c. If there are minor children of the Petitioner and Respondent, a completed Declaration Under Uniform Child Custody Jurisdiction and Enforcement Act (UCCJEA) (form FL-105) must be attached.
  d. ☐ A completed voluntary declaration of paternity regarding minor children born to the Petitioner and Respondent prior to the marriage is attached.

4. SEPARATE PROPERTY
  Petitioner requests that the assets and debts listed ☐ in Property Declaration (form FL-160) ☐ in Attachment 4
  ☐ below be confirmed as separate property.
  Item   Confirm to

NOTICE: You may redact (black out) social security numbers from any written material filed with the court in this case other than a form used to collect child or spousal support.

Page 1 of 2

Form Adopted for Mandatory Use
Judicial Council of California
FL-100 [Rev. January 1, 2005]

PETITION—MARRIAGE
(Family Law)

Family Code, §§ 2330, 3409;
www.courtinfo.ca.gov

Item 3c. Fill out the Declaration Under UCCJEA form as shown in Figures 10.3 and 10.4 and attach it to the Petition.

Item 3d. Refers to the Voluntary Declaration of Paternity available in many hospitals for the last two or three years. If you happen to have one, you can check this box.

Items 7a–c. Read chapter 4.

- To request pure joint custody, check 7a and 7b at the boxes under the "Joint" column.
- To request joint legal custody with sole physical custody to one parent, check 7a under the "Joint" column and check 7b to indicate who is to have primary physical custody.
- To request sole custody (both legal and physical) for one parent, check both 7a and 7b under the column that indicates who is to have custody.
- Check 7c to indicate which parent is to have a visitation schedule.
- **Optional attachments:** If you want to specify custody or visitation in some detail—which is not generally recommended unless you plan to ask for something unusual, which Respndent would have a right to know about—check a box or boxes below 7c and attach one of the listed forms, which can be found on the companion CD. Take a look at those forms to see what's possible. **Note.** FL-312 is a request for orders to prevent the abduction of a child, which is not something you should try to handle yourself. If you face this threat, get help from a family law attorney.

Item 7d—Determine parentage. If a child of the parties was born before the marriage, you *must* check 7d for a determination of parentage. When you apply for your judgment, you will have to attach a declaration stating facts that establish who the biological parents are. A form for your declaration, titled Nolo-1, is included in the companion CD in the forms folder.

ASSETS and DEBTS

Read chapter 3 very carefully. The way the court will relate to your property depends upon how you fill out the Petition. Items 4 and 5 in the Petition are where you tell the court about your property. Remember that "property" includes both assets and debts. Also remember that if you want an *unequal* division of community property worth more than $5,000, you *must* have a settlement agreement.

Item 4, Confirmation of separate assets and debts. If you want any item of property confirmed as the separate asset or debt of either you or your spouse, then check Items 4 and 7h. List each item and indicate to whom it is to be confirmed (Petitioner or Respondent). Be sure to include any retirement plan or fund if no part was earned between marriage and separation. Do *not* list any community property that has already been informally divided by the spouses—it is not separate until divided by the court and must be listed under Item 5. If you need more room, use the Property Declaration form (see chapter 15 for instructions) and call it "Attachment 4."

Option: If you expect to work out an agreement, check "below" then type in, "To be determined by written agreement of the parties." Read discussion below for 5b, "Agreement Coming."

Item 5, Declaration regarding . . . assets and debts.

5a. There are no such assets or debts subject to disposition by the court in this proceeding. Only check this box if there is *truly* no property or so little that it just doesn't matter. Property of any significance *must* be dealt with in 5b even if you have already informally divided it, because it remains community property and you both own it as tenants in common until it is divided by court order. Do *not* check this

Figure 10.2 **PETITION**
Form FL-100 (page 2)

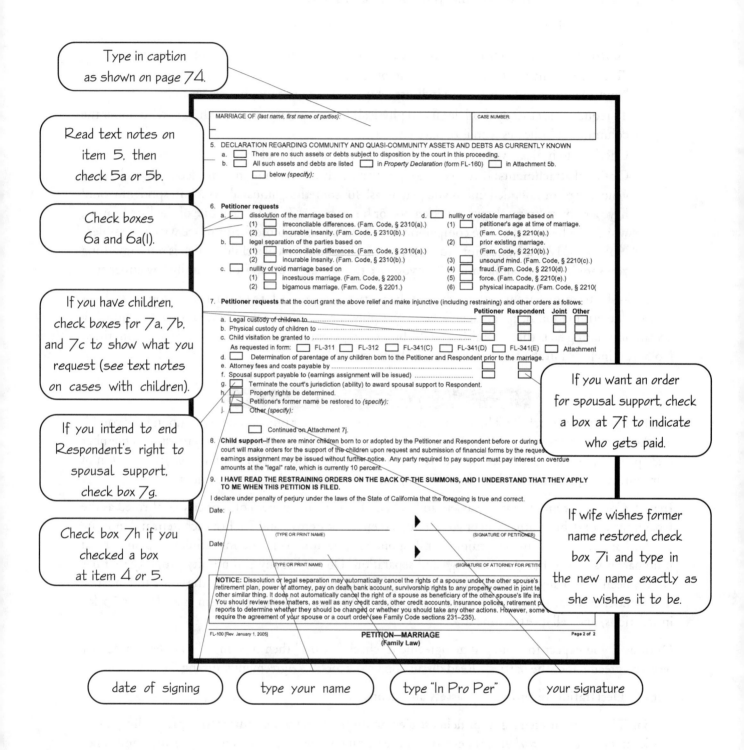

Type in caption as shown on page 74.

Read text notes on item 5, then check 5a or 5b.

Check boxes 6a and 6a(1).

If you have children, check boxes for 7a, 7b, and 7c to show what you request (see text notes on cases with children).

If you intend to end Respondent's right to spousal support, check box 7g.

Check box 7h if you checked a box at item 4 or 5.

If you want an order for spousal support, check a box at 7f to indicate who gets paid.

If wife wishes former name restored, check box 7i and type in the new name exactly as she wishes it to be.

date of signing

type your name

type "In Pro Per"

your signature

box if there is or may *ever* be a disagreement about some item that you care about, or where there is any real estate, or if there is a community interest in a pension plan (see chapter 3.6(b)). When you check box 5a, the court will not inquire about property or make orders about it.

5b. All such assets and debts are listed . . . Check boxes 5b and 7h if you have property or debts that have not yet been divided in a written agreement. You can still put together a settlement agreement with your spouse at a later time and present it to the court when you get your Judgment.

Now, you have a choice to make: you can either list your assets and debts here and now, or you can indicate that they will be determined later in a written agreement.

> **Agreement coming.** If you plan to have a settlement agreement or are promising Respondent you won't proceed without one, check boxes for 5b and "below" then type in, "To be determined by written agreement of the parties."

> If you indicate here or in item 4 that there will be an agreement, then you can *only* proceed by agreement. This should make your spouse feel secure because you can't go forward without either a written agreement or filing and serving an amended Petition, so there can't be any tricks or surprises.

> **Amended Petition.** If you do *not* get an agreement, in order to move your case forward you have to file an Amended Petition. Prepare another Petition but this time check the "AMENDED" box in the caption, check 5b and list all community property and debts, file it with a new Summons with the words "FOR FIRST AMENDED PETITION" typed under the title "SUMMONS," have the papers served on Respondent as you did the first time, then file the new Proof of Service, as before. This might cost you and additional filing fee of about $75 and it takes more time. It is not a terrible burden, but if in doubt about getting an agreement and you don't need to soothe Respondent, then list your community assets and debts in item 5.

> **Listed.** If you decide to list all community assets and debts, you have three ways to do it:

> – **below.** If you have only a few items, you can check this box and enter your list right on the Petition. Most people need more space and will use either of the next two options.

> – **in Property Declaration (form FL-160).** Check this box, then fill out and attach the Property Declaration form as shown in chapter 15.

> – **in Attachment 5b.** Check this box to use the Additional Page form (page 74). Type in a heading, "Attachment 5b." Review the Property Declaration to see how items should be grouped and as a check list for your assets and debts. Major items should be individually listed, such as cars, bank accounts, pension plans, stocks, accumulated vacation pay, trusts, and things of special importance to you. Real estate is identified by its common address and assessor's parcel number. Household goods and appliances can simply be lumped together as such.

Item 9. Read the back of the Summons carefully; don't take the kids out of state without written permission and don't transfer funds or do those other things "by accident."

Figure 10.3 DECLARATION UNDER UCCJEA
Form FL-105 (page 1)

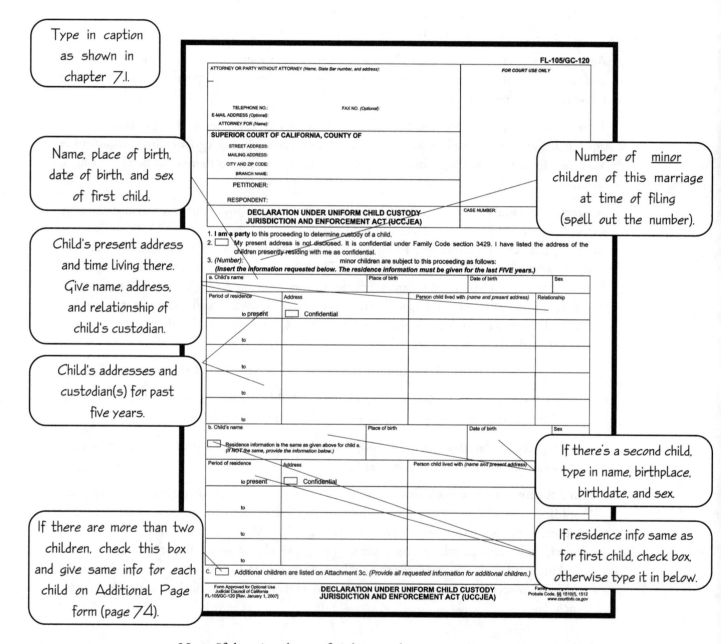

Type in caption as shown in chapter 7.1.

Name, place of birth, date of birth, and sex of first child.

Child's present address and time living there. Give name, address, and relationship of child's custodian.

Child's addresses and custodian(s) for past five years.

If there are more than two children, check this box and give same info for each child on Additional Page form (page 74).

Number of minor children of this marriage at time of filing (spell out the number).

If there's a second child, type in name, birthplace, birthdate, and sex.

If residence info same as for first child, check box, otherwise type it in below.

Note: If there is a threat of violence or harassment in your case, you can keep your address(es) secret. Check the box at item 2, and for each child who lives with you, check the "confidential" box in the address column and do not give your address. There is a slight chance this will cause you to be called in for a hearing when you apply to get your Judgment by mail (chapter 20).

Figure 10.4 DECLARATION UNDER UCCJEA
Form FL-105 (page 2)

Check first box of items 4 and 5 if there have been _no_ custody proceedings anywhere re: the minor child(ren).

If there have been custody proceedings, check second box and fill in requested info.

Check first box if no person (other than you or spouse) claims custody or visitation...

....otherwise, check second box and give requested info.

date of signing

If you used extra pages to complete this form, check this box and type in the number of pages attached.

Fill in this caption as shown on page 74

If a restraining order is in effect, check box 6 and provide requested info

your signature

type your name

FL-105/GC-120

SHORT TITLE: CASE NUMBER:

4. Have you participated as a party or a witness or in some other capacity in another litigation or custody proceeding, in California or elsewhere, concerning custody of a child subject to this proceeding?
☐ No ☑ Yes   *(If yes, provide the following information):*
a. Name of each child:

b. I was a: ☐ party ☐ witness ☐ other *(specify):*

c. Court *(specify name, state, location):*

d. Court order or judgment *(date):*

5. Do you have information about a custody proceeding pending in a California court or any other court concerning a child in this case, other than that stated in item 4?
☐ No ☑ Yes *(If yes, provide the following information):*

a. Name of each child:
b. Nature of proceeding: ☐ dissolution or divorce ☐ guardianship ☐ adoption
c. Court *(specify name, state, location):*
d. Status of proceeding:

6. ☐ One or more domestic violence restraining /protective orders are now in effect. (Attach a copy of the orders if you have one.)
The orders are from the following court or courts *(specify county and state):*
a. ☐ Criminal: County/state: _____   c. ☐ Juvenile: County/state: _____
     Case No. *(if known):* _____   Case No. *(if known):* _____
b. ☐ Family: County/state: _____   d. ☐ Other: County/state: _____
     Case No. *(if known):* _____   Case No. *(if known):* _____

7. Do you know of any person who is not a party to this proceeding who has physical custody or claims to have custody of or visitation rights with any child in this case?
☐ No ☑ Yes *(If yes, provide the following information):*

a. Name and address of person	b. Name and address of person	c. Name and address of person
☐ Has physical custody ☐ Claims custody rights ☐ Claims visitation rights	☐ Has physical custody ☐ Claims custody rights ☐ Claims visitation rights	☐ Has physical custody ☐ Claims custody rights ☐ Claims visitation rights
Name of each child	Name of each child	Name of each child

I declare under penalty of perjury under the laws of the State of California that the foregoing is true and correct.
Date:

_____   ▶   _____
(TYPE OR PRINT NAME)   (SIGNATURE OF DE...)

8. ☐ Number of pages attached after this page: _____

NOTICE TO DECLARANT: You have a continuing duty to inform this court if you obtain any informa... proceeding in a California court or any other court concerning a child s...

FL-105/GC-120 [Rev. January 1, 2007]   **DECLARATION UNDER UNIFORM CHILD CUSTODY JURISDICTION AND ENFORCEMENT ACT (UCCJEA)**

11
THE RESPONSE

About the Response

The Response lets everyone know that you have officially joined the case. Depending on how you fill it out, it might also give notice that you want some separate property confirmed to you, or have a different view of the basic facts, or the ultimate outcome. Once the Response is filed and served, you and Petitioner are exact equals in the legal proceedings and have equal ability to go ahead with any legal procedure.

Time to file. Once you are served with the Petition, you have thirty days to file your Response. However, if Petitioner sends you a letter stating that you can have a specific amount of extra time, or better, that he/she will not proceed in the case without giving you thirty days written notice to Respond, then you can put off filing the Response and concentrate on getting an agreement worked out.

Study the Summons and Petition.

Restraining orders. Once you are served, you and Petitioner are bound by the automatic restraining orders on the back of the Summons (see chapter 2.7). Examine them carefully. Until the Judgment, do not take the kids out of state without written permission and don't transfer funds or do any of those other things "by accident."

Facts. Check every fact stated in the Petition. You get to state your version of facts in your Response.

Property. If assets and debts are actually listed on the Petition or on an attached list, then Petitioner will be able to go to court and get a Judgment if you do not Respond on time. **However,** if items 4 or 5 say "to be determined by written agreement," or something similar, this means Petitioner can't get a Judgment without your written agreement, so you can decide not to Respond and focus on working out an agreement, because the case can't go forward without either an agreement or until Amended Petition listing all property is filed and served on you, giving you another chance to Respond.

Requests. Study item 8 very carefully, as this is where Petitioner indicates in general terms what kind of orders are being requested of the court. You can request whatever you want in the Response.

What to do

First, read Part One of *How to Do Your Own Divorce*. Prepare the original and 3 copies. L.A. County wants an extra copy of the front of the Response.

- **Married people:** Fill out FL-120 Response, as shown in Figs. 11.1 and 11.2.
- **Domestic partners:** Use FL-123 Response, which is almost identical to FL-120 except for language referring to registered domestic partners. Follow the instructions for FL-120 below.

NOTES FOR THE RESPONSE

If you need more space to complete any item, use an Additional Page form (chapter 7.1) with the heading "Continuation of Response." Add a sub-heading that reads "Attachment (number of item being continued)," and complete your list. Staple the original and copies to the original and copies of your Response.

Caption. If the Petition asks for Legal Separation and you want a divorce, check the boxes "and Request For," and "Dissolution of Marriage." Divorce trumps separation; you'll almost certainly get it.

Figure 11.1 **RESPONSE**
Form FL-120 (page 1)

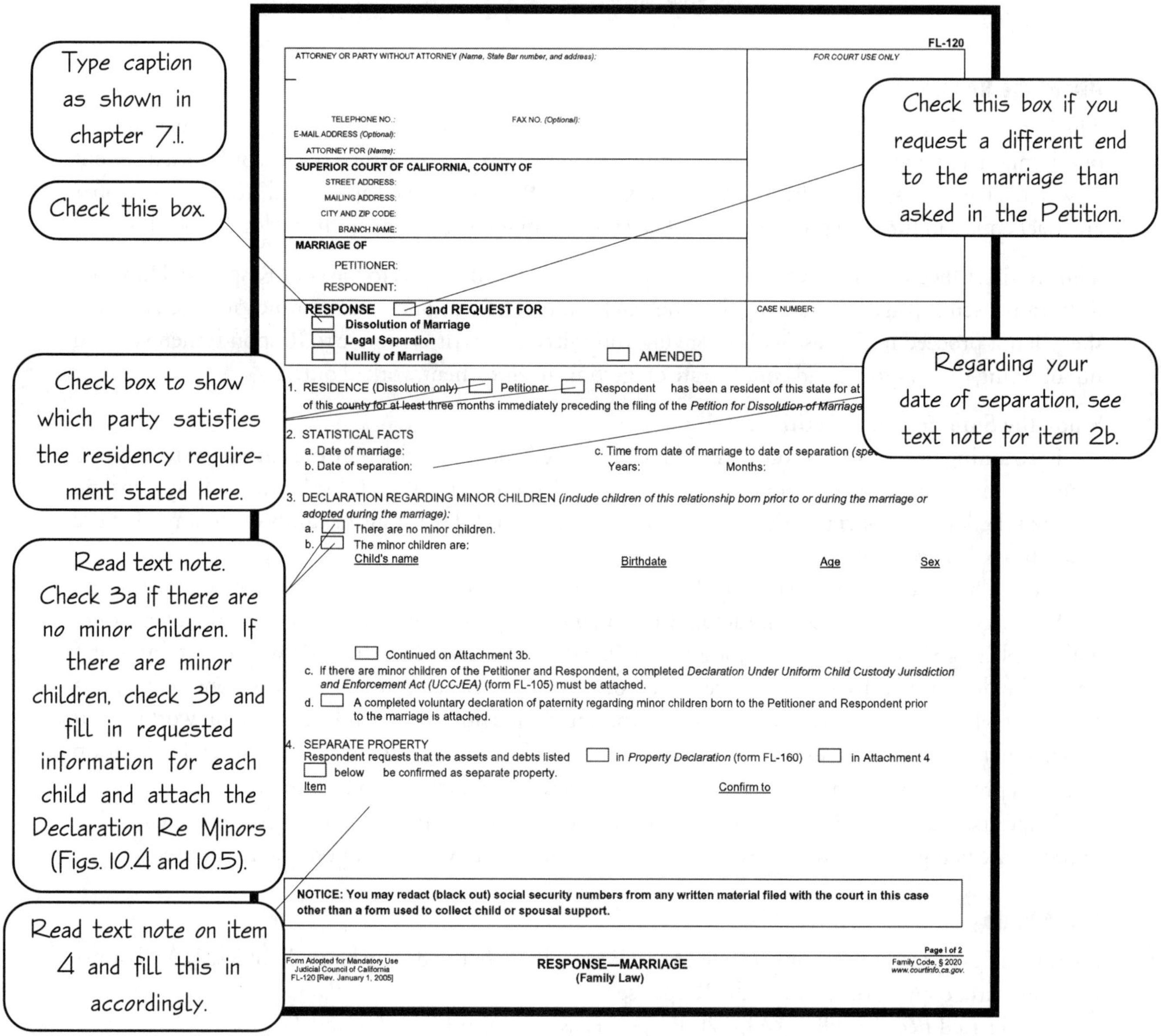

Type caption as shown in chapter 7.1.

Check this box.

Check this box if you request a different end to the marriage than asked in the Petition.

Check box to show which party satisfies the residency requirement stated here.

Regarding your date of separation, see text note for item 2b.

Read text note. Check 3a if there are no minor children. If there are minor children, check 3b and fill in requested information for each child and attach the Declaration Re Minors (Figs. 10.4 and 10.5).

Read text note on item 4 and fill this in accordingly.

FL-120

ATTORNEY OR PARTY WITHOUT ATTORNEY (Name, State Bar number, and address):

FOR COURT USE ONLY

TELEPHONE NO.:   FAX NO. (Optional):
E-MAIL ADDRESS (Optional):
ATTORNEY FOR (Name):

SUPERIOR COURT OF CALIFORNIA, COUNTY OF
STREET ADDRESS:
MAILING ADDRESS:
CITY AND ZIP CODE:
BRANCH NAME:

MARRIAGE OF
PETITIONER:
RESPONDENT:

RESPONSE ☐ and REQUEST FOR   CASE NUMBER:
☐ Dissolution of Marriage
☐ Legal Separation
☐ Nullity of Marriage   ☐ AMENDED

1. RESIDENCE (Dissolution only) ☐ Petitioner ☐ Respondent has been a resident of this state for at least of this county for at least three months immediately preceding the filing of the *Petition for Dissolution of Marriage*

2. STATISTICAL FACTS
   a. Date of marriage: c. Time from date of marriage to date of separation (spe
   b. Date of separation: Years: Months:

3. DECLARATION REGARDING MINOR CHILDREN *(include children of this relationship born prior to or during the marriage or adopted during the marriage):*
   a. ☐ There are no minor children.
   b. ☐ The minor children are:

   Child's name   Birthdate   Age   Sex

   ☐ Continued on Attachment 3b.
   c. If there are minor children of the Petitioner and Respondent, a completed *Declaration Under Uniform Child Custody Jurisdiction and Enforcement Act (UCCJEA)* (form FL-105) must be attached.
   d. ☐ A completed voluntary declaration of paternity regarding minor children born to the Petitioner and Respondent prior to the marriage is attached.

4. SEPARATE PROPERTY
   Respondent requests that the assets and debts listed ☐ in *Property Declaration* (form FL-160) ☐ in Attachment 4
   ☐ below be confirmed as separate property.
   Item   Confirm to

NOTICE: You may redact (black out) social security numbers from any written material filed with the court in this case other than a form used to collect child or spousal support.

Form Adopted for Mandatory Use
Judicial Council of California
FL-120 [Rev. January 1, 2005]

RESPONSE—MARRIAGE
(Family Law)

Page 1 of 2
Family Code, § 2020
www.courtinfo.ca.gov.

Item 2b. The date of your separation is the last day you were living together as husband and wife or partners. If there is any question in your mind about what date to use, read about the date of separation in chapter 3.1. If you still don't have an exact date, just get as close as you can. If you have separated several times, use the most recent date. Merely sleeping together does not affect separation or dissolution.

Item 7. Check this box to deny the grounds for divorce stated in the Petition at item 6. If Petitioner selected "irreconcilable differences," there's no reason whatever to contest this, as the mere fact that Petitioner wants a divorce is enough to show that your relationship is irreconcilable.

Item 8. Most people should check 8(a)(1) to request a divorce on the grounds of "irreconcilable differences." If one party asks for a legal separation and the other asks for a divorce, the divorce wins. It's hard to stop a divorce if one party wants it. Do *not* check any of the other boxes without legal advice.

Item 9. This is where you tell the court and Petitioner what you are asking for in your case. If you don't check it here, you can't get it in your Judgment.

Item 9e, Spousal support. If there will be some spousal support in your case, check box 9e and check a box to indicate who will be the recipient of the support, Petitioner or Respondent.

Item 9g, Terminate . . . spousal support to petitioner. Check this box to notify Petitioner that you are going to ask the court to terminate all possibility of any spousal support, either now or in the future.

Amended Response. If you need to file an amended Response (see notes for Item 5b), it must be done before the case is "at issue" or trial date is set. Prepare another Response, but this time check the "AMENDED" box in the caption, fill it out with the changed information, file it with a new Summons with the words "FOR FIRST AMENDED RESPONSE" typed under the title "SUMMONS," have the papers served on Petitioner as you did the first time, then file the new Proof of Service, as before.

CASES WITH CHILDREN

Item 3b. The children you list here will include only those presently under 18 (or 18, enrolled full-time in high school and not self-supporting) who were born to or adopted by both you and your spouse. Don't include stepchildren who have not been formally adopted. If the wife is pregnant, include the unborn child by putting "one unborn" in the space provided for the name of child. However, if you want to challenge the paternity, call Divorce Helpline.

Item 3c. Fill out the Declaration Re: Minors (UCCJEA) form as shown in Figures 10.4 and 10.5 and attach it to the Response.

Item 3d. Refers to the Voluntary Declaration of Paternity available in many hospitals for the last two or three years. If you happen to have one, you can check this box.

Items 9a-d. Read chapter 4.

- To request pure joint custody, check 9a and 9b at the boxes under the "Joint" column.
- To request joint legal custody with sole physical custody to one parent, check 9a under the "Joint" column and check 9b to indicate who is to have primary physical custody.
- To request sole custody (both legal and physical) for one parent, check both 9a and 9b under the column that indicates who is to have custody, and 9c to indicate who will have visitation rights.
- Check 9c to indicate which parent is to have a visitation schedule.
- **Optional attachments:** If you want to specify custody or visitation in some detail—which is not generally recommended unless you plan to ask for something unusual, which Respndent would have a right to know about—check a box or boxes below 9c and attach one of the listed forms, which can be found on the companion CD. Take a look at those forms to see what's possible.
  Note. FL-312 is a request for orders to prevent the abduction of a child, which is not something you should try to handle yourself. If you face this threat, get help from a family law attorney.

- If a child of the parties was born before marriage, check 9d for a determination of parentage.

Figure 11.2 **RESPONSE**
Form FL-120 (page 2)

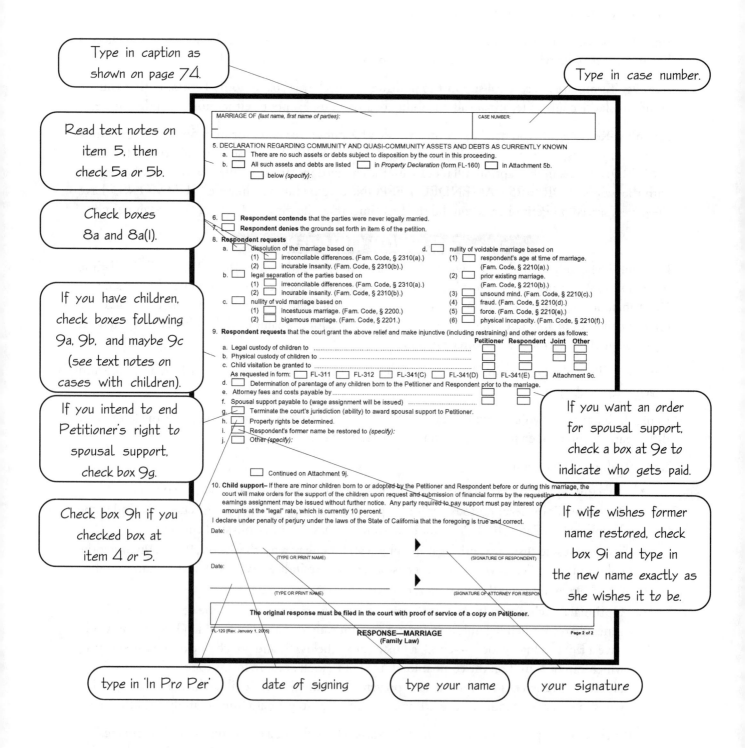

Type in caption as shown on page 74.

Type in case number.

Read text notes on item 5, then check 5a or 5b.

Check boxes 8a and 8a(1).

If you have children, check boxes following 9a, 9b, and maybe 9c (see text notes on cases with children).

If you intend to end Petitioner's right to spousal support, check box 9g.

Check box 9h if you checked box at item 4 or 5.

If you want an order for spousal support, check a box at 9e to indicate who gets paid.

If wife wishes former name restored, check box 9i and type in the new name exactly as she wishes it to be.

type in 'In Pro Per'

date of signing

type your name

your signature

Read chapter 3 very carefully. The way the court will relate to your property depends upon how you fill out the Response. Items 4 and 5 in the Response are where you tell the court about your property. Remember that "property" includes both assets and debts.

Item 4, Confirmation of separate assets and debts. If you want any item of property confirmed as the separate asset or debt of either you or your spouse, then check Items 4 and 9h. List each item and indicate to whom it is to be confirmed (Petitioner or Respondent). Be sure to include any retirement plan or fund if no part was earned between marriage and separation. Do *not* list any community property that has already been informally divided by the spouses—it is not separate until divided by the court and must be listed under Item 5. If you need more room, use the Property Declaration form (see chapter 15 for instructions) and call it "Attachment 4."

Option: If you expect to work out an agreement, check "below" then type in, "To be determined by written agreement of the parties." Read discussion below for 5b, "Agreement Coming."

Item 5, Declaration regarding . . . assets and debts.

    5a. There are no such assets or debts subject to disposition by the court in this proceeding. Only check this box if there is truly no property or so little that it just doesn't matter. When you check box 5a, the court will not inquire about your property nor make orders about it. Property of any significance *must* be listed even if you have already informally divided it—it is still community property and technically you both own it all as tenants in common until divided by a court order. Do *not* check this box if there is or may *ever* be a disagreement between you about some item of property that you care about, or where there is any real estate, or if there is a community interest in a pension plan (see chapter 3.6(b)).

    5b. All such assets and debts are listed . . . Check boxes 5b and 9h if you have property or debts that have not yet been divided in a written agreement. You can still put together a settlement agreement with your spouse at a later time and present it to the court when you get your Judgment.

        Agreement coming. If the Petition, at either item 4 or 5, indicates that property and debts will be determined in a written agreement, and if you, too, are reasonably sure you will have one, check boxes for "5b" and "below" then type in, "To be determined by written agreement of the parties." If both you and Petitioner do this, the case cannot move forward without an agreement unless either an Amended Petition or an Amended Response is filed listing all property and debts.

        Listed. If you decide to list all community assets and debts, you have three ways to do it:

      – **below.** If you have only a few items, you can check this box and enter your list right on the Response. Most people need more space and will use either of the next two options.

      – **in Property Declaration (form FL-160).** Check this box, then fill out and attach the Property Declaration form as shown in chapter 15.

      – **in Attachment 5b.** Check this box and use the Additional Page form (page 74). Type in a heading, "Attachment 5b." Review the Property Declaration to see how items should be grouped. Major items should be individually listed, such as cars, bank accounts, pension plans, stocks, accumulated vacation pay, trusts, and things of special importance to you. Real estate is identified by its common address and assessor's parcel number. Household goods and appliances can simply be lumped together as such.

What next?

- Serve the Response on Petitioner by mail (see chapter 12.6) along with a copy of the Proof of Service by Mail (FL-335, chapter 13, Figure 13.3).

- Once the papers have been mailed, the server signs the Proof of Service by Mail, then you file the Response and the Proof of Servce with the court along with the Response filing fee (chapter 7.3).

- Respondent is now on equal footing with Petitioner and can do any of the things Petitioner can do described in this book or in Book 2 to move the case toward completion.

- If you have trouble settling issues in your divorce, you should both read my book *Make Any Divorce Better* and learn how to reduce upset, talk to your spouse, and negotiate a settlement. If your case seems headed to court anyway, get Book 2, *How to Solve Divorce Problems,* and learn how to use the legal process to reach your goals or supervise your attorney if you decide to retain one.

Case Management or Status Conference?

Courts are very concerned with the management of their case load and they worry about the large number of cases in their files that are inactive for long periods of time. If a Response is filed, many counties will start scheduling hearings to find out what's going on with your case. These are called Case Management or Status Conferences. Typically, they will send you a form to gather information about your case. Somewhere in there you can tell them you are currently in negotiation or mediation and expect to settle everything by agreement. For example, if they ask you to list the issues, you can check a box for "other" and type in, "None—the parties are in mediation," or "None—the parties are negotiating a settlement." This will usually get you a continuance for a few months, at which time you might have to repeat the process if your case is not yet moving toward Judgment.

HOW TO SERVE PAPERS

Giving formal notice to the other side is called "service of process." To start a case, the Petition and other papers must be correctly served on the other spouse. If a Response is filed, it must be served on Petitioner. As the case progresses, there will be a few times when you have to give formal notice of some step to the other side. If your case moves into legal conflict, serving papers will happen many times. We will tell you each time when service is required. In this chapter, we explain the general rules for getting it done.

12.1 Who serves whom and when

Who can serve? Papers must be served by someone who is at least 18 years old and not a party to the action, so neither spouse can do it and almost anyone else can. A relative can do it, but it would look better if the person were unrelated. You can hire a professional process server (see yellow pages) but don't use a Sheriff, Marshal, or Constable if you are in a hurry, or if it might take diligence to find your spouse. Being a citizen is not a requirement. Each time papers are served, the person who does it must sign a Proof of Service form so you can prove when, where, how and by whom it was done.

Who gets served? The Summons and Petition set is always served directly on the spouse. For everything else, papers are always served on the "attorney of record." Look on the caption of the most recent court document you received (if any) from your spouse and the name that appears there is the "attorney of record." If you were never served with court documents, keep serving your spouse directly. Just because your ex consulted an attorney does *not* make that attorney "of record" unless his/her name appears on a court document that is served on you. Whoever is "of record," your spouse or your spouse's attorney, you *must* use that name and address on all your proofs of service, *exactly* as it appears in the captions.

Order of events. For the first step—the Summons, Petition and related documents—you need to file your papers first, then have the papers served, then file your Proof of Service.

12.2 Serving the Petition

You *must* serve your spouse with:
- a *copy* (not the original) of the Summons,
- a copy of the Petition (plus any attachments you filed with it, *e.g.*, the Declaration Re: Minors), and
- a blank Response form.

Optional: Serve your Preliminary Disclosure papers at this time (Check List, step 3; chapter 14) . This saves you having to serve them later by mail and having to do another Proof of Service for them. However, don't unduly delay filing your Petition in order to do this step, too.

Recommended: Unless your spouse is an abuser/controller, consider also sending a cover letter with the papers being served saying there's no hurry to Respond, that you want to work out an agreement and won't go further in the case without giving 30 days' written notice. Consider sending copies of this book and a copy of *Make Any Divorce Better*. This is all designed to reduce chances for conflict.

Recommended: This is a logical time to get Respondent involved with the Declarations of Disclosure (chapter 14). In a separate envelope, send blanks of the Declaration of Disclosure, the Declaration Re: Service, the Income and Expense Forms, and a copy of chapter 14. Send a note explaining that Respondent's rights will best be protected and the case will go easier if Respondent completes first the Preliminary and, later, the Final Declarations of Disclosure and files a Declaration that it was done. If you like, you can offer to help Respondent fill out the forms.

12.3 Choosing the method of service

The Summons and Petition (first set)

1. **If your spouse is located inside California:**
   • Personal service (12.4), or
   • Service by Notice and Acknowledgment (12.5), or

2. **If your spouse is located outside California:**
   • Any of the methods above (12.4 or 12.5), or
   • Service by certified or registered mail (12.6).

   Note: important! See chapter 2.6. The court's power (jurisdiction) to order your spouse to pay support or to do or not do certain acts (hand over property or not to harass you, for example) is most clear when your spouse (a) files a Response or the Appearance & Waiver, or (b) is served personally inside California. If neither of these is possible, the court's jurisdiction to make orders against your spouse *might* be limited. What to do? Use one of the other methods and hope for the best or consult an attorney or call Divorce Helpline for advice.

3. **The Appearance & Waiver—for cooperative and military spouses:**

   If your spouse is on *active* military duty, you can*not* use any other method—you *must* use the Appearance & Waiver and your spouse must be willing to sign it. If your spouse is on active military duty and will not sign and return this form, you should consult an attorney.

4. **If your spouse files a Response:**

   If your spouse files a Response, you do not need to serve the Petition or file a Proof of Service. You *do* need to return the original Summons the next time you file papers. However, don't wait around for the Response—it's better to go ahead and serve the first papers rather than wait for something that might never come.

5. **If your spouse cannot be located anywhere:**

   If you can't find your spouse, the service of process becomes much more difficult. You are required to try *very* hard to locate your spouse. Get the most recent address you can and try serving papers by mail as described in 12.5 or 12.6—maybe they will get through. If that fails, try to contact relatives and friends who might know where your spouse is, the last-known employer, and the County Tax Assessor. If nothing works, then you can proceed by Publication of Summons. You will find forms and instructions for publishing your Summons in the Kits section of the companion CD. You can also call Divorce Helpline if you need more information, advice or help with service.

Look over the various methods and decide which to use. If your spouse will be cooperative, then service by Notice and Acknowledgment (12.5) is easiest and cheapest, but it does not clearly give the court personal jurisdiction to make enforceable support and other orders against your spouse. If your spouse is out-of-state and will not try to avoid a certified letter, service by certified or registered mail (12.6) is good. If you know where your spouse is located, but aren't sure how much cooperation you will get, then personal service (12.4) is most certain. It's okay to try one method, then another if the first fails.

All other papers

If the other party has not filed a Petition or Response, papers should always be served personally (12.4). If your spouse *has* filed either a Petition or Response, you can serve papers by mail (12.6) sent to the attorney of record (see 12.1), the name and address exactly as it appears in the caption of court documents. An attorney who represents your spouse (of record) can be served either by mail or in person. Personal service on an attorney is easier than on a non-attorney (Code of Civil Procedure 1011). The server can simply (1) go to the attorney's office any time it is open and hand an envelope containing the papers (with the attorney's name on the envelope) to a receptionist or any adult in charge, or (2) from 9 a.m. to 5 p.m., if nobody is there, leave the envelope in a conspicuous place. Where the Proof of Personal Service form asks for the name of the person served, type in "Receptionist at the office of Attorney (name)." Instead of "receptionist" you could also use "adult in charge." If no one was present, type in "Attorney (name), papers left at address in conspicuous place."

12.4 Personal service

If you know where your spouse can be located, you can have papers served personally. This means that some person (over 18, not you) must personally hand your spouse the package of papers being served.

Whoever is going to serve your spouse must be given the following items:

1. For servers who don't know your spouse personally, a photo and description of your spouse.

2. Complete information about where your spouse can be found, including work schedules, addresses at home and work.

3. The papers to be served (for the Petition, those listed in 12.2).

4. The Proof of Service form, filled out, to be signed by the person who serves the papers:

> **When serving the Petition and papers along with it:** use the Proof of Service of Summons form (Fig. 13.1).

> **When serving other papers at other times:** use the Proof of Personal Service form (Fig. 13.4)

If you want to use a professional process server, look in the yellow pages of the phone book for the area near your spouse (big libraries and some phone companies keep national sets of phone books), or check with a process server in the area near you and see if they can recommend someone near your spouse. Call around for the best price. Call the one you select and discuss delivery of papers and the items they want sent.

If you are in *no* hurry, it might be cheaper to use a Sheriff, Marshal, or Constable. Just mail the items listed above to one of those officials nearest your spouse, and request that they serve him. Include a money order for $20 with a request to refund any unused portion. Be prepared to wait patiently.

If you decide to have a friend or relative make service, deliver the items listed above and tell that person all they have to do is to personally hand the package of papers being served to your spouse. If your spouse may possibly be a bit sticky about being served, the process server should know this: Once your spouse has been located and identified, the server should say, "I have court papers for you." If your spouse won't open the door, or if he turns and runs, or in any other way tries to avoid service, the server can just put the papers in the nearest convenient spot where they can be picked up, then leave, and service will have been effectively completed.

Make sure the Proof of Service is filled out properly (see chapter 13). If service is made outside California, it must be proved by a sworn and notarized affidavit so you should not send a Proof of Service. Use only a professional or an official and request that he send his affidavit of service to you. Attach this to the Proof of Service when you file it.

12.5 Service by Notice and Acknowledgment

This is only for the Petition. If you know your spouse's address, and if your ex will cooperate to the extent of signing an Acknowledgment, then your job is easy.

A copy of papers to be served (12.2) should be mailed by first class mail, postage prepaid, to your spouse, together with the original and one copy of the Acknowledgment *and* a return envelope, postage prepaid, addressed to the sender. You can't mail this yourself; someone over 18 must do it for you. Fill it out as shown in Figure 13.2 and make 3 copies.

All your spouse needs to do is enter the date the papers were received (that date *must* be after the date the Summons was filed), then date and sign the original Acknowledgment and return it to the sender. It is not necessary for Respondent to fill out, file or return any of the other papers that were sent. The sender then completes the Proof of Service (chapter 13) and the job is complete. Be sure to attach the original Acknowledgment to the original Proof of Service when you file it. Service by this method is effective on the date the papers are signed by your spouse.

12.6 Service by mail

The Petition

If you know your spouse's address and it is *outside* California, you can have the server mail papers to be served (12.2) along with a copy of the Proof of Service by Mail (FL-335, chapter 13, Fig. 13.3), by registered or certified mail, with a return receipt requested. Make sure the sender indicates "restricted delivery" or "deliver to addressee only" on the post office form. When the return receipt comes back with your spouse's signature, it must be filed as a part of the Proof of Service of Summons (Fig. 13.1) which must be signed by the person who mailed the papers. When using this method, the effective date of service is the 10th day after mailing. Use that date as the "date of service" on forms and in court.

All other papers

Once a party has made a general appearance—that is, filed a Petition or Response or the Appearance and Waiver form (see next section) with item 1 checked—then you can serve all documents other than a Summons by ordinary mail, addressed exactly as the name appears on the caption of the most recent court documents you received from your spouse. When you serve by mail, you *must* always include a copy of the Proof of Service by Mail (FL-335, chapter 13, Fig. 13.3) with the papers served. The copy served must be completely filled out, though it need not be signed. This is so the recipient knows the date, time and manner papers were mailed. The person who did the mailing must sign a Proof of Service by Mail (Fig. 13.3) immediately after posting the papers.

If your spouse has *not* made a general appearance, everything should be served personally (12.4).

12.7 Appearance, Stipulations, and Waivers

This form is signed by both parties. Respondent can make a general appearance and waive military rights and/or the parties can agree to let the case go without contest according to their settlement agreement. The A&W form appears at this point in the book because it may have to be used with the Proof of Service as a military waiver. It is more typically used after an agreement is completed.

- If Respondent is on active military duty, you can only proceed if Respondent will sign at least the military waiver portion of this form.

- If a Response has been filed, the case can only proceed by trial or by agreement. After you resolve all issues in your agreement, one party files this form to allow the other party to get the Judgment.

Good news. If Respondent makes an appearance with this form (by checking item 1), the need for service of process is eliminated, just as would the filing of a Response. It also eliminates having to file the Request for Default, and avoids the 30 days wait before you can go on to the next steps.

Less-good news. The Response filing fee (chapter 7.3) will be charged if it hasn't already been paid for filing a Response. However, no fee can be charged for filing the A&W if the form is used solely as a military waiver, that is, if *only* box 3 is checked.

Caution. In cases with property, support or any unresolved issues, Respondent should hesitate to waive rights other than the military waiver (box 3) *before* a settlement agreement has been signed. If a settlement agreement has not yet been signed, Respondent should file a Response within 30 days of being served— or any time before a Request for Default is filed by Petitioner—and file this A&W form *after* the agreement is completed.

How to do it. Fill out the A&W form using Figure 12.1 as a guide. Prepare the original and 3 copies. It is okay if you prepare and file the form for Respondent. Send all but one copy to Respondent with a copy of the Petition and a self-addressed, stamped envelope. Respondent should date and sign the original and a copy exactly as his or her name appears in the caption, then return it to you.

When this form is used, you should return the *original* Summons to the court when it is filed. No Proof of Service is necessary and no Request for Default is necessary. Service by this method is effective on the date the A&W is filed.

Note: The date of Respondent's signature must be *after* the date your Petition was filed. Respondent keeps a copy of the A&W form and the copy of the Petition, but has no further responsibility in the case except for possibly completing a Declaration of Disclosure.

Note: Once either a Response has been filed or Respondent makes a general appearance with the A&W, the parties are equal; either spouse can take care of the business of finishing the case.

Figure 12.1 **APPEARANCE, STIPULATIONS, AND WAIVERS**
Form FL-130

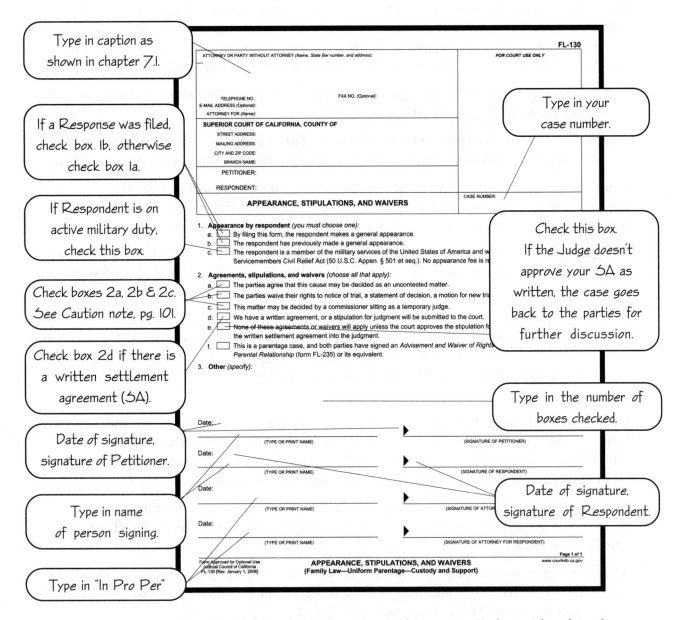

Type in caption as shown in chapter 7.1.

If a Response was filed, check box 1b, otherwise check box 1a.

If Respondent is on active military duty, check this box.

Check boxes 2a, 2b & 2c. See Caution note, pg. 101.

Check box 2d if there is a written settlement agreement (SA).

Date of signature, signature of Petitioner.

Type in name of person signing.

Type in "In Pro Per"

Type in your case number.

Check this box. If the Judge doesn't approve your SA as written, the case goes back to the parties for further discussion.

Type in the number of boxes checked.

Date of signature, signature of Respondent.

Note: Check box 2c unless you have some special reason not to. You have a right to demand a judge, but you also don't want to upset the system without a good reason.

PROOF OF SERVICE

What they are

A Proof of Service (POS) is a declaration swearing that certain steps were carried out to serve papers on the other side. This is so the court is certain that notice of the action was actually given correctly.

1. **The Proof of Service of Summons** (Fig. 13.1) is used after the Summons and Petition have been served.
2. **The Notice and Acknowledgment of Receipt** (Fig. 13.2) is used with the POS above when you have a cooperative spouse who will sign this form and return it to the sender.
3. **The Proof of Service by Mail** (Fig. 13.3) is used when serving any documents (other than the Summons and Petition) by mail.
4. **The Proof of Personal Service** (Fig. 13.4) is used when serving any documents (other than the Summons and Petition) when serving papers personally.

How to fill them in

Fill forms out as shown in Figures 13.1 to 13.4. Prepare the original and two copies. The form can be filed immediately. However, if you are doing an ordinary uncontested dissolution with no motions or other legal action, some courts prefer you to wait and file all papers at one time when you file for your Judgment (chapter 20). That's also more convenient, but be sure to keep papers safe until filed.

Note on personal service (chapter 12.4). If service is done by a friend, you can fill out the Proof of Service, but he or she must sign it. If service is made in California by an official or a professional, send the Proof of Service form for them to fill out and return. If service is made outside California by an official or professional, simply request that they send you their notarized affidavit of service and file that as your Proof of Service.

Summons: the Effective Date of Service

1. Personal Service (12.4) becomes effective on the date papers were handed to Respondent.
2. Service by Notice and Acknowledgment (12.5) becomes effective on the date Respondent signs the papers. Attach the original Acknowledgment to the Proof of Service.
3. Service by certified or registered mail (12.6) becomes effective on the 10th day after the date mailed. Attach the returned signature receipt to the Proof of Service.
4. The Appearance & Waiver (12.7) becomes effective on the date it is filed.

Figure 13.1 PROOF OF SERVICE OF SUMMONS
Form FL-115 (page 1)

Type in the caption as shown in 7.1.

your case number

Check one of these boxes.

Kids, check this box.

Check boxes to show what other forms were served with the Petition.

In every case, type address where Respondent was served.

If Respondent was served personally (ch. 12.4), check box 3a and type in date & time of delivery.

FL-115

ATTORNEY OR PARTY WITHOUT ATTORNEY (Name, State Bar number, and address):

TELEPHONE NO.:   FAX NO. (Optional):
E-MAIL ADDRESS (Optional):
ATTORNEY FOR (Name):

SUPERIOR COURT OF CALIFORNIA, COUNTY OF
STREET ADDRESS:
MAILING ADDRESS:
CITY AND ZIP CODE:
BRANCH NAME:

PETITIONER:

RESPONDENT:

FOR COURT USE ONLY

PROOF OF SERVICE OF SUMMONS

CASE NUMBER:

1. At the time of service I was at least 18 years of age and not a party to this action. **I served the respondent with copies of:**
   a. ☐ Family Law: *Petition* (form FL-100), *Summons* (form FL-110), and blank *Response* (form FL-120)
   —or—
   b. ☐ Family Law—Domestic Partnership: *Petition—Domestic Partnership* (form FL-103), *Summons* (form FL-110), and blank *Response—Domestic Partnership* (form FL-123)
   —or—
   c. ☐ Uniform Parentage: *Petition to Establish Parental Relationship* (form FL-200), *Summons* (form FL-2__) Response to Petition to Establish Parental Relationship (form FL-220)
   —or—
   d. ☐ Custody and Support: *Petition for Custody and Support of Minor Children* (form FL-260), *Summons* (form FL-210), and blank *Response to Petition for Custody and Support of Minor Children* (form FL-270)

   and

   e. ☐ (1) ☐ Completed and blank *Declaration Under Uniform Child Custody Jurisdiction and Enforcement Act* (form FL-105)
   (2) ☐ Completed and blank *Declaration of Disclosure* (form FL-140)
   (3) ☐ Completed and blank *Schedule of Assets and Debts* (form FL-142)
   (4) ☐ Completed and blank *Income and Expense Declaration* (form FL-150)

   (5) ☐ Completed and blank *Finan___ (Simplified)* (form FL-155)
   (6) ☐ Completed and blank *Prope___ Declaration* (form FL-160)
   (7) ☐ Order to Show Cause (form ___ for Order and Supporting Decl___ FL-310), and blank *Responsive Declaration to Order to Show Cause or Notice of Motion* (form FL-320)
   (8) ☐ Other (specify):

2. Address where respondent was served:

3. I served the respondent by the following means (check proper box):
   a. ☐ **Personal service.** I personally delivered the copies to the respondent (Code Civ. Proc., § 415.10) on (date):   at (time):
   b. ☐ **Substituted service.** I left the copies with or in the presence of (name):
      who is (specify title or relationship to respondent):
      (1) ☐ **(Business)** a person at least 18 years of age who was apparently in charge at the office or usual place of business of the respondent. I informed him or her of the general nature of the papers
      (2) ☐ **(Home)** a competent member of the household (at least 18 years of age) at the home of the respondent. I informed him or her of the general nature of the papers

Page 1 of 2

Form Approved for Optional Use
Judicial Council of California
FL-115 [Rev. January 1, 2005]

PROOF OF SERVICE OF SUMMONS
(Family Law—Uniform Parentage—Custody and Support)

Code of Civil Procedure, § 417.10
www.courtinfo.ca.gov

Figure 13.1a PROOF OF SERVICE OF SUMMONS
Form FL-115 (page 2)

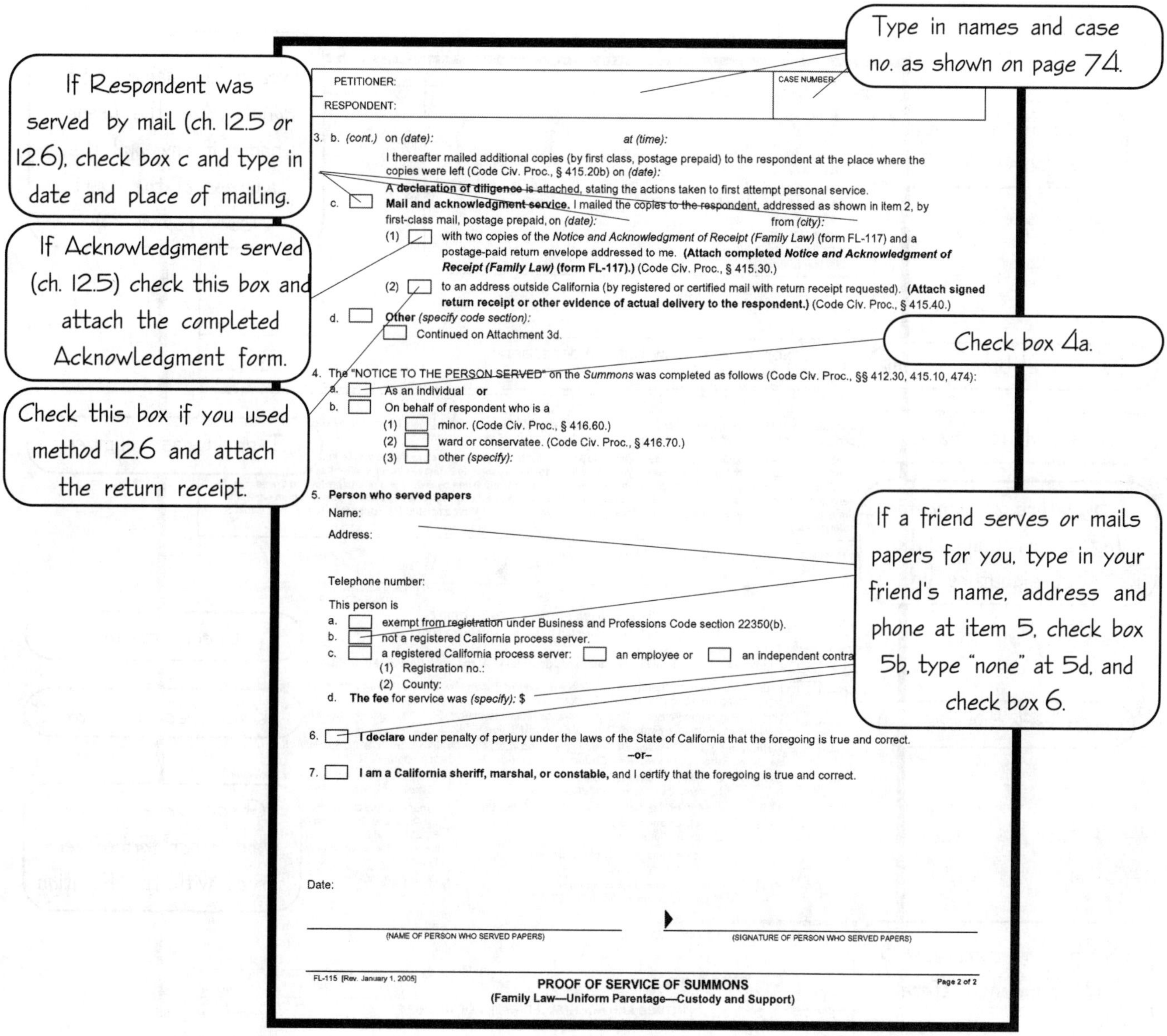

Type in names and case no. as shown on page 74.

If Respondent was served by mail (ch. 12.5 or 12.6), check box c and type in date and place of mailing.

If Acknowledgment served (ch. 12.5) check this box and attach the completed Acknowledgment form.

Check this box if you used method 12.6 and attach the return receipt.

If a friend serves or mails papers for you, type in your friend's name, address and phone at item 5, check box 5b, type "none" at 5d, and check box 6.

Check box 4a.

PETITIONER:

RESPONDENT:

CASE NUMBER:

3. b. *(cont.)* on *(date):*   at *(time):*

I thereafter mailed additional copies (by first class, postage prepaid) to the respondent at the place where the copies were left (Code Civ. Proc., § 415.20b) on *(date):*

A declaration of diligence is attached, stating the actions taken to first attempt personal service.

c. ☐ **Mail and acknowledgment service.** I mailed the copies to the respondent, addressed as shown in item 2, by first-class mail, postage prepaid, on *(date):*   from *(city):*

(1) ☐ with two copies of the *Notice and Acknowledgment of Receipt (Family Law)* (form FL-117) and a postage-paid return envelope addressed to me. **(Attach completed *Notice and Acknowledgment of Receipt (Family Law)* (form FL-117).)** (Code Civ. Proc., § 415.30.)

(2) ☐ to an address outside California (by registered or certified mail with return receipt requested). **(Attach signed return receipt or other evidence of actual delivery to the respondent.)** (Code Civ. Proc., § 415.40.)

d. ☐ **Other** *(specify code section):*
☐ Continued on Attachment 3d.

4. The "NOTICE TO THE PERSON SERVED" on the *Summons* was completed as follows (Code Civ. Proc., §§ 412.30, 415.10, 474):
a. ☐ As an individual **or**
b. ☐ On behalf of respondent who is a
(1) ☐ minor. (Code Civ. Proc., § 416.60.)
(2) ☐ ward or conservatee. (Code Civ. Proc., § 416.70.)
(3) ☐ other *(specify):*

5. **Person who served papers**
Name:
Address:

Telephone number:
This person is
a. ☐ exempt from registration under Business and Professions Code section 22350(b).
b. ☐ not a registered California process server.
c. ☐ a registered California process server: ☐ an employee or ☐ an independent contra
(1) Registration no.:
(2) County:
d. **The fee** for service was *(specify):* $

6. ☐ **I declare** under penalty of perjury under the laws of the State of California that the foregoing is true and correct.
–or–
7. ☐ **I am a California sheriff, marshal, or constable,** and I certify that the foregoing is true and correct.

Date:

_____   ▶ _____
(NAME OF PERSON WHO SERVED PAPERS)   (SIGNATURE OF PERSON WHO SERVED PAPERS)

FL-115 [Rev. January 1, 2005]   **PROOF OF SERVICE OF SUMMONS**   Page 2 of 2
(Family Law—Uniform Parentage—Custody and Support)

Figure 13.2 NOTICE AND ACKNOWLEDGMENT OF RECEIPT
Form FL-117

Note: When you use this form, also send a self-addressed stamped envelope for the Respondent to use to return the form to you.

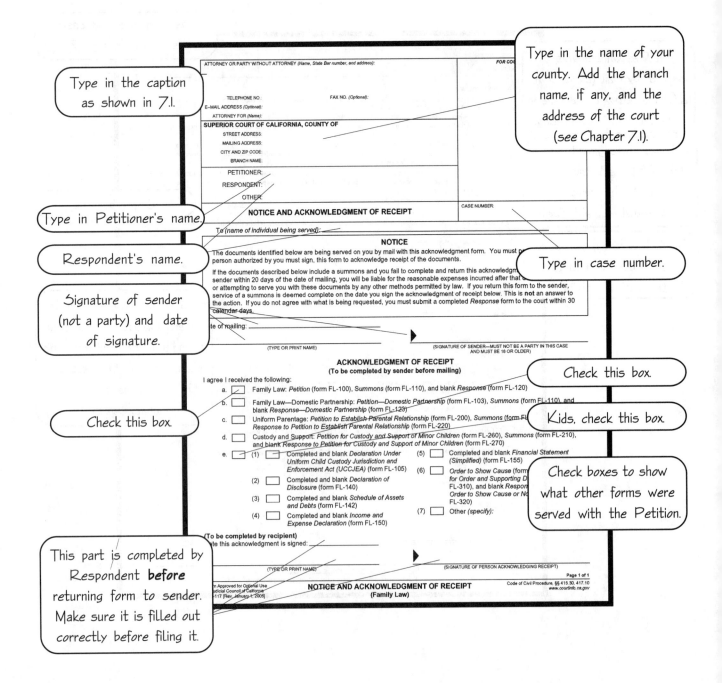

Type in the caption as shown in 7.1.

Type in the name of your county. Add the branch name, if any, and the address of the court (see Chapter 7.1).

Type in Petitioner's name.

Respondent's name.

Type in case number.

Signature of sender (not a party) and date of signature.

Check this box.

Check this box.

Kids, check this box.

Check boxes to show what other forms were served with the Petition.

This part is completed by Respondent **before** returning form to sender. Make sure it is filled out correctly before filing it.

Figure 13.3 PROOF OF SERVICE BY MAIL
Form FL-335

Note: Always include a copy of this form along with whatever papers are being served. The copy must be completely filled out but need not be signed. This is to give the other side notice of the time, place and manner of mailing.

* Note: When this form is used by Respondent for the Declarations of Disclosure (chapter 14), if Respondent is not filing any papers other than proofs of service of Disclosure Declarations, you can improve the chances for not paying the Response fee if Respondent puts Petitioner's name and address in the caption and has Petitioner file it. In other words, although signed by Respondent, this would be treated as just another document in Petitioner's case.

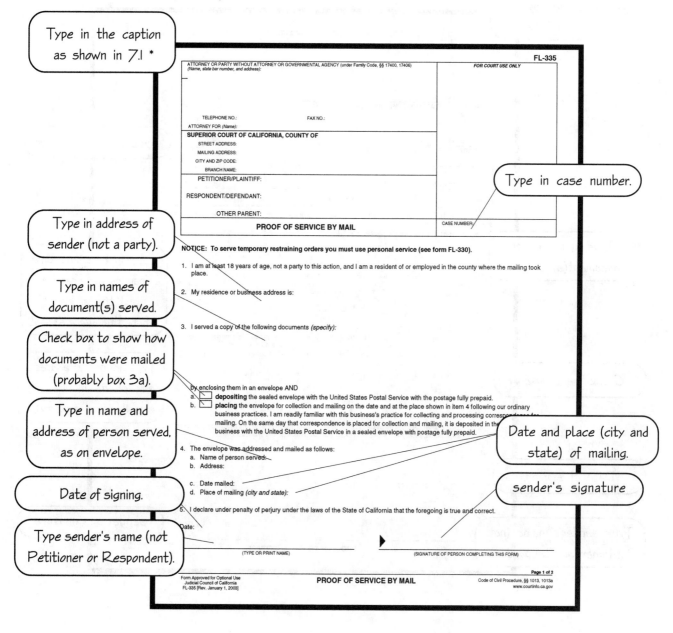

Callouts around the form:

- Type in the caption as shown in 7.1 *
- Type in case number.
- Type in address of sender (not a party).
- Type in names of document(s) served.
- Check box to show how documents were mailed (probably box 3a).
- Type in name and address of person served, as on envelope.
- Date and place (city and state) of mailing.
- Date of signing.
- sender's signature
- Type sender's name (not Petitioner or Respondent).

Form text:

ATTORNEY OR PARTY WITHOUT ATTORNEY OR GOVERNMENTAL AGENCY (under Family Code, §§ 17400, 17406) (Name, state bar number, and address):

FOR COURT USE ONLY

FL-335

TELEPHONE NO.: FAX NO.:
ATTORNEY FOR (Name):

SUPERIOR COURT OF CALIFORNIA, COUNTY OF
STREET ADDRESS:
MAILING ADDRESS:
CITY AND ZIP CODE:
BRANCH NAME:

PETITIONER/PLAINTIFF:

RESPONDENT/DEFENDANT:

OTHER PARENT:

PROOF OF SERVICE BY MAIL

CASE NUMBER:

NOTICE: To serve temporary restraining orders you must use personal service (see form FL-330).

1. I am at least 18 years of age, not a party to this action, and I am a resident of or employed in the county where the mailing took place.

2. My residence or business address is:

3. I served a copy of the following documents (specify):

by enclosing them in an envelope AND
a. □ depositing the sealed envelope with the United States Postal Service with the postage fully prepaid.
b. □ placing the envelope for collection and mailing on the date and at the place shown in item 4 following our ordinary business practices. I am readily familiar with this business's practice for collecting and processing correspondence for mailing. On the same day that correspondence is placed for collection and mailing, it is deposited in the ordinary course of business with the United States Postal Service in a sealed envelope with postage fully prepaid.

4. The envelope was addressed and mailed as follows:
a. Name of person served:
b. Address:

c. Date mailed:
d. Place of mailing (city and state):

5. I declare under penalty of perjury under the laws of the State of California that the foregoing is true and correct.

Date:

(TYPE OR PRINT NAME)

(SIGNATURE OF PERSON COMPLETING THIS FORM)

Page 1 of 2

Form Approved for Optional Use
Judicial Council of California
FL-335 [Rev. January 1, 2003]

PROOF OF SERVICE BY MAIL

Code of Civil Procedure, §§ 1013, 1013a
www.courtinfo.ca.gov

Figure 13.4 **PROOF OF PERSONAL SERVICE**
Form FL-330

Type in the caption as shown in 7.1.

Type in case number.

Type in names of document(s) served.

Type in date and time papers were served and the address where they were served.

Check these boxes.

Type in name, address and phone number of sender (not a party).

Date of signing.

sender's signature

Type sender's name (not Petitioner or Respondent).

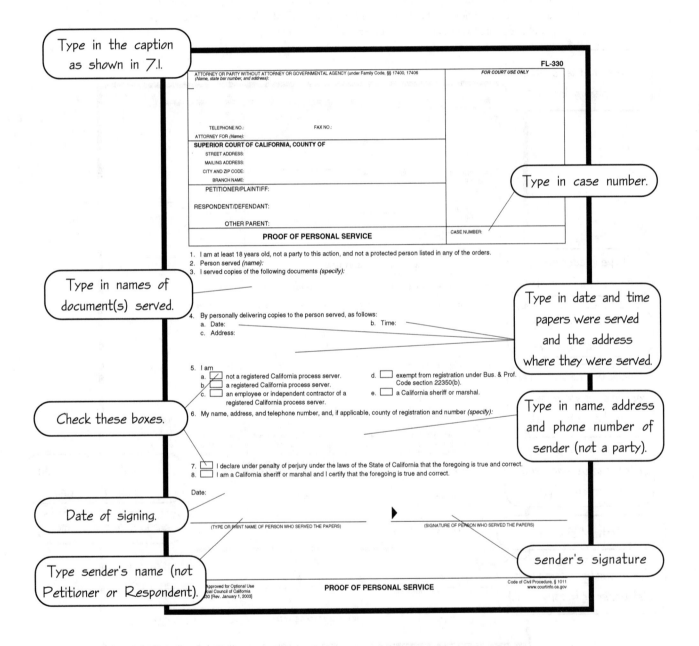

FL-330

ATTORNEY OR PARTY WITHOUT ATTORNEY OR GOVERNMENTAL AGENCY (under Family Code, §§ 17400, 17406
(Name, state bar number, and address):

FOR COURT USE ONLY

TELEPHONE NO.:   FAX NO.:
ATTORNEY FOR *(Name):*

SUPERIOR COURT OF CALIFORNIA, COUNTY OF
STREET ADDRESS:
MAILING ADDRESS:
CITY AND ZIP CODE:
BRANCH NAME:

PETITIONER/PLAINTIFF:

RESPONDENT/DEFENDANT:

OTHER PARENT:

PROOF OF PERSONAL SERVICE

CASE NUMBER:

1. I am at least 18 years old, not a party to this action, and not a protected person listed in any of the orders.
2. Person served *(name):*
3. I served copies of the following documents *(specify):*

4. By personally delivering copies to the person served, as follows:
   a. Date: b. Time:
   c. Address:

5. I am
   a. ☑ not a registered California process server.   d. ☐ exempt from registration under Bus. & Prof.
   b. ☐ a registered California process server.   Code section 22350(b).
   c. ☐ an employee or independent contractor of a   e. ☐ a California sheriff or marshal.
       registered California process server.
6. My name, address, and telephone number, and, if applicable, county of registration and number *(specify):*

7. ☐ I declare under penalty of perjury under the laws of the State of California that the foregoing is true and correct.
8. ☐ I am a California sheriff or marshal and I certify that the foregoing is true and correct.

Date:

_____   ▶ _____
(TYPE OR PRINT NAME OF PERSON WHO SERVED THE PAPERS)   (SIGNATURE OF PERSON WHO SERVED THE PAPERS)

Approved for Optional Use   **PROOF OF PERSONAL SERVICE**   Code of Civil Procedure, § 1011
cial Council of California   www.courtinfo.ca.gov
30 [Rev. January 1, 2003]

DECLARATIONS OF DISCLOSURE

To get a divorce, both spouses *must* exchange Declarations of Disclosure listing all information about their property, debts, income and expenses. This is an extension of the fiduciary duty (discussed in chapter 3.2 and 3.3) requiring spouses to always be completely open and honest in their dealings with each other. Keep in mind that any property or important information about property that is concealed, misrepresented, or mistakenly overlooked can result in your agreement or judgment being set aside, even years after you think the divorce is over, and penalties can be imposed. One woman lost her entire $1.3 million lottery prize because she intentionally failed to disclose it. Another judgment was set aside because the Disclosure stated "unknown" for the value of one spouse's pension. So, be very careful.

14.1 The law and how it works

The disclosure law

1. **Preliminary Declaration** of Disclosure (PD). When the Petition is filed, or some unspecified time afterward, each spouse must serve the other with a Preliminary Declaration of Disclosure, which consists of a list of all assets and debts, including both community and separate property, no matter where located, in which the spouse has or may have an interest, along with a completed Income and Expense declaration set (I&E). **Note:** The PD can't be waived. Petitioner *must* do it. However, there is no automatic penalty for being late or if Respondent doesn't comply at all.

2. **Final Declaration** of Disclosure (FD). At or before the time you enter into a settlement agreement, each spouse must serve on the other a Final Declaration of Disclosure. The FD must include "all material facts and information" regarding the character of each asset or debt (whether community or separate), the value of community assets and debts, and income and expenses of each party.

3. Each spouse has a *continuing* duty to update information so the other spouse has accurate information whenever support or the division of property is settled by written agreement or by judgment.

4. In addition, each party must disclose in writing any income-producing opportunities that arise after separation which result directly from the income-producing activities of either spouse during the marriage. The disclosure must be in time to allow the other spouse to decide whether to participate in the opportunity.

5. **Waiver of FD.** The Final Disclosure can be waived by Petitioner unilaterally where there is no settlement agreement and Respondent has not filed a Response. If there is an agreement, both parties can mutually agree to waive it using form FL-144 (back of book but not illustrated as it is so easy to fill out). However, if you have significant assets or debts, we recommend that you avoid waiving the FD if at all possible.

How it works

• Disclosures are served but *not* filed with the court. Only the parties see the disclosures. The court sees only proofs of service.

• If a declaration is incomplete or inadequate, the other party can object in court, either immediately or in the future.

• Omitted community property is owned by the spouses as tenants in common and can be divided later by the court, whenever the omission is discovered. A party who makes incorrect or inadequate disclosure risks having the case reopened in the future, perhaps *much* later (see chapter 2.9). However, it takes time, money and energy to do this, so it has to be worth the effort. Therefore, the risk created by inadequate disclosure increases with the value of the property and the degree of upset involved.

• Assuming all the right information is included (very big assumption), it is okay for one spouse to prepare lists and documents for the other spouse to sign, or to make one set of documents serve as both the Preliminary and Final Disclosures and file one Declaration re Service to cover both.

1. If Respondent *will* participate:

• If you had no significant property or debts to divide when you separated, no minor children, and no spousal support to be arranged, there is no advantage to having the other spouse pay a filing fee to enter the case formally as Respondent. Go to item 2, below.

• If you have significant property or debts to divide, or minor children, or spousal support to be arranged, you should make a written settlement agreement (SA) to settle all issues. Both parties should complete Preliminary and Final Declarations of Disclosure, and file a Proof of Service for each one to prove they were delivered, along with a Declaration Re Service of Disclosure (Fig. 14.4).

2. If Respondent will *not* participate:

Petitioner *must* serve the Preliminary Declaration on Respondent in every case.

• If there is no SA, Petitioner can complete the case by default (chapter 17) and waive the Final Disclosure (FD) by checking box 6(b) in the Declaration for Default Dissolution (Fig. 20.1).

• If you are going to have an SA, try hard to get your spouse to sign an FD beforehand or at the same time, even if you have to prepare it yourself. If he/she will not do an FD, you have a problem. In order to complete your case, either: (1) waive the FD with form FL-144 (not recommended in cases with significant property because you *want* the other party's sworn info before you sign) *and* check box 6(b)in the Declaration for Default Dissolution (Fig. 20.1), or (2) try using the Declaration of Compliance (chapter 20.2), understanding that this might not work.

• If you want to *force* compliance and go for your other remedies, you will need an attorney.

14.2 Doing the declarations

The Preliminary Declaration

The Preliminary Declaration (PD) includes the Declaration of Disclosure, the Schedule of Assets and Debts, and the Income and Expense Declarations. Petitioner serves these documents on Respondent either along with the Summons and Petition or soon afterward. If possible, Respondent should also complete the PD and have someone mail it to Petitioner and file a Proof of Service by Mail (Figure 13.3) with the court.

How to do it:

• Complete the Declaration of Disclosure (Fig. 14.1) and attach to it the following:

• Schedule of Assets and Debts (Fig. 14.2 and 14.3). Indicate what property and debts you have. It is not necessary *at this time* to provide values, indicate whether the property is separate, or any requested attachments, but you can if you wish. List separately major items, items that have some special significance to you, and items that have title documents (land, cars) or account numbers. Include account or ID numbers, wherever applicable.

• Complete a set of Income and Expense forms (chapter 16).

The Final Declaration

The Final Declaration should be completed before you sign your settlement agreement. If no agreement, do it before you file the final papers. The FD includes statements of "all material facts and information regarding . . ." (a) the value of all community assets and debts; and (b) the character of each asset or debt. So, for every item of significant value, you must indicate whether you think it is separate (in which case, who it belongs to) or community property. If property is mixed, a brief statement of facts should be added to clarify its mixed character and what part belongs to each.

Who knows exactly what "all material facts" includes? You don't have to do any guessing, but if you *do* know something that might even *possibly* make a difference, you'd better write it down and include it in your disclosure.

How to do it:

• Complete the Declaration of Disclosure (Fig. 14.1) and attach to it the following:

• The Schedule of Assets and Debts (Fig. 14.2 and 14.3) with all columns completed and in indication of the character of each asset and debt (whether community, separate, or mixed).

• Attach updated I&E forms if anything has changed since the Preliminary Declaration.

Statements *must* be made in *every* case for items 3 and 4 on the Declaration of Disclosure (Figure 14.1). Minimum statements can be typed on the face of the Declaration form. A minimum statement for item 3 or 4 would be, "Regarding item __, I know of no special facts or other information regarding this subject other than what is contained in the Schedule of Assets and Debts attached to this Final Declaration." To be safe, some corporate officers might have occasion to state, "Certain information cannot be disclosed due to SEC rules against insider trading."

More than minimum information. If you *do* have some "material facts or information" to disclose about any item, it should be typed on an Additional Page form (page 74) with the heading, "Statement Regarding Item __ of the (Schedule of Assets and Debts) (or Declaration of Final Disclosure)." Use any number of pages to be complete.

Service and Proofs of Service

Preliminary Disclosure. Each party should have someone serve the PD on the other party, by mail or personally, then sign either a Proof of Service by Mail (Figure 13.3) or Proof of Personal Service (Figure 13.4). Optionally, Petitioner can include the PD with the first papers served and enter it on the Proof of Service of Summons. Also complete the Declaration Regarding Service of Declaration of Disclosure (Fig. 14.4) and file it along with the Proof of Service.

Final Disclosure. Each party should have someone serve the FD on the other party, by mail or personally, then sign either a Proof of Service by Mail (Figure 13.3) or a Proof of Personal Service (Figure 13.4). Option: some counties are satisfied if you state in your settlement agreement that the Final Disclosures were served. We suggest you do both. Each party signs a Declaration Regarding Service of Declaration of Disclosure (Fig. 14.4) which should then be filed with the court along with the Proofs of Service.

Figure 14.1 **DECLARATION OF DISCLOSURE**
Form FL-140

Note: In the instructions below,
PD = Preliminary Declaration
FD = Final Declaration

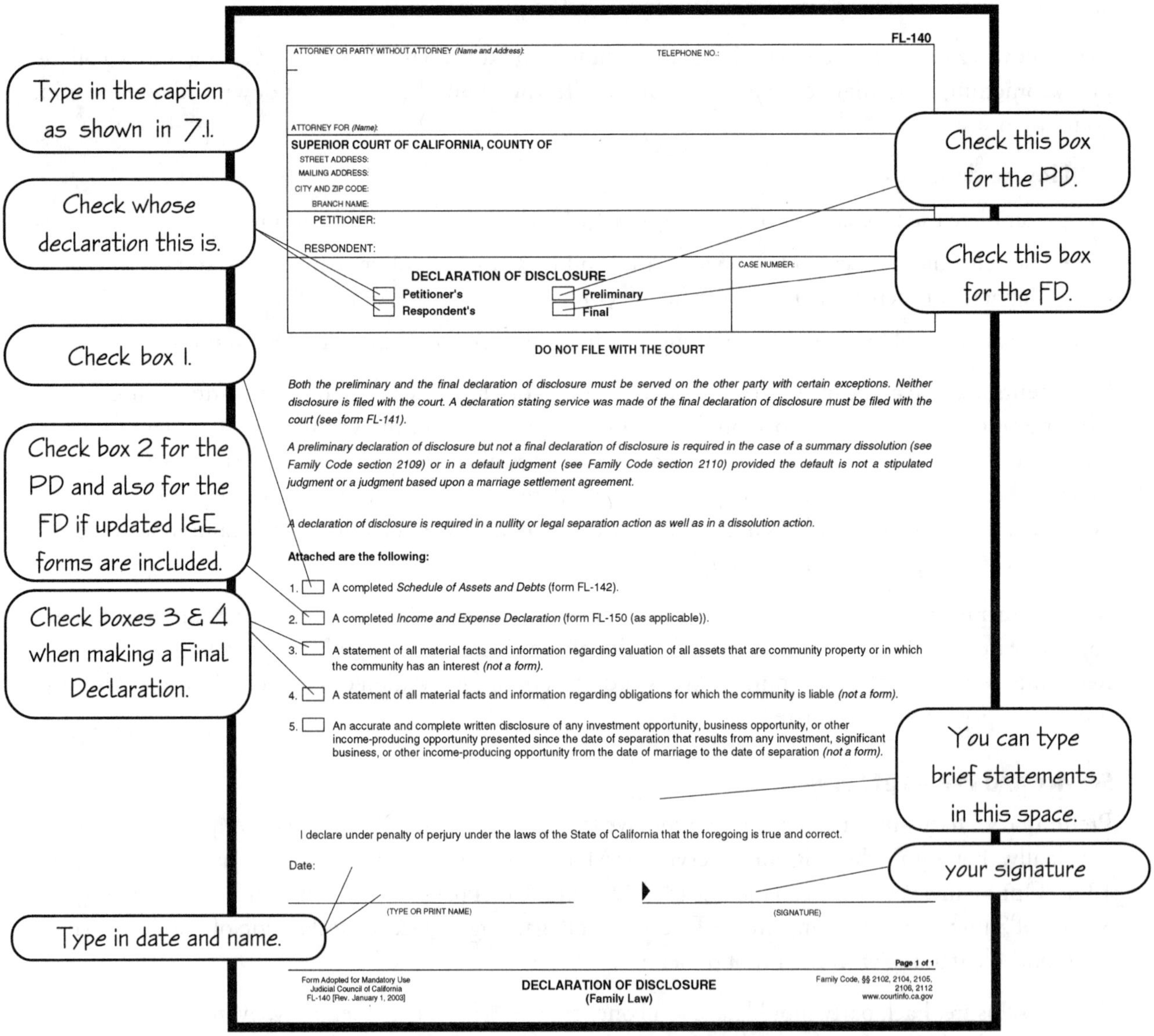

Type in the caption as shown in 7.1.

Check whose declaration this is.

Check box 1.

Check box 2 for the PD and also for the FD if updated I&E forms are included.

Check boxes 3 & 4 when making a Final Declaration.

Type in date and name.

Check this box for the PD.

Check this box for the FD.

You can type brief statements in this space.

your signature

FL-140

ATTORNEY OR PARTY WITHOUT ATTORNEY *(Name and Address)*:   TELEPHONE NO.:

ATTORNEY FOR *(Name)*:

SUPERIOR COURT OF CALIFORNIA, COUNTY OF
STREET ADDRESS:
MAILING ADDRESS:
CITY AND ZIP CODE:
BRANCH NAME:
PETITIONER:
RESPONDENT:

DECLARATION OF DISCLOSURE   CASE NUMBER:
☐ Petitioner's   ☐ Preliminary
☐ Respondent's   ☐ Final

DO NOT FILE WITH THE COURT

Both the preliminary and the final declaration of disclosure must be served on the other party with certain exceptions. Neither disclosure is filed with the court. A declaration stating service was made of the final declaration of disclosure must be filed with the court (see form FL-141).

A preliminary declaration of disclosure but not a final declaration of disclosure is required in the case of a summary dissolution (see Family Code section 2109) or in a default judgment (see Family Code section 2110) provided the default is not a stipulated judgment or a judgment based upon a marriage settlement agreement.

A declaration of disclosure is required in a nullity or legal separation action as well as in a dissolution action.

Attached are the following:

1. ☐ A completed *Schedule of Assets and Debts* (form FL-142).

2. ☐ A completed *Income and Expense Declaration* (form FL-150 as applicable)).

3. ☐ A statement of all material facts and information regarding valuation of all assets that are community property or in which the community has an interest *(not a form)*.

4. ☐ A statement of all material facts and information regarding obligations for which the community is liable *(not a form)*.

5. ☐ An accurate and complete written disclosure of any investment opportunity, business opportunity, or other income-producing opportunity presented since the date of separation that results from any investment, significant business, or other income-producing opportunity from the date of marriage to the date of separation *(not a form)*.

I declare under penalty of perjury under the laws of the State of California that the foregoing is true and correct.

Date:

_____   ▶   _____
(TYPE OR PRINT NAME)   (SIGNATURE)

Page 1 of 1

Form Adopted for Mandatory Use   **DECLARATION OF DISCLOSURE**   Family Code, §§ 2102, 2104, 2105,
Judicial Council of California   **(Family Law)**   2106, 2112
FL-140 [Rev. January 1, 2003]   www.courtinfo.ca.gov

Schedule of Assets and Debts

When to use it

This form is used as part of the Preliminary and Final Declarations of Disclosure. It is also used as part of formal discovery when you need to formally require information from the other side (see chapter 17 in Book 2: *How to Solve Divorce Problems*).

How to fill it out

Make extra copies of the blank form to use as work sheets. Fill it out as shown in Figures 14.2 and 14.3. Prepare the original and make 3 copies. Don't guess about anything; if you don't know some piece of information, put "Unknown."

Listing property. Type entries to show what assets and debts you or your spouse have or might have, individually or together. List separately any items that have title documents, registration numbers or account numbers, special personal importance to you, or high monetary value. For information you don't have access to, put "Known only to my spouse." On the Preliminary Disclosure, if you have no other choice, put "To be provided on the Final Disclosure" in place of identifying numbers that you haven't been able to determine.

If you run out of room in any asset category, use another sheet and type in "Continuation of item __." On the Schedule form, put in a line "Value from continuation sheet" and include the value from the continuation for that item. At item 27 on page 4, type in the number of all continuation pages attached.

Attachments. Many items on this form request attachments to document the items entered. These are *required* for purposes of discovery (Book 2, chapter 17) but not, strictly speaking, required as part of disclosure. However, it would be a good idea to attach whatever documents you can get in order to inspire trust and to avoid giving the other side a good reason to start formal discovery procedures.

Completing the columns. The Preliminary Declaration requires only a simple list, but for the Final Declaration you must complete the columns:

> **Sep. Prop.** For each item or group, enter a H or W to indicate that you think Husband or Wife has a separate interest, or HW to indicate that both do. For some items, it might help to attach an explanatory note, but if you do, enter "see attached note" in the left column headed "Description."

> **Date acquired.** This is an important indicator of the character of an asset or debt. For each item or group, give the date if you can, otherwise enter "UNK" if you don't know. They should have asked if it was acquired before marriage, during the marriage, or after separation (which is what really counts) or over a period of time covering two or more of those periods. Here again, in order to be clear, you might want to attach an explanatory note, in the same manner as described above.

> **Gross fair market value.** This is what the item could get on the open market if sold right now. Put down what you know or believe to be the value, but don't just guess because you might be held responsible for it later. Get a professional appraisal on major items, talk to dealers, scan the want ads, try to estimate what you could get. If you simply don't know, put "Unknown."

> **Money owed.** Make an entry for each item, either a value, $0 if nothing owed, or "Unknown," if you don't know and can't easily find out. If you can find out with a phone call, do it.

> **Totals.** When finished, total the columns at items 18 and 26.

Explain contradictions. For example, if an asset was acquired during marriage but you believe it is separate or partly separate, attach a note explaining why you think this is so.

Figure 14.2 SCHEDULE OF ASSETS AND DEBTS
Form FL-142 (page 1)

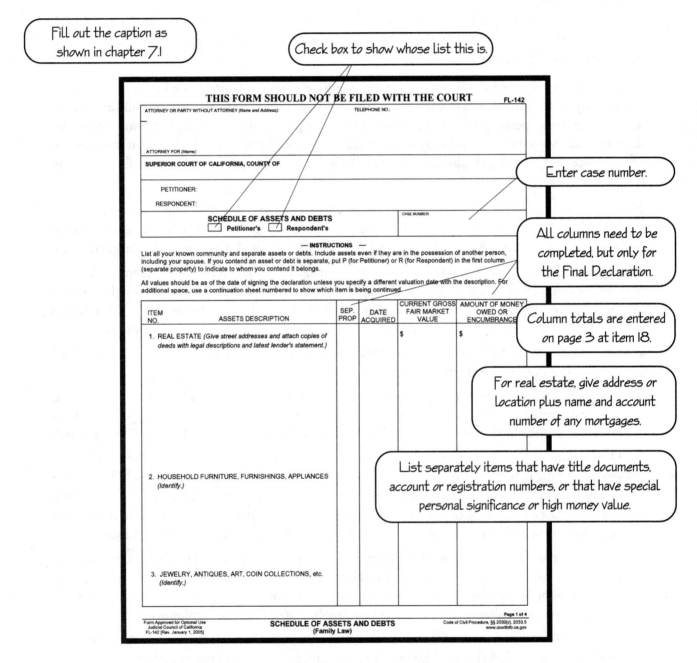

Fill out the caption as shown in chapter 7.1

Check box to show whose list this is.

Enter case number.

All columns need to be completed, but only for the Final Declaration.

Column totals are entered on page 3 at item 18.

For real estate, give address or location plus name and account number of any mortgages.

List separately items that have title documents, account or registration numbers, or that have special personal significance or high money value.

Note: Pages 2 and 3 of this form are not illustrated. They are similar to this one and easy to understand.

Figure 14.3 SCHEDULE OF ASSETS AND DEBTS
Form FL-142 (page 4)

ITEM NO.	DEBTS—SHOW TO WHOM OWED	SEP. PROP.	TOTAL OWING	DATE INCURRED
19. STUDENT LOANS *(Give details.)*			$	
20. TAXES *(Give details.)*				
21. SUPPORT ARREARAGES *(Attach copies of orders and statements.)*				
22. LOANS—UNSECURED *(Give bank name and loan number and attach copy of latest statement.)*				
23. CREDIT CARDS *(Give creditor's name and address and the account number. Attach copy of latest statement.)*				
24. OTHER DEBTS *(Specify.):*				
25. TOTAL DEBTS FROM CONTINUATION SHEET				
26. TOTAL DEBTS			$	

27. ☐ *(Specify number):* _____ pages are attached as continuation sheets.

I declare under penalty of perjury under the laws of the State of California that the foregoing is true and correct.

Date: _____

_____   ▶   _____
(TYPE OR PRINT NAME)   (SIGNATURE OF DECLARANT)

FL-142 [Rev. January 1, 2005]   **SCHEDULE OF ASSETS AND DEBTS**   Page 4 of 4
(Family Law)

List all debts that are owed or may be owed by either spouse or both.

Columns need to be completed only for the Final Declaration.

If you attached continuation pages, check box 27 and indicate how many.

Enter totals.

Type date signed.

Type your name.

your signature

Figure 14.4 DECLARATION RE SERVICE OF DECLARATION OF DISCLOSURE

Form FL-141

Note: This form is *almost* a proof of service, but not quite. That's why it is also best if you file a proof of service at the same time.

Note: When filed on behalf of a spouse who is not the Petitioner, if that spouse is not filing any papers other than proofs of service of disclosure and this declaration form, you can avoid any chance of being asked to pay a response filing fee if you put Petitioner's name and address in the caption of each document and have Petitioner file them. In other words, although signed by the other spouse, these documents would be treated as just another document in Petitioner's case.

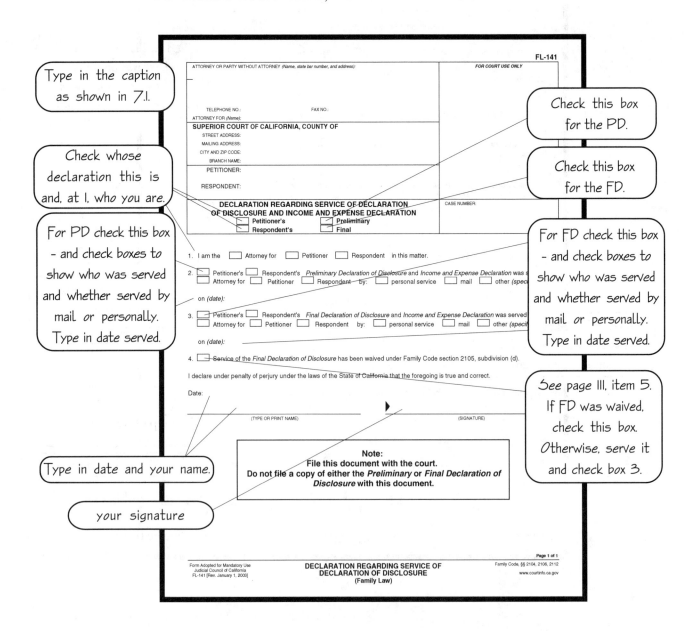

THE PROPERTY DECLARATION

What it is

The Property Declaration is a detailed list and valuation of your property designed to give you, your spouse and the court a good idea of what you have, how much you owe, and how you would like things to be divided.

When required

If you have community property and/or debts to be divided or separate property to confirm, you *must* file a Property Declaration with your Request to Enter Default (chapter 17) *unless* you have a settlement agreement or unless you listed everything in the tiny spaces provided on the Petition form itself at items 4 and 5.

How to fill it out

Make extra copies of the *blank* form to use as worksheets. Fill it out as shown in Figures 15.1 and 15.2. Prepare the original and make 3 copies.

Listing property. List separately any major items or items with title; minor things can go in a group, like "household goods." If you have no property in a category, put "none." Don't guess about anything: if you don't know some piece of information, put "unknown."

Need more room? If you run out of room for an item, use the Continuation of Property Declaration form (back of book and companion CD) or the Additional Page form (page 74).

Values on Property Declaration. In the first column, you *must* value each item or group of items so the judge can divide your property. The "fair market value" of an item or group is the amount you could get if sold on the open market. Put down what you know or believe to be the value, but don't just guess because you might be held responsible later. If you don't know, put "unknown."Get a professional appraisal on major items, talk to dealers, scan the want ads, try to estimate what you could get. The judge might ask how you arrived at your figures. In the second column, put the amount of any debt owed on that item or group, deduct it from the first column and enter the balance in the third column. In the fourth and fifth columns, show the value of property as you wish it to be divided between you and Respondent. The total value, considering all debts and property, should come out about equal unless your total property value is under $5,000.

Community and separate property. If you have both types of property, community and separate property must go on two separate forms.

Figure 15.1 **PROPERTY DECLARATION**
Form FL-160 (page 1)

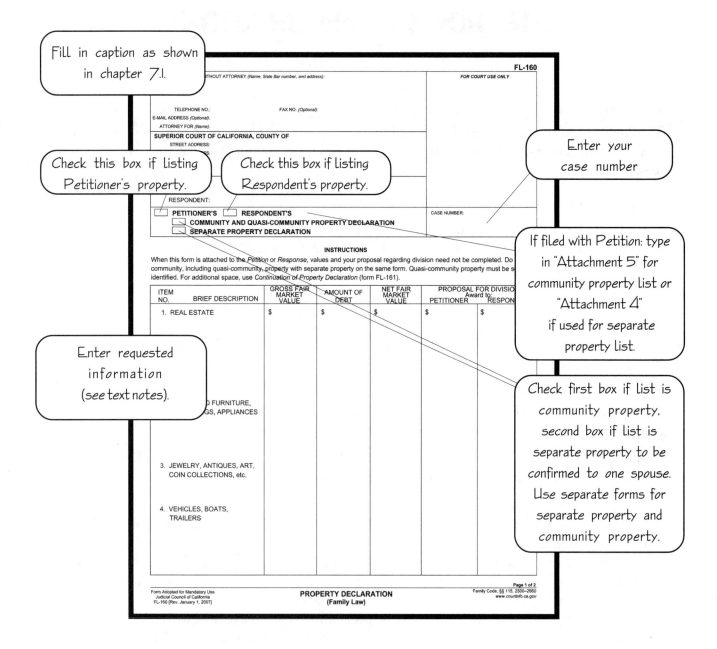

Fill in caption as shown in chapter 7.1.

Check this box if listing Petitioner's property.

Check this box if listing Respondent's property.

Enter your case number

If filed with Petition: type in "Attachment 5" for community property list or "Attachment 4" if used for separate property list.

Enter requested information (see text notes).

Check first box if list is community property, second box if list is separate property to be confirmed to one spouse. Use separate forms for separate property and community property.

Figure 15.2 PROPERTY DECLARATION
Form FL-160 (page 2)

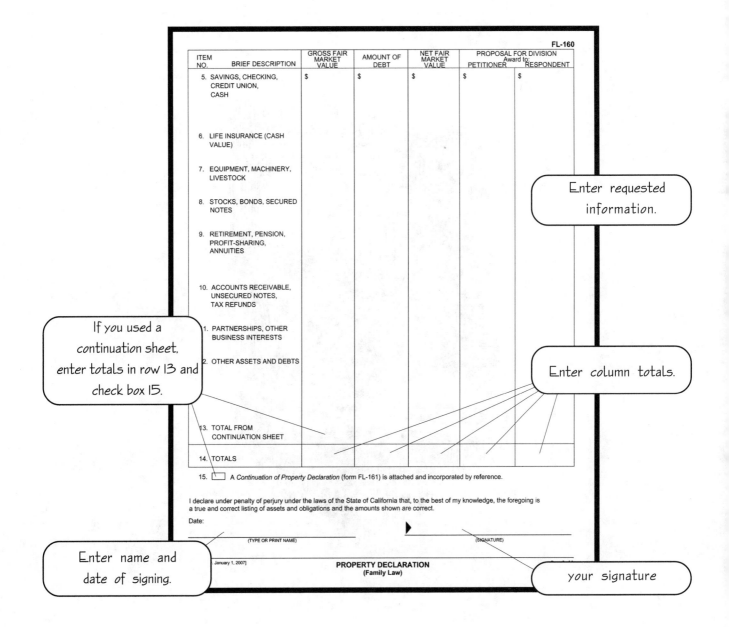

Enter requested information.

If you used a continuation sheet, enter totals in row 13 and check box 15.

Enter column totals.

Enter name and date of signing.

your signature

THE INCOME AND EXPENSE DECLARATION

What it is

The Income & Expense Declaration structures a detailed look at your income and expenses. There are four pages to this form (Figures 16.1 to 16.4), each of which is a different financial statement.

When the Income and Expense Declaration is required

Child support information. The fourth page (Figure 16.4) is specifically about child support. If you have minor children, you *must* complete this page; otherwise, you do not complete it.

The Income and Expense Declaration is used in *every* case as part of the Declaration of Disclosure (chapter 14). Don't forget, disclosures are served on your spouse but not filed with the court. However, if your case involves any kind of support, you have to file this form with the court *unless* you have a settlement agreement. Even if you have an agreement, some counties (Alameda, Contra Costa, Monterey, San Francisco, Santa Clara, Solano) want it anyway. If required in your county, include it when you mail your papers for the Judgment (chapter 20.1) or take it with you if you go to a hearing (20.3). Don't forget, if you have minor children, you *must* also include the fourth page, Child Support Information.

How to fill it out

Make a *blank* copy of the form to use as a worksheet and another to give to your spouse to complete and return to you as part of mandatory disclosure. If you need to file this form with the court, be aware that a few counties want financial forms on colored paper; see chapter 7.1 and ask your clerk.

Prepare the original and make 3 copies. Read the instructions on each page *very* carefully and follow them *exactly*. Every blank should have an entry. Either put down the information or figure requested, "zero" or "none" if not any, "not applicable" if the item is not relevant according to previous answers, "est." where you are estimating, or "unknown" if you have no idea at all.

Privacy. If filed with the court, this form will be a public record, so you should use a code for any Social Security or financial account numbers. This is true wherever such information appears in any document filed with the court or on any document attached to a form filed in court. Instructions for how to do this can be found in chapter 7.2.

Need more space? If more information is requested than will fit on the page, use the Additional Page form as shown on page 74. Type the heading, 'Continuation Sheet for (name of form),' and identify each item with the heading, 'Continuation of Item Number ___.' At the bottom of page one, in the space provided, enter the total number of extra pages attached to the form.

Your spouse's figures: The judge needs information about your spouse's income, mandatory deductions, and hardship expenses, if any. You are entitled by law to get this information in your spouse's disclosures. You are also entitled by law to see your spouse's current pay stubs, the last two state income tax returns, and other relevant documents.

If you do *not* get information voluntarily from your spouse, make estimates based on whatever you know from past records or past experience and mark these entries "est." If you have no figures at all and no facts from the past to use for a guess, put "unknown" wherever necessary, then go to a hearing with blanks left in the orders for support and let the judge decide the amount for support.

In Book 2, *How to Solve Divorce Problems,* chapters 8, 17 and 18, tell you how to get information from your spouse, either with or without court action.

Financial Statement (Simplified) FL–155

If you are eligible, you might want to use the simplified form instead of the more detailed Income and Expense Declaration illustrated in this chapter. You are **not** eligible to use the simplified form if either party is asking for spousal support or attorney fees, if you have any self-employment income, or if you receive *any* money from *any* source other than: salary or wages, interest, welfare, disability, unemployment, worker's compensation, Social Security or retirement income. We recommend the longer version illustrated here for most people, but if you want to take a look, you will find the simplified form in the back of this book and on the companion CD in the "forms" folder.

Figure 16.1 INCOME AND EXPENSE DECLARATION
Form FL-150 (page 1)

Type in caption as shown in chapter 7.1.

your case number

Enter the personal and financial information requested in these items.

See note on previous page, "Your spouse's figures."

Number of extra pages attached to this form, if any.

your signature

Type in your name and the date.

FL-150

ATTORNEY OR PARTY WITHOUT ATTORNEY *(Name, State Bar number, and address):*

FOR COURT USE ONLY

TELEPHONE NO.:
E-MAIL ADDRESS *(Optional):*
ATTORNEY FOR *(Name):*

SUPERIOR COURT OF CALIFORNIA, COUNTY OF
STREET ADDRESS:
MAILING ADDRESS:
CITY AND ZIP CODE:
BRANCH NAME:

PETITIONER/PLAINTIFF:
RESPONDENT/DEFENDANT:
OTHER PARENT/CLAIMANT:

INCOME AND EXPENSE DECLARATION

CASE NUMBER:

1. **Employment** *(Give information on your current job or, if you're unemployed, your most recent job.)*

Attach copies of your pay stubs for last two months (black out social security numbers).

   a. Employer:
   b. Employer's address:
   c. Employer's phone number:
   d. Occupation:
   e. Date job started:
   f. If unemployed, date job ended:
   g. I work about _____ hours per week.
   h. I get paid $ _____ gross (before taxes) ☐ per month ☐ per week ☐ per hour.

(If you have more than one job, attach an 8½-by-11-inch sheet of paper and list the same information as above for your other jobs. Write "Question 1—Other Jobs" at the top.)

2. **Age and education**
   a. My age is *(specify):*
   b. I have completed high school or the equivalent: ☐ Yes ☐ No   If no, highest grade completed *(specify):*
   c. Number of years of college completed *(specify):* ☐ Degree(s) obtained *(specify):*
   d. Number of years of graduate school completed *(specify):* ☐ Degree(s) obtained *(specify):*
   e. I have: ☐ professional/occupational license(s) *(specify):*
      ☐ vocational training *(specify):*

3. **Tax information**
   a. ☐ I last filed taxes for tax year *(specify year):*
   b. My tax filing status is ☐ single ☐ head of household ☐ married, filing separately
      ☐ married, filing jointly with *(specify name):*
   c. I file state tax returns in ☐ California ☐ other *(specify state):*
   d. I claim the following number of exemptions (including myself) on my taxes *(specify):*

4. **Other party's income.** I estimate the gross monthly income (before taxes) of the other party in this case at *(sp* This estimate is based on *(explain):*

(If you need more space to answer any questions on this form, attach an 8½-by-11-inch sheet of paper an question number before your answer.) Number of pages attached: _____

I declare under penalty of perjury under the laws of the State of California that the information contained on all pages of this form and any attachments is true and correct.

Date: _____

_____
(TYPE OR PRINT NAME)

▶ _____
(SIGNATURE OF DECLARANT)

Form Adopted for Mandatory Use
Judicial Council of California
FL-150 [Rev. January 1, 2007]

INCOME AND EXPENSE DECLARATION

Page 1 of 4
Family Code, §§ 2030–2032,
2100–2113, 3552, 3620–3634,
4050–4076, 4300–4339
www.courtinfo.ca.gov

Figure 16.2 INCOME AND EXPENSE DECLARATION (Income)

Form FL-150 (page 2)

Type in names as shown on page 74.

Type in your case number.

Enter the income information requested in items 5-10 and asset info at item 11.

For wage earners, amounts for items 10(a)-(c) will be on your paycheck stubs.

FL-150

PETITIONER/PLAINTIFF:	CASE NUMBER:
RESPONDENT/DEFENDANT:	
OTHER PARENT/CLAIMANT:	

Attach copies of your pay stubs for the last two months and proof of any other income. Take a copy of your latest federal tax return to the court hearing. *(Black out your social security number on the pay stub and tax return.)*

5. **Income** *(For average monthly, add up all the income you received in each category in the last 12 months and divide the total by 12.)*

                                                                       Last month   Average monthly

   a. Salary or wages (gross, before taxes)............................ $_____ _____

   b. Overtime (gross, before taxes)................................. $_____ _____

   c. Commissions or bonuses...................................... $_____ _____

   d. Public assistance (for example: TANF, SSI, GA/GR) ☐ currently receiving ...... $_____ _____

   e. Spousal support ☐ from this marriage ☐ from a different marriage .... $_____ _____

   f. Partner support ☐ from this domestic partnership ☐ from a different domestic partnership $_____ _____

   g. Pension/retirement fund payments............................. $_____ _____

   h. Social security retirement (not SSI)........................... $_____ _____

   i. Disability: ☐ Social security (not SSI) ☐ State disability (SDI) ☐ Private insurance . $_____ _____

   j. Unemployment compensation................................. $_____ _____

   k. Workers' compensation...................................... $_____ _____

   l. Other (military BAQ, royalty payments, etc.) *(specify):* .... $_____ _____

6. **Investment income** *(Attach a schedule showing gross receipts less cash expenses for each piece of property.)*

   a. Dividends/interest... $_____ _____

   b. Rental property income...................................... $_____ _____

   c. Trust income... $_____ _____

   d. Other *(specify):* .... $_____ _____

7. **Income from self-employment, after business expenses for all businesses**.............. $_____ _____

   I am the ☐ owner/sole proprietor ☐ business partner ☐ other *(specify):*

   Number of years in this business *(specify):*

   Name of business *(specify):*

   Type of business *(specify):*

   Attach a profit and loss statement for the last two years or a Schedule C from your last federal tax return. Black out your social security number. If you have more than one business, provide the information above for each of your businesses.

8. ☐ **Additional income.** I received one-time money (lottery winnings, inheritance, etc.) in the last 12 months *(specify source and amount):*

9. ☐ **Change in income.** My financial situation has changed significantly over the last 12 months because *(specify):*

10. **Deductions**   Last month

   a. Required union dues .... $_____

   b. Required retirement payments (not social security, FICA, 401(k), or IRA)............ $_____

   c. Medical, hospital, dental, and other health insurance premiums *(total monthly amount)*...... $_____

   d. Child support that I pay for children from other relationships................. $_____

   e. Spousal support that I pay by court order from a different marriage.............. $_____

   f. Partner support that I pay by court order from a different domestic partnership .... $_____

   g. Necessary job-related expenses not reimbursed by my employer *(attach explanation labeled "Question 10g")* ..... $_____

11. **Assets**   Total

   a. Cash and checking accounts, savings, credit union, money market, and other deposit accounts .... $_____

   b. Stocks, bonds, and other assets I could easily sell .... $_____

   c. All other property, ☐ real and ☐ personal *(estimate fair market value minus the debts you owe)* .... $_____

FL-150 [Rev. January 1, 2007]	**INCOME AND EXPENSE DECLARATION**	Page 2 of 4

Figure 16.3 **INCOME AND EXPENSE DECLARATION**
(Expenses)
Form FL-150 (page 3)

Type in your names as shown on page 74.

your case number

FL-150

PETITIONER/PLAINTIFF:	CASE NUMBER:
RESPONDENT/DEFENDANT:	
OTHER PARENT/CLAIMANT:	

12. **The following people live with me:**

Name	Age	How the person is related to me? (ex: son)	That person's gross monthly income	Pays some of the household expenses?
a.				Yes ☐ No ☐
b.				Yes ☐ No ☐
c.				Yes ☐ No ☐
d.				Yes ☐ No ☐
e.				Yes ☐ No ☐

For each person, indicate income from all sources, not just work and wages.

13. **Average monthly expenses** ☐ Estimated expenses ☐ Actual expenses ☐ Proposed needs

a. Home:

(1) ☐ Rent or ☐ mortgage. . . $ _____

If mortgage:

(a) average principal: $ _____
(b) average interest: $ _____

(2) Real property taxes . . . . $ _____

(3) Homeowner's or renter's insurance (if not included above) . . . . $ _____

(4) Maintenance and repair . . . . $ _____

b. Health-care costs not paid by insurance. . . $ _____

c. Child care . . . . $ _____

d. Groceries and household supplies. . . . . . . $ _____

e. Eating out. . . . . $ _____

f. Utilities (gas, electric, water, trash) . . . . . . $ _____

g. Telephone, cell phone, and e-mail . . . . $ _____

h. Laundry and cleaning . . . . $ _____
i. Clothes . . . . $ _____
j. Education . . . . $ _____
k. Entertainment, gifts, and vacation. . . . . . . $ _____
l. Auto expenses and transportation (insurance, gas, repairs, bus, etc.) . . . . $ _____
m. Insurance (life, accident, etc.; do not include auto, home, or health insurance). . . $ _____
n. Savings and investments. . . . . $ _____
o. Charitable contributions. . . . . $ _____
p. Monthly payments listed in item 14 (itemize below in 14 and insert total here). . $ _____
q. Other (specify): . . . . $ _____

r. **TOTAL EXPENSES** (a–q) (do not add in the amounts in a(1)(a) and (b)) $ _____

s. **Amount of expenses paid by others** $ _____

Total for Item 13 expenses.

14. **Installment payments and debts not listed above**

Paid to	For	Amount	Balance	Date of last payment
		$	$	
		$	$	
		$	$	
		$	$	
		$	$	
		$	$	

If not enough room here, check box and continue on separate sheet titled "Attachment 14."

15. **Attorney fees** (This is required if either party is requesting attorney fees.):

a. To date, I have paid my attorney this amount for fees and costs (specify): $
b. The source of this money was (specify):
c. I still owe the following fees and costs to my attorney (specify total owed): $
d. My attorney's hourly rate is (specify): $

I confirm this fee arrangement.

Date:

_____ ▶ _____
(TYPE OR PRINT NAME OF ATTORNEY)   (SIGNATURE OF ATTORNEY)

FL-150 [Rev. January 1, 2007]   **INCOME AND EXPENSE DECLARATION**   Page 3 of 4

Figure 16.4 INCOME AND EXPENSE DECLARATION
(Child Support Information)
Form FL-150 (page 4)

Type in names of parties..

Type in your case number.

FL-150

PETITIONER/PLAINTIFF:	CASE NUMBER:
RESPONDENT/DEFENDANT:	
OTHER PARENT/CLAIMANT:	

CHILD SUPPORT INFORMATION
(NOTE: Fill out this page only if your case involves chi

16. **Number of children**
   a. I have (specify number): _____ children under the age of 18 with the other parent in this case.
   b. The children spend _____ percent of their time with me and _____ percent of their time with the other parent.
      (If you're not sure about percentage or it has not been agreed on, please describe your parenting schedule here.)

Enter number of minors.

Part of child support calculation. Timeshare should add up to 100%. See chapter 5.3 - 5.4.

17. **Children's health-care expenses**
   a. ☐ I do   ☐ I do not   have health insurance available to me for the chil
   b. Name of insurance company:
   c. Address of insurance company:

   d. The monthly cost for the **children's** health insurance is or would be (specify): $ _____
      (Do not include the amount your employer pays.)

Read very carefully then enter the information requested.

18. **Additional expenses for the children in this case**   Amount per month
   a. Child care so I can work or get job training. . . . . $ _____
   b. Children's health care not covered by insurance . . . . $ _____
   c. Travel expenses for visitation . . . . $ _____
   d. Children's educational or other special needs (specify below): . . . . $ _____

19. **Special hardships.** I ask the court to consider the following special financial circumstances
   (attach documentation of any item listed here, including court orders):   Amount per month   For how many months?
   a. Extraordinary health expenses not included in 18b. . . . . $ _____   _____
   b. Major losses not covered by insurance (examples: fire, theft, other
      insured loss) . . . . $ _____   _____
   c. (1) Expenses for my minor children who are from other relationships and
          are living with me . . . . $ _____   _____
      (2) Names and ages of those children (specify):

      (3) Child support I receive for those children. . . . . $ _____

   The expenses listed in a, b, and c create an extreme financial hardship because (explain):

20. **Other information I want the court to know concerning support in my case** (specify):

FL-150 [Rev. January 1, 2007]   **INCOME AND EXPENSE DECLARATION**   Page 4 of 4

THE REQUEST TO ENTER DEFAULT

What it is

This form declares Respondent in default because no Response has been filed. After this, Respondent can no longer file legal documents in this case. If Respondent has filed a Response, this form is not used—you should proceed by settlement agreement and the Appearance & Waiver (chapter 12.7).

When used, file this form along with all your other papers in Step 4 (chapter 8), that is, when you are ready to get your Judgment. If you wish, you can request a date for your hearing when you file this form, or at a later time. Along with this form, you must also include a stamped envelope addressed to Respondent with the court clerk's return address.

The five parts in the Request To Enter Default:

Item 1 requests the Clerk to enter the default of Respondent.

Item 2 declares which, if any, of the Financial Declarations are attached (see note below).

Item 3 is an oath, swearing that a copy of this form and the indicated attachments was provided to the court with an envelope addressed to Respondent's last known address.

Item 4 itemizes your costs in the action. Put down "not claimed."

Item 5 is your oath that Respondent is not on active military duty. If you cannot swear to this, you cannot proceed this way (see chapter 12.3(3)).

How to fill it out

As shown in Figure 17.1. Prepare the original and make 3 copies.

Item 2: If you have no settlement agreement, a completed Property Declaration (ch. 15) *must* be attached to the original and all copies. If support is an issue, you must also attach Income & Expense forms (ch. 16). If you do have an agreement, Santa Clara wants these forms anyway. The signature on item 2 must be dated *at least* 31 days after the effective date of service on Respondent. In fact, you should wait until you have both completed the Declarations of Disclosure (chapter 14) or it appears certain that Respondent will not do the Declarations.

Item 3: With this form, include an envelope addressed to Respondent's attorney or, if no attorney, to Respondent's last known address, stamped with sufficient postage to mail the form and all attachments, return address to the clerk's office. If service was by publication, this is not required.

Figure 17.1 REQUEST TO ENTER DEFAULT
Form FL-165

Type in caption as shown in chapter 7.1.

Check box to show if the Income & Expense forms are attached or not

If either the I&E or Property Decl. are _not_ attached, check a box to explain why. Check (a) if a form was previously filed with the court. Check (b) if there is a written agreement. Check (c) and/or (d) and/or (e) if you are _not_ requesting an order which makes the omitted form relevant.

Type in date and name.

Type in case number.

Check box to show if the Property Declaration is attached or not (see text note).

Type your name and date of signing (not earlier than date next section signed).

your signature

If Respondent was served by publication check (a), otherwise check (b) and type in Respondent's name and Last known address.

your signature

FL-165

ATTORNEY OR PARTY WITHOUT ATTORNEY *(Name, State Bar number, and address):*

FOR COURT USE ONLY

TELEPHONE NO.:   FAX NO. *(Optional):*
E-MAIL ADDRESS *(Optional):*
ATTORNEY FOR *(Name):*

SUPERIOR COURT OF CALIFORNIA, COUNTY OF
STREET ADDRESS:
MAILING ADDRESS:
CITY AND ZIP CODE:
BRANCH NAME:

PETITIONER:

RESPONDENT:

REQUEST TO ENTER DEFAULT   CASE NUMBER:

1. **To the clerk:** Please enter the default of the respondent who has failed to respond to the petition.

2. A completed *Income and Expense Declaration* (form FL-150) or *Financial Statement (Simplified)* (form FL-☐ is attached ☐ is not attached.
   A completed *Property Declaration* (form FL-160) ☐ is attached ☐ is not attached
   because *(check at least one of the following):*
   (a) ☐ there have been no changes since the previous filing.
   (b) ☐ the issues subject to disposition by the court in this proceeding are the subject of a written agreement.
   (c) ☐ there are no issues of child, spousal, or partner support or attorney fees and costs subject to determination by the court.
   (d) ☐ the petition does not request money, property, costs, or attorney fees. (Fam. Code, § 2330.5.)
   (e) ☐ there are no issues of division of community property.
   (f) ☐ this is an action to establish parental relationship.
   Date:

   _____   ▶   _____
   (TYPE OR PRINT NAME)   (SIGNATURE OF ATTORNEY FO

3. **Declaration**
   a. ☐ No mailing is required because service was by publication or posting and the address of the resp
   b. ☐ A copy of this *Request to Enter Default*, including any attachments and an envelope with sufficient provided to the court clerk, with the envelope addressed as follows *(address of the respondent's attorney or, if none, the respondent's last known address):*

   I declare under penalty of perjury under the laws of the State of California that the foregoing is true and correc
   Date:

   _____   ▶   _____
   (TYPE OR PRINT NAME)   (SIGNATURE OF DECL

   FOR COURT USE ONLY
   ☐ *Request to Enter Default* mailed to the respondent or the respondent's attorney on *(date):*
   ☐ Default entered as requested on *(date):*
   ☐ Default **not** entered. Reason:

                                        Clerk, by _____

Form Adopted for Mandatory Use   **REQUEST TO ENTER DEFAULT**   Code of Civil Procedure, §§ 585, 587;
Judicial Council of California   Family Code, § 2335.5
FL-165 [Rev. January 1, 2005]   **(Family Law—Uniform Parentage)**   www.courtinfo.ca.gov

---

How to fill out the back

Item 4, Memorandum of Costs: Check box 4a (costs waived). On the line for Total, type in "not claimed." Date and sign as for previous section.

Item 5, Declaration of Nonmilitary Status: Assuming the statement is true, date and sign as shown for previous sections.

HOW TO FILL OUT THE JUDGMENT

What it is

The Judgment is your most critical document. It is the final resolution of all legal issues in your case, so take your time, be careful, get it right. The Judgment does not become effective until (1) you prepare it, (2) the judge signs it, and (3) it is entered into court records. Upon *entry* of Judgment, every part of it becomes effective and the Judgment can only be modified by stipulation of the parties or after a hearing on a motion to modify the Judgment.

Note: When the Judgment is entered, the automatic restraining orders (2.7) are ended.

How to fill it out

Fill it out as shown in Figure 18.1. Prepare an original and 3 copies.

Date marital status ends. The Judgment *must* specify exactly when your marital status will be terminated. "Date marital status ends" is six months plus one day after the date the service of process became effective. See the note on page 105 to determine effective date of service and enter that date at item 3, then add six months plus one day and enter that date in the caption where indicated and also at item 4(a)(1) on the Judgment. In San Mateo, do not use a holiday or weekend date! **If the date has already passed,** type in "upon entry of Judgment" except as follows: Alameda and Marin, "forthwith;" Contra Costa, "date of filing;" Santa Clara, "date Judgment is filed;" leave it blank in Fresno, Los Angeles, Orange, San Diego, San Luis Obispo, and Santa Cruz counties. If the field provided is too small, abbreviate Judgment = Jdgmnt.

Now or later? In some cases, there might be big advantages (Social Security, military benefits, taxes, etc.) to ending the marriage at a later date. To end your marriage at some date beyond the six month waiting period, you must either leave it to be determined later—by checking box 4(a)(2)—or by filing a stipulated Judgment (signed by your spouse as shown page 134) setting the date you want. If the date is left to be determined, then to end the marriage you will have to make a formal motion or file a consent Judgment. A stipulation will cost the response fee, if it has not already been paid. You can find a stipulation form in the Kits section of the companion CD.

Very important! Serve the Judgment on Respondent. To enforce an order, especially by using "contempt of court," you *must* be able to prove Respondent knew of the order. So, if Respondent has been ordered to pay support, deliver property, or do or not do any act in the future, then once the Judgment has been signed and entered (chapter 21), it is *very* important to have a copy of the Judgment *personally* served on Respondent (chapter 12.4) and a Proof of Personal Service filed with the court (Figure 13.4).

Figure 18.1 **JUDGMENT**
Form FL-180   (Page 1)

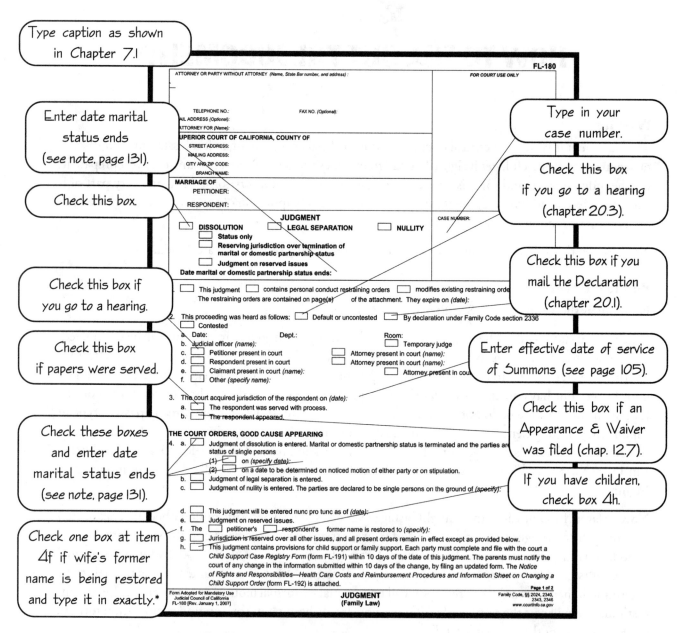

Type caption as shown in Chapter 7.1

Enter date marital status ends (see note, page 131).

Check this box.

Check this box if you go to a hearing.

Check this box if papers were served.

Check these boxes and enter date marital status ends (see note, page 131).

Check one box at item 4f if wife's former name is being restored and type it in exactly.*

Type in your case number.

Check this box if you go to a hearing (chapter 20.3).

Check this box if you mail the Declaration (chapter 20.1).

Enter effective date of service of Summons (see page 105).

Check this box if an Appearance & Waiver was filed (chap. 12.7).

If you have children, check box 4h.

*Note: If Husband is applying for the Judgment, some judges will not restore Wife's former name unless she agreed to it in the settlement agreement or has signed her consent to the Judgment (page 134).

18.1   How to add further orders

What they are

If you have property, debts, kids or spousal support, then you *must* add orders to your Judgment to spell out every decision the judge makes in your case. These are called "further orders." If you have a settlement agreement, some counties do not require further orders, while others do, so the way you add further orders to your Judgment will depend on which county you are in, as explained in section 18.2 below.

Two ways to add further orders

A. Write your own. You can add further orders that you prepare yourself on addtional pages, using as a guide the order language shown in sections 18.3–18.6. Use parts that apply to your case and change wording to fit your particular situation. You can also borrow language from the Judgment Attachments described below. If you need help with your Judgment, call Divorce Helpline.

On the Judgment form, fill out items 4 and 5 as shown in Figures 18.1 and 18.2. Check boxes to show which items (4k – 4m) are the subject of further orders. Next, check the box under the judge's signature line to show that the Judge's signature now appears at the end of the last attachment.

Put the rest of your orders on Additional Page forms (chapter 7.1) and use a new Additional Page to start each separate item. Type the heading: "Continuation of Judgment For Item 4(k)," or 4(l) or 4(m). Below that, type your further orders, one right after the other, on as many Additional Pages as necessary. Further orders should be typed double-spaced on numbered lines only, one side only. Always refer to the parties as Petitioner and Respondent unless we tell you otherwise below. At the end of all of your further orders, type a line for the date and judge's signature, just like the one on the Judgment form. Nothing else should follow the judge's signature.

B. Use Judgment attachments. The Judicial Council continues to expand the Judgment attachment forms that you can use to define further orders and, for the most part, you simply check boxes and fill in blanks to define your orders. Because they must cover almost every case, they are fairly bulky—there are ten of these Judgment attachment forms in the forms folder on the companion CD that comes with this book. In the order in which the appear on page 2 of the Judgment, they are:

- FL-341 Child Custody and Visitation Order Attachment (used alone or under FL-355)
- FL-355 Stipulation and Order for Custody/Visitation, which can have the following attachments: FL-341, 341(C), 341(D), 341(E). **Note** that FL-341(A) and 341(B)—supervised visits and abduction orders—are found in Book 2 where cases with conflict are treated.
- FL-342 Child Support Information and Order Attachment
- FL-342(A) Non-Guideline Child Support Findings Attachment
- FL-350 Stipulation to Establish or Modify Child Support and Order
- FL-343 Spousal or Family Support Order Attachment
- FL-345 Property Order Attachment

You can use these for your Judgment, or just study them for ideas and language for your written further orders, or combine the two methods, or ignore them entirely.

If you decide to use any of the Judgment attachment forms, at items 4k – 4m you must check boxes to show which items have further orders and which Judgment attachment you are using.

For either method A or method B, you will be adding more pages to the Judgment, so in item 5 you must indicate the number of pages attached. This means how many pages of additional orders you use, but do *not* include the pages of any attached settlement agreement or separate written parenting plan; just pages with further orders written on them.

Privacy rules. To protect yourself, your Ex and your children from identity theft, your further orders should be modified to have all Social Security and financial account numbers replaced with a code plus the last four digits of the account. See chapter 7.2.

Special rule for Los Angeles, San Bernardino & Solano Counties

When you file a settlement agreement (SA) in these counties, both spouses must sign their approval of the Judgment, so have the Judgment ready to sign when the settlement agreement is signed. The approval goes at the very end of your further orders and is followed only by the judge's signature line, which is the very last thing on the Judgment.

Here's how to do it. On the Judgment form, check the box under the Judge's signature line to show that this will now follow the last attachment. At the end of any further orders you might add, type in the language shown below followed by the Judge's signature line, as shown. You will need the original and three copies to take to court, plus a copy to give Respondent when the document is signed.

The foregoing is agreed to by

Dated: _____
                          Respondent, in pro per

Dated: _____
                          Petitioner, in pro per

                        _____
                          Judge of the Superior Court

In Los Angeles County, we recently learned, if Respondent has had his/her default taken, that signature must be notarized, so leave several inches for this purpose between the parties' signatures and the judge's signature line. It wouldn't do any harm to notarize them both in any county.

Figure 18.2 JUDGMENT
Form FL-180 (Page 2)

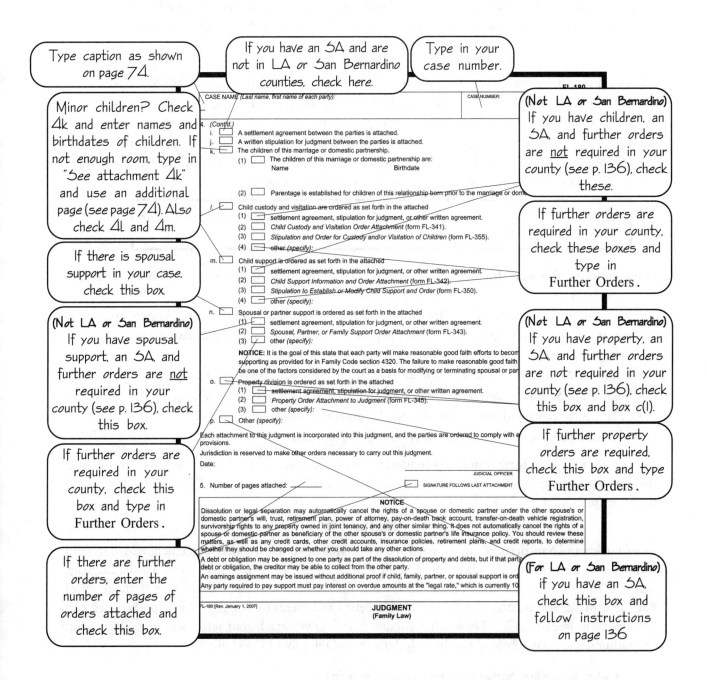

Type caption as shown on page 74.

If you have an SA and are not in LA or San Bernardino counties, check here.

Type in your case number.

Minor children? Check 4k and enter names and birthdates of children. If not enough room, type in "See attachment 4k" and use an additional page (see page 74). Also check 4l and 4m.

If there is spousal support in your case, check this box.

(Not LA or San Bernardino) If you have spousal support, an SA, and further orders are not required in your county (see p. 136), check this box.

If further orders are required in your county, check this box and type in Further Orders.

If there are further orders, enter the number of pages of orders attached and check this box.

(Not LA or San Bernardino) If you have children, an SA, and further orders are not required in your county (see p. 136), check these.

If further orders are required in your county, check these boxes and type in Further Orders.

(Not LA or San Bernardino) If you have property, an SA, and further orders are not required in your county (see p. 136), check this box and box c(1).

If further property orders are required, check this box and type Further Orders.

(For LA or San Bernardino) if you have an SA, check this box and follow instructions on page 136

FL-180

CASE NAME *(Last name, first name of each party):*

CASE NUMBER:

4. *(Cont'd.)*

i. ☐ A settlement agreement between the parties is attached.

j. ☐ A written stipulation for judgment between the parties is attached.

k. ☐ The children of this marriage or domestic partnership.
    (1) ☐ The children of this marriage or domestic partnership are:
        Name   Birthdate

    (2) ☐ Parentage is established for children of this relationship born prior to the marriage or dom

l. ☐ Child custody and visitation are ordered as set forth in the attached
    (1) ☐ settlement agreement, stipulation for judgment, or other written agreement.
    (2) ☐ *Child Custody and Visitation Order Attachment* (form FL-341).
    (3) ☐ *Stipulation and Order for Custody and/or Visitation of Children* (form FL-355).
    (4) ☐ other *(specify):*

m. ☐ Child support is ordered as set forth in the attached
    (1) ☐ settlement agreement, stipulation for judgment, or other written agreement.
    (2) ☐ *Child Support Information and Order Attachment* (form FL-342).
    (3) ☐ *Stipulation to Establish or Modify Child Support and Order* (form FL-350).
    (4) ☐ other *(specify):*

n. ☐ Spousal or partner support is ordered as set forth in the attached
    (1) ☐ settlement agreement, stipulation for judgment, or other written agreement.
    (2) ☐ *Spousal, Partner, or Family Support Order Attachment* (form FL-343).
    (3) ☐ other *(specify):*

NOTICE: It is the goal of this state that each party will make reasonable good faith efforts to becom supporting as provided for in Family Code section 4320. The failure to make reasonable good faith be one of the factors considered by the court as a basis for modifying or terminating spousal or par

o. ☐ Property division is ordered as set forth in the attached
    (1) ☐ settlement agreement, stipulation for judgment, or other written agreement.
    (2) ☐ *Property Order Attachment to Judgment* (form FL-345).
    (3) ☐ other *(specify):*

p. ☐ Other *(specify):*

Each attachment to this judgment is incorporated into this judgment, and the parties are ordered to comply with e provisions.

Jurisdiction is reserved to make other orders necessary to carry out this judgment.

Date:

                                    JUDICIAL OFFICER

5. Number of pages attached: _____   ☐ SIGNATURE FOLLOWS LAST ATTACHMENT

NOTICE

Dissolution or legal separation may automatically cancel the rights of a spouse or domestic partner under the other spouse's or domestic partner's will, trust, retirement plan, power of attorney, pay-on-death bank account, transfer-on-death vehicle registration, survivorship rights to any property owned in joint tenancy, and any other similar thing. It does not automatically cancel the rights of a spouse or domestic partner as beneficiary of the other spouse's or domestic partner's life insurance policy. You should review these matters, as well as any credit cards, other credit accounts, insurance policies, retirement plans, and credit reports, to determine whether they should be changed or whether you should take any other actions.

A debt or obligation may be assigned to one party as part of the dissolution of property and debts, but if that party debt or obligation, the creditor may be able to collect from the other party.

An earnings assignment may be issued without additional proof if child, family, partner, or spousal support is ord

Any party required to pay support must pay interest on overdue amounts at the "legal rate," which is currently 10

FL-180 [Rev. January 1, 2007]   **JUDGMENT**
                            (Family Law)

⓲.2 If you have a settlement agreement

Privacy rules. To protect yourself, your Ex and your children from identity theft, the copy of your agreement that is submitted to the court should be modified to have all Social Security and financial account numbers replaced with a code plus the last four digits of the account. See chapter 7.2.

Agreements and Judgments. You *must* include the terms of your agreement in your Judgment. There are two ways for doing this, one for LA and San Bernardino, and one for all other counties.

Method A

Most counties simply want you to attach your agreement to the Judgment, check box 4(i), and:
- If you have minor children, check boxes 4(k), 4(l) and 4(m) and also check the first box below each of them, the one that says "Settlement agreement . . ."
- If you have spousal support, check 4(n) and the first box below, "Settlement agreement . . ."
- If property is being divided, check 4(o) and the first box below, "Settlement agreement . . ."
- In every case, also check box 4(p) and type in the following language:

```
All warranties and contract remedies in the settlement agreement
shall be preserved.
```

Some counties also want further orders. See sections 18.3–18.5 (or the Judgment attachments) for language that you can use for your own further orders.
- Contra Costa, Marin, San Luis Obispo, Santa Clara, Solano and Stanislaus want you to attach your agreement and also include further orders spelling out provisions for child custody and visitation, child support and spousal support.
- Fresno and Sutter want the same and also further orders on the division of property and debts.
- Solano and Stanislaus also want orders for any agreed medical or other insurance.
- Solano also wants both spouses to sign the Judgment as shown on page 134.
- Alameda wants further orders on every term of the agreement.

In counties that want further orders, you need to check the boxes a little differently. For each item 4(k) through 4(o) that applies to your case, check the last box, "Other," and type in "Further Orders" in the field next to "Other."

Method B

Los Angeles and San Bernardino counties want all terms of your settlement agreement added to your Judgment as Further Orders. Therefore, at item 4(p) enter "See further orders." Then use the language below as your first Further Order, then add as many further orders as required to reflect all the terms of your agreement. See sections 18.3–18.6 and Judgment attachments for language. Both spouses *must* sign the Judgment (see page 134). Do *not* check item 4(i) and do *not* attach your agreement to the Judgment, but rather file it separately along with the Judgment and refer to it as "Exhibit 1."

LA-San Bernardino, further order for settlement agreement

```
The settlement agreement, received in evidence as Petitioner's
Exhibit 1, is approved, ordered placed in the case file and,
pursuant thereto, it is ordered as follows below.
```

18.3 Orders for cases with property and debts

1. None: If you checked box 5a in the Petition, then you will not need any orders regarding property in the Judgment.

2. Divided by agreement: If you and your spouse have a written settlement agreement, then use method A or B in the section above. If you use method B, or if you are in Alameda, Fresno or Sutter counties, insert further orders as shown below.

3. Divided by the court: If you listed community property at item 5 on the Petition and do not have a settlement agreement, insert the following order into your Judgment:

order dividing community property

```
    It is further ordered that the community property and obli-
gations of the parties, in order to effectuate a substantially
equal division (say 'fair division' if you are seeking an
unequal division), is divided as follows:

    Petitioner is awarded the following:

    Respondent is awarded the following:

    Petitioner is ordered to pay:

    Respondent is ordered to pay:

    The parties are ordered to do whatever acts and sign
whatever documents may be necessary to carry out these
orders.
```

List & describe in detail. Identify with account numbers, license and VIN for vehicles. For real estate, use Legal description and assessor's parcel number.

List & describe debts in detail - use account numbers when possible.

Note about pension plans: If the community has an interest in a retirement plan, then it can be awarded to the employee-spouse under items 2 or 3 above. Read chapter 3.6(b) very carefully. If you want some other disposition of a retirement or pension benefit, you should see an attorney or call the Divorce Helpline for assistance.

Note about the family home: See chapter 3.6(c). If there are minor children and you want to keep them in the house for some period of time, you can order title changed to tenants-in-common and defer the sale until all child-support obligations are terminated, or other dates or conditions. The percentage interest of each spouse would be half the community interest plus any reimbursable separate contributions divided by total equity in the house. Use the order below, or adapt it to fit your needs.

Note about Auto IDs: If Respondent won't sign a pink slip to transfer ownership of an auto that goes to Petitioner, add the VIN (vehicle identification number) to the auto's description in this order and use the Judgment to transfer the auto title.

It is further ordered that the family residence, located at **(give full street address),** assessor's parcel number **(give number)**, also known as **(give legal description taken from deed)**, is awarded to the Parties as tenants-in-common, with a ___ percent undivided interest to Petitioner and a ___ percent undivided interest to Respondent. As additional child support, the Petitioner (or Respondent), hereafter called in-spouse, shall have exclusive occupancy of the residence until (1) all children reach 18 or are otherwise emancipated **(or some other date or specific condition)**, (2) the in-spouse no longer has custody of any minor child(ren) of the parties, (3) death or remarriage of the in-spouse, (4) the sale of the residence by mutual agreement of the parties, (5) the in-spouse becomes 60 days delinquent in any payment set forth below, (6) further order of this court. During the period of occupancy, the in-spouse shall maintain in force a policy of fire, casualty and liability insurance, naming both parties as insureds, in an amount sufficient to protect the parties' interest in the residence. The in-spouse shall also be liable for all payments of principal and interest on existing encum-brance on the property, together with all taxes, assessments, and ordinary maintenance and upkeep, without right to reim-bursement. Individual outlays in excess of $500 shall be deemed capital expenditures, and when made by written agreement of the parties shall be divided equally between them. On termination of the right of the in-spouse to occupy the residence, it shall be sold and the net proceeds distributed according to their percentage ownership.

Note about awards of real property: After the hearing, be sure to file a certified copy of the Judgment with the County Recorder, along with the Preliminary Change of Ownership form (see chapter 3.6(c)). This makes the Judgment work as a legal transfer of title.

4. Separate property: If you used Item 4 in the Petition, insert the following order in your Judgment:

It is further ordered that the following described prop-erty be confirmed as (Petitioner's/Respondent's) separate property: **(list property in detail and with full legal descriptions as described in item 3 above).**

Orders for cases with children

If there are children, your Judgment *must* include orders for their custody, support, and health insurance. Use the language below, or take a look at order attachment forms FL-341, FL-342 and FL-342(A) on the companion CD, which might be useful. If you use an order attachment, simply check boxes at items 4(k)(1) or 4(l)(1) to show the attachment. **Agreement?** If you covered these subjects in an agreement, you need further orders only in the counties listed on page 136 that require them. The list can change, so check with your Clerk's office to see if they do or do not want further orders in cases with an agreement.

Required language in every Judgment concerning children

Item 4l. The Judgment must now contain certain statements about notice and jurisdiction. Therefore, on the Judgment form at item 4l, do one of the following:

a. Use FL-341 (on the CD) for all custody/visitation orders (it contains required statements), or

b. If you do **not** include Further Orders, then in addition to following the other instructions, check the box for Other, and type in "Order Attachment 4(l)," and add the language below using the Additional Page form (page 74), or

c. If you **do** include Further Orders, then in addition to following the other instructions, check the box for Other, and type in "Order Attachment 4(l) and Further Orders," and attach the page below **in front of** your Further Orders.

Order Attachment 4(l) (Family Code Sec. 3048)

Jurisdiction: This court has jurisdiction to make child custody orders in this case under the Uniform Child Custody Jurisdiction and Enforcement Act (part 3 of the California Family Code commencing with section 3400).

Notice and Opportunity to Be Heard: The responding party was given notice and opportunity to be heard as provided by the laws of the State of California.

Country of Habitual Residence: The country of habitual residence of the child or children in this case is (the United States of America) (other).

Penalties for Violating This Order: If you violate this order you may be subject to civil or criminal penalties, or both.

Two more required forms for cases with children

• **FL-192 Notice of Rights and Responsibilities.** Attach to the Judgment. This form contains information about health care and changing a child support order.

• **FL-191 Case Registry form.** This form is presented along with the Judgment but *not* attached to it. Filling it out is straightforward. Do the caption like most of the other forms and enter as much of the requested personal information as you can dig up as it may help you enforce your support order some day. This form is not on public view, so you **should** include complete Social Security numbers.

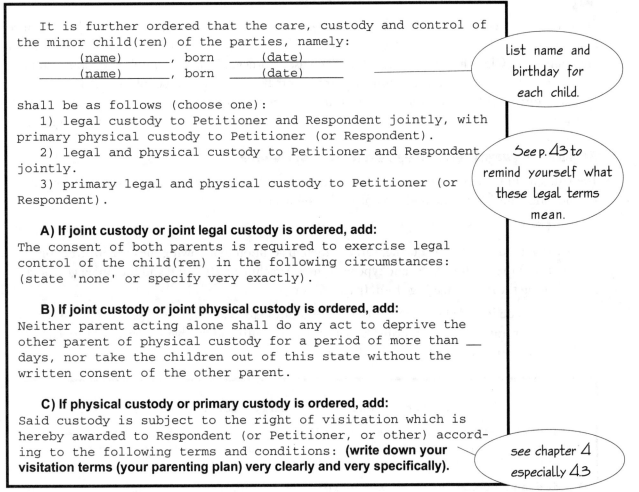

It is further ordered that the care, custody and control of the minor child(ren) of the parties, namely:

_____(name)_____, born _____(date)_____

_____(name)_____, born _____(date)_____

(list name and birthday for each child.)

shall be as follows (choose one):

1) legal custody to Petitioner and Respondent jointly, with primary physical custody to Petitioner (or Respondent).

2) legal and physical custody to Petitioner and Respondent jointly.

3) primary legal and physical custody to Petitioner (or Respondent).

(See p. 43 to remind yourself what these legal terms mean.)

A) If joint custody or joint legal custody is ordered, add:

The consent of both parents is required to exercise legal control of the child(ren) in the following circumstances: (state 'none' or specify very exactly).

B) If joint custody or joint physical custody is ordered, add:

Neither parent acting alone shall do any act to deprive the other parent of physical custody for a period of more than __ days, nor take the children out of this state without the written consent of the other parent.

C) If physical custody or primary custody is ordered, add:

Said custody is subject to the right of visitation which is hereby awarded to Respondent (or Petitioner, or other) according to the following terms and conditions: **(write down your visitation terms (your parenting plan) very clearly and very specifically).**

(see chapter 4 especially 4.3)

Note for welfare parents about custody: If joint physical custody is awarded, you should add this language to the custody order: "It is further ordered that for the purpose of determining eligibility for public assistance, the Petitioner (or Respondent) shall be considered the primary caretaker of the child, and Petitioner's (or Respondent's) home is the primary home of the child(ren)."

It is further ordered that (Respondent/Petitioner) shall pay to (Petitioner/Respondent/other) as and for child support, a total of $_____ per month, payable on the___ day of each month, beginning (some date after the hearing), and continuing until further order of this court or until said child marries, dies, is emancipated, reaches the age of 19, or reaches 18 and is not a full-time high school student, whichever occurs first. **(If more than one child, unless there's different timeshare for different children, add:)** Of the total amount ordered, the amount of support for the youngest child is $____, referred to hereafter as (CS). Support has been added for additional children as follows:

.6 times (CS) for the second youngest child, or $_____, plus

.4 times (CS) for the third youngest child, or $_____, plus

.3 times (CS) for the fourth youngest child, or $_____, plus

(and so on for each additional child: .2 for the 5th child; .125 for the 6th and 7th; .063 for the 8th; .031 for the 9th and .016 for the 10th. Use as many steps as there are additional children in your case and make sure it all adds up to the total support ordered.)

If child care is being paid to allow a parent to work: As additional child support, it is further ordered that (Respondent/Petitioner) shall pay to (Petitioner/Respondent) for child care, a total of $_____ per month, payable on the___ day of each month, beginning on _____, 20_, and continuing as long as child care is necessary and actually being paid.

Optional: It is further ordered that the all child support obligation shall terminate upon the death of the recipient if the payor assumes full custody of the children.

Note: (CS) comes from the guideline calculation (chapter 5.4). (CS) plus all additional support *must* add up to total support ordered.

Health insurance must be ordered! If either parent can get it at reasonable cost—say, as a group plan through employment—use order A below. If health care not available now, you must include the alternative order B. Also, dental & vision coverage is to be included if available.

It is further ordered that reasonable health expenses for the child not paid for by insurance shall be shared as follows:

Mother ____% Father ___%. **Proportional to net income? Equally? See p. 51.**

(A)

It is further ordered that during the term of the support obligation for each child, (Respondent/ Petitioner) shall carry and maintain health, hospital, (dental, vision) insurance for the benefit of said child.

(B)

It is further ordered that during the term of the support obligation for each child, should health (dental, vision) insurance coverage for the benefit of the child become available at a reasonable cost to either party, that party shall provide such coverage and notify the other party in writing.

```
   It is further ordered that during the term of the child
support obligation, (Respondent/Petitioner) shall maintain a
policy of insurance on his/her life in the amount of $_____
and shall name said minor child(children)as beneficiary (ben-
eficiaries).
```

CHILD SUPPORT NOTES

Mandatory wage assignments. If you have a child support order, you *must* also use the wage assignment order described in section 18.6, below. You must also prepare the wage assignment form described in chapter 19 and present it along with your Judgment.

Tax savings? If there is a significant difference in income levels between spouses, the family as a whole can very likely save some money on taxes by combining child and spousal support and calling it "family support." This way, Uncle Sam will chip in on your support payments. An order for family support is too tricky to draft without help. You can call Divorce Helpline to order a computerized calculation of possible tax savings, or you can get your own copy of Nolo's CalSupport™ software and do it yourself.

Changes. If you want the amount of child support to change, you must formally modify the court order. This can be done by stipulation (agreement) or by making a motion in court.

Welfare cases:

1) If the recipient of child support gets public assistance, child support *must* be paid to the State Disbursement Unit. Add these words at the end of the child support order: "Payments are to be made through the State Disbursement Unit, P.O. Box 989067, West Sacramento, CA 95798-9067." Your Wage Assignment Order must be made payable to the same office. Find your local DCSS under "Links" on the companion CD or at **www.nolodivorce.com/links**. Contact them well ahead of Judgment to open a file.

2) The Department of Child Support Services of the county where children are receiving aid must sign off on the proposed Judgment before you file it or take it to court. Put a line at the end of the orders after the Judge's signature, as shown below, then take it in and get it signed:

```
The Department of Child Support Services for _____ County
approves the above child support order.

Dated:_____Signed: _____
```

Stipulation to Establish Child Support

What it is

The Stipulation to Establish Child Support is an agreement signed by both parents setting the amount of child support. It can be used to set support in cases of pure joint custody or when for any reason parents want to agree to less support than is required by state guidelines, yet do not want to go to the trouble of making a complete settlement agreement. The response fee (chapter 7.3) might be charged unless it has already been paid for filing other documents. If parents stipulate to an amount below California guidelines, no change of circumstances need be shown on a future motion to modify the support order to bring it up to guideline level.

When required

If used at all, this form is filed when you file the Judgment. If you want to agree to an amount of child support—especially if it is less than the guideline figure—you will need either a settlement agreement (chapter 6) or the Stipulation to Establish Child Support. In fact, in at least six counties, you need the Stipulation even if you *do* have a settlement agreement: Imperial, Santa Barbara, Santa Cruz, Solano, Stanislaus —and also Alameda, if the amount is above or below the guideline.

How to fill it out

Fill it out as shown in Figures 18.3 and 18.4. Prepare the original and make 3 copies.

Your spouse's figures for income and deductions are taken from the data you already entered in the Income and Expense Declarations, discussed in Chapter 16.

Welfare cases: If either spouse is receiving or has applied for welfare for the minor children of this case, this form will have to be signed by the DA of the county where your case is filed.

Note: FYI, what used to be called AFDC is now called TANF/CalWORKS. In either case, it refers to welfare for children.

Figure 18.3 STIPULATION TO ESTABLISH CHILD SUPPORT
Form FL-350 (Page 1)

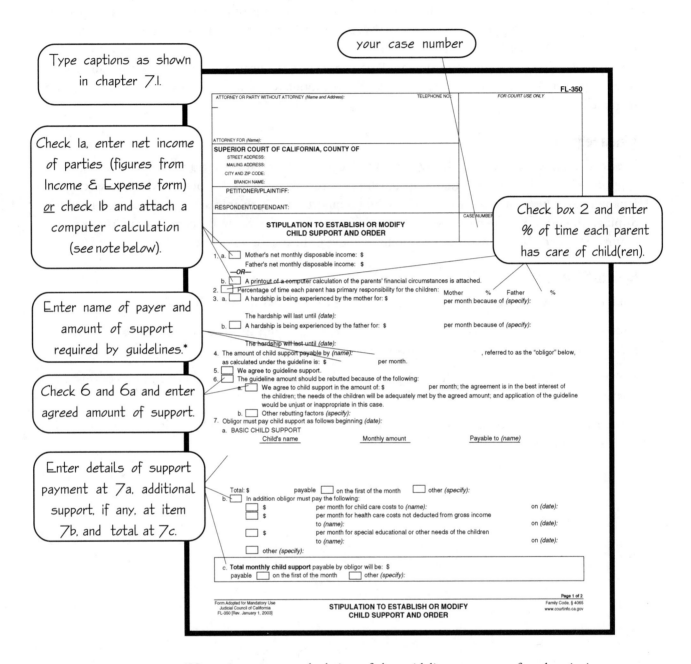

Type captions as shown in chapter 7.1.

your case number

Check 1a, enter net income of parties (figures from Income & Expense form) or check 1b and attach a computer calculation (see note below).

Check box 2 and enter % of time each parent has care of child(ren).

Enter name of payer and amount of support required by guidelines.*

Check 6 and 6a and enter agreed amount of support.

Enter details of support payment at 7a, additional support, if any, at item 7b, and total at 7c.

Within the form:

FL-350

ATTORNEY OR PARTY WITHOUT ATTORNEY *(Name and Address):*   TELEPHONE NO.:   FOR COURT USE ONLY

ATTORNEY FOR *(Name):*

SUPERIOR COURT OF CALIFORNIA, COUNTY OF
STREET ADDRESS:
MAILING ADDRESS:
CITY AND ZIP CODE:
BRANCH NAME:

PETITIONER/PLAINTIFF:

RESPONDENT/DEFENDANT:

CASE NUMBER

STIPULATION TO ESTABLISH OR MODIFY CHILD SUPPORT AND ORDER

1. a. ☐ Mother's net monthly disposable income: $
   Father's net monthly disposable income: $
   —OR—
   b. ☐ A printout of a computer calculation of the parents' financial circumstances is attached.
2. ☐ Percentage of time each parent has primary responsibility for the children: Mother ___ %   Father ___ %
3. a. ☐ A hardship is being experienced by the mother for: $ per month because of *(specify):*

   The hardship will last until *(date):*
   b. ☐ A hardship is being experienced by the father for: $ per month because of *(specify):*

   The hardship will last until *(date):*
4. The amount of child support payable by *(name):*   , referred to as the "obligor" below,
   as calculated under the guideline is: $ per month.
5. ☐ We agree to guideline support.
6. ☐ The guideline amount should be rebutted because of the following:
   a. ☐ We agree to child support in the amount of: $ per month; the agreement is in the best interest of
   the children; the needs of the children will be adequately met by the agreed amount; and application of the guideline
   would be unjust or inappropriate in this case.
   b. ☐ Other rebutting factors *(specify):*
7. Obligor must pay child support as follows beginning *(date):*
   a. BASIC CHILD SUPPORT
   Child's name   Monthly amount   Payable to *(name)*

   Total: $ payable ☐ on the first of the month   ☐ other *(specify):*
   b. ☐ In addition obligor must pay the following:
   ☐ $ per month for child care costs to *(name):*   on *(date):*
   ☐ $ per month for health care costs not deducted from gross income
   to *(name):*   on *(date):*
   ☐ $ per month for special educational or other needs of the children
   to *(name):*   on *(date):*
   ☐ other *(specify):*
   c. **Total monthly child support** payable by obligor will be: $
   payable ☐ on the first of the month   ☐ other *(specify):*

Form Adopted for Mandatory Use
Judicial Council of California
FL-350 [Rev. January 1, 2003]

STIPULATION TO ESTABLISH OR MODIFY CHILD SUPPORT AND ORDER

Page 1 of 2
Family Code, § 4065
www.courtinfo.ca.gov

*Note: A computer calculation of the guideline amount, referred to in items 1b and 4, is available from Divorce Helpline. Or you can calculate it yourself with CalSupport™ software (see inside front cover). Or you can try to calculate the guideline figure by hand with the formula and instructions in chapter 5.4.

Figure 18.4 STIPULATION TO ESTABLISH CHILD SUPPORT
Form FL-350 (Page 2)

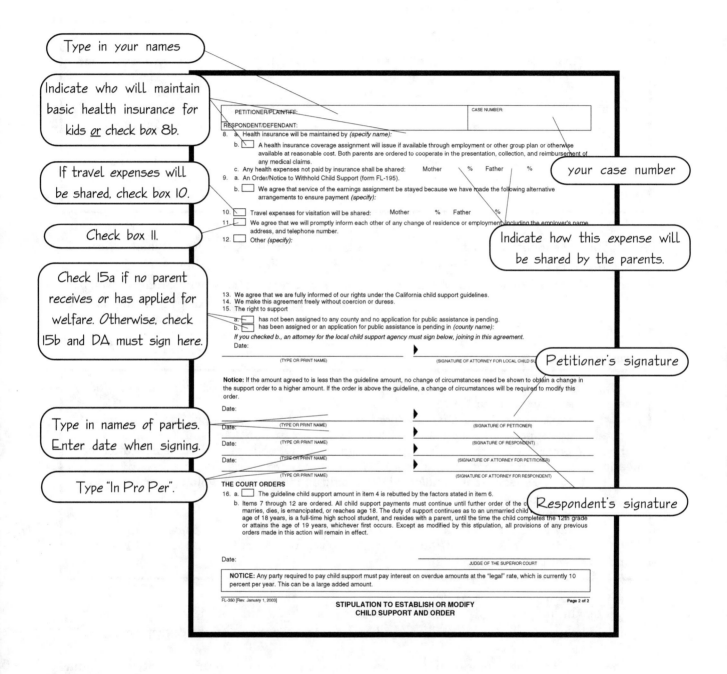

Type in your names

Indicate who will maintain basic health insurance for kids *or* check box 8b.

If travel expenses will be shared, check box 10.

Check box 11.

Check 15a if no parent receives or has applied for welfare. Otherwise, check 15b and DA must sign here.

Type in names of parties. Enter date when signing.

Type "In Pro Per".

your case number

Indicate how this expense will be shared by the parents.

Petitioner's signature

Respondent's signature

18.5 Orders for spousal support

1. None: If no spousal support was requested or desired at this time, use option A below, but if it was waived either in open court or in writing, use option B:

no spousal support or spousal support waived

> **A.** No spousal support shall be awarded at this time.
>
> **B. For marriages over 5 years, add this before the next bit:** The parties are informed and aware that, if requested by either party, the court is required to reserve spousal support for long-term marriages of over ten years and may choose to do so for some marriages shorter than ten years. They each waive the right to receive spousal support now or at any time in the future.
>
> **All cases use this:** Spousal support having been waived by Petitioner (or Respondent, or Petitioner *and* Respondent), the court hereby terminates jurisdiction therein and no court shall have jurisdiction to order spousal support in the future regardless of any circumstances that may arise. *

2. Spousal support ordered: Use the language below or take a look at order attachment form FL-343 on the companion CD, which might be helpful. If you use the order attachment, check the box at item 4(n) to show the attachment. **Agreement?** If you covered this in a settlement agreement, you need further orders only in counties listed on page 136 that require them. The list keeps changing, so check with your Clerk's office to see if they do or do not want further orders in cases with an agreement.

order for spousal support

> The court (also) finds that the needs of Petitioner (or Respondent) are/ are not met by this order.
>
> It is hereby ordered that Respondent (or Petitioner) shall pay to Petitioner (or Respondent) the sum of $_____ per month, as and for spousal support, payable on the ____ day of each month, beginning **(some date after the hearing)**, 20__, and continuing until death or remarriage of the recipient, or until **(some specific date, and/or other specific conditions upon which payments stop)**, whichever occurs first,
>
> .... or until further order of the court.
>
> .... and following said time (or event), no court shall have jurisdiction to modify the (amount/ duration/ amount or duration) of spousal support, regardless of circumstances. *

*Note: In long marriages (roughly 10 years or more), the court *must* retain jurisdiction indefinitely unless the parties have agreed otherwise in a very specific writing (see chapter 5.2).

Options: There are many possibilities for customizing spousal support to suit your needs, including automatic decreases at set times, tying the amount to either spouse's income, posting security or obtaining life insurance to benefit the recipient, and so on. If you need advice on this subject, call Divorce Helpline.

Mandatory wage assignments. If you have an order for spousal support, you *must* also use the assignment order described in section 18.6, below. You must also prepare the wage assignment form described in chapter 19 and present it along with your Judgment.

18.6 Mandatory wage assignment

Order for wage assignment cases

If you have an order for child support or spousal support, the following order *must* be inserted in your Judgment immediately after your other orders for either child or spousal support.

```
   It is further ordered that, pursuant to Family Code 5230,
obligor is ordered to assign to obligee that portion of (his/
her) earnings sufficient to pay the amount of support ordered by
the Court. The obligor is ordered to give written notice to the
obligee of any change in employment within ten days of said
change, together with the name and address of any new employer.
```

Order staying wage assignment

If you can satisfy the requirements for a stay of the wage assignment (chapter 20), try adding this order after the one above. It could work.

```
   It is further ordered that, service of the Wage Assignment
Order is stayed provided that the Payor is not more than ___
days late in the payment of spousal/family support.
```

18.7 Personal service of the Judgment

To enforce an order, especially by using contempt of court, you have to be able to prove Respondent had notice of the order. So, if Respondent has been ordered to pay support, deliver property, or do or not do any act in the future, *and* was not personally present in court when the order was made, then once the Judgment has been signed by the Judge and entered (chapter 20), it is very important to have a copy of the Judgment *personally* served on Respondent as described in chapter 12.4. The person who served the papers signs this Proof of Personal Service which you then file with the clerk.

WAGE AND EARNINGS ASSIGNMENT

What it is

The best way to make sure you get paid by an employed ex-spouse is to use the Wage Assignment Order (WAO). It is served on the employer who must take support out of the employee's earnings and pay it directly to the recipient. In child support cases the recipient can choose to have payments made to the State Disbursement Unit, which takes over enforcement and forwards all payments to the recipient. If public assistance is being recieved or has been applied for, support *must* be paid to the SDU.

Wage assignment is mandatory. In any case where support is ordered, you *must* include one of the Wage Assignment Orders below with your Judgment. No exceptions. After the order is signed by the Judge, you can then *choose* to have it served on the paying spouse's employer. If served, the employer will withhold up to 50% of the payer's wages at each pay period to make support payments. This is now the routine way of handling support and employers are accustomed to it. It is against the law for any employer to refuse to hire, to discipline, or to fire an employee because of a wage assignment.

The WAO is binding against present or future employers. So, even if the paying spouse is unemployed or self-employed or whereabouts unknown, the order must still be issued—then you just wait until your spouse has an employer (or a big customer) you can locate, whenever that might happen.

Staying service of the Wage Assignment Order:

Formal stay by court order is possible if the parties make a written agreement that says the WAO will not be immediately served on the payor's employer. If support is being ordered through a county officer, this agreement must signed by the Department of Child Support Services. If the court *does* stay the service of the wage assignment, the recipient can later terminate the stay simply by filing a simple declaration under penalty of perjury that the payments are in arrears in any amount.

Informal stay. It is always entirely in the control of the recipient to serve the Order whenever he or she chooses to do so. If the spouses are cooperative, the Order need never be served. This understanding can be made part of a settlement agreement (see chapter 6). It pays to cooperate and it pays to keep payments current.

Which wage assignment form to use

- If there's child support, use FL-195, Order/Notice to Withhold Income For Child Support. If you also have spousal support, it can be included. This is a Federally mandated form.
- Spousal support alone, no child support, use the Earnings Assignment Order For Spousal Support.

How to fill out the forms

Fill the forms out as shown in Figures 19.1 or 19.2. Make the original and four copies. Attach this order to the Judgment and present it for the Judge's signature at the same time, in the same way. When using FL-195, a local cover sheet form is required in Santa Cruz County to act as a caption. Don't forget: you should disguise Social Security numbers on papers filed with the court (chapter 7.2), but not on copies given to the other side or served on an employer.

Service of the wage assignment order and blank Request for Hearing

Unless there is a written agreement or an order that the wage assignment will not be served, then immediately after it is signed by the judge, you should serve the WAO on the paying spouse's employer along with a blank copy of form FL-450 Request For Hearing Re Wage Assignment (copy in back of book and on CD). Technically, employers are to be served personally, but most will honor papers served by mail. So, unless your spouse is a big wheel in a small company, serve these documents on the employer by mail (chapter 12.6) and file a Proof of Service by Mail (Fig.13.3) with the court.

Whenever the paying spouse changes jobs, the new employer must be served as soon as possible with copies of the same documents and another Proof of Service must be filed.

Troubleshooting

Self-employed people. Wage assignment is not effective against self-employed people unless they happen to have one primary client or customer, in which case the order can be served on that client or customer.

Can't find spouse or employer? If you don't know the location of your spouse or spouse's employer, take the Judgment and the WAO to your county Department of Child Support Services and they will try to help you. They can conduct a parent locator search. If your spouse is working but you can't find out who the employer is, go to the DCSS office in your county.

Problem payers. If your spouse is often unemployed or frequently changes jobs or might otherwise be difficult to chase down for *child* support payments, go see your your local office of the Department of Child Support Services and open a case, and make your Wage Assignment Order payable to the State Disbursement Unit at the address below. If your order is for spousal support only, contact the local District Attorney and ask if they have a support enforcement service that can help you.

How long does it take to get paid? You get paid when the employee does. Most employees are paid every two weeks. Depending on the company's pay period and when in that cycle the employer receives the WAO, it could take several weeks for the order to take effect and for you to start receiving payments. If three or four weeks go by and you don't see any money, call the employer's payroll department and ask if there is a problem and when you will see your check.

If the employer does not obey the order. It has been known to happen that in some small companies where the employee is very important, or friends with the boss, the company will try to disregard the WAO. In that case, contact your local office of the Department of Child Support Services.

Changes of address or employment

The recipient must notify the employer of changes in address if being paid directly, or notify the State Disbursement Unit if payments are being made through that office. If payments are undeliverable for six months because the recipient failed to provide a current address, the employer or SDU will stop making payments and refund all undelivered money to the paying spouse.

If the paying spouse terminates employment, the employer *must* notify the recipient by mail on or before the date the next payment would be due. The paying spouse must notify the recipient of any changes in employment within ten days, and provide the name and address of the new employer.

Payments through the State Disbursement Unit

When you want child support (or both child and spousal support) paid through the SDU, on your WAO, the recipient is: State Disbursement Unit, P.O. Box 989067, West Sacramento, CA 95798-9067.

Figure 19.1
ORDER/NOTICE TO WITHHOLD INCOME FOR CHILD SUPPORT
Form FL-195   (OMB No: 0970-0154)

Note: "Employer" in the instructions also refers to any other withholder upon whom the order might be served.

Check these.

Enter your county.

your case number

employee's name (last name first) and Soc. Security number

employer's name and address

Employer's Federal EIN number, if you know it.

recipient's name (last name first)

Enter amounts for: child support past-due support spousal support Total

Enter total to be withheld, figured for **each** of these four pay periods.

If past due amounts are ordered, check yes if over 12 weeks overdue, otherwise check "no."

For each order item you use, and for the total, enter pay period: weekly, biweekly, semi-monthly, or monthly.

Enter 50% unless a different amount has been ordered.

Name and address of recipient (or the SDU—address on previous page). If the address won't fit (most won't), put "see below," and hand-print the address at the bottom.

☐ ORDER/NOTICE TO WITHHOLD INCOME FOR CHILD SUPPORT
☐ NOTICE OF AN ORDER TO WITHHOLD INCOME FOR CHILD SUPPORT

☐ Original   ☐ Amended   ☐ Termination   Date: _____
State/Tribe/Territory _____
City/Co./Dist./Reservation _____
☐ Non-governmental entity or Individual _____
Case Number _____

RE :

Employer's/Withholder's   Name _____   Employee's/Obligor's Name (Last, First, MI) _____

Employer's/Withholders   Address _____   Employee's/Obligees Social Security Number _____

                                               Employee's/Obligors Case Identifier _____

Employers/Withholder's Federal EIN Number (if known) _____   Obligee's Name (Last, First, MI) _____

ORDER INFORMATION: *This document is based on the support or withholding order from* ___California___.
You are required by law to deduct these amounts from the employee's/obligor's income until further notice.
$ _____ Per _____ current child support
$ _____ Per _____ past-due child support - Arrears greater than 12 weeks? ☐ yes ☐ no
$ _____ Per _____ current Cash medical support
$ _____ Per _____ past-due cash medical support
$ _____ Per _____ spousal support
$ _____ Per _____ past-due spousal support
$ _____ Per _____ other (specify) _____
for a total of _____ per _____ to be forwarded to the payee below.
You do not have to vary your pay cycle to be in compliance with the support order. If your pay cycle does not match the ordered payment cycle, withhold one of the following amounts:
$ _____ per weekly pay period. $ _____ per semimonthly pay period.
$ _____ per biweekly pay period (every two weeks). $ _____ per monthly pay period.

REMITTANCE INFORMATION. When remitting payment, provide the pay date/date of withholding.
If the employee's/obligor's principal place of employment is in California, begin withholding no later than the first pay period occurring 10 days after the date of this order. Send payment within 10 working days of the pay date/date of withholding.
The total withheld amount, including your fee, may not exceed ___% of the employee's/obligor's aggregate disposable weekly earnings.

If the employee's/obligor's principal place of employment is not ___in California___, obtain withholding limitations, time requirements, and any allowable employer fees, follow the laws of the employee's/obligor's principal place of employment (see #3 and #9, ADDITIONAL INFORMATION FOR EMPLOYERS AND OTHER WITHHOLDERS).

Make check payable to: _____   Send check to: _____. If remitting payment by EFT/EDI, call _____ before first submission. Use this FIPS code: _____
Bank routing number: _____   Bank account number: _____

If this is an Order/Notice to Withhold: **If this is a Notice of an Order:**
Print Name _____   Print Name _____
Title of Issuing Official _____   Title (if appropriate) _____
Signature and Date _____   Signature and Date _____
☐ IV-D Agency ☐ Court   ☐ Attorney ☐ Individual ☐ Private Entity
☐ Attorney with authority under state law to issue order/notice.

NOTE: Non-IV-D Attorneys, individuals, and non-governmental entities must submit a Notice and include a copy of the income withholding order unless, under a state's law, an attorney in that case may submit an withholding order. In that case, the attorney may submit an Order/Notice to Withhold and include a copy.

IMPORTANT: The person completing this form is advised that the information on this form may be shared with authorizing the attorney to issue an income withholding order/notice.

FL-195 Page 1 of 2

OMB 0970-0154

How to fill out the back

Item 9. Enter the full names of children being supported by this order.

Item 10: Fill in contact information for recipient of support payments, which would be either you or the State Disbursement Unit (address on previous page). This is who employer contacts with questions.

Figure 19.2

EARNINGS ASSIGNMENT ORDER FOR SPOUSAL SUPPORT

Form FL-435

Note: Use this form only when there is no child support in your case, just spousal support.

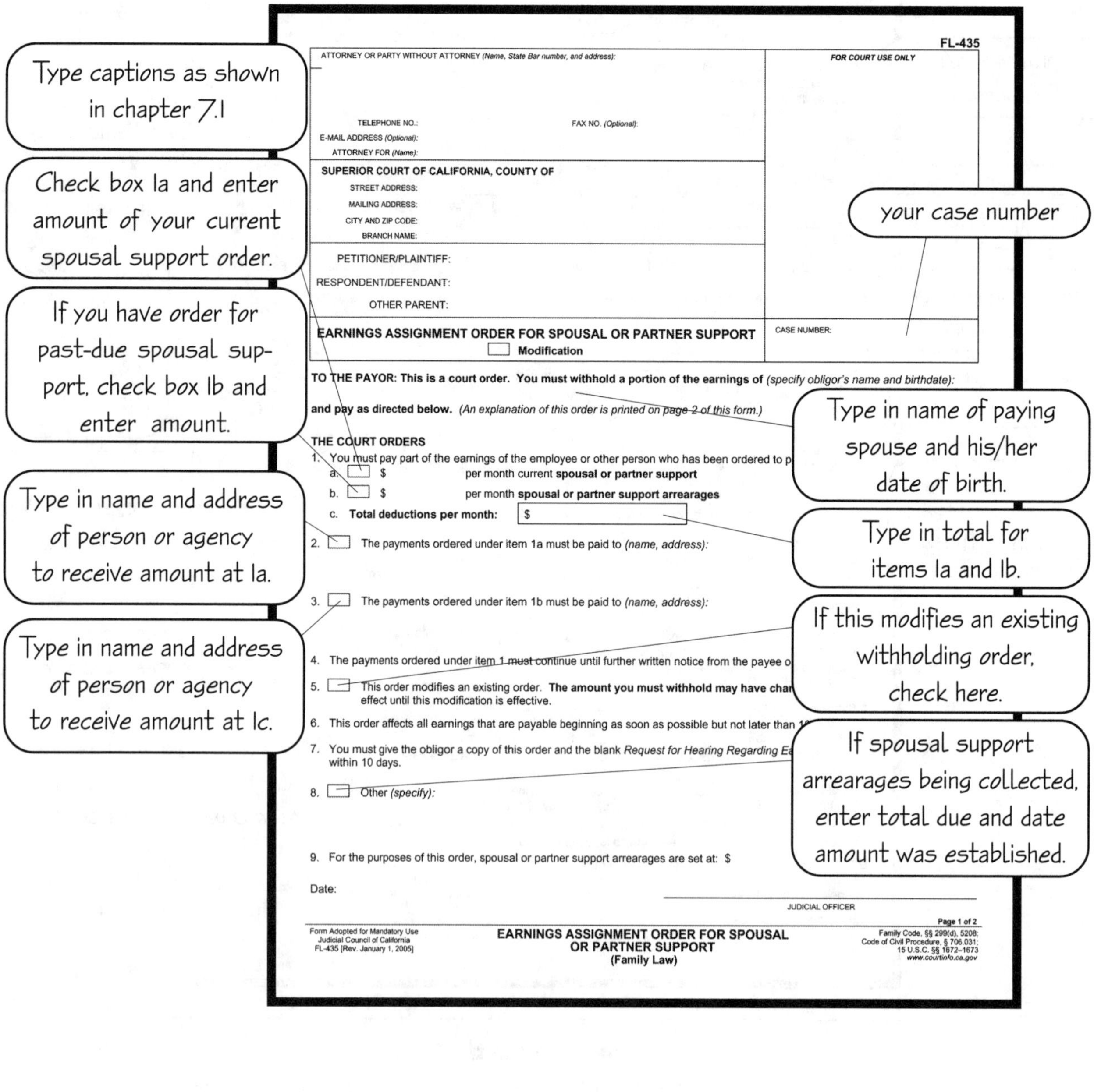

FL-435

ATTORNEY OR PARTY WITHOUT ATTORNEY *(Name, State Bar number, and address):*

FOR COURT USE ONLY

TELEPHONE NO.: FAX NO. *(Optional):*
E-MAIL ADDRESS *(Optional):*
ATTORNEY FOR *(Name):*

SUPERIOR COURT OF CALIFORNIA, COUNTY OF
STREET ADDRESS:
MAILING ADDRESS:
CITY AND ZIP CODE:
BRANCH NAME:

PETITIONER/PLAINTIFF:
RESPONDENT/DEFENDANT:
OTHER PARENT:

EARNINGS ASSIGNMENT ORDER FOR SPOUSAL OR PARTNER SUPPORT
☐ **Modification**

CASE NUMBER:

TO THE PAYOR: This is a court order. You must withhold a portion of the earnings of *(specify obligor's name and birthdate):*

and pay as directed below. *(An explanation of this order is printed on page 2 of this form.)*

THE COURT ORDERS

1. You must pay part of the earnings of the employee or other person who has been ordered to p
   a. ☐ $ per month current **spousal or partner support**
   b. ☐ $ per month **spousal or partner support arrearages**
   c. **Total deductions per month:** $
2. ☐ The payments ordered under item 1a must be paid to *(name, address):*
3. ☐ The payments ordered under item 1b must be paid to *(name, address):*
4. The payments ordered under item 1 must continue until further written notice from the payee o
5. ☐ This order modifies an existing order. **The amount you must withhold may have char** effect until this modification is effective.
6. This order affects all earnings that are payable beginning as soon as possible but not later than 1
7. You must give the obligor a copy of this order and the blank *Request for Hearing Regarding Ea* within 10 days.
8. ☐ Other *(specify):*
9. For the purposes of this order, spousal or partner support arrearages are set at: $

Date:

JUDICIAL OFFICER

Form Adopted for Mandatory Use
Judicial Council of California
FL-435 [Rev. January 1, 2005]

EARNINGS ASSIGNMENT ORDER FOR SPOUSAL OR PARTNER SUPPORT
(Family Law)

Page 1 of 2
Family Code, §§ 299(d), 5208;
Code of Civil Procedure, § 706.031;
15 U.S.C. §§ 1672–1673
www.courtinfo.ca.gov

Type captions as shown in chapter 7.1
Check box 1a and enter amount of your current spousal support order.
If you have order for past-due spousal support, check box 1b and enter amount.
Type in name and address of person or agency to receive amount at 1a.
Type in name and address of person or agency to receive amount at 1c.
your case number
Type in name of paying spouse and his/her date of birth.
Type in total for items 1a and 1b.
If this modifies an existing withholding order, check here.
If spousal support arrearages being collected, enter total due and date amount was established.

HOW TO GET YOUR JUDGMENT

The goal of all your paperwork is to get a Judgment that will settle the legal issues of your case and order the marriage dissolved. There are two ways you can go about getting your Judgment: (A) by filing the Declaration form (below) with your final papers, or (B) by going to a hearing. Read the discussion below on both methods before choosing which to try first.

Method A: Filing the Declaration Form

This is the preferred method for getting your Judgment. All you have to do is prepare a simple form, the Declaration for Default or Uncontested Dissolution (below), and file it with the Judgment and a Notice of Entry of Judgment. You can file it by mail or personally deliver it to the Clerk's Office (see chapter 7.3). A judge or commissioner will examine your orders and settlement agreement, if you have one. They like to avoid hearings, but if there are unusual features in your case, such as support that is too low or a very unequal division of property, and those features are not explained in an agreement, then it is possible that a judge will set a hearing where you can explain things in person.

Preliminary Declarations of Disclosure (PD) and Final Declaration of Disclosure (FD):

- **Cases with no settlement agreement.** If you have no SA and no Response was filed, then—assuming you served your spouse with a PD and filed a proof of service and the Declaration in Fig. 14.4—you can waive the FD by checking box 6(b) on the Declaration for Default Dissolution (Fig. 20.1).
- **Cases with an agreement.** If you *do* have a settlement agreement, the judge must be able to look in your file and find proofs of service and the Declaration re Service in Fig. 14.4 for the PD, and same for the FD unless the FD was waived using form FL-144. If disclosure requirements were satisfied but your file is not complete on this point, you can file a declaration that clarifies things for the court. We invented a Declaration of Compliance (20.2, below) that might increase your chances for getting your mailed-in paperwork accepted in irregular cases. However, if you have an agreement and the FD was neither completed by both parties nor mutually waived, you better call an attorney.

Item 14—Parentage. If a child was born before marriage, check this box and attach a Declaration of Parentage (Nolo 1 on CD in forms directory) stating facts to establish who are the biological parents.

Rejected Declarations: In the unlikely event that your Declaration for Default or Uncontested Dissolution is rejected, all that happens is that you have to either correct your paperwork or, if the courts asks it, go to a hearing (see Method B). The Declaration is more likely to work in cases that are routine—that is, if your requests appear normal, the property division appears equal, and support is reasonable—otherwise the judge might want you to come in and be examined in person so he can ask questions and be satisfied that everything is fair and correct.

Los Angeles and Solano counties. To proceed by Declaration, Respondent must approve your Judgment as to form and content as shown on page 134. Because this signature is required by the county, there should be no response fee charged for filing the document.

Welfare. If the recipient of support is receiving welfare, the DA must also sign the Judgment.

Patience. Many courts are backed up to the point that it can take 10–12 weeks to get default papers processed, so you have to be patient. Call and ask the clerk how long it might take. If you are are in a hurry, ask if you or an agent can come down and hand-walk the papers through. A few counties allow this. If not, ask how soon you can schedule a hearing, because papers are generally signed and filed on the spot after a hearing. This way, you can tell if a hearing might be faster.

Method B: Going to a Hearing

Most counties do not want hearings in uncontested divorce cases. However, if you are asked to go, don't worry; the hearing is easier than you might think. Since this is not a contested case, your spouse will not appear in court. The hearing will be very brief, almost a mere formality, and most of your time will be spent just waiting for it to start. The judge sees a lot of cases and will take no special notice of yours unless it is unusual. You won't be grilled mercilessly—the judge just wants to ask about the facts.

First, you have to arrange a date for your hearing, as described in section 20.3. When you appear, your name is called, you take the stand and make statements about the facts in your case. Your job is to present evidence to the court that will allow the judge to make decisions. Your testimony is evidence, but be sure to take with you any documents you have about the title and value of property (or debts) to be divided and, if there is to be support, take recent pay stubs, accounting statements and tax returns to show the income of you and your spouse.

Further instructions, including what to say at a hearing, are set out below in section 20.3.

20.1 Method A: Filing the Declaration Form

You can usually avoid going to a hearing by filing a sworn statement—the Declaration for Default Dissolution—to take the place of your testimony in court. This is the preferred method in most counties for cases where there is a settlement agreement or cases without property, debts, children or spousal support. If you have property, debts, or kids but no settlement agreement, it might still work if your paperwork is clear, complete and shows that you made full disclosure, property is divided equally, and the amount of support is backed up with a computer calculation such as CalSupport's Bench Report.

How to do it

You can file the Declaration for Default Dissolution at the same time as the Request for Entry of Default (see check list, page 82) or any time thereafter. If filed after, include a copy of the stamped Request for Default form. One source in LA tells us it's safer to file it *shortly after* the Default papers rather than with them; less confusing to the bureaucratic mind.

Fill out the Declaration as shown in Figures 20.1 and 20.2. Prepare the original and make three copies. You *must* also file the Judgment (chapter 18), wage assignment papers (chapter 19) if requried in your case, and the Notice of Entry of Judgment (chapter 21). Don't forget to include stamped envelopes addressed to you and the Respondent with the clerk's return address. File these papers in person or by mail. If all goes well, you will get the signed Judgment back in the mail. If not, the court will tell you the reason why and ask you to arrange a hearing. If that happens, go on to the next section.

Note 1. If you have no settlement agreement and you have property or debts to divide, you must attach a completed Property Declaration (chapter 15) showing estimated values and your proposed division.

Note 2. If you have no settlement agreement and there are children or a request for spousal support, you must attach a completed Income and Expense Declaration (chapter 16). If, on this form, you were not able to provide an estimate of the other party's income, you must state why you don't know it at item 13(c) on the Declaration Form (Figure 20.2).

Santa Clara. If you have no settlement agreement but there are children, you must attach a sworn declaration stating basic financial facts: gross and net incomes of each party, the date support is to begin, amount of support requested for the spouse, amount requested for each child and in total, whether the recipient gets welfare, the name and birth date of each child, when the parties separated and who has been the primary caretaker since, that the parties are fit parents, and, for joint physical custody, what contact the Respondent will have with the child. Ask the clerk if they have local rules that spell out this requirement. For spousal support, you must include information relevant to the spousal support factors under Family Code § 4320, stated in chapter 5.2. A computer printout of guideline calculation, including the findings page, can be used in place of the support portion information on the required declaration.

Pre-judgment checklist

The following list is adapted from Marin County's Family Law Judgment Checklist, a required local form. Make sure you have checked the items on this list before you file your final papers.

1. ❑ Parties have complied with disclosure laws:
   - ❑ Proof of service of preliminary and final disclosure on file.
   - ❑ Proof of service of final disclosure on file or waiver of final disclosure in proper form included.
   - ❑ Settlement agreement **not signed** before service of final disclosure.

2. ❑ Jurisdiction date on Judgment agrees with information in file, and correct date for termination of marital status inserted on judgment.

3. ❑ If an Appearance, Stipulation and Waivers form is filed, a check must be attached for the Response filing fee if this is Respondent's first appearance.

4. ❑ Declaration for Default or Uncontested Dissolution form is included. *[Figure 20.1]*

5. ❑ If you have kids, statement of guideline child support included *[for example, CalSupport's Bench Report]*. If you have a support agreement for less than guideline, special language must be included (FC § 4065) *[see agreement in ch. 6, item V, or use the Stipulation form, Figure 18.3]*.

6. ❑ If you have kids, support modification information and health care cost reimbursement information is attached *[Form FL-192]*.

7. ❑ If you have kids, file the Child Support Case Registry Form *[FL-191]*.

8. ❑ If there's no agreement, the Judgment does not contain relief not requested in the Petition.

9. ❑ Your Judgment must not terminate marital status before the date of your uncontested hearing or the date of filing your Declaration for Default Dissolution *[FL-170]*.

10. ❑ If Respondent's default was taken *[chapter 17] then Respondent's* signature on any agreement must be notarized. *[See note on page 62.]*

13. ❑ If public assistance is paid to a parent, or there is an Order of Limited Appointment, the Department of Child Support Services has signed their approval on the Judgment.

All items must be completed either by checking each box to indicate compliance or by marking "NA" to verify that an item is not applicable.

Figure 20.1
DECLARATION FOR DEFAULT OR UNCONTESTED DISSOLUTION

Form FL-170 (Page 1)

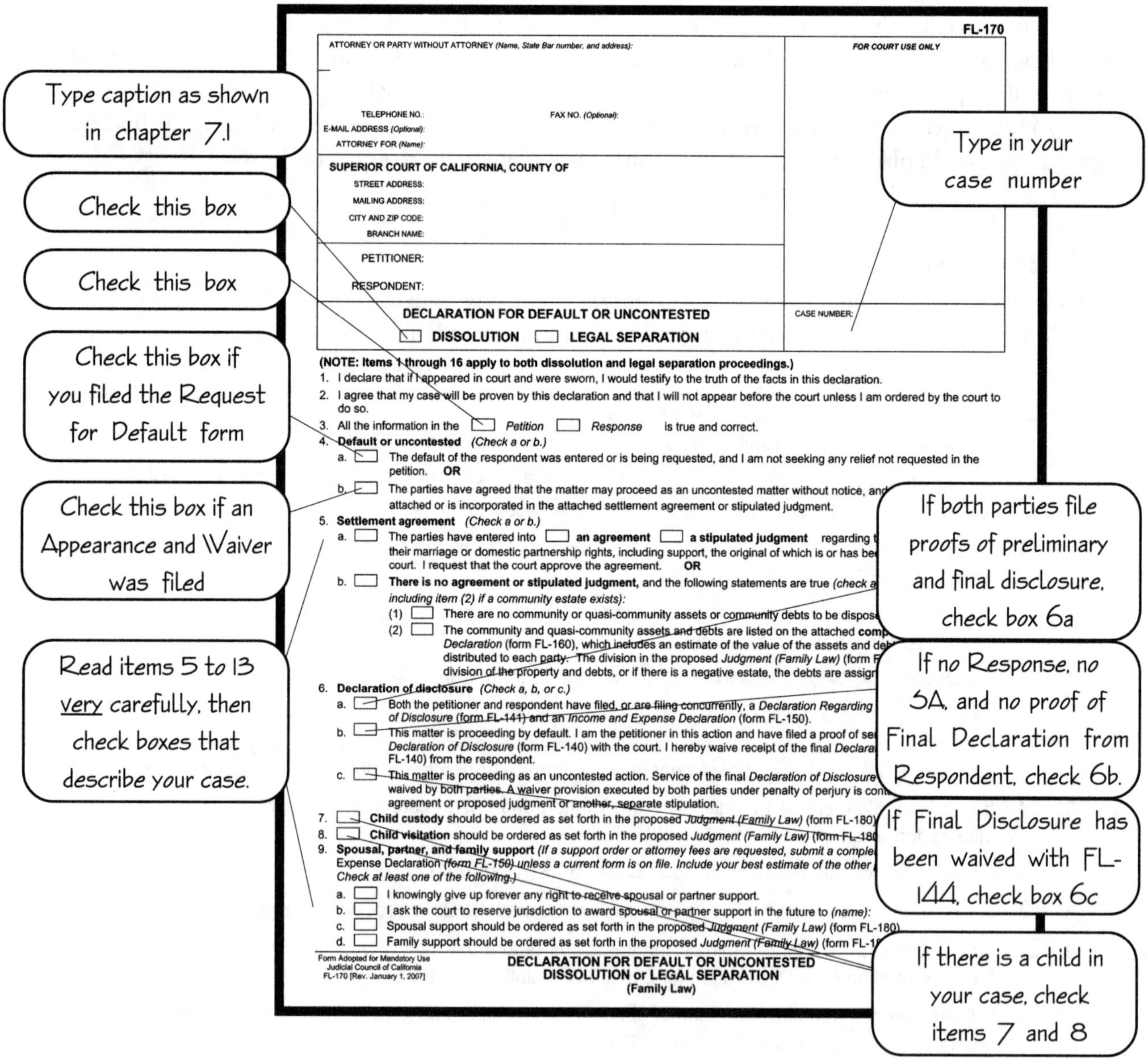
FL-170

ATTORNEY OR PARTY WITHOUT ATTORNEY (Name, State Bar number, and address): FOR COURT USE ONLY

TELEPHONE NO.: FAX NO. (Optional):
E-MAIL ADDRESS (Optional):
ATTORNEY FOR (Name):

SUPERIOR COURT OF CALIFORNIA, COUNTY OF
STREET ADDRESS:
MAILING ADDRESS:
CITY AND ZIP CODE:
BRANCH NAME:

PETITIONER:
RESPONDENT:

DECLARATION FOR DEFAULT OR UNCONTESTED
☐ DISSOLUTION ☐ LEGAL SEPARATION

CASE NUMBER:

(NOTE: Items 1 through 16 apply to both dissolution and legal separation proceedings.)

1. I declare that if I appeared in court and were sworn, I would testify to the truth of the facts in this declaration.
2. I agree that my case will be proven by this declaration and that I will not appear before the court unless I am ordered by the court to do so.
3. All the information in the ☐ *Petition* ☐ *Response* is true and correct.
4. **Default or uncontested** *(Check a or b.)*
   a. ☐ The default of the respondent was entered or is being requested, and I am not seeking any relief not requested in the petition. **OR**
   b. ☐ The parties have agreed that the matter may proceed as an uncontested matter without notice, and … attached or is incorporated in the attached settlement agreement or stipulated judgment.
5. **Settlement agreement** *(Check a or b.)*
   a. ☐ The parties have entered into ☐ **an agreement** ☐ **a stipulated judgment** regarding … their marriage or domestic partnership rights, including support, the original of which is or has be… court. I request that the court approve the agreement. **OR**
   b. ☐ **There is no agreement or stipulated judgment,** and the following statements are true *(check a… including item (2) if a community estate exists):*
      (1) ☐ There are no community or quasi-community assets or community debts to be dispos…
      (2) ☐ The community and quasi-community assets and debts are listed on the attached comp… *Declaration* (form FL-160), which includes an estimate of the value of the assets and de… distributed to each party. The division in the proposed *Judgment (Family Law)* (form F… division of the property and debts, or if there is a negative estate, the debts are assig…
6. **Declaration of disclosure** *(Check a, b, or c.)*
   a. ☐ Both the petitioner and respondent have filed, or are filing concurrently, a *Declaration Regarding … of Disclosure* (form FL-141) and an *Income and Expense Declaration* (form FL-150).
   b. ☐ This matter is proceeding by default. I am the petitioner in this action and have filed a proof of se… *Declaration of Disclosure* (form FL-140) with the court. I hereby waive receipt of the final *Declara…* FL-140) from the respondent.
   c. ☐ This matter is proceeding as an uncontested action. Service of the final *Declaration of Disclosure* … waived by both parties. A waiver provision executed by both parties under penalty of perjury is con… agreement or proposed judgment or another, separate stipulation.
7. ☐ **Child custody** should be ordered as set forth in the proposed *Judgment (Family Law)* (form FL-180)…
8. ☐ **Child visitation** should be ordered as set forth in the proposed *Judgment (Family Law)* (form FL-18…
9. **Spousal, partner, and family support** *(If a support order or attorney fees are requested, submit a comple… Expense Declaration (form FL-150) unless a current form is on file. Include your best estimate of the other … Check at least one of the following.)*
   a. ☐ I knowingly give up forever any right to receive spousal or partner support.
   b. ☐ I ask the court to reserve jurisdiction to award spousal or partner support in the future to *(name)*:
   c. ☐ Spousal support should be ordered as set forth in the proposed *Judgment (Family Law)* (form FL-180)
   d. ☐ Family support should be ordered as set forth in the proposed *Judgment (Family Law)* (form FL-1…

Form Adopted for Mandatory Use
Judicial Council of California
FL-170 [Rev. January 1, 2007]

DECLARATION FOR DEFAULT OR UNCONTESTED
DISSOLUTION or LEGAL SEPARATION
(Family Law)
Type caption as shown in chapter 7.1
Check this box
Check this box
Check this box if you filed the Request for Default form
Check this box if an Appearance and Waiver was filed
Read items 5 to 13 very carefully, then check boxes that describe your case.
Type in your case number
If both parties file proofs of preliminary and final disclosure, check box 6a
If no Response, no SA, and no proof of Final Declaration from Respondent, check 6b.
If Final Disclosure has been waived with FL-144, check box 6c
If there is a child in your case, check items 7 and 8

Note on Item 5(b)(2): If you have property or bills to divide but no settlement agreement (SA), you must attach a copy of the completed Property Declaration (chapter 15) to this form unless a completed one was already filed with the Request for Default (chapter 17).

Figure 20.2
DECLARATION FOR
DEFAULT OR UNCONTESTED DISSOLUTION
Form FL-170   (Page 2)

Type in names of parties as shown on page 74

If there is a child in your case, check box 10 and one box in both items 11a and 11b. Also complete 13a and 13b or 13c.

Check box 14 if Petition listed a child who was born before marriage.

Check one of these boxes if wife's former name is being restored.

Type in case number.

If support is to be paid to a party on welfare, check a box at item 12.

Date and sign as indicated on form.

FL-170

PETITIONER:

RESPONDENT:

CASE NUMBER:

10. ☑ **Child support** should be ordered as set forth in the proposed *Judgment (Family Law)* (form FL-180).

11. a. I ☐ am receiving ☐ am not receiving ☐ intend to apply for   public assistance for the child or in the proposed order.

   b. To the best of my knowledge, the other party ☐ is ☐ is not   receiving public assistance.

12. ☐ The petitioner ☐ respondent   is presently receiving public assistance, and all support should be made payable to the local child support agency at the address set forth in the proposed judgment. A representative of the local child support agency has signed the proposed judgment.

13. If there are minor children, check and complete item a and item b or c:

   a. My gross (before taxes) monthly income is *(specify):* $

   b. ☐ The estimated gross monthly income of the other party is *(specify):* $

   c. ☐ I have no knowledge of the estimated monthly income of the other party for the following reasons *(specify):*

   d. ☐ I request that this order be based on the ☐ petitioner's ☐ respondent's   earning ab my estimate of earning ability are *(specify):*

      ☐ Continued on Attachment 13d.

14. ☑ **Parentage** of the children of the petitioner and respondent born prior to their marriage or domestic ordered as set forth in the proposed *Judgment (Family Law)* (form FL-180). A declaration regarding p

15. ☐ **Attorney fees** should be ordered as set forth in the proposed *Judgment (Family Law)* (form FL-180).

16. ☑ The petitioner ☐ respondent   requests restoration of his or her former name as set forth in the proposed *Judgment (Family Law)* (form FL-180).

17. There are irreconcilable differences that have led to the irremediable breakdown of the marriage or domestic partnership, and there is no possibility of saving the marriage or domestic partnership through counseling or other means.

18. This declaration may be reviewed by a commissioner sitting as a temporary judge, who may determine whether to grant this request or require my appearance under Family Code section 2336.

STATEMENTS IN THIS BOX APPLY ONLY TO DISSOLUTIONS—Items 19 through 21

19. If this is a dissolution of marriage or of a domestic partnership created in another state, the petitioner and/or the respondent has been a resident of this county for at least three months and of the state of California for at least six months continuously and immediately preceding the date of the filing of the petition for dissolution of marriage or domestic partnership.

20. I ask that the court grant the request for a judgment for dissolution of marriage or domestic partnership based upon irreconcilable differences and that the court make the orders set forth in the proposed *Judgment (Family Law)* (form FL-180) submitted with this declaration.

21. ☐ **This declaration is for the termination of marital or domestic partner status only.** I ask the court to reserve jurisdiction over all issues whose determination is not requested in this declaration.

THIS STATEMENT APPLIES ONLY TO LEGAL SEPARATIONS

22. I ask that the court grant the request for a judgment for legal separation based upon irreconcilable differences and that the court make the orders set forth in the proposed *Judgment (Family Law)* (form FL-180) submitted with this declaration.

   I understand that a judgment of legal separation does not terminate a marriage or domestic partnership and that I am still married or a partner in a domestic partnership.

23. ☐ Other *(specify):*

I declare under penalty of perjury under the laws of the State of California that the foregoing is true and correct.

Date:

▶

_____
(TYPE OR PRINT NAME)

_____
(SIGNATURE OF DECLARANT)

FL-170 [Rev. January 1, 2007]

DECLARATION FOR DEFAULT OR UNCONTESTED DISSOLUTION or LEGAL SEPARATION
(Family Law)

Page 2 of 2

20.2 The Declaration of Compliance

If Respondent did not file a Proof of Service for the Preliminary or Final Disclosures along with a Declaration Re Service of Declaration (Fig. 14.4) for each, you might want to file this Declaration of Compliance to help the court make its determination without requiring a hearing. However, if you have an agreement but could not get a Final Disclosure from Respondent, and it wasn't waived with FL-144, you have an irregular situation that cannot be cured by this declaration, so you better call an attorney.

Type your declaration on an Additional Page form (page 74), as shown below. Type in statements and facts that describe the situation in your case, using the following as an example.

DECLARATION OF COMPLIANCE RE: DISCLOSURE DECLARATIONS

1. I am _____, the Petitioner in the within case.

2. The parties have (I have) complied or substantially complied with the disclosure requirements under Family Code 2100 et. seq., as stated below.

3. The Preliminary Declaration of Disclosure with an Income and Expense Declaration:

   a) was served by Petitioner on Respondent on (date). **If a Proof of Service was filed, add:** ...and a Proof of Service for same was filed with this court on (date).

   b) was served by Respondent on Petitioner on (date), receipt of which is acknowledged by Petitioner. **If Respondent didn't comply, state:** ...was not served on Petitioner by Respondent and no such Preliminary Declaration has been received by Petitioner.

4. The Final Declaration of Disclosure (use any of the following that apply to your case):

   a) was served by Petitioner on Respondent on (date **If a Proof of Service was filed, add**: ...and a Proof of Service for same was filed with this court on (date).

   b) was served by Respondent on Petitioner on (date), receipt of which is acknowledged by Petitioner. **If a Proof of Service was filed, add:** ...and a Proof of Service for same was filed with this court on (date).

   c) I have entered into a written settlement agreement with Respondent that has been submitted with the proposed Judgment **If FD was waived, add:** ...and the parties mutually waived the Final Disclosure therein.

5. I have complied with all disclosure requirements and am entitled to Judgment in that I would be unfairly prejudiced, and it would not be in the interests of justice, if the Judgment were not entered in this case. I understand that I can return to court if I discover undisclosed assets in the future, therefore I request that Judgment be entered at this time.

I declare under penalty of perjury under the laws of the State of California that the foregoing is true and correct.

Date: (Signed)

20.3 **Going to a hearing**

Going to a hearing is easier than you might think. Thousands of people before you have done it by themselves with little trouble and great success, so just follow the instructions below and you'll be okay.

Setting the hearing date. To get a date for your hearing, you have to ask the Clerk's office to "set" your case on their trial calendar. You can request a hearing date when you file the Request for Default (see check list, page 82) or any time thereafter. In some counties, you merely call the Clerk's office on the phone any time after they receive your second papers and ask for a hearing date, but others require a local form to be filed when you request a hearing. The clerk will tell you this when you call. The L.A. local form is at the end of this chapter for purposes of illustration, but if you run into one that you can't figure out, just send two blank copies to Nolo Press Occidental, 501 Mission Street, Suite 2, Santa Cruz, CA 95060, with a stamped, self-addressed envelope and we will send instructions.

Paperwork. In general, you bring all papers to hand over for the judge to examine and sign, but some counties want them filed sooner. When you call to set your hearing, ask when they want the Judgment, Notice of Entry of Judgment, and, if you use them, the Wage Assignment papers.

Preview. If you can take the time, it could be very helpful to watch some uncontested divorces before your own hearing day. This will give you a good idea of what to expect when your case comes up, what sort your judge is (if you know ahead who it will be), how the courtroom is run, and so on. Ask a clerk when and where uncontested dissolutions are usually heard.

The day of the hearing—how to go and what to say

The way you look might matter, so dress cleanly and neatly. If you own any, wear business-type clothing. Get to the courthouse a little before your case is scheduled to give yourself time to find the right place.

Most counties have more than one Superior Court judge. Each judge has his own courtroom, called a "department," which is identified by a number or letter. In some counties you go straight to the assigned department for your hearing. In larger counties, you may go first to a "presiding" or "master calendar" department. In such a case, go there and listen for the name of your case to be called, stand up and answer, "Ready!" and your case will then be sent to some other department for the hearing. Sometimes they will want you to pick up your file and carry it to the hearing—find out by asking the clerk or bailiff when you appear for the hearing, or call and ask the clerk ahead of time.

Don't give the bailiff or the court clerk any grief, no matter how they act toward you. They're the judge's staff and in too important a position for you to take any chances. Be extra nice.

When you get to the proper courtroom for your hearing, tell the clerk or bailiff that you are present. If you haven't already filed them, hand the clerk the original and three copies of your proposed Judgment, the Notice of Entry of Judgment, wage attachment forms if you use them, and stamped envelopes addressed to you and Respondent. If you have a settlement agreement that has not been previously filed, hand it over.

When your case is called, answer "Ready!" Go right on up, get sworn, and take the stand. Take time to arrange your papers. Relax. Some judges will ask you questions to get the information they want, but most will just tell you to begin. Tell the judge facts and information about your case and the orders you want made. Always call the judge "Your Honor."

The outline below is your guide; use the portions that apply to you. Don't take this book to the stand, but *do* make complete notes or cut out these pages and take them up with you. Check each item as you go along to make sure you don't forget to say any part of it. Take your time. If the judge asks questions, it is only in order to become better informed and be satisfied that justice, as he or she understands it, is being done. Don't worry, just answer *briefly and exactly* what is asked. Don't volunteer information that is not asked for.

I. IN EVERY CASE, GIVE THE FOLLOWING INFORMATION:

A. "Your Honor, my name is _____ , and I am the Petitioner in this case."

B. "All of the facts stated in my Petition are true and correct."

C. "(I/ Respondent) resided in California for more than six months, and in *(County your court is in)* County for more than three months, immediately prior to the filing of the Petition."

D. *Using exactly these words, tell the judge:* "During the course of our marriage, there arose irreconcilable differences which led to the irremediable breakdown of our marriage. There is no chance for a reconciliation. Your honor, I ask that the marriage be dissolved."

II. USE THE PORTIONS THAT APPLY TO YOUR CASE:

If you have a settlement agreement, you say:

"Your Honor, the original copy of our settlement agreement has been submitted with the Judgment. My signature is on it, and I recognize the other signature as that of Respondent. I ask that it be admitted into evidence. I request that the court make the orders set out in the Judgment which I have submitted for your signature, which correspond to the terms of our settlement agreement."

Ask the judge if he or she would like more detail on the orders you have set out in the proposed Judgment and, if so, go on as described below.

If you have no settlement agreement, you say:

A. CHILDREN:

    1. None: "Your Honor, the Respondent and I have no minor children, and none are expected."

    2. If you have children:

        a. "Your Honor, the Respondent and I have ___ child(ren)." *Give the full name, age, and birth date of each child.*

---

b. "I know that (I am/ Respondent is/ Respondent and I are both) fit and proper to have custody of the child(ren), and it would be in the best interest of the child(ren) to have the court award

i. legal custody to both parents jointly with primary physical custody to (me/ Respondent)."

ii. primary legal and physical custody to (me/ Respondent)."

iii. both legal and physical custody to both parents jointly."

For joint physical and legal custody, the judge may ask for reasons why this is suitable in your case and may want details about how it will work in actual practice.

c. Visitation: *Say,* "I request that the court order the parenting arrangements described in the parenting plan set forth in the proposed Judgment." *(Be prepared to describe and discuss your plan if the Judge wants you to.)*

B. CHILD SUPPORT AND SPOUSAL SUPPORT:

1. No children and no request for spousal support:

a. Where Petitioner is the wife: "Your Honor, I do not want spousal support and I understand that if I waive my claim to it now I lose all claim to it forever."

b. Where Petitioner is the husband: *If you have a written waiver of spousal support, hand the original to the judge and say,* "I recognize the signature on this waiver of spousal support to be that of Respondent, and I request that it be admitted into evidence." *If the waiver is part of a settlement agreement, say nothing. If you don't have a written waiver or a settlement agreement with Respondent, the court may retain jurisdiction or make a nominal support award.*

2. If you want spousal support and/or child support:

a. "The information in the Income & Expense Declaration(s) is true and accurate to the best of my knowledge and belief. Before separation our gross combined family income was $_____ per month with average expenses of $_____ per month. The current net monthly disposable income of the parties is $_____ for myself and $_____ for my spouse *state amount on line 16 of Income Info form (Figure 16.2)."*

b. If there are children: "Under the proposed parenting plan, the custodial parent will have physical custody of the child ____% of the time. After the divorce my actual federal tax filing status will be _____ and my spouse's will be ____. The total number of exemptions claimed by each party will be ____for myself and ____ for my spouse." *This should be enough, but be prepared to give more details if the judge asks. Don't worry, just tell it the best you can. If you get stuck, ask for a continuance.*

c. "I request that (Petitioner/ Respondent) be ordered to pay (Respondent/ Petitioner) $___ per month for spousal support, to continue until _____."

d. "For child support, I request that (Petitioner/ Respondent) be ordered to pay to (Respondent/ Petitioner) $____ per month for one child and $____ per month for the next child and... *state the amount for each additional child*, a total of $____ per month." *If support is to continue beyond the age of 18, that must be stated here. If the child is being supported with welfare funds, say* "(I am/ Respondent is) receiving welfare to help support the child(ren), so support payments should be made through *(title of officer for your county)*."

e. "Your Honor, I request that the parties be ordered to share uninsured health care costs for the child(ren) as follows: Mother to pay __% and Father to pay __%.

f. (Respondent/Petitoner) (has/does not have) health insurance available at a reasonable cost so I now request that health (life, other) insurance be ordered at this (a future) time as set forth in the proposed Judgment." *Be prepared to give details about what is or is not available through employment, and costs.*

g. "Finally, I request that the Order for Wage Assignment be issued."

C. PROPERTY AND BILLS:

1. None: *If you checked box 5a on the Petition, then tell the judge,* "There is no property subject to disposition by the court."

2. Divided by agreement: *If you checked box 5b on the Petition and have an agreement, then say,* "Our property is divided in the agreement previously received in evidence."

3. Divided by the Court: *If you listed property at item 5b on the Petition, then tell the judge,* "The information in the Property Declaration is true, accurate, and complete, to the best of my knowledge and belief. I request that the property be divided as set forth in the Judgment which has been submitted for Your Honor's signature." *Be prepared to answer questions about the property or your requested division of it if the judge wants to go into it in more detail.*

Notes on pension plans: *If there is a community interest in a retirement plan, take care of it by one of the following methods (see chapter 3.6(b)). If you have it, bring an expert's report or other papers to show the value of the community share.*

a) Trade-off: *The pension is listed and valued with the other property in the Property Declaration. Say nothing unless the judge asks questions.*

b) Waiver by Petitioner: *Tell the judge,* "Your Honor, I know I may have some right to part of Respondent's pension plan which is listed in the Property Declaration, but I have thought it over and I don't want or need any part of it. I waive any and all rights I may have in that pension plan."

c) Written waiver by Respondent: *Hand the judge the original and one copy of the waiver and say,* "Your Honor, this is Respondent's waiver of rights to my pension plan. I recognize the signature as the Respondent's. Would you please admit this into evidence?"

Note on family home: *If the home is awarded to one spouse, say nothing unless asked. If, however, you want an order for a deferred sale, say* "In order to benefit the minor child(ren), I request that the sale of the family home be deferred as set forth in the proposed Judgment."

4. Separate property: *If you checked box 4 in the Petition, then say,* "The property listed under item 4 of the Petition is separate property, and I ask that it be confirmed as such." *The judge may want to ask questions about how some item was acquired or debt incurred, so be prepared, and bring any related documents you may have.*

D. DECLARATIONS OF DISCLOSURE:

1. Both parties have complied: "Your honor, the case file will show that both parties have complied and served each other with the Preliminary and Final Declarations of Disclosure."

2. Respondent has not complied: "Your honor, the case file will show that I have served Respondent with the Preliminary and Final Declarations of Disclosure but Respondent has not complied. I waive the Final Disclosure requirement and ask that you enter the Judgment in this case without it."

E. RESTORATION OF WIFE'S MAIDEN NAME:

"Your Honor, (I want my/ Respondent wants her) former name restored as set forth in the Judgment."

F. CONCLUSION: "Your Honor, that concludes my statement."

When your testimony is finished, the judge will recite the orders being made in your case; take notes. You do not need any witnesses. The clerk may hand you your signed copy of the Judgment. If not, it will be mailed to you, as will your copy of the Notice of Entry.

The Judgment you prepared *must* correspond to the judge's spoken orders. If the judge orders something different from what is in your prepared form, take careful notes on what the judge says; ask him to repeat if necessary. Then get your forms back from the clerk, make the necessary changes, and return them as soon as possible for the judge's signature. The orders in your Judgment do *not* become effective until the Judgment is signed by the judge *and* entered in the clerk's record book.

Troubleshooting guide

We said it before and say it again: 99 times out of 100 there will be no trouble with a hearing. However, it will make you feel better if you know what to do in case you are that unfortunate 1 out of the 100.

1. Before the hearing begins.

It sometimes happens that the people who work in the court forget that they are there to serve the public. It usually does no good to remind them. Rather, if the clerk or bailiff (or even the judge) is less than helpful or polite, just keep calm, be nice, and quietly but firmly pursue your goal. You have a right to be there and a right to represent yourself. Whatever you do, don't get short with the judge's clerk or bailiff even if you don't like the way they are treating you—these people work with the judge every day and you have enough problems without getting on their bad side. Walk softly. Be polite no matter what. Consider it a mark of your new maturity.

If someone is making things difficult for you, it is very possible that there is a reason. If so, you must find it out and correct the problem. Ask what is the matter, and at least try to get some hint about the general area of the problem. If necessary, ask to speak to another clerk or to a supervisor. Don't get upset. What is important is to correct the problem. Go over this book and double check everything. You can always return to the Clerk's office or to court another day.

2. After your hearing begins.

This is a scary time for something to go wrong, but don't worry, you have an excellent escape hatch (or panic button) that you can use if all else fails. Lawyers use it all the time. It is called the continuance.

If the judge is very difficult, or refuses to grant your dissolution, this means he or she thinks you have left out something essential. Ask the judge, politely, to explain, as it is likely that you can give additional testimony that will solve the problem. If things go very wrong and you can't figure out what your problem is, or if you get into any kind of situation you can't handle, just tell the judge, *"Your Honor, I request that this matter be taken off calendar, to be reset for hearing at another time, so that I may have time to seek advice and further prepare this case for presentation."* During the next recess, see if the clerk or bailiff can help you, or ask to see the judge in chambers. Go over this book and double check everything.

Assuming you figure out what went wrong, have your case set for hearing again, just like you did the first time, and do the hearing over again. If you think the problem was personal to that judge, ask the clerk if there is an informal way to avoid a judge who doesn't seem to like you or people who represent themselves.

3. After the hearing.

If the judge grants your dissolution but refuses to sign your Judgment, this means the judge thinks there is something wrong with it. Probably it is different from the orders announced in court. Ask the clerk what is wrong (or look at the clerk's docket sheet or minute order, a public record) and make up a new Judgment form. Do it as soon as possible, and bring it in for the judge's signature.

Figure 20.3
REQUEST FOR DEFAULT SETTING
Local form for Los Angeles County

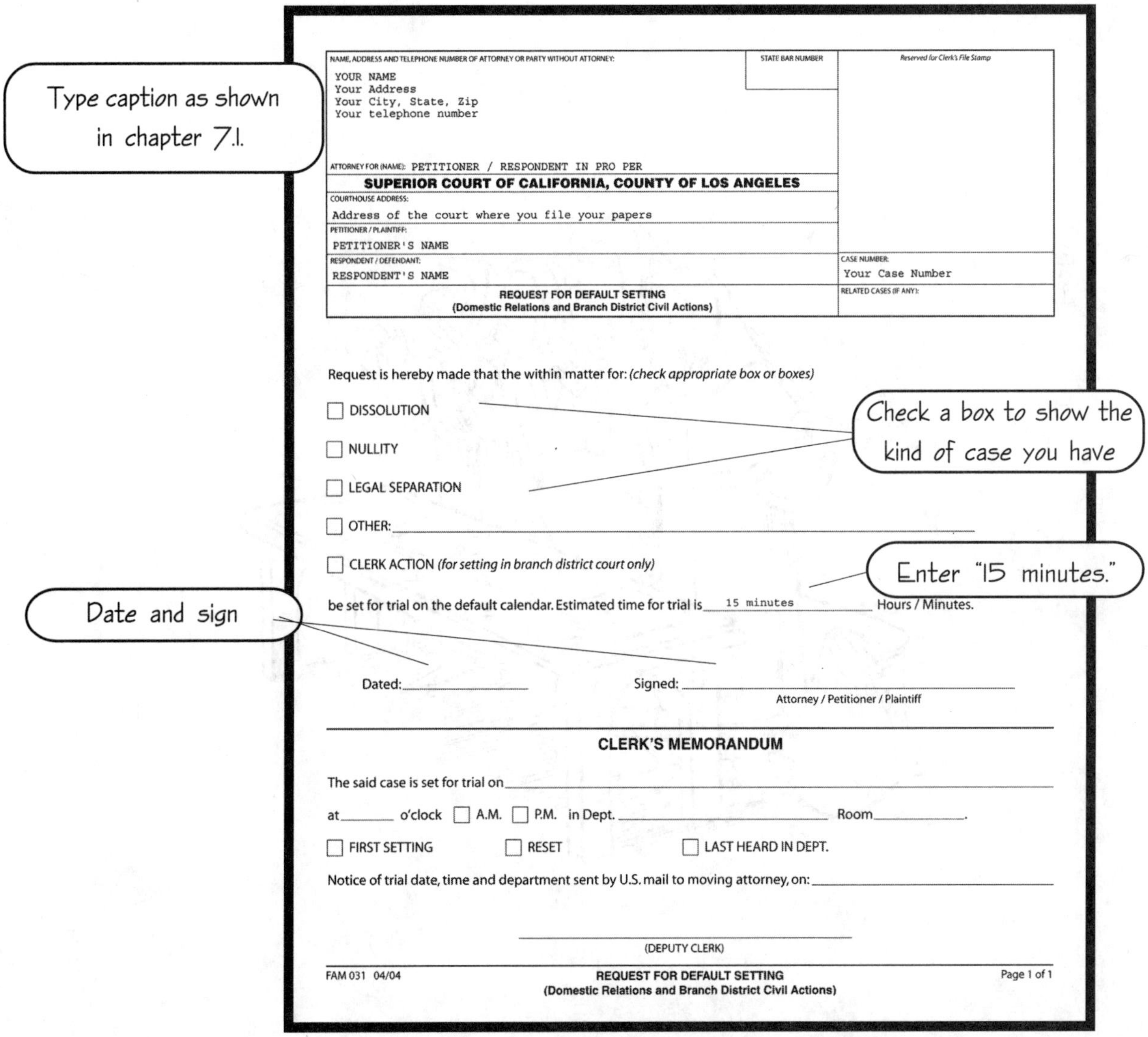

> Type caption as shown in chapter 7.1.

> Check a box to show the kind of case you have

> Enter "15 minutes."

> Date and sign

NAME, ADDRESS AND TELEPHONE NUMBER OF ATTORNEY OR PARTY WITHOUT ATTORNEY: YOUR NAME Your Address Your City, State, Zip Your telephone number	STATE BAR NUMBER	Reserved for Clerk's File Stamp

ATTORNEY FOR (NAME): PETITIONER / RESPONDENT IN PRO PER

SUPERIOR COURT OF CALIFORNIA, COUNTY OF LOS ANGELES

COURTHOUSE ADDRESS:
Address of the court where you file your papers

PETITIONER / PLAINTIFF:
PETITIONER'S NAME

RESPONDENT / DEFENDANT:
RESPONDENT'S NAME

CASE NUMBER:
Your Case Number

REQUEST FOR DEFAULT SETTING
(Domestic Relations and Branch District Civil Actions)

RELATED CASES (IF ANY):

Request is hereby made that the within matter for: *(check appropriate box or boxes)*

☐ DISSOLUTION

☐ NULLITY

☐ LEGAL SEPARATION

☐ OTHER: _____

☐ CLERK ACTION *(for setting in branch district court only)*

be set for trial on the default calendar. Estimated time for trial is ___15 minutes___ Hours / Minutes.

Dated: _____   Signed: _____
                                                            Attorney / Petitioner / Plaintiff

CLERK'S MEMORANDUM

The said case is set for trial on _____

at _____ o'clock ☐ A.M. ☐ P.M. in Dept. _____ Room _____.

☐ FIRST SETTING   ☐ RESET   ☐ LAST HEARD IN DEPT.

Notice of trial date, time and department sent by U.S. mail to moving attorney, on: _____

_____
(DEPUTY CLERK)

FAM 031 04/04   **REQUEST FOR DEFAULT SETTING**   Page 1 of 1
                        (Domestic Relations and Branch District Civil Actions)

THE NOTICE OF ENTRY OF JUDGMENT

What it is

To become effective, the written order of the court *must* be entered in the Clerk's Judgment Book. To let you know that the entry has been made, and when it was made, a clerk mails a notice to both parties. You prepare this form for the Clerk's office, but leaving blanks which they fill in.

After the Judgment is entered and returned to you, make sure to mail Respondent a court-stamped copy of the Judgment and Notice of Entry to show when the Judgment was correctly completed.

How to fill it out

Fill it out as shown in Figure 21.1. Prepare the original and make 3 copies.

Note: When you file this form, you *must* also include two stamped envelopes with the court clerk's return address: one addressed to you, and one addressed to your spouse's last known address. Weigh your packet of papers and include enough postage.

Note: If divorce will end your group health coverage under your ex-spouse's plan, you have 60 days to give written notice of your divorce to the Plan Administrator and your desire to continue at your own expense under the plan.

Figure 21.1 NOTICE OF ENTRY OF JUDGMENT
Form FL-190

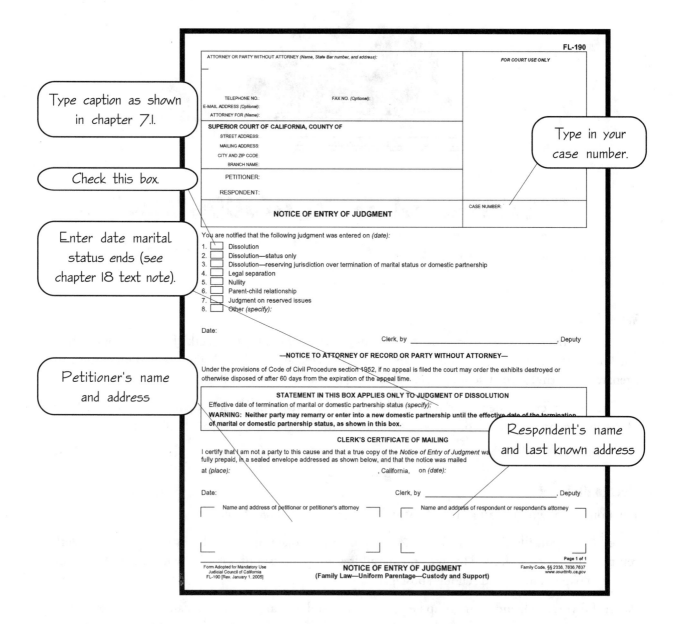

Type caption as shown in chapter 7.1.

Check this box.

Enter date marital status ends (see chapter 18 text note).

Petitioner's name and address

Type in your case number.

Respondent's name and last known address

Part Three:
Summary Procedures

22
THE SUMMARY DISSOLUTION

If you haven't already done so, read chapter 2.2 about the advantages and disadvantages of the Summary Dissolution. You should also read through all of Part One, no matter which procedure you choose.

After many years of experience, we find it striking how *little* the Summary Dissolution is being used. We think this is because of the disadvantages pointed out in chapter 2.2. Now that we have the burden of the disclosure requirements (chapter 14) added to the Summary Dissolution, it loses a lot of its advantage of ease of use. Please remember our main advice: don't do it if you think your spouse may file a revocation during the long waiting period, and don't rush into it just to make the deadline. The Regular Dissolution is not much harder to do and it has some advantages over this shorter method.

If you are qualified to use the Summary Dissolution procedure, and if you choose to use it instead of doing a Regular Dissolution, then you will need the the official *Summary Dissolution Booklet*, form FL-810 (in Spanish, form FL-812), forms FL-800, FL-820 and FL-830, and a sheet of instructions for filling out FL-800.

The law *requires* both spouses to read this booklet before you can file, so you may as well do it now. Get these materials from your clerk's office, from the companion CD that comes with this book in the forms folder in their own separate folder, or download them from **www.courtinfo.ca.gov/selfhelp/family/ divorce/summary.htm**. The Summary Dissolution Booklet is clear and easy to read, but it urges you too often and too strongly into an attorney's office. We think it is best if you do *not* retain a lawyer unless you have a specific question or problem, or if your spouse is raising problems you can't solve on your own. Lawyers cost a lot and have a way of making simple things more complicated.

To file a Summary Dissolution you must follow the instructions in the booklet. Unfortunately, the booklet fails to tell you much about filling out the Request for Judgment or the Revocation forms, so we have included some instructions and details in the next chapter.

Captions

The "captions" of all forms are done just as shown in the instructions for form FL-800, or as shown in this book in chapter 7.1.

Request for Final Judgment & Notice

Six months after the Petition is filed, one of the spouses *must* remember to file the Request for Final Judgment. Either spouse can do it, but you are not divorced until this form is filed and returned to you.

Do the caption as described above. Don't forget to put in the case number stamped on your Petition.

Item 3: Check box (a). Box (b) is for cases where the final Judgment was not properly requested and/or entered when you first had a right to it, and for some good reason you need to have it made effective as of the earlier date. For example: If you were told and believed that your spouse entered the final Judgment then got married again and later found out your divorce was not entered, you might get the Judgment made effective as of the end of the waiting period, *if* the proceeding has not since been revoked or dismissed.

Item 4: If the wife's former name was not requested on the Petition, it can be requested here, but *only* if the wife is the one filing this form. Check this box and type in the full name you wish to have restored.

Put in the date and place where the form is signed, type your name on the dotted line, and put your signature on the solid line.

On the back of the form, fill in only the boxes with the husband's and wife's name and last known address.

The Notice of Revocation

This form, FL-830, is used to stop the dissolution. Either spouse can file it. *Do not* file it unless you want the divorce proceeding to be permanently stopped.

The caption is filled out as shown above. Don't forget the case number. In the first paragraph, put in the date the Petition was filed (the date stamped at the clerk's office). Then put in the date and place signed, type your name on the dotted line and add your signature on the solid line.

Fill in Husband's and Wife's name and last known address in the boxes provided.

23

TERMINATION OF DOMESTIC PARTNERSHIP

If you haven't already done so, read chapter 2.2, which discusses who is qualified to use the summary procedure and, for those who are qualified, the advantages and disadvantages of doing it that way. You should also read through all of Part One, no matter which procedure you choose.

Please remember our main advice: even if you are qualified to use it, don't proceed by Notice of Termination of Domestic Partnership if you think your partner might file a revocation during the long waiting period, and don't rush into it just to make the deadline. The Regular Dissolution is not terribly difficult and it has some advantages over this shorter method.

If you are qualified to use the Notice of Termination procedure, and if you choose to use it instead of doing a Regular Dissolution, then here's how you will need to obtain and carefully read the Termination brochure prepared by the Secretary of State and the Termination forms. These can be found on our CD in the forms folder in their own separate folder, or you can download the latest brochure and forms from the Secretary of State's Web site at **www.ss.ca.gov/dpregistry.**

For your convenience, the full text of the statute that defines the summary procedure to terminate a domestic partnership is reproduced below.

Family Code § 299: Termination of Domestic Partnership

(a) A domestic partnership may be terminated without filing a proceeding for dissolution of domestic partnership by the filing of a Notice of Termination of Domestic Partnership with the Secretary of State pursuant to this section, provided that all of the following conditions exist at the time of the filing:

(1) The Notice of Termination of Domestic Partnership is signed by both domestic partners.

(2) There are no children of the relationship of the parties born before or after registration of the domestic partnership or adopted by the parties after registration of the domestic partnership, and neither of the domestic partners, to their knowledge, is pregnant.

(3) The domestic partnership is not more than five years in duration.

(4) Neither party has any interest in real property wherever situated, with the exception of the lease of a residence occupied by either party which satisfies the following requirements:
    (A) The lease does not include an option to purchase.
    (B) The lease terminates within one year from the date of filing of the Notice of Termination of Domestic Partnership.

(5) There are no unpaid obligations in excess of the amount described in paragraph (6) of subdivision (a) of Section 2400, as adjusted by subdivision (b) of Section 2400, incurred by either or both of the parties after registration of the domestic partnership, excluding the amount of any unpaid obligation with respect to an automobile.

(6) The total fair market value of community property assets, excluding all encumbrances and automobiles, including any deferred compensation or retirement plan, is less than the amount described in paragraph (7) of subdivision (a) of Section 2400, as

adjusted by subdivision (b) of Section 2400, and neither party has separate property assets, excluding all encumbrances and automobiles, in excess of that amount.

(7) The parties have executed an agreement setting forth the division of assets and the assumption of liabilities of the community property, and have executed any documents, title certificates, bills of sale, or other evidence of transfer necessary to effectuate the agreement.

(8) The parties waive any rights to support by the other domestic partner.

(9) The parties have read and understand a brochure prepared by the Secretary of State describing the requirements, nature, and effect of terminating a domestic partnership.

(10) Both parties desire that the domestic partnership be terminated.

(b) The domestic partnership shall be terminated effective six months after the date of filing of the Notice of Termination of Domestic Partnership with the Secretary of State pursuant to this section, provided that neither party has, before that date, filed with the Secretary of State a notice of revocation of the termination of domestic partnership, in the form and content as shall be prescribed by the Secretary of State, and sent to the other party a copy of the notice of revocation by first-class mail, postage prepaid, at the other party's last known address. The effect of termination of a domestic partnership pursuant to this section shall be the same as, and shall be treated for all purposes as, the entry of a judgment of dissolution of a domestic partnership.

(c) The termination of a domestic partnership pursuant to subdivision (b) does not prejudice nor bar the rights of either of the parties to institute an action in the superior court to set aside the termination for fraud, duress, mistake, or any other ground recognized at law or in equity. A court may set aside the termination of domestic partnership and declare the termination of the domestic partnership null and void upon proof that the parties did not meet the requirements of subdivision (a) at the time of the filing of the Notice of Termination of Domestic Partnership with the Secretary of State.

(d) The superior courts shall have jurisdiction over all proceedings relating to the dissolution of domestic partnerships, nullity of domestic partnerships, and legal separation of partners in a domestic partnership. The dissolution of a domestic partnership, nullity of a domestic partnership, and legal separation of partners in a domestic partnership shall follow the same procedures, and the partners shall possess the same rights, protections, and benefits, and be subject to the same responsibilities, obligations, and duties, as apply to the dissolution of marriage, nullity of marriage, and legal separation of spouses in a marriage, respectively, except as provided in subdivision (a), and except that, in accordance with the consent acknowledged by domestic partners in the Declaration of Domestic Partnership form, proceedings for dissolution, nullity, or legal separation of a domestic partnership registered in this state may be filed in the superior courts of this state even if neither domestic partner is a resident of, or maintains a domicile in, the state at the time the proceedings are filed.

Order of Forms

All Judicial Council forms in this book (and more) are also on the companion CD
in the forms folder and can be filled out and printed on any Mac or PC.

Chapter	Form Number		
9	FL-110	•	Summons
10	FL-100	•	Petition
10	FL-103		Petition—Domestic Partnership
10	FL-105		Declaration Under UCCJEA
7.1	MC-020		Additional Page
11	FL-120	•	Response
11	FL-123		Response—Domestic Partnership
12.7	FL-130		Appearance, Stipulations, and Waivers
13	FL-115	•	Proof of Service of Summons
13	FL-117		Notice and Acknowledgment of Receipt
13	FL-335		Proof of Service by Mail
13	FL-330		Proof of Personal Service
14	FL-140	•	Declaration of Disclosure
14	FL-142	•	Schedule of Assets and Debts *(4 pages)*
14	FL-141	•	Declaration Re Service of Declaration of Disclosure
14	FL-144		Stipulation and Waiver of Final Declaration of Disclosure
15	FL-160		Property Declaration *(used if there's no written agreement)*
15	FL-161		Continuation of Property Declaration "
16	FL-150/1	•	Income and Expense Declaration
16	FL-150/2	•	Income Information
16	FL-150/3	•	Expense Information
16	FL-150/4	*	Child Support Information
16	FL-155		Financial Statement (Simplified)
17	FL-165	•	Request to Enter Default
18	FL-180	•	Judgment
18.4	FL-350		Stipulation to Establish Child Support *(in a few counties)*
18.4	FL-191	*	Child Support Case Registry Form
18.4	FL-192	*	Notice of Rights and Responsibilities, Health Care Costs
18.4	FL-192/2	*	Information Sheet on Changing a Child Support Order
19	FL-195	†	Order/Notice to Withhold Income for Child Support
19	FL-435	†	Earnings Assignment Order for Spousal or Partner Support
19	FL-450	†	Request for Hearing Re Earnings Assignment *(blank sent to Respondent)*
20.1	FL-170	•	Declaration for Default or Uncontested Dissolution *(not used if you go to court)*
21	FL-190	•	Notice of Entry of Judgment
6			Nolo Arbitration Rules *(required if you use our settlement agreement)*

* • *Used in every case. Forms not marked are used only in special circumstances.*
* † *Used in every case with either child or spousal support.*
* * *Used in every case with child support.*

SUMMONS (Family Law)

CITACIÓN (Derecho familiar)

NOTICE TO RESPONDENT *(Name):*

AVISO AL DEMANDADO *(Nombre):*

FOR COURT USE ONLY
(SÓLO PARA USO DE LA CORTE)

You are being sued. *Lo están demandando.*

Petitioner's name is:

Nombre del demandante:

CASE NUMBER *(NÚMERO DE CASO):*

You have **30 calendar days** after this *Summons* and *Petition* are served on you to file a *Response* (form FL-120 or FL-123) at the court and have a copy served on the petitioner. A letter or phone call will not protect you.

If you do not file your *Response* on time, the court may make orders affecting your marriage or domestic partnership, your property, and custody of your children. You may be ordered to pay support and attorney fees and costs. If you cannot pay the filing fee, ask the clerk for a fee waiver form.

If you want legal advice, contact a lawyer immediately. You can get information about finding lawyers at the California Courts Online Self-Help Center *(www.courtinfo.ca.gov/selfhelp)*, at the California Legal Services Web site *(www.lawhelpcalifornia.org)*, or by contacting your local county bar association.

*Tiene **30 días corridos** después de haber recibido la entrega legal de esta Citación y Petición para presentar una Respuesta (formulario FL-120 ó FL-123) ante la corte y efectuar la entrega legal de una copia al demandante. Una carta o llamada telefónica no basta para protegerlo.*

Si no presenta su Respuesta a tiempo, la corte puede dar órdenes que afecten su matrimonio o pareja de hecho, sus bienes y la custodia de sus hijos. La corte también le puede ordenar que pague manutención, y honorarios y costos legales. Si no puede pagar la cuota de presentación, pida al secretario un formulario de exención de cuotas.

Si desea obtener asesoramiento legal, póngase en contacto de inmediato con un abogado. Puede obtener información para encontrar a un abogado en el Centro de Ayuda de las Cortes de California (www.sucorte.ca.gov), en el sitio Web de los Servicios Legales de California (www.lawhelpcalifornia.org) o poniéndose en contacto con el colegio de abogados de su condado.

NOTICE: The restraining orders on page 2 are effective against both spouses or domestic partners until the petition is dismissed, a judgment is entered, or the court makes further orders. These orders are enforceable anywhere in California by any law enforcement officer who has received or seen a copy of them.

AVISO: *Las órdenes de restricción que figuran en la página 2 valen para ambos cónyuges o pareja de hecho hasta que se despida la petición, se emita un fallo o la corte dé otras órdenes. Cualquier autoridad de la ley que haya recibido o visto una copia de estas órdenes puede hacerlas acatar en cualquier lugar de California.*

1. The name and address of the court are *(El nombre y dirección de la corte son):*

2. The name, address, and telephone number of the petitioner's attorney, or the petitioner without an attorney, are:
   (El nombre, dirección y número de teléfono del abogado del demandante, o del demandante si no tiene abogado, son):

Date *(Fecha):* _____ Clerk, by *(Secretario, por)* _____, Deputy *(Asistente)*

[SEAL]

NOTICE TO THE PERSON SERVED: You are served

AVISO A LA PERSONA QUE RECIBIÓ LA ENTREGA: *Esta entrega se realiza*

a. ☐ as an individual. *(a usted como individuo.)*

b. ☐ on behalf of respondent who is a *(en nombre de un demandado que es):*

    (1) ☐ minor *(menor de edad)*

    (2) ☐ ward or conservatee *(dependiente de la corte o pupilo)*

    (3) ☐ other *(specify) (otro – especifique):*

(Read the reverse for important information.)

(Lea importante información al dorso.)

Form Adopted for Mandatory Use
Judicial Council of California
FL-110 [Rev. January 1, 2006]

SUMMONS
(Family Law)

Family Code §§ 232, 233, 2040,7700;
Code of Civil Procedure, §§ 412.20, 416.60–416.90
www.courtinfo.ca.gov

WARNING—IMPORTANT INFORMATION

WARNING: California law provides that, for purposes of division of property upon dissolution of a marriage or domestic partnership or upon legal separation, property acquired by the parties during marriage or domestic partnership in joint form is presumed to be community property. If either party to this action should die before the jointly held community property is divided, the language in the deed that characterizes how title is held (i.e., joint tenancy, tenants in common, or community property) will be controlling, and not the community property presumption. You should consult your attorney if you want the community property presumption to be written into the recorded title to the property.

STANDARD FAMILY LAW RESTRAINING ORDERS

Starting immediately, you and your spouse or domestic partner are restrained from

1. removing the minor child or children of the parties, if any, from the state without the prior written consent of the other party or an order of the court;

2. cashing, borrowing against, canceling, transferring, disposing of, or changing the beneficiaries of any insurance or other coverage, including life, health, automobile, and disability, held for the benefit of the parties and their minor child or children;

3. transferring, encumbering, hypothecating, concealing, or in any way disposing of any property, real or personal, whether community, quasi-community, or separate, without the written consent of the other party or an order of the court, except in the usual course of business or for the necessities of life; and

4. creating a nonprobate transfer or modifying a nonprobate transfer in a manner that affects the disposition of property subject to the transfer, without the written consent of the other party or an order of the court. Before revocation of a nonprobate transfer can take effect or a right of survivorship to property can be eliminated, notice of the change must be filed and served on the other party.

You must notify each other of any proposed extraordinary expenditures at least five business days prior to incurring these extraordinary expenditures and account to the court for all extraordinary expenditures made after these restraining orders are effective. However, you may use community property, quasi-community property, or your own separate property to pay an attorney to help you or to pay court costs.

ADVERTENCIA – INFORMACIÓN IMPORTANTE

ADVERTENCIA: De acuerdo a la ley de California, las propiedades adquiridas por las partes durante su matrimonio o pareja de hecho en forma conjunta se consideran propiedad comunitaria para los fines de la división de bienes que ocurre cuando se produce una disolución o separación legal del matrimonio o pareja de hecho. Si cualquiera de las partes de este caso llega a fallecer antes de que se divida la propiedad comunitaria de tenencia conjunta, el destino de la misma quedará determinado por las cláusulas de la escritura correspondiente que describen su tenencia (por ej., tenencia conjunta, tenencia en común o propiedad comunitaria) y no por la presunción de propiedad comunitaria. Si quiere que la presunción comunitaria quede registrada en la escritura de la propiedad, debería consultar con un abogado.

ÓRDENES DE RESTRICCIÓN NORMALES DE DERECHO FAMILIAR

En forma inmediata, usted y su cónyuge o pareja de hecho tienen prohibido:

1. Llevarse del estado de California a los hijos menores de las partes, si los hubiera, sin el consentimiento previo por escrito de la otra parte o de una orden de la corte;

2. Cobrar, pedir prestado, cancelar, transferir, deshacerse o cambiar el nombre de los beneficiarios de cualquier seguro u otro tipo de cobertura, tal como de vida, salud, vehículo y discapacidad, que tenga como beneficiario(s) a las partes y su(s) hijo(s) menor(es);

3. Transferir, gravar, ocultar o deshacerse de cualquier manera de cualquier propiedad, inmueble o personal, ya sea comunitaria, cuasicomunitaria o separada, sin el consentimiento escrito de la otra parte o de una orden de la corte, con excepción las operaciones realizadas en el curso normal de actividades o para satisfacer las necesidades de la vida; y

4. Crear o modificar una transferencia no testamentaria de manera que afecte el destino de una propiedad sujeta a transferencia, sin el consentimiento por escrito de la otra parte o de una orden de la corte. Antes de que se pueda eliminar la revocación de una transferencia no testamentaria, se debe presentar ante la corte un aviso del cambio y hacer una entrega legal de dicho aviso a la otra parte.

Cada parte tiene que notificar a la otra sobre cualquier gasto extraordinario propuesto, por lo menos cinco días laborales antes de realizarlo, y rendir cuenta a la corte de todos los gastos extraordinarios realizados después de que estas órdenes de restricción hayan entrado en vigencia. No obstante, puede usar propiedad comunitaria, cuasicomunitaria o suya separada para pagar a un abogado o para ayudarle a pagar los costos de la corte.

ATTORNEY OR PARTY WITHOUT ATTORNEY *(Name, State Bar number, and address):*	*FOR COURT USE ONLY*
TELEPHONE NO.: FAX NO. *(Optional):*	
E-MAIL ADDRESS *(Optional):*	
ATTORNEY FOR *(Name):*	

SUPERIOR COURT OF CALIFORNIA, COUNTY OF
STREET ADDRESS:
MAILING ADDRESS:
CITY AND ZIP CODE:
BRANCH NAME:

MARRIAGE OF
PETITIONER:

RESPONDENT:

PETITION FOR	CASE NUMBER:
[ ] **Dissolution of Marriage** [ ] **Legal Separation** [ ] **Nullity of Marriage** [ ] **AMENDED**	

1. RESIDENCE (Dissolution only) [ ] Petitioner [ ] Respondent has been a resident of this state for at least six months and of this county for at least three months immediately preceding the filing of this *Petition for Dissolution of Marriage.*

2. STATISTICAL FACTS
   a. Date of marriage:
   b. Date of separation:
   c. Time from date of marriage to date of separation *(specify):*
      Years: Months:

3. DECLARATION REGARDING MINOR CHILDREN *(include children of this relationship born prior to or during the marriage or adopted during the marriage):*
   a. [ ] There are no minor children.
   b. [ ] The minor children are:

Child's name	Birthdate	Age	Sex

   [ ] Continued on Attachment 3b.
   c. If there are minor children of the Petitioner and Respondent, a completed *Declaration Under Uniform Child Custody Jurisdiction and Enforcement Act (UCCJEA)* (form FL-105) must be attached.
   d. [ ] A completed voluntary declaration of paternity regarding minor children born to the Petitioner and Respondent prior to the marriage is attached.

4. SEPARATE PROPERTY
   Petitioner requests that the assets and debts listed [ ] in *Property Declaration* (form FL-160) [ ] in Attachment 4
   [ ] below be confirmed as separate property.

Item	Confirm to

NOTICE: You may redact (black out) social security numbers from any written material filed with the court in this case other than a form used to collect child or spousal support.

Form Adopted for Mandatory Use
Judicial Council of California
FL-100 [Rev. January 1, 2005]

PETITION—MARRIAGE
(Family Law)

Family Code, §§ 2330, 3409;
www.courtinfo.ca.gov

5. DECLARATION REGARDING COMMUNITY AND QUASI-COMMUNITY ASSETS AND DEBTS AS CURRENTLY KNOWN
   a. ☐ There are no such assets or debts subject to disposition by the court in this proceeding.
   b. ☐ All such assets and debts are listed ☐ in *Property Declaration* (form FL-160) ☐ in Attachment 5b.
      ☐ below (specify):

6. **Petitioner requests**
   a. ☐ dissolution of the marriage based on
      (1) ☐ irreconcilable differences. (Fam. Code, § 2310(a).)
      (2) ☐ incurable insanity. (Fam. Code, § 2310(b).)
   b. ☐ legal separation of the parties based on
      (1) ☐ irreconcilable differences. (Fam. Code, § 2310(a).)
      (2) ☐ incurable insanity. (Fam. Code, § 2310(b).)
   c. ☐ nullity of void marriage based on
      (1) ☐ incestuous marriage. (Fam. Code, § 2200.)
      (2) ☐ bigamous marriage. (Fam. Code, § 2201.)
   d. ☐ nullity of voidable marriage based on
      (1) ☐ petitioner's age at time of marriage. (Fam. Code, § 2210(a).)
      (2) ☐ prior existing marriage. (Fam. Code, § 2210(b).)
      (3) ☐ unsound mind. (Fam. Code, § 2210(c).)
      (4) ☐ fraud. (Fam. Code, § 2210(d).)
      (5) ☐ force. (Fam. Code, § 2210(e).)
      (6) ☐ physical incapacity. (Fam. Code, § 2210(f).)

7. **Petitioner requests** that the court grant the above relief and make injunctive (including restraining) and other orders as follows:

	Petitioner	Respondent	Joint	Other
a. Legal custody of children to	☐	☐	☐	☐
b. Physical custody of children to	☐	☐	☐	☐
c. Child visitation be granted to	☐	☐		☐

   As requested in form: ☐ FL-311 ☐ FL-312 ☐ FL-341(C) ☐ FL-341(D) ☐ FL-341(E) ☐ Attachment 7c.
   d. ☐ Determination of parentage of any children born to the Petitioner and Respondent prior to the marriage.
   e. Attorney fees and costs payable by .... ☐ ☐
   f. Spousal support payable to (earnings assignment will be issued) .... ☐ ☐
   g. ☐ Terminate the court's jurisdiction (ability) to award spousal support to Respondent.
   h. ☐ Property rights be determined.
   i. ☐ Petitioner's former name be restored to (specify):
   j. ☐ Other (specify):

      ☐ Continued on Attachment 7j.

8. **Child support**–If there are minor children born to or adopted by the Petitioner and Respondent before or during this marriage, the court will make orders for the support of the children upon request and submission of financial forms by the requesting party. An earnings assignment may be issued without further notice. Any party required to pay support must pay interest on overdue amounts at the "legal" rate, which is currently 10 percent.

9. **I HAVE READ THE RESTRAINING ORDERS ON THE BACK OF THE SUMMONS, AND I UNDERSTAND THAT THEY APPLY TO ME WHEN THIS PETITION IS FILED.**

I declare under penalty of perjury under the laws of the State of California that the foregoing is true and correct.

Date:

▶

_____   _____
(TYPE OR PRINT NAME)   (SIGNATURE OF PETITIONER)

Date:

▶

_____   _____
(TYPE OR PRINT NAME)   (SIGNATURE OF ATTORNEY FOR PETITIONER)

NOTICE: Dissolution or legal separation may automatically cancel the rights of a spouse under the other spouse's will, trust, retirement plan, power of attorney, pay on death bank account, survivorship rights to any property owned in joint tenancy, and any other similar thing. It does not automatically cancel the right of a spouse as beneficiary of the other spouse's life insurance policy. You should review these matters, as well as any credit cards, other credit accounts, insurance polices, retirement plans, and credit reports to determine whether they should be changed or whether you should take any other actions. However, some changes may require the agreement of your spouse or a court order (see Family Code sections 231–235).

ATTORNEY OR PARTY WITHOUT ATTORNEY *(Name, State Bar number, and address):*

FOR COURT USE ONLY

TELEPHONE NO. :   FAX NO. *(Optional):*

E-MAIL ADDRESS *(Optional):*

ATTORNEY FOR *(Name):*

SUPERIOR COURT OF CALIFORNIA, COUNTY OF

STREET ADDRESS:

MAILING ADDRESS:

CITY AND ZIP CODE:

BRANCH NAME:

DOMESTIC PARTNERSHIP OF

PETITIONER:

RESPONDENT:

PETITION FOR	CASE NUMBER:

☐ **Dissolution of Domestic Partnership**
☐ **Legal Separation of Domestic Partnership**
☐ **Nullity of Domestic Partnership**   ☐ **AMENDED**

1. STATISTICAL FACTS
   a. Date of registration of domestic partnership or equivalent:
   b. Date of separation:
   c. Time from date of registration of domestic partnership to date of separation *(specify):*   Years   Months

2. RESIDENCE (Partnerships established out of state only)
   a. ☐ Our domestic partnership was established in another state *(specify state):*
   b. ☐ Petitioner ☐ Respondent has been a resident of this state of California for at least six months and of this county for at least three months immediately preceding the filing of this *Petition for Dissolution of Domestic Partnership.*

3. DECLARATION REGARDING MINOR CHILDREN *(include children of this relationship born prior to or during this domestic partnership or adopted during this domestic partnership):*
   a. ☐ There are no minor children.
   b. ☐ The minor children are:

Child's name	Birthdate	Age	Sex

☐ Continued on Attachment 3b.
   c. If there are minor children of the petitioner and respondent, a completed *Declaration Under Uniform Child Custody Jurisdiction and Enforcement Act (UCCJEA)* (form FL-105) must be attached.

4. SEPARATE PROPERTY
   Petitioner requests that the assets and debts listed ☐ in *Property Declaration* (form FL-160) ☐ in Attachment 4
   ☐ below   be confirmed as separate property.

Item	Confirm to

NOTICE: You may redact (black out) social security numbers from any written material filed with the court in this case other than a form used to collect child or partner support.

Form Adopted for Mandatory Use
Judicial Council of California
FL-103 [New January 1, 2005]

PETITION—DOMESTIC PARTNERSHIP
(Family Law)

Family Code, §§ 299, 2330;
Cal. Rules of Court, rule 5.28
www.courtinfo.ca.gov

DOMESTIC PARTNERSHIP OF (Last name, first name of each party):	CASE NUMBER:

5. DECLARATION REGARDING COMMUNITY AND QUASI-COMMUNITY ASSETS AND DEBTS AS CURRENTLY KNOWN

a. ☐ There are no such assets or debts subject to disposition by the court in this proceeding.

b. ☐ All such assets and debts are listed ☐ in *Property Declaration* (form FL-160) ☐ in Attachment 5b. ☐ below (specify):

6. Petitioner requests

a. ☐ dissolution of the domestic partnership based on
   (1) ☐ irreconcilable differences. (Fam. Code, § 2310(a).)
   (2) ☐ incurable insanity. (Fam. Code, § 2310(b).)

b. ☐ legal separation of the domestic partnership based on
   (1) ☐ irreconcilable differences. (Fam. Code, § 2310(a).)
   (2) ☐ incurable insanity. (Fam. Code, § 2310(b).)

c. ☐ nullity of void domestic partnership based on
   (1) ☐ incest. (Fam. Code, § 2200.)
   (2) ☐ bigamy. (Fam. Code, § 2201.)

d. ☐ nullity of voidable domestic partnership based on
   (1) ☐ petitioner's age at time of registration of domestic partnership. (Fam. Code, § 2210(a).)
   (2) ☐ prior existing marriage or domestic partnership. (Fam. Code, § 2210(b).)
   (3) ☐ unsound mind. (Fam. Code, § 2210(c).)
   (4) ☐ fraud. (Fam. Code, § 2210(d).)
   (5) ☐ force. (Fam. Code, § 2210(e).)
   (6) ☐ physical incapacity. (Fam. Code, § 2210(f).)

7. Petitioner requests that the court grant the above relief and make injunctive (including restraining) and other orders as follows:

	Petitioner	Respondent	Joint	Other
a. Legal custody of children to	☐	☐	☐	☐
b. Physical custody of children to	☐	☐	☐	☐
c. Child visitation granted to	☐	☐	☐	☐

As requested in form: ☐ FL-311 ☐ FL-312 ☐ FL-341(C) ☐ FL-341(D) ☐ FL-341(E) ☐ Attachment 7c.

d. ☐ Determination of parentage of any children born to the Petitioner and Respondent prior to the domestic partnership.
e. ☐ Attorney fees and costs payable by ....
f. ☐ Partner support payable to ....
g. ☐ Terminate court's jurisdiction (ability) to award partner support to respondent.
h. ☐ Property rights be determined.
i. ☐ Petitioner's former name be restored to (specify):
j. ☐ Other (specify):

☐ Continued on Attachment 7j.

8. Child support—If there are minor children who were born to or adopted by the petitioner and respondent before or during this domestic partnership, the court will make orders for the support of the children upon request and submission of financial forms by the requesting party. An earnings assignment may be issued without further notice. Any party required to pay support must pay interest on overdue amounts at the "legal" rate, which is currently 10 percent.

9. I HAVE READ THE RESTRAINING ORDERS ON THE BACK OF THE SUMMONS, AND I UNDERSTAND THAT THEY APPLY TO ME WHEN THIS PETITION IS FILED.

I declare under penalty of perjury under the laws of the State of California that the foregoing is true and correct.

Date:

_____ ▶ _____
(TYPE OR PRINT NAME) (SIGNATURE OF PETITIONER)

Date:

_____ ▶ _____
(TYPE OR PRINT NAME) (SIGNATURE OF ATTORNEY FOR PETITIONER)

NOTICE: Dissolution or legal separation may automatically cancel the rights of a domestic partner under the other domestic partner's will, trust, retirement plan, power of attorney, pay-on-death bank account, survivorship rights to any property owned in joint tenancy, and any other similar thing. It does not automatically cancel the right of a domestic partner as beneficiary of the other partner's life insurance policy. You should review these matters, as well as any credit cards, other credit accounts, insurance policies, retirement plans, and credit reports, to determine whether they should be changed or whether you should take any other actions. However, some changes may require the agreement of your partner or a court order (see Fam. Code, §§ 231–235).

ATTORNEY OR PARTY WITHOUT ATTORNEY *(Name, State Bar number, and address):*	FOR COURT USE ONLY
TELEPHONE NO.: FAX NO. *(Optional):* E-MAIL ADDRESS *(Optional):* ATTORNEY FOR *(Name):*	

SUPERIOR COURT OF CALIFORNIA, COUNTY OF

STREET ADDRESS:

MAILING ADDRESS:

CITY AND ZIP CODE:

BRANCH NAME:

PETITIONER:

RESPONDENT:

DECLARATION UNDER UNIFORM CHILD CUSTODY JURISDICTION AND ENFORCEMENT ACT (UCCJEA)	CASE NUMBER:

1. **I am a party** to this proceeding to determine custody of a child.
2. ☐ My present address is not disclosed. It is confidential under Family Code section 3429. I have listed the address of the children presently residing with me as confidential.
3. *(Number):* minor children are subject to this proceeding as follows:
   (Insert the information requested below. The residence information must be given for the last FIVE years.)

a. Child's name		Place of birth	Date of birth	Sex
Period of residence	**Address**	**Person child lived with** *(name and present address)*		**Relationship**
to present	☐ Confidential			
to				
to				
to				

b. Child's name		Place of birth	Date of birth	Sex
☐ Residence information is the same as given above for child a. *(If NOT the same, provide the information below.)*				
Period of residence	**Address**	**Person child lived with** *(name and present address)*		**Relationship**
to present	☐ Confidential			
to				
to				

c. ☐ Additional children are listed on Attachment 3c. *(Provide all requested information for additional children.)*

Form Approved for Optional Use
Judicial Council of California
FL-105/GC-120 [Rev. January 1, 2007]

**DECLARATION UNDER UNIFORM CHILD CUSTODY
JURISDICTION AND ENFORCEMENT ACT (UCCJEA)**

Family Code, § 3400 et seq.
Probate Code, §§ 1510(f), 1512
www.courtinfo.ca.gov

SHORT TITLE:	CASE NUMBER:

4. Have you participated as a party or a witness or in some other capacity in another litigation or custody proceeding, in California or elsewhere, concerning custody of a child subject to this proceeding?

☐ No ☐ Yes *(If yes, provide the following information):*

a. Name of each child:

b. I was a: ☐ party ☐ witness ☐ other *(specify):*

c. Court *(specify name, state, location):*

d. Court order or judgment *(date):*

5. Do you have information about a custody proceeding pending in a California court or any other court concerning a child in this case, other than that stated in item 4?

☐ No ☐ Yes *(If yes, provide the following information):*

a. Name of each child:

b. Nature of proceeding: ☐ dissolution or divorce ☐ guardianship ☐ adoption ☐ other *(specify):*

c. Court *(specify name, state, location):*

d. Status of proceeding:

6. ☐ One or more domestic violence restraining /protective orders are now in effect. (Attach a copy of the orders if you have one.)
The orders are from the following court or courts *(specify county and state):*

a. ☐ Criminal: County/state: _____
Case No. (*if known*): _____

b. ☐ Family: County/state: _____
Case No. (*if known*): _____

c. ☐ Juvenile: County/state: _____
Case No. (*if known*): _____

d. ☐ Other: County/state: _____
Case No. (*if known*): _____

7. Do you know of any person who is not a party to this proceeding who has physical custody or claims to have custody of or visitation rights with any child in this case?

☐ No ☐ Yes *(If yes, provide the following information):*

a. Name and address of person	b. Name and address of person	c. Name and address of person
☐ Has physical custody ☐ Claims custody rights ☐ Claims visitation rights	☐ Has physical custody ☐ Claims custody rights ☐ Claims visitation rights	☐ Has physical custody ☐ Claims custody rights ☐ Claims visitation rights
Name of each child	Name of each child	Name of each child

I declare under penalty of perjury under the laws of the State of California that the foregoing is true and correct.

Date:

▶

_____
(TYPE OR PRINT NAME)

_____
(SIGNATURE OF DECLARANT)

8. ☐ Number of pages attached after this page: _____

NOTICE TO DECLARANT: You have a continuing duty to inform this court if you obtain any information about a custody proceeding in a California court or any other court concerning a child subject to this proceeding.

DECLARATION UNDER UNIFORM CHILD CUSTODY JURISDICTION AND ENFORCEMENT ACT (UCCJEA)

1
2
3
4
5
6
7
8
9
10
11
12
13
14
15
16
17
18
19
20
21
22
23
24
25
26 *(Required for verified pleading)* The items on this page stated on information and belief are *(specify item numbers, **not** line numbers)*:
27

This page may be used with any Judicial Council form or any other paper filed with the court.

Page _____

Form Approved by the
Judicial Council of California
MC-020 [New January 1, 1987]

ADDITIONAL PAGE
Attach to Judicial Council Form or Other Court Paper

CRC 201, 501

ATTORNEY OR PARTY WITHOUT ATTORNEY *(Name, State Bar number, and address)*:

TELEPHONE NO.: FAX NO. *(Optional)*:

E-MAIL ADDRESS *(Optional)*:

ATTORNEY FOR *(Name)*:

FOR COURT USE ONLY

SUPERIOR COURT OF CALIFORNIA, COUNTY OF

STREET ADDRESS:

MAILING ADDRESS:

CITY AND ZIP CODE:

BRANCH NAME:

MARRIAGE OF

PETITIONER:

RESPONDENT:

RESPONSE ☐ **and REQUEST FOR**
☐ **Dissolution of Marriage**
☐ **Legal Separation**
☐ **Nullity of Marriage** ☐ AMENDED

CASE NUMBER:

1. RESIDENCE (Dissolution only) ☐ Petitioner ☐ Respondent has been a resident of this state for at least six months and of this county for at least three months immediately preceding the filing of the *Petition for Dissolution of Marriage.*

2. STATISTICAL FACTS
   a. Date of marriage:
   b. Date of separation:
   c. Time from date of marriage to date of separation *(specify)*:
   Years: Months:

3. DECLARATION REGARDING MINOR CHILDREN *(include children of this relationship born prior to or during the marriage or adopted during the marriage)*:
   a. ☐ There are no minor children.
   b. ☐ The minor children are:

Child's name	Birthdate	Age	Sex

   ☐ Continued on Attachment 3b.
   c. If there are minor children of the Petitioner and Respondent, a completed *Declaration Under Uniform Child Custody Jurisdiction and Enforcement Act (UCCJEA)* (form FL-105) must be attached.
   d. ☐ A completed voluntary declaration of paternity regarding minor children born to the Petitioner and Respondent prior to the marriage is attached.

4. SEPARATE PROPERTY
   Respondent requests that the assets and debts listed ☐ in *Property Declaration* (form FL-160) ☐ in Attachment 4
   ☐ below be confirmed as separate property.

Item	Confirm to

NOTICE: You may redact (black out) social security numbers from any written material filed with the court in this case other than a form used to collect child or spousal support.

Form Adopted for Mandatory Use
Judicial Council of California
FL-120 [Rev. January 1, 2005]

RESPONSE—MARRIAGE
(Family Law)

Family Code, § 2020
www.courtinfo.ca.gov.

RESPONSE—MARRIAGE
(Family Law)

MARRIAGE OF (last name, first name of parties):	CASE NUMBER:

5. **DECLARATION REGARDING COMMUNITY AND QUASI-COMMUNITY ASSETS AND DEBTS AS CURRENTLY KNOWN**

   a. ☐ There are no such assets or debts subject to disposition by the court in this proceeding.

   b. ☐ All such assets and debts are listed ☐ in *Property Declaration* (form FL-160) ☐ in Attachment 5b. ☐
below (specify):

6. ☐ **Respondent contends** that the parties were never legally married.

7. ☐ **Respondent denies** the grounds set forth in item 6 of the petition.

8. **Respondent requests**

   a. ☐ dissolution of the marriage based on

      (1) ☐ irreconcilable differences. (Fam. Code, § 2310(a).)

      (2) ☐ incurable insanity. (Fam. Code, § 2310(b).)

   b. ☐ legal separation of the parties based on

      (1) ☐ irreconcilable differences. (Fam. Code, § 2310(a).)

      (2) ☐ incurable insanity. (Fam. Code, § 2310(b).)

   c. ☐ nullity of void marriage based on

      (1) ☐ incestuous marriage. (Fam. Code, § 2200.)

      (2) ☐ bigamous marriage. (Fam. Code, § 2201.)

   d. ☐ nullity of voidable marriage based on

      (1) ☐ respondent's age at time of marriage.
(Fam. Code, § 2210(a).)

      (2) ☐ prior existing marriage.
(Fam. Code, § 2210(b).)

      (3) ☐ unsound mind. (Fam. Code, § 2210(c).)

      (4) ☐ fraud. (Fam. Code, § 2210(d).)

      (5) ☐ force. (Fam. Code, § 2210(e).)

      (6) ☐ physical incapacity. (Fam. Code, § 2210(f).)

9. **Respondent requests** that the court grant the above relief and make injunctive (including restraining) and other orders as follows:

	Petitioner	Respondent	Joint	Other
a. Legal custody of children to	☐	☐	☐	☐
b. Physical custody of children to	☐	☐	☐	☐
c. Child visitation be granted to	☐	☐	☐	☐

     As requested in form: ☐ FL-311 ☐ FL-312 ☐ FL-341(C) ☐ FL-341(D) ☐ FL-341(E) ☐ Attachment 9c.

   d. ☐ Determination of parentage of any children born to the Petitioner and Respondent prior to the marriage.

   e. ☐ Attorney fees and costs payable by .... ☐ ☐

   f. ☐ Spousal support payable to (wage assignment will be issued) .... ☐ ☐

   g. ☐ Terminate the court's jurisdiction (ability) to award spousal support to Petitioner.

   h. ☐ Property rights be determined.

   i. ☐ Respondent's former name be restored to (specify):

   j. ☐ Other (specify):

   ☐ Continued on Attachment 9j.

10. **Child support—** If there are minor children born to or adopted by the Petitioner and Respondent before or during this marriage, the court will make orders for the support of the children upon request and submission of financial forms by the requesting party. An earnings assignment may be issued without further notice. Any party required to pay support must pay interest on overdue amounts at the "legal" rate, which is currently 10 percent.

I declare under penalty of perjury under the laws of the State of California that the foregoing is true and correct.

Date:

_____   ►   _____

(TYPE OR PRINT NAME)   (SIGNATURE OF RESPONDENT)

Date:

_____   ►   _____

(TYPE OR PRINT NAME)   (SIGNATURE OF ATTORNEY FOR RESPONDENT)

The original response must be filed in the court with proof of service of a copy on Petitioner.

ATTORNEY OR PARTY WITHOUT ATTORNEY *(Name, State Bar number, and address)*:	FOR COURT USE ONLY
TELEPHONE NO.: FAX NO. *(Optional)*: E–MAIL ADDRESS *(Optional)*: ATTORNEY FOR *(Name)*:	

SUPERIOR COURT OF CALIFORNIA, COUNTY OF

STREET ADDRESS:

MAILING ADDRESS:

CITY AND ZIP CODE:

BRANCH NAME:

DOMESTIC PARTNERSHIP OF

PETITIONER:

RESPONDENT:

RESPONSE ☐ and **REQUEST FOR** ☐ **Dissolution of Domestic Partnership** ☐ **Legal Separation of Domestic Partnership** ☐ **Nullity of Domestic Partnership** ☐ **AMENDED**	CASE NUMBER:

1. STATISTICAL FACTS
   a. Date of registration of domestic partnership:
   b. Date of separation:
   c. Time from date of registration of domestic partnership to date of separation *(specify)*:   Years   Months

2. RESIDENCE (Partnerships established out of state only)
   a. ☐ Our domestic partnership was established in another state *(specify state)*:
   b. ☐ Petitioner ☐ Respondent has been a resident of this state of California for at least six months and of this county for at least three months immediately preceding the filing of this *Petition for Dissolution of Domestic Partnership.*

3. DECLARATION REGARDING MINOR CHILDREN *(include children of this relationship born prior to or during this domestic partnership or adopted during this domestic partnership)*:
   a. ☐ There are no minor children.
   b. ☐ The minor children are:

Child's name	Birthdate	Age	Sex

   ☐ Continued on Attachment 3b.
   c. If there are minor children of the petitioner and the respondent, a completed *Declaration Under Uniform Child Custody Jurisdiction and Enforcement Act (UCCJEA)* (form FL-105) must be attached.

4. SEPARATE PROPERTY
   Respondent requests that the assets and debts listed ☐ in *Property Declaration* (form FL-160) ☐ in Attachment 4
   ☐ below   be confirmed as separate property.

Item	Confirm to

NOTICE: You may redact (black out) social security numbers from any written material filed with the court in this case other than a form used to collect child or partner support.

Form Adopted for Mandatory Use
Judicial Council of California
FL-123 [New January 1, 2005]

RESPONSE—DOMESTIC PARTNERSHIP
(Family Law)

Family Code, §§ 299, 2020
www.courtinfo.ca.gov

5. DECLARATION REGARDING COMMUNITY AND QUASI-COMMUNITY ASSETS AND DEBTS AS CURRENTLY KNOWN
    a. ☐ There are no such assets or debts subject to disposition by the court in this proceeding.
    b. ☐ All such assets and debts are listed ☐ in *Property Declaration* (form FL-160) ☐ in Attachment 5b.
          ☐ below (specify):

6. ☐ **Respondent contends** that there is not a valid domestic partnership or equivalent.

7. ☐ **Respondent denies** the grounds set forth in item 6 of the petition.

8. **Respondent requests**
    a. ☐ dissolution of the domestic partnership based on   d. ☐ nullity of voidable domestic partnership based on
        (1) ☐ irreconcilable differences. (Fam. Code, § 2310(a).)   (1) ☐ respondent's age at time of domestic
        (2) ☐ incurable insanity. (Fam. Code, § 2310(b).)   partnership. (Fam. Code, § 2210(a).)
    b. ☐ legal separation of the domestic partners based on   (2) ☐ prior existing marriage or domestic
        (1) ☐ irreconcilable differences. (Fam. Code, § 2310(a).)   partnership. (Fam. Code, § 2210(b).)
        (2) ☐ incurable insanity. (Fam. Code, § 2310(b).)   (3) ☐ unsound mind. (Fam. Code, § 2210(c).)
    c. ☐ nullity of void domestic partnership based on   (4) ☐ fraud. (Fam. Code, § 2210(d).)
        (1) ☐ incest. (Fam. Code, § 2200.)   (5) ☐ force. (Fam. Code, § 2210(e).)
        (2) ☐ bigamy. (Fam. Code, § 2201.)   (6) ☐ physical incapacity. (Fam. Code, § 2210(f).)

9. **Respondent requests** that the court grant the above relief and make injunctive (including restraining) and other orders as follows:

	Petitioner	Respondent	Joint	Other
a. Legal custody of children to	☐	☐	☐	☐
b. Physical custody of children to	☐	☐	☐	☐
c. Child visitation granted to	☐	☐		☐

        As requested in form: ☐ FL-311 ☐ FL-312 ☐ FL-341(C) ☐ FL-341(D) ☐ FL-341(E) ☐ Attachment 9c.
    d. ☐ Determination of parentage of any children born to the petitioner and respondent prior to the domestic partnership.
    e. Attorney fees and costs payable by .... ☐ ☐
    f. Partner support payable to .... ☐ ☐
    g. ☐ Terminate court's jurisdiction (ability) to award partner support to the petitioner.
    h. ☐ Property rights be determined.
    i. ☐ Respondent's former name be restored to (specify):
    j. ☐ Other (specify):

        ☐ Continued on Attachment 9j.

10. **Child support** –If there are minor children who were born to or adopted by the petitioner and the respondent before or during this domestic partnership, the court will make orders for the support of the children upon request and submission of financial forms by the requesting party. An earnings assignment may be issued without further notice. Any party required to pay support must pay interest on overdue amounts at the "legal" rate, which is currently 10 percent.

I declare under penalty of perjury under the laws of the State of California that the foregoing is true and correct.

Date:

▶

_____
(TYPE OR PRINT NAME)

Date:

_____
(SIGNATURE OF RESPONDENT)

▶

_____
(TYPE OR PRINT NAME)

_____
(SIGNATURE OF ATTORNEY FOR RESPONDENT)

The original response must be filed in the court with proof of service of a copy on petitioner.

ATTORNEY OR PARTY WITHOUT ATTORNEY *(Name, State Bar number, and address):*

FOR COURT USE ONLY

TELEPHONE NO.:

FAX NO. *(Optional):*

E-MAIL ADDRESS *(Optional):*

ATTORNEY FOR *(Name):*

SUPERIOR COURT OF CALIFORNIA, COUNTY OF

STREET ADDRESS:

MAILING ADDRESS:

CITY AND ZIP CODE:

BRANCH NAME:

PETITIONER:

RESPONDENT:

APPEARANCE, STIPULATIONS, AND WAIVERS	CASE NUMBER:

1. **Appearance by respondent** *(you must choose one):*
   a. ☐ By filing this form, the respondent makes a general appearance.
   b. ☐ The respondent has previously made a general appearance.
   c. ☐ The respondent is a member of the military services of the United States of America and waives all rights under the Servicemembers Civil Relief Act (50 U.S.C. Appen. § 501 et seq.). No appearance fee is required.

2. **Agreements, stipulations, and waivers** *(choose all that apply):*
   a. ☐ The parties agree that this cause may be decided as an uncontested matter.
   b. ☐ The parties waive their rights to notice of trial, a statement of decision, a motion for new trial, and the right to appeal.
   c. ☐ This matter may be decided by a commissioner sitting as a temporary judge.
   d. ☐ We have a written agreement, or a stipulation for judgment will be submitted to the court.
   e. ☐ None of these agreements or waivers will apply unless the court approves the stipulation for judgment or incorporates the written settlement agreement into the judgment.
   f. ☐ This is a parentage case, and both parties have signed an *Advisement and Waiver of Rights Re: Establishment of Parental Relationship* (form FL-235) or its equivalent.

3. **Other** *(specify):*

Date: _____

_____
(TYPE OR PRINT NAME)

▶ _____
(SIGNATURE OF PETITIONER)

Date: _____

_____
(TYPE OR PRINT NAME)

▶ _____
(SIGNATURE OF RESPONDENT)

Date: _____

_____
(TYPE OR PRINT NAME)

▶ _____
(SIGNATURE OF ATTORNEY FOR PETITIONER)

Date: _____

_____
(TYPE OR PRINT NAME)

▶ _____
(SIGNATURE OF ATTORNEY FOR RESPONDENT)

Page 1 of 1

Form Approved for Optional Use
Judicial Council of California
FL-130 [Rev. January 1, 2006]

APPEARANCE, STIPULATIONS, AND WAIVERS
(Family Law—Uniform Parentage—Custody and Support)

www.courtinfo.ca.gov

ATTORNEY OR PARTY WITHOUT ATTORNEY *(Name, State Bar number, and address)*:	*FOR COURT USE ONLY*
TELEPHONE NO.: FAX NO. *(Optional)*: E–MAIL ADDRESS *(Optional)*: ATTORNEY FOR *(Name)*:	

SUPERIOR COURT OF CALIFORNIA, COUNTY OF
STREET ADDRESS:
MAILING ADDRESS:
CITY AND ZIP CODE:
BRANCH NAME:

PETITIONER:

RESPONDENT:

PROOF OF SERVICE OF SUMMONS	CASE NUMBER:

1. At the time of service I was at least 18 years of age and not a party to this action. **I served the respondent with copies of:**

    a. ☐ Family Law: *Petition* (form FL-100), *Summons* (form FL-110), and blank *Response* (form FL-120)

    –or–

    b. ☐ Family Law—Domestic Partnership: *Petition—Domestic Partnership* (form FL-103), *Summons* (form FL-110), and blank *Response—Domestic Partnership* (form FL-123)

    –or–

    c. ☐ Uniform Parentage: *Petition to Establish Parental Relationship* (form FL-200), *Summons* (form FL-210), and blank *Response to Petition to Establish Parental Relationship* (form FL-220)

    –or–

    d. ☐ Custody and Support: *Petition for Custody and Support of Minor Children* (form FL-260), *Summons* (form FL-210), and blank *Response to Petition for Custody and Support of Minor Children* (form FL-270)

    and

    e. ☐ (1) ☐ Completed and blank *Declaration Under Uniform Child Custody Jurisdiction and Enforcement Act* (form FL-105)

    (2) ☐ Completed and blank *Declaration of Disclosure* (form FL-140)

    (3) ☐ Completed and blank *Schedule of Assets and Debts* (form FL-142)

    (4) ☐ Completed and blank *Income and Expense Declaration* (form FL-150)

    (5) ☐ Completed and blank *Financial Statement (Simplified)* (form FL-155)

    (6) ☐ Completed and blank *Property Declaration* (form FL-160)

    (7) ☐ *Order to Show Cause* (form FL-300), *Application for Order and Supporting Declaration* (form FL-310), and blank *Responsive Declaration to Order to Show Cause or Notice of Motion* (form FL-320)

    (8) ☐ Other *(specify)*:

2. Address where respondent was served:

3. I served the respondent by the following means *(check proper box)*:

    a. ☐ **Personal service.** I personally delivered the copies to the respondent (Code Civ. Proc., § 415.10)
    on *(date)*: at *(time)*:

    b. ☐ **Substituted service.** I left the copies with or in the presence of *(name)*:
    who is *(specify title or relationship to respondent)*:

    (1) ☐ **(Business)** a person at least 18 years of age who was apparently in charge at the office or usual place of business of the respondent. I informed him or her of the general nature of the papers

    (2) ☐ **(Home)** a competent member of the household (at least 18 years of age) at the home of the respondent. I informed him or her of the general nature of the papers

Page 1 of 2

PROOF OF SERVICE OF SUMMONS
(Family Law—Uniform Parentage—Custody and Support)

PETITIONER:	CASE NUMBER:
RESPONDENT:	

3. b. (cont.) on (date): ___ at (time): ___

I thereafter mailed additional copies (by first class, postage prepaid) to the respondent at the place where the copies were left (Code Civ. Proc., § 415.20b) on (date):

A declaration of diligence is attached, stating the actions taken to first attempt personal service.

c. ☐ **Mail and acknowledgment service.** I mailed the copies to the respondent, addressed as shown in item 2, by first-class mail, postage prepaid, on (date): ___ from (city):

(1) ☐ with two copies of the Notice and Acknowledgment of Receipt (Family Law) (form FL-117) and a postage-paid return envelope addressed to me. **(Attach completed Notice and Acknowledgment of Receipt (Family Law) (form FL-117).)** (Code Civ. Proc., § 415.30.)

(2) ☐ to an address outside California (by registered or certified mail with return receipt requested). **(Attach signed return receipt or other evidence of actual delivery to the respondent.)** (Code Civ. Proc., § 415.40.)

d. ☐ **Other (specify code section):**

☐ Continued on Attachment 3d.

4. The "NOTICE TO THE PERSON SERVED" on the *Summons* was completed as follows (Code Civ. Proc., §§ 412.30, 415.10, 474):

a. ☐ As an individual

b. ☐ On behalf of respondent who is a

(1) ☐ minor. (Code Civ. Proc., § 416.60.)

(2) ☐ ward or conservatee. (Code Civ. Proc., § 416.70.)

(3) ☐ other (specify):

5. **Person who served papers**

Name:

Address:

or

Telephone number:

This person is

a. ☐ exempt from registration under Business and Professions Code section 22350(b).

b. ☐ not a registered California process server.

c. ☐ a registered California process server: ☐ an employee or   ☐ an independent contractor

(1) Registration no.:

(2) County:

d. **The fee for service was (specify):** $

6. ☐ **I declare under penalty of perjury under the laws of the State of California that the foregoing is true and correct.**

—or—

7. ☐ **I am a California sheriff, marshal, or constable, and I certify that the foregoing is true and correct.**

Date:

_____   ▶   _____
(NAME OF PERSON WHO SERVED PAPERS)   (SIGNATURE OF PERSON WHO SERVED PAPERS)

ATTORNEY OR PARTY WITHOUT ATTORNEY *(Name, State Bar number, and address):*	*FOR COURT USE ONLY*

TELEPHONE NO.:   FAX NO. *(Optional):*

E–MAIL ADDRESS *(Optional):*

ATTORNEY FOR *(Name):*

SUPERIOR COURT OF CALIFORNIA, COUNTY OF

STREET ADDRESS:

MAILING ADDRESS:

CITY AND ZIP CODE:

BRANCH NAME:

PETITIONER:

RESPONDENT:

OTHER:

NOTICE AND ACKNOWLEDGMENT OF RECEIPT	CASE NUMBER:

To *(name of individual being served):* _____

NOTICE

The documents identified below are being served on you by mail with this acknowledgment form. You must personally sign, or a person authorized by you must sign, this form to acknowledge receipt of the documents.

If the documents described below include a summons and you fail to complete and return this acknowledgment form to the sender within 20 days of the date of mailing, you will be liable for the reasonable expenses incurred after that date in serving you or attempting to serve you with these documents by any other methods permitted by law. If you return this form to the sender, service of a summons is deemed complete on the date you sign the acknowledgment of receipt below. This is **not** an answer to the action. If you do not agree with what is being requested, you must submit a completed *Response* form to the court within 30 calendar days.

Date of mailing: _____

▶

_____   _____
(TYPE OR PRINT NAME)   (SIGNATURE OF SENDER—MUST NOT BE A PARTY IN THIS CASE
AND MUST BE 18 OR OLDER)

ACKNOWLEDGMENT OF RECEIPT
(To be completed by sender before mailing)

I agree I received the following:

a. ☐ Family Law: *Petition* (form FL-100), *Summons* (form FL-110), and blank *Response* (form FL-120)

b. ☐ Family Law—Domestic Partnership: *Petition—Domestic Partnership* (form FL-103), *Summons* (form FL-110), and blank *Response—Domestic Partnership* (form FL-123)

c. ☐ Uniform Parentage: *Petition to Establish Parental Relationship* (form FL-200), *Summons* (form FL-210), and blank *Response to Petition to Establish Parental Relationship* (form FL-220)

d. ☐ Custody and Support: *Petition for Custody and Support of Minor Children* (form FL-260), *Summons* (form FL-210), and blank *Response to Petition for Custody and Support of Minor Children* (form FL-270)

e. ☐ (1) ☐ Completed and blank *Declaration Under Uniform Child Custody Jurisdiction and Enforcement Act (UCCJEA)* (form FL-105)

(2) ☐ Completed and blank *Declaration of Disclosure* (form FL-140)

(3) ☐ Completed and blank *Schedule of Assets and Debts* (form FL-142)

(4) ☐ Completed and blank *Income and Expense Declaration* (form FL-150)

(5) ☐ Completed and blank *Financial Statement (Simplified)* (form FL-155)

(6) ☐ *Order to Show Cause* (form FL-300), *Application for Order and Supporting Declaration* (form FL-310), and blank *Responsive Declaration to Order to Show Cause or Notice of Motion* (form FL-320)

(7) ☐ Other *(specify):*

(To be completed by recipient)

Date this acknowledgment is signed: _____

▶

_____   _____
(TYPE OR PRINT NAME)   (SIGNATURE OF PERSON ACKNOWLEDGING RECEIPT)

Page 1 of 1

Form Approved for Optional Use Judicial Council of California FL-117 [Rev. January 1, 2005]	**NOTICE AND ACKNOWLEDGMENT OF RECEIPT** **(Family Law)**	Code of Civil Procedure, §§ 415.30, 417.10 *www.courtinfo.ca.gov*

ATTORNEY OR PARTY WITHOUT ATTORNEY OR GOVERNMENTAL AGENCY (under Family Code, §§ 17400, 17406)
(Name, state bar number, and address):

	FOR COURT USE ONLY

TELEPHONE NO.:   FAX NO.:

ATTORNEY FOR *(Name):*

SUPERIOR COURT OF CALIFORNIA, COUNTY OF

STREET ADDRESS:

MAILING ADDRESS:

CITY AND ZIP CODE:

BRANCH NAME:

PETITIONER/PLAINTIFF:

RESPONDENT/DEFENDANT:

OTHER PARENT:

PROOF OF SERVICE BY MAIL	CASE NUMBER:

NOTICE: To serve temporary restraining orders you must use personal service (see form FL-330).

1. I am at least 18 years of age, not a party to this action, and I am a resident of or employed in the county where the mailing took place.

2. My residence or business address is:

3. I served a copy of the following documents *(specify):*

by enclosing them in an envelope AND

   a. ☐ **depositing** the sealed envelope with the United States Postal Service with the postage fully prepaid.

   b. ☐ **placing** the envelope for collection and mailing on the date and at the place shown in item 4 following our ordinary business practices. I am readily familiar with this business's practice for collecting and processing correspondence for mailing. On the same day that correspondence is placed for collection and mailing, it is deposited in the ordinary course of business with the United States Postal Service in a sealed envelope with postage fully prepaid.

4. The envelope was addressed and mailed as follows:

   a. Name of person served:

   b. Address:

   c. Date mailed:

   d. Place of mailing *(city and state):*

5. I declare under penalty of perjury under the laws of the State of California that the foregoing is true and correct.

Date:

▶

_____
(TYPE OR PRINT NAME)

_____
(SIGNATURE OF PERSON COMPLETING THIS FORM)

Page 1 of 2

Form Approved for Optional Use
Judicial Council of California
FL-335 [Rev. January 1, 2003]

PROOF OF SERVICE BY MAIL

Code of Civil Procedure, §§ 1013, 1013a
www.courtinfo.ca.gov

INFORMATION SHEET FOR PROOF OF SERVICE BY MAIL

Use these instructions to complete the *Proof of Service by Mail* (form FL-335).

A person at least 18 years of age or older must serve the documents. There are two ways to serve documents: (1) personal delivery and (2) by mail. See the *Proof of Personal Service* (form FL-330) if the documents are being personally served. The person who serves the documents must complete a proof of service form for the documents being served. **You cannot serve documents if you are a party to the action.**

INSTRUCTIONS FOR THE PERSON WHO SERVES THE DOCUMENTS (TYPE OR PRINT IN BLACK INK)

You must complete a proof of service for each package of documents you serve. For example, if you serve the Respondent and the Other Parent, you must complete two proofs of service, one for the Respondent and one for the Other Parent.

Complete the top section of the proof of service forms as follows:

First box, left side: In this box print the name, address, and phone number of the person for whom you are serving the documents.

Second box, left side: Print the name of the county in which the legal action is filed and the court's address in this box. Use the same address for the court that is on the documents you are serving.

Third box, left side: Print the names of the Petitioner/Plaintiff, Respondent/Defendant, and Other Parent in this box. Use the same names listed on the documents you are serving.

First box, top of form, right side: Leave this box blank for the court's use.

Second box, right side: Print the case number in this box. This number is also stated on the documents you are serving.

You cannot serve a temporary restraining order by mail. You must serve those documents by personal service.

1. You are stating that you are at least 18 years old and that you are not a party to this action. You are also stating that you either live in or are employed in the county where the mailing took place.
2. Print your home or business address.
3. List the name of each document that you mailed (the exact names are listed on the bottoms of the forms).
  a. Check this box if you put the documents in the regular U.S. mail.
  b. Check this box if you put the mail at your place of employment.
4. a. Print the name you put on the envelope containing the documents.
  b. Print the address you put on the envelope containing the documents.
  c. Write in the date that you put the envelope containing the documents in the mail.
  d. Write in the city and state you were in when you mailed the envelope containing the documents.
5. You are stating under penalty of perjury that the information you have provided is true and correct.

Print your name, fill in the date, and sign the form.

If you need additional assistance with this form, contact the Family Law Facilitator in your county.

ATTORNEY OR PARTY WITHOUT ATTORNEY OR GOVERNMENTAL AGENCY (under Family Code, §§ 17400, 17406
(Name, state bar number, and address):

FOR COURT USE ONLY

TELEPHONE NO.:   FAX NO.:

ATTORNEY FOR *(Name):*

SUPERIOR COURT OF CALIFORNIA, COUNTY OF

STREET ADDRESS:

MAILING ADDRESS:

CITY AND ZIP CODE:

BRANCH NAME:

PETITIONER/PLAINTIFF:

RESPONDENT/DEFENDANT:

OTHER PARENT:

PROOF OF PERSONAL SERVICE

CASE NUMBER:

1. I am at least 18 years old, not a party to this action, and not a protected person listed in any of the orders.

2. Person served *(name):*

3. I served copies of the following documents *(specify):*

4. By personally delivering copies to the person served, as follows:
   a. Date: b. Time:
   c. Address:

5. I am
   a. ☐ not a registered California process server.
   b. ☐ a registered California process server.
   c. ☐ an employee or independent contractor of a registered California process server.
   d. ☐ exempt from registration under Bus. & Prof. Code section 22350(b).
   e. ☐ a California sheriff or marshal.

6. My name, address, and telephone number, and, if applicable, county of registration and number *(specify):*

7. ☐ I declare under penalty of perjury under the laws of the State of California that the foregoing is true and correct.

8. ☐ I am a California sheriff or marshal and I certify that the foregoing is true and correct.

Date:

▶

_____
(TYPE OR PRINT NAME OF PERSON WHO SERVED THE PAPERS)

_____
(SIGNATURE OF PERSON WHO SERVED THE PAPERS)

Form Approved for Optional Use
Judicial Council of California
FL-330 [Rev. January 1, 2003]

PROOF OF PERSONAL SERVICE

Code of Civil Procedure, § 1011
www.courtinfo.ca.gov

INFORMATION SHEET FOR PROOF OF PERSONAL SERVICE

Use these instructions to complete the *Proof of Personal Service* (form FL-330).

A person at least 18 years of age or older must serve the documents. There are two ways to serve documents: (1) personal delivery and (2) by mail. See the *Proof of Service by Mail* (form FL-335) if the documents are being served by mail. The person who serves the documents must complete a proof of service form for the documents being served. **You cannot serve documents if you are a party to the action.**

INSTRUCTIONS FOR THE PERSON WHO SERVES THE DOCUMENTS (TYPE OR PRINT IN BLACK INK)

You must complete a proof of service for each package of documents you serve. For example, if you serve the Respondent and the Other Parent, you must complete two proofs of service, one for the Respondent and one for the Other Parent.

Complete the top section of the proof of service forms as follows:

First box, left side: In this box print the name, address, and phone number of the person for whom you are serving the documents.

Second box, left side: Print the name of the county in which the legal action is filed and the court's address in this box. Use the same address for the court that is on the documents you are serving.

Third box, left side: Print the names of the Petitioner/Plaintiff, Respondent/Defendant, and Other Parent in this box. Use the same names listed on the documents you are serving.

First box, top of form, right side: Leave this box blank for the court's use.

Second box, right side: Print the case number in this box. This number is also stated on the documents you are serving.

1. You are stating that you are over the age of 18 and that you are neither a party of this action nor a protected person listed in any of the orders.
2. Print the name of the party to whom you handed the documents.
3. List the name of each document that you delivered to the party.
4. a. Write in the date that you delivered the documents to the party.
   b. Write in the time of day that you delivered the documents to the party.
   c. Print the address where you delivered the documents.
5. Check the box that applies to you. If you are a private person serving the documents for a party, check box "a."
6. Print your name, address, and telephone number. If applicable, include the county in which you are registered as a process server and your registration number.
7. You must check this box if you are not a California sheriff or marshal. You are stating under penalty of perjury that the information you have provided is true and correct.
8. Do not check this box unless you are a California sheriff or marshal.

Print your name, fill in the date, and sign the form.

If you need additional assistance with this form, contact the Family Law Facilitator in your county.

ATTORNEY OR PARTY WITHOUT ATTORNEY *(Name and Address)*:

TELEPHONE NO.:

ATTORNEY FOR *(Name)*:

SUPERIOR COURT OF CALIFORNIA, COUNTY OF

STREET ADDRESS:

MAILING ADDRESS:

CITY AND ZIP CODE:

BRANCH NAME:

PETITIONER:

RESPONDENT:

	CASE NUMBER:
DECLARATION OF DISCLOSURE ☐ **Petitioner's** ☐ **Preliminary** ☐ **Respondent's** ☐ **Final**	

DO NOT FILE WITH THE COURT

Both the preliminary and the final declaration of disclosure must be served on the other party with certain exceptions. Neither disclosure is filed with the court. A declaration stating service was made of the final declaration of disclosure must be filed with the court (see form FL-141).

A preliminary declaration of disclosure but not a final declaration of disclosure is required in the case of a summary dissolution (see Family Code section 2109) or in a default judgment (see Family Code section 2110) provided the default is not a stipulated judgment or a judgment based upon a marriage settlement agreement.

A declaration of disclosure is required in a nullity or legal separation action as well as in a dissolution action.

Attached are the following:

1. ☐ A completed *Schedule of Assets and Debts* (form FL-142).

2. ☐ A completed *Income and Expense Declaration* (form FL-150 (as applicable)).

3. ☐ A statement of all material facts and information regarding valuation of all assets that are community property or in which the community has an interest *(not a form)*.

4. ☐ A statement of all material facts and information regarding obligations for which the community is liable *(not a form)*.

5. ☐ An accurate and complete written disclosure of any investment opportunity, business opportunity, or other income-producing opportunity presented since the date of separation that results from any investment, significant business, or other income-producing opportunity from the date of marriage to the date of separation *(not a form)*.

I declare under penalty of perjury under the laws of the State of California that the foregoing is true and correct.

Date:

_____

(TYPE OR PRINT NAME)

▶

_____

(SIGNATURE)

Page 1 of 1

DECLARATION OF DISCLOSURE
(Family Law)

ATTORNEY OR PARTY WITHOUT ATTORNEY *(Name and Address):*	TELEPHONE NO.:

ATTORNEY FOR *(Name):*

SUPERIOR COURT OF CALIFORNIA, COUNTY OF

PETITIONER:

RESPONDENT:

SCHEDULE OF ASSETS AND DEBTS ☐ **Petitioner's** ☐ **Respondent's**	CASE NUMBER:

— **INSTRUCTIONS** —

List all your known community and separate assets or debts. Include assets even if they are in the possession of another person, including your spouse. If you contend an asset or debt is separate, put P (for Petitioner) or R (for Respondent) in the first column (separate property) to indicate to whom you contend it belongs.

All values should be as of the date of signing the declaration unless you specify a different valuation date with the description. For additional space, use a continuation sheet numbered to show which item is being continued.

ITEM NO.	ASSETS DESCRIPTION	SEP. PROP	DATE ACQUIRED	CURRENT GROSS FAIR MARKET VALUE	AMOUNT OF MONEY OWED OR ENCUMBRANCE
1.	REAL ESTATE *(Give street addresses and attach copies of deeds with legal descriptions and latest lender's statement.)*			$	$
2.	HOUSEHOLD FURNITURE, FURNISHINGS, APPLIANCES *(Identify.)*				
3.	JEWELRY, ANTIQUES, ART, COIN COLLECTIONS, etc. *(Identify.)*				

Form Approved for Optional Use
Judicial Council of California
FL-142 [Rev. January 1, 2005]

SCHEDULE OF ASSETS AND DEBTS
(Family Law)

Code of Civil Procedure, §§ 2030(c), 2033.5
www.courtinfo.ca.gov

ITEM NO.	ASSETS DESCRIPTION	SEP. PROP	DATE ACQUIRED	CURRENT GROSS FAIR MARKET VALUE	AMOUNT OF MONEY OWED OR ENCUMBRANCE
				$	$
4.	VEHICLES, BOATS, TRAILERS *(Describe and attach copy of title document.)*				
5.	SAVINGS ACCOUNTS *(Account name, account number, bank, and branch. Attach copy of latest statement.)*				
6.	CHECKING ACCOUNTS *(Account name and number, bank, and branch. Attach copy of latest statement.)*				
7.	CREDIT UNION, OTHER DEPOSIT ACCOUNTS *(Account name and number, bank, and branch. Attach copy of latest statement.)*				
8.	CASH *(Give location.)*				
9.	TAX REFUND				
10.	LIFE INSURANCE WITH CASH SURRENDER OR LOAN VALUE *(Attach copy of declaration page for each policy.)*				

SCHEDULE OF ASSETS AND DEBTS
(Family Law)

ITEM NO.	ASSETS DESCRIPTION	SEP. PROP	DATE ACQUIRED	CURRENT GROSS FAIR MARKET VALUE	AMOUNT OF MONEY OWED OR ENCUMBRANCE
11.	STOCKS, BONDS, SECURED NOTES, MUTUAL FUNDS *(Give certificate number and attach copy of the certificate or copy of latest statement.)*			$	$
12.	RETIREMENT AND PENSIONS *(Attach copy of latest summary plan documents and latest benefit statement.)*				
13.	PROFIT - SHARING, ANNUITIES, IRAS, DEFERRED COMPENSATION *(Attach copy of latest statement.)*				
14.	ACCOUNTS RECEIVABLE AND UNSECURED NOTES *(Attach copy of each.)*				
15.	PARTNERSHIPS AND OTHER BUSINESS INTERESTS *(Attach copy of most current K-1 form and Schedule C.)*				
16.	OTHER ASSETS				
17.	TOTAL ASSETS FROM CONTINUATION SHEET				
18.	TOTAL ASSETS			$	$

SCHEDULE OF ASSETS AND DEBTS
(Family Law)

ITEM NO.	DEBTS—SHOW TO WHOM OWED	SEP. PROP.	TOTAL OWING	DATE INCURRED
19.	STUDENT LOANS *(Give details.)*		$	
20.	TAXES *(Give details.)*			
21.	SUPPORT ARREARAGES *(Attach copies of orders and statements.)*			
22.	LOANS—UNSECURED *(Give bank name and loan number and attach copy of latest statement.)*			
23.	CREDIT CARDS *(Give creditor's name and address and the account number. Attach copy of latest statement.)*			
24.	OTHER DEBTS *(Specify.):*			
25.	TOTAL DEBTS FROM CONTINUATION SHEET			
26.	TOTAL DEBTS		$	

27. ☐ *(Specify number):* _____ pages are attached as continuation sheets.

I declare under penalty of perjury under the laws of the State of California that the foregoing is true and correct.

Date:

▶

_____
(TYPE OR PRINT NAME)

_____
(SIGNATURE OF DECLARANT)

SCHEDULE OF ASSETS AND DEBTS
(Family Law)

ATTORNEY OR PARTY WITHOUT ATTORNEY *(Name, state bar number, and address):*

FOR COURT USE ONLY

TELEPHONE NO.:   FAX NO.:

ATTORNEY FOR *(Name):*

SUPERIOR COURT OF CALIFORNIA, COUNTY OF

STREET ADDRESS:

MAILING ADDRESS:

CITY AND ZIP CODE:

BRANCH NAME:

PETITIONER:

RESPONDENT:

DECLARATION REGARDING SERVICE OF DECLARATION OF DISCLOSURE AND INCOME AND EXPENSE DECLARATION ☐ **Petitioner's** ☐ **Preliminary** ☐ **Respondent's** ☐ **Final**	CASE NUMBER:

1. I am the ☐ Attorney for ☐ Petitioner ☐ Respondent   in this matter.

2. ☐ Petitioner's ☐ Respondent's *Preliminary Declaration of Disclosure* and *Income and Expense Declaration* was served on:
☐ Attorney for ☐ Petitioner ☐ Respondent by: ☐ personal service ☐ mail ☐ other *(specify):*

   on *(date):*

3. ☐ Petitioner's ☐ Respondent's *Final Declaration of Disclosure* and *Income and Expense Declaration* was served on:
☐ Attorney for ☐ Petitioner ☐ Respondent by: ☐ personal service ☐ mail ☐ other *(specify):*

   on *(date):*

4. ☐ Service of the *Final Declaration of Disclosure* has been waived under Family Code section 2105, subdivision (d).

I declare under penalty of perjury under the laws of the State of California that the foregoing is true and correct.

Date:

_____
(TYPE OR PRINT NAME)

▶ _____
(SIGNATURE)

Note:
File this document with the court.
Do not file a copy of either the *Preliminary* or *Final Declaration of Disclosure* with this document.

Form Adopted for Mandatory Use
Judicial Council of California
FL-141 [Rev. January 1, 2003]

DECLARATION REGARDING SERVICE OF DECLARATION OF DISCLOSURE
(Family Law)

Family Code, §§ 2104, 2106, 2112
www.courtinfo.ca.gov

ATTORNEY OR PARTY WITHOUT ATTORNEY (Name, State Bar number, and address):	FOR COURT USE ONLY
TELEPHONE NO: FAX NO. (Optional): E–MAIL ADDRESS (Optional): ATTORNEY FOR (Name):	

SUPERIOR COURT OF CALIFORNIA, COUNTY OF
STREET ADDRESS:
MAILING ADDRESS:
CITY AND ZIP CODE:
BRANCH NAME:

PLAINTIFF/ PETITIONER:
DEFENDANT/ RESPONDENT:
OTHER:

STIPULATION AND WAIVER OF FINAL DECLARATION OF DISCLOSURE	CASE NUMBER:

1. Under Family Code section 2105(d), the parties agree to waive the requirements of Family Code section 2105(a) concerning the final declaration of disclosure.

2. The parties agree as follows:

   a. We have complied with Family Code section 2104, and the preliminary declarations of disclosure have been completed and exchanged.

   b. We have completed and exchanged a current *Income and Expense Declaration* (form FL-150) that includes all material facts and information on each party's earnings, accumulations, and expenses.

   c. We have fully complied with Family Law section 2102 and have fully augmented the preliminary declarations of disclosure, including disclosure of all material facts and information on

      (1) the characterization of all assets and liabilities,

      (2) the valuation of all assets that are community property or in which the community has an interest, and

      (3) the amounts of all community debts and obligations.

   d. Each of the parties enters into this waiver knowingly, intelligently, and voluntarily.

   e. Each party understands that this waiver does not limit the legal disclosure obligations of the parties but rather is a statement under penalty of perjury that those obligations have been fulfilled.

   f. The parties also understand that if they do not comply with these obligations, the court will set aside the judgment.

The petitioner and respondent declare under penalty of perjury under the laws of the State of California that the foregoing is true and correct.

Date:

_____
(TYPE OR PRINT NAME)

_____
(SIGNATURE OF PETITIONER)

_____
(TYPE OR PRINT NAME)

_____
(SIGNATURE OF RESPONDENT)

Page 1 of 1

Form Approved for Optional Use
Judicial Council of California
FL-144 [Rev. January 1, 2007]

**STIPULATION AND WAIVER OF FINAL
DECLARATION OF DISCLOSURE**

Family Code, §§ 2102, 2104, 2105(d)
www.courtinfo.ca.gov

ATTORNEY OR PARTY WITHOUT ATTORNEY *(Name, State Bar number, and address):*

FOR COURT USE ONLY

TELEPHONE NO.:   FAX NO. *(Optional):*

E-MAIL ADDRESS *(Optional):*

ATTORNEY FOR *(Name):*

SUPERIOR COURT OF CALIFORNIA, COUNTY OF

STREET ADDRESS:

MAILING ADDRESS:

CITY AND ZIP CODE:

BRANCH NAME:

PETITIONER:

RESPONDENT:

☐ **PETITIONER'S** ☐ **RESPONDENT'S**

    ☐ **COMMUNITY AND QUASI-COMMUNITY PROPERTY DECLARATION**

    ☐ **SEPARATE PROPERTY DECLARATION**

CASE NUMBER:

INSTRUCTIONS

When this form is attached to the *Petition* or *Response,* values and your proposal regarding division need not be completed. Do not list community, including quasi-community, property with separate property on the same form. Quasi-community property must be so identified. For additional space, use *Continuation of Property Declaration* (form FL-161).

ITEM NO.	BRIEF DESCRIPTION	GROSS FAIR MARKET VALUE	AMOUNT OF DEBT	NET FAIR MARKET VALUE	PROPOSAL FOR DIVISION Award to:	
					PETITIONER	RESPONDENT
1.	REAL ESTATE	$	$	$	$	$
2.	HOUSEHOLD FURNITURE, FURNISHINGS, APPLIANCES					
3.	JEWELRY, ANTIQUES, ART, COIN COLLECTIONS, etc.					
4.	VEHICLES, BOATS, TRAILERS					

Form Adopted for Mandatory Use
Judicial Council of California
FL-160 [Rev. January 1, 2007]

PROPERTY DECLARATION
(Family Law)

Family Code, §§ 115, 2500–2660
www.courtinfo.ca.gov

ITEM NO.	BRIEF DESCRIPTION	GROSS FAIR MARKET VALUE	AMOUNT OF DEBT	NET FAIR MARKET VALUE	PROPOSAL FOR DIVISION Award to:	
					PETITIONER	RESPONDENT
5.	SAVINGS, CHECKING, CREDIT UNION, CASH	$	$	$	$	$
6.	LIFE INSURANCE (CASH VALUE)					
7.	EQUIPMENT, MACHINERY, LIVESTOCK					
8.	STOCKS, BONDS, SECURED NOTES					
9.	RETIREMENT, PENSION, PROFIT-SHARING, ANNUITIES					
10.	ACCOUNTS RECEIVABLE, UNSECURED NOTES, TAX REFUNDS					
11.	PARTNERSHIPS, OTHER BUSINESS INTERESTS					
12.	OTHER ASSETS AND DEBTS					
13.	TOTAL FROM CONTINUATION SHEET					
14.	TOTALS					

15. ☐ A *Continuation of Property Declaration* (form FL-161) is attached and incorporated by reference.

I declare under penalty of perjury under the laws of the State of California that, to the best of my knowledge, the foregoing is a true and correct listing of assets and obligations and the amounts shown are correct.

Date:

_____
(TYPE OR PRINT NAME)

► _____
(SIGNATURE)

MARRIAGE OF (Last name—first names of parties)	CASE NUMBER

☐ **PETITIONER'S**   ☐ **RESPONDENT'S**

☐ **COMMUNITY AND QUASI-COMMUNITY PROPERTY DECLARATION**

☐ **SEPARATE PROPERTY DECLARATION**

ITEM NO.	BRIEF DESCRIPTION	GROSS FAIR MARKET VALUE	AMOUNT OF DEBT	NET FAIR MARKET VALUE	PROPOSAL FOR DIVISION AWARD TO	
					PETITIONER	RESPONDENT
		$	$	$	$	$

Form Adopted for Mandatory Use
Judicial Council of California
FL-161 [Rev. January 1, 2003]

CONTINUATION OF PROPERTY DECLARATION
(FAMILY LAW)

Family Code, §§ 2500–2600
www.courtinfo.ca.gov

CONTINUATION OF PROPERTY DECLARATION
(FAMILY LAW)

ITEM NO.	BRIEF DESCRIPTION	GROSS FAIR MARKET VALUE	AMOUNT OF DEBT	NET FAIR MARKET VALUE	PROPOSAL FOR DIVISION AWARD TO PETITIONER	RESPONDENT
		$	$	$	$	$

ATTORNEY OR PARTY WITHOUT ATTORNEY *(Name, State Bar number, and address)*:	*FOR COURT USE ONLY*

TELEPHONE NO.:

E-MAIL ADDRESS *(Optional)*:

ATTORNEY FOR *(Name)*:

SUPERIOR COURT OF CALIFORNIA, COUNTY OF

STREET ADDRESS:

MAILING ADDRESS:

CITY AND ZIP CODE:

BRANCH NAME:

PETITIONER/PLAINTIFF:

RESPONDENT/DEFENDANT:

OTHER PARENT/CLAIMANT:

INCOME AND EXPENSE DECLARATION	CASE NUMBER:

1. **Employment** *(Give information on your current job or, if you're unemployed, your most recent job.)*

> Attach copies of your pay stubs for last two months (black out social security numbers).

   a. Employer:

   b. Employer's address:

   c. Employer's phone number:

   d. Occupation:

   e. Date job started:

   f. If unemployed, date job ended:

   g. I work about   hours per week.

   h. I get paid $ gross (before taxes) ☐ per month ☐ per week ☐ per hour.

(If you have more than one job, attach an 8½-by-11-inch sheet of paper and list the same information as above for your other jobs. Write "Question 1—Other Jobs" at the top.)

2. **Age and education**

   a. My age is *(specify)*:

   b. I have completed high school or the equivalent: ☐ Yes ☐ No   If no, highest grade completed *(specify)*:

   c. Number of years of college completed *(specify)*:   ☐ Degree(s) obtained *(specify)*:

   d. Number of years of graduate school completed *(specify)*:   ☐ Degree(s) obtained *(specify)*:

   e. I have: ☐ professional/occupational license(s) *(specify)*:

         ☐ vocational training *(specify)*:

3. **Tax information**

   a. ☐ I last filed taxes for tax year *(specify year)*:

   b. My tax filing status is ☐ single ☐ head of household ☐ married, filing separately

        ☐ married, filing jointly with *(specify name)*:

   c. I file state tax returns in ☐ California ☐ other *(specify state)*:

   d. I claim the following number of exemptions (including myself) on my taxes *(specify)*:

4. **Other party's income.** I estimate the gross monthly income (before taxes) of the other party in this case at *(specify)*: $
This estimate is based on *(explain)*:

(If you need more space to answer any questions on this form, attach an 8½-by-11-inch sheet of paper and write the question number before your answer.) Number of pages attached: _____

I declare under penalty of perjury under the laws of the State of California that the information contained on all pages of this form and any attachments is true and correct.

Date:

_____   ▶   _____
(TYPE OR PRINT NAME)   (SIGNATURE OF DECLARANT)

Page 1 of 4

Form Adopted for Mandatory Use
Judicial Council of California
FL-150 [Rev. January 1, 2007]

INCOME AND EXPENSE DECLARATION

Family Code, §§ 2030–2032,
2100–2113, 3552, 3620–3634,
4050–4076, 4300–4339
www.courtinfo.ca.gov

PETITIONER/PLAINTIFF:	CASE NUMBER:
RESPONDENT/DEFENDANT:	
OTHER PARENT/CLAIMANT:	

Attach copies of your pay stubs for the last two months and proof of any other income. Take a copy of your latest federal tax return to the court hearing. (Black out your social security number on the pay stub and tax return.)

5. **Income** *(For average monthly, add up all the income you received in each category in the last 12 months and divide the total by 12.)*
  Last month   Average monthly

  a. Salary or wages (gross, before taxes). . . . . $_____ _____

  b. Overtime (gross, before taxes) . . . . $_____ _____

  c. Commissions or bonuses. . . . . $_____ _____

  d. Public assistance (for example: TANF, SSI, GA/GR) ☐ currently receiving . . . . $_____ _____

  e. Spousal support ☐ from this marriage ☐ from a different marriage . . . . $_____ _____

  f. Partner support ☐ from this domestic partnership ☐ from a different domestic partnership $_____ _____

  g. Pension/retirement fund payments. . . . . $_____ _____

  h. Social security retirement (not SSI) . . . . $_____ _____

  i. Disability: ☐ Social security (not SSI) ☐ State disability (SDI) ☐ Private insurance . $_____ _____

  j. Unemployment compensation . . . . $_____ _____

  k. Workers' compensation . . . . $_____ _____

  l. Other (military BAQ, royalty payments, etc.) *(specify):* . . . . $_____ _____

6. **Investment income** *(Attach a schedule showing gross receipts less cash expenses for each piece of property.)*

  a. Dividends/interest. . . . . $_____ _____

  b. Rental property income . . . . $_____ _____

  c. Trust income. . . . . $_____ _____

  d. Other *(specify):* . . . . $_____ _____

7. **Income from self-employment, after business expenses for all businesses.** . . . . $_____ _____

  I am the ☐ owner/sole proprietor ☐ business partner ☐ other *(specify):*

  Number of years in this business *(specify):*

  Name of business *(specify):*

  Type of business *(specify):*

  Attach a profit and loss statement for the last two years or a Schedule C from your last federal tax return. Black out your social security number. If you have more than one business, provide the information above for each of your businesses.

8. ☐ **Additional income.** I received one-time money (lottery winnings, inheritance, etc.) in the last 12 months *(specify source and amount):*

9. ☐ **Change in income.** My financial situation has changed significantly over the last 12 months because *(specify):*

10. **Deductions**
  Last month

  a. Required union dues . . . . $ _____

  b. Required retirement payments (not social security, FICA, 401(k), or IRA). . . . . $ _____

  c. Medical, hospital, dental, and other health insurance premiums *(total monthly amount).* . . . . $ _____

  d. Child support that I pay for children from other relationships. . . . . $ _____

  e. Spousal support that I pay by court order from a different marriage. . . . . $ _____

  f. Partner support that I pay by court order from a different domestic partnership . . . . $ _____

  g. Necessary job-related expenses not reimbursed by my employer *(attach explanation labeled "Question 10g")* . . . . . $ _____

11. **Assets**
  Total

  a. Cash and checking accounts, savings, credit union, money market, and other deposit accounts . . . . $ _____

  b. Stocks, bonds, and other assets I could easily sell . . . . $ _____

  c. All other property, ☐ real and ☐ personal *(estimate fair market value minus the debts you owe)* . . . . $ _____

PETITIONER/PLAINTIFF:	CASE NUMBER:
RESPONDENT/DEFENDANT:	
OTHER PARENT/CLAIMANT:	

12. The following people live with me:

Name	Age	How the person is related to me? *(ex: son)*	That person's gross monthly income	Pays some of the household expenses?
a.				☐ Yes ☐ No
b.				☐ Yes ☐ No
c.				☐ Yes ☐ No
d.				☐ Yes ☐ No
e.				☐ Yes ☐ No

13. Average monthly expenses ☐ Estimated expenses ☐ Actual expenses ☐ Proposed needs

a. Home:

  (1) ☐ Rent or ☐ mortgage... $ _____

    If mortgage:

    (a) average principal: $ _____

    (b) average interest: $ _____

  (2) Real property taxes .... $ _____

  (3) Homeowner's or renter's insurance (if not included above) .... $ _____

  (4) Maintenance and repair .... $ _____

b. Health-care costs not paid by insurance. . . $ _____

c. Child care .... $ _____

d. Groceries and household supplies....... $ _____

e. Eating out......................... $ _____

f. Utilities (gas, electric, water, trash) ...... $ _____

g. Telephone, cell phone, and e-mail .... $ _____

h. Laundry and cleaning .... $ _____

i. Clothes .... $ _____

j. Education .... $ _____

k. Entertainment, gifts, and vacation........ $ _____

l. Auto expenses and transportation (insurance, gas, repairs, bus, etc.) .... $ _____

m. Insurance (life, accident, etc.; do not include auto, home, or health insurance). . . $ _____

n. Savings and investments............... $ _____

o. Charitable contributions................ $ _____

p. Monthly payments listed in item 14 *(itemize below in 14 and insert total here)*. . $ _____

q. Other *(specify):* .... $ _____

r. **TOTAL EXPENSES** (a–q) *(do not add in the amounts in a(1)(a) and (b))* $ _____

s. **Amount of expenses paid by others** $ _____

14. Installment payments and debts not listed above

Paid to	For	Amount	Balance	Date of last payment
		$	$	
		$	$	
		$	$	
		$	$	
		$	$	
		$	$	

15. Attorney fees *(This is required if either party is requesting attorney fees.):*

a. To date, I have paid my attorney this amount for fees and costs *(specify):* $

b. The source of this money was *(specify):*

c. I still owe the following fees and costs to my attorney *(specify total owed):* $

d. My attorney's hourly rate is *(specify):* $

I confirm this fee arrangement.

Date:

▶

_____
(TYPE OR PRINT NAME OF ATTORNEY)

_____
(SIGNATURE OF ATTORNEY)

	CASE NUMBER:
PETITIONER/PLAINTIFF:	
RESPONDENT/DEFENDANT:	
OTHER PARENT/CLAIMANT:	

CHILD SUPPORT INFORMATION
(NOTE: Fill out this page only if your case involves child support.)

16. **Number of children**

a. I have (specify number): _____ children under the age of 18 with the other parent in this case.

b. The children spend _____ percent of their time with me and _____ percent of their time with the other parent.
(If you're not sure about percentage or if it has not been agreed on, please describe your parenting schedule here.)

17. **Children's health-care expenses**

a. I do ☐   I do not ☐   have health insurance available to me for the children through my job.

b. Name of insurance company:

c. Address of insurance company:

d. The monthly cost for the **children's** health insurance is or would be (specify): $ _____
(Do not include the amount your employer pays.)

18. **Additional expenses for the children in this case**   Amount per month

a. Child care so I can work or get job training. . . . . $ _____

b. Children's health care not covered by insurance . . . . $ _____

c. Travel expenses for visitation. . . . . $ _____

d. Children's educational or other special needs (specify below): . . . . $ _____

19. **Special hardships.** I ask the court to consider the following special financial circumstances
(attach documentation of any item listed here, including court orders):

	Amount per month	For how many months?
a. Extraordinary health expenses not included in 18b.	$ _____	_____
b. Major losses not covered by insurance (examples: fire, theft, other insured loss) . . .	$ _____	_____
c. (1) Expenses for my minor children who are from other relationships and are living with me . . .	$ _____	_____

(2) Names and ages of those children (specify):

(3) Child support I receive for those children. . . . . $ _____

The expenses listed in a, b, and c create an extreme financial hardship because (explain):

20. **Other information I want the court to know concerning support in my case** (specify):

Your name and address or attorney's name and address:

TELEPHONE NO.:

FOR COURT USE ONLY

ATTORNEY FOR (Name):

SUPERIOR COURT OF CALIFORNIA, COUNTY OF

STREET ADDRESS:

MAILING ADDRESS:

CITY AND ZIP CODE:

BRANCH NAME:

PETITIONER/PLAINTIFF:

RESPONDENT/DEFENDANT:

OTHER PARENT:

FINANCIAL STATEMENT (SIMPLIFIED)

CASE NUMBER:

NOTICE: Read page 2 to find out if you qualify to use this form and how to use it.

1. a. ☐ My only source of income is TANF, SSI, or GA/GR.

   b. ☐ I have applied for TANF, SSI, or GA/GR.

2. I am the parent of the following number of natural or adopted children from this relationship .... ___

3. a. The children from this relationship are with me this amount of time .... ___ %

   b. The children from this relationship are with the other parent this amount of time .... ___ %

   c. Our arrangement for custody and visitation is (specify, using extra sheet if necessary):

4. My tax filing status is: ☐ single ☐ married filing jointly ☐ head of household ☐ married filing separately.

5. My current gross income (before taxes) per month is .... $ ___

   Attach 1 copy of pay stubs for last 2 months here (cross out social security numbers)

   This income comes from the following:

   ☐ Salary/wages: Amount before taxes per month .... $ ___
   ☐ Retirement: Amount before taxes per month .... $ ___
   ☐ Unemployment compensation: Amount per month .... $ ___
   ☐ Workers' compensation: Amount per month .... $ ___
   ☐ Social security: ☐ SSI ☐ Other Amount per month .... $ ___
   ☐ Disability: Amount per month .... $ ___
   ☐ Interest income (from bank accounts or other): Amount per month .... $ ___

   ☐ I have no income other than as stated in this paragraph.

6. I pay the following monthly expenses for the children in this case:

   a. ☐ Day care or preschool to allow me to work or go to school .... $ ___
   b. ☐ Health care not paid for by insurance .... $ ___
   c. ☐ School, education, tuition, or other special needs of the child .... $ ___
   d. ☐ Travel expenses for visitation .... $ ___

7. ☐ There are (specify number) ___ other minor children of mine living with me. Their monthly expenses that I pay are .... $ ___

8. I spend the following average monthly amounts (please attach proof):

   a. ☐ Job-related expenses that are not paid by my employer (specify reasons for expenses on separate sheet) $ ___
   b. ☐ Required union dues .... $ ___
   c. ☐ Required retirement payments (not social security, FICA, 401k or IRA) .... $ ___
   d. ☐ Health insurance costs .... $ ___
   e. ☐ Child support I am paying for other minor children of mine who are not living with me .... $ ___
   f. ☐ Spousal support I am paying because of a court order for another relationship .... $ ___
   g. ☐ Monthly housing costs: ☐ rent or ☐ mortgage .... $ ___

   If mortgage: interest payments $ ___ real property taxes $ ___

9. Information concerning ☐ my current employment ☐ my most recent employment:

   Employer:

   Address:

   Telephone number:

   My occupation:

   Date work started:

   Date work stopped (if applicable): What was your gross income (before taxes) before work stopped?:

Form Approved for Optional Use
Judicial Council of California
FL-155 [Rev. January 1, 2004]

FINANCIAL STATEMENT (SIMPLIFIED)

Family Code, § 4068(b)
www.courtinfo.ca.gov

PETITIONER/PLAINTIFF:		CASE NUMBER:
RESPONDENT/DEFENDANT:		
OTHER PARENT:		

10. My estimate of the other party's gross monthly income (*before taxes*) is . . . . $ _____

11. My current spouse's monthly income (*before taxes*) is . . . . $ _____

12. Other information I want the court to know concerning child support in my case (*attach extra sheet with the information*). _____

13. ☐ I am attaching a copy of page 3 of form FL-150, *Income and Expense Declaration* showing my expenses.

I declare under penalty of perjury under the laws of the State of California that the information contained on all pages of this form and any attachments is true and correct.

Date:

▶

_____   _____
(TYPE OR PRINT NAME)   (SIGNATURE OF DECLARANT)

☐ PETITIONER/PLAINTIFF   ☐ RESPONDENT/DEFENDANT

INSTRUCTIONS

Step 1: Are you eligible to use this form? *If your answer is YES to any of the following questions, you may NOT use this form:*

- Are you asking for spousal support (alimony) or a change in spousal support?
- Is your spouse or former spouse asking for spousal support (alimony) or a change in spousal support?
- Are you asking the other party to pay your attorney fees?
- Is the other party asking you to pay his or her attorney fees?
- Do you receive money (*income*) from any source other than the following?

  - Welfare (such as TANF, GR, or GA)
  - Interest
  - Salary or wages
  - Workers' compensation
  - Disability
  - Social security
  - Unemployment
  - Retirement
  - Are you self-employed?

If you are eligible to use this form and choose to do so, you do not need to complete the *Income and Expense Declaration* (form FL-150). Even if you are eligible to use this form, you may choose instead to use the *Income and Expense Declaration* (form FL-150).

Step 2: Make 2 copies of each of your pay stubs for the last two months. If you received money from other than wages or salary, include copies of the pay stub received with that money.

Privacy notice: If you wish, you may cross out your social security number if it appears on the pay stub, other payment notice or your tax return.

Step 3: Make 2 copies of your most recent federal income tax form.

Step 4: Complete this form with the required information. Type the form if possible or complete it neatly and clearly in black ink. If you need additional room, please use plain or lined paper, 8½-by-11", and staple to this form.

Step 5: Make 2 copies of each side of this completed form and any attached pages.

Step 6: Serve a copy on the other party. Have someone other than yourself mail to the attorney for the other party, the other party, and the local child support agency, if they are handling the case, 1 copy of this form, 1 copy of each of your pay stubs for the last two months, and 1 copy of your most recent federal income tax return.

Step 7: File the original with the court. Staple this form with 1 copy of each of your pay stubs for the last two months. Take this document and give it to the clerk of the court. Check with your local court about how to submit your return.

Step 8: Keep the remaining copies of the documents for your file.

Step 9: Take the copy of your latest federal income tax return to the court hearing.

It is very important that you attend the hearings scheduled for this case. If you do not attend a hearing, the court may make an order without considering the information you want the court to consider.

ATTORNEY OR PARTY WITHOUT ATTORNEY *(Name, State Bar number, and address):*

FOR COURT USE ONLY

TELEPHONE NO.: FAX NO. *(Optional):*

E-MAIL ADDRESS *(Optional):*

ATTORNEY FOR *(Name):*

SUPERIOR COURT OF CALIFORNIA, COUNTY OF

STREET ADDRESS:

MAILING ADDRESS:

CITY AND ZIP CODE:

BRANCH NAME:

PETITIONER:

RESPONDENT:

REQUEST TO ENTER DEFAULT	CASE NUMBER:

1. **To the clerk:** Please enter the default of the respondent who has failed to respond to the petition.

2. A completed *Income and Expense Declaration* (form FL-150) or *Financial Statement (Simplified)* (form FL-155)
   ☐ is attached ☐ is not attached.

   A completed *Property Declaration* (form FL-160) ☐ is attached ☐ is not attached

   because *(check at least one of the following):*

   (a) ☐ there have been no changes since the previous filing.

   (b) ☐ the issues subject to disposition by the court in this proceeding are the subject of a written agreement.

   (c) ☐ there are no issues of child, spousal, or partner support or attorney fees and costs subject to determination by the court.

   (d) ☐ the petition does not request money, property, costs, or attorney fees. (Fam. Code, § 2330.5.)

   (e) ☐ there are no issues of division of community property.

   (f) ☐ this is an action to establish parental relationship.

Date: _____

▶

_____   _____
(TYPE OR PRINT NAME)   (SIGNATURE OF [ATTORNEY FOR] PETITIONER)

3. **Declaration**

   a. ☐ No mailing is required because service was by publication or posting and the address of the respondent remains unknown.

   b. ☐ A copy of this *Request to Enter Default,* including any attachments and an envelope with sufficient postage, was provided to the court clerk, with the envelope addressed as follows *(address of the respondent's attorney or, if none, the respondent's last known address):*

I declare under penalty of perjury under the laws of the State of California that the foregoing is true and correct.

Date: _____

▶

_____   _____
(TYPE OR PRINT NAME)   (SIGNATURE OF DECLARANT)

FOR COURT USE ONLY

☐ *Request to Enter Default* mailed to the respondent or the respondent's attorney on *(date):*

☐ Default entered as requested on *(date):*

☐ Default **not** entered. Reason:

Clerk, by _____ , Deputy

Form Adopted for Mandatory Use
Judicial Council of California
FL-165 [Rev. January 1, 2005]

REQUEST TO ENTER DEFAULT
(Family Law—Uniform Parentage)

Code of Civil Procedure, §§ 585, 587;
Family Code, § 2335.5
www.courtinfo.ca.gov

CASE NAME (Last name, first name of each party):	CASE NUMBER:

4. **Memorandum of costs**

  a. ☐ Costs and disbursements are waived.

  b. Costs and disbursements are listed as follows:

    (1) ☐ Clerk's fees .... $ ....

    (2) ☐ Process server's fees .... $ ....

    (3) ☐ Other (specify): .... $ ....

    .... $ ....

    .... $ ....

    TOTAL .... $ ....

  c. I am the attorney, agent, or party who claims these costs. To the best of my knowledge and belief, the foregoing items of cost are correct and have been necessarily incurred in this cause or proceeding.

I declare under penalty of perjury under the laws of the State of California that the foregoing is true and correct.

Date:

_____ ▶ _____
(TYPE OR PRINT NAME)   (SIGNATURE OF DECLARANT)

5. **Declaration of nonmilitary status.** The respondent is not in the military service of the United States as defined in section 511 et seq. of the Servicemembers Civil Relief Act (50 U.S.C. Appen. § 501 et seq.), and is not entitled to the benefits of such act.

I declare under penalty of perjury under the laws of the State of California that the foregoing is true and correct.

Date:

_____ ▶ _____
(TYPE OR PRINT NAME)   (SIGNATURE OF DECLARANT)

ATTORNEY OR PARTY WITHOUT ATTORNEY *(Name, State Bar number, and address)* :

FOR COURT USE ONLY

TELEPHONE NO.:   FAX NO. *(Optional)*:

E-MAIL ADDRESS *(Optional)*:

ATTORNEY FOR *(Name)*:

SUPERIOR COURT OF CALIFORNIA, COUNTY OF

STREET ADDRESS:

MAILING ADDRESS:

CITY AND ZIP CODE:

BRANCH NAME:

MARRIAGE OF

PETITIONER:

RESPONDENT:

JUDGMENT	CASE NUMBER:

☐ **DISSOLUTION**   ☐ **LEGAL SEPARATION**   ☐ **NULLITY**

    ☐ **Status only**

    ☐ **Reserving jurisdiction over termination of marital or domestic partnership status**

    ☐ **Judgment on reserved issues**

Date marital or domestic partnership status ends:

1. ☐ This judgment ☐ contains personal conduct restraining orders ☐ modifies existing restraining orders.
   The restraining orders are contained on page(s)   of the attachment. They expire on *(date)*:

2. This proceeding was heard as follows: ☐ Default or uncontested ☐ By declaration under Family Code section 2336
   ☐ Contested
   a. Date: Dept.:   Room:
   b. Judicial officer *(name)*:   ☐ Temporary judge
   c. ☐ Petitioner present in court   ☐ Attorney present in court *(name)*:
   d. ☐ Respondent present in court   ☐ Attorney present in court *(name)*:
   e. ☐ Claimant present in court *(name)*:   ☐ Attorney present in court *(name)*:
   f. ☐ Other *(specify name)*:

3. The court acquired jurisdiction of the respondent on *(date)*:
   a. ☐ The respondent was served with process.
   b. ☐ The respondent appeared.

THE COURT ORDERS, GOOD CAUSE APPEARING

4. a. ☐ Judgment of dissolution is entered. Marital or domestic partnership status is terminated and the parties are restored to the status of single persons
       (1) ☐ on *(specify date)*:
       (2) ☐ on a date to be determined on noticed motion of either party or on stipulation.
   b. ☐ Judgment of legal separation is entered.
   c. ☐ Judgment of nullity is entered. The parties are declared to be single persons on the ground of *(specify)*:

   d. ☐ This judgment will be entered nunc pro tunc as of *(date)*:
   e. ☐ Judgment on reserved issues.
   f. The ☐ petitioner's ☐ respondent's former name is restored to *(specify)*:
   g. ☐ Jurisdiction is reserved over all other issues, and all present orders remain in effect except as provided below.
   h. ☐ This judgment contains provisions for child support or family support. Each party must complete and file with the court a *Child Support Case Registry Form* (form FL-191) within 10 days of the date of this judgment. The parents must notify the court of any change in the information submitted within 10 days of the change, by filing an updated form. The *Notice of Rights and Responsibilities—Health Care Costs and Reimbursement Procedures and Information Sheet on Changing a Child Support Order* (form FL-192) is attached.

Form Adopted for Mandatory Use
Judicial Council of California
FL-180 [Rev. January 1, 2007]

JUDGMENT
(Family Law)

Family Code, §§ 2024, 2340,
2343, 2346
www.courtinfo.ca.gov

CASE NAME (Last name, first name of each party):

CASE NUMBER:

4. (Cont'd.)

i. ☐ A settlement agreement between the parties is attached.

j. ☐ A written stipulation for judgment between the parties is attached.

k. ☐ The children of this marriage or domestic partnership.

    (1) ☐ The children of this marriage or domestic partnership are:

Name	Birthdate

    (2) ☐ Parentage is established for children of this relationship born prior to the marriage or domestic partnership.

l. ☐ Child custody and visitation are ordered as set forth in the attached

    (1) ☐ settlement agreement, stipulation for judgment, or other written agreement.

    (2) ☐ Child Custody and Visitation Order Attachment (form FL-341).

    (3) ☐ Stipulation and Order for Custody and/or Visitation of Children (form FL-355).

    (4) ☐ other (specify):

m. ☐ Child support is ordered as set forth in the attached

    (1) ☐ settlement agreement, stipulation for judgment, or other written agreement.

    (2) ☐ Child Support Information and Order Attachment (form FL-342).

    (3) ☐ Stipulation to Establish or Modify Child Support and Order (form FL-350).

    (4) ☐ other (specify):

n. ☐ Spousal or partner support is ordered as set forth in the attached

    (1) ☐ settlement agreement, stipulation for judgment, or other written agreement.

    (2) ☐ Spousal, Partner, or Family Support Order Attachment (form FL-343).

    (3) ☐ other (specify):

NOTICE: It is the goal of this state that each party will make reasonable good faith efforts to become self-supporting as provided for in Family Code section 4320. The failure to make reasonable good faith efforts may be one of the factors considered by the court as a basis for modifying or terminating spousal or partner support.

o. ☐ Property division is ordered as set forth in the attached

    (1) ☐ settlement agreement, stipulation for judgment, or other written agreement.

    (2) ☐ Property Order Attachment to Judgment (form FL-345).

    (3) ☐ other (specify):

p. ☐ Other (specify):

Each attachment to this judgment is incorporated into this judgment, and the parties are ordered to comply with each attachment's provisions.

Jurisdiction is reserved to make other orders necessary to carry out this judgment.

Date:

_____
JUDICIAL OFFICER

5. Number of pages attached: _____   ☐ SIGNATURE FOLLOWS LAST ATTACHMENT

NOTICE

Dissolution or legal separation may automatically cancel the rights of a spouse or domestic partner under the other spouse's or domestic partner's will, trust, retirement plan, power of attorney, pay-on-death bank account, transfer-on-death vehicle registration, survivorship rights to any property owned in joint tenancy, and any other similar thing. It does not automatically cancel the rights of a spouse or domestic partner as beneficiary of the other spouse's or domestic partner's life insurance policy. You should review these matters, as well as any credit cards, other credit accounts, insurance policies, retirement plans, and credit reports, to determine whether they should be changed or whether you should take any other actions.

A debt or obligation may be assigned to one party as part of the dissolution of property and debts, but if that party does not pay the debt or obligation, the creditor may be able to collect from the other party.

An earnings assignment may be issued without additional proof if child, family, partner, or spousal support is ordered.

Any party required to pay support must pay interest on overdue amounts at the "legal rate," which is currently 10 percent.

ATTORNEY OR PARTY WITHOUT ATTORNEY *(Name and Address):*	TELEPHONE NO.:	FOR COURT USE ONLY

ATTORNEY FOR *(Name):*

SUPERIOR COURT OF CALIFORNIA, COUNTY OF
   STREET ADDRESS:
   MAILING ADDRESS:
   CITY AND ZIP CODE:
   BRANCH NAME:

PETITIONER/PLAINTIFF:

RESPONDENT/DEFENDANT:

STIPULATION TO ESTABLISH OR MODIFY CHILD SUPPORT AND ORDER	CASE NUMBER:

1. a. ☐ Mother's net monthly disposable income: $

    Father's net monthly disposable income: $
    —*OR*—
   b. ☐ A printout of a computer calculation of the parents' financial circumstances is attached.
2. ☐ Percentage of time each parent has primary responsibility for the children: Mother   %   Father   %
3. a. ☐ A hardship is being experienced by the mother for: $ per month because of *(specify):*

    The hardship will last until *(date):*
   b. ☐ A hardship is being experienced by the father for: $ per month because of *(specify):*

    The hardship will last until *(date):*
4. The amount of child support payable by *(name):*   , referred to as the "obligor" below,
   as calculated under the guideline is: $ per month.
5. ☐ We agree to guideline support.
6. ☐ The guideline amount should be rebutted because of the following:
   a. ☐ We agree to child support in the amount of: $ per month; the agreement is in the best interest of
       the children; the needs of the children will be adequately met by the agreed amount; and application of the guideline
       would be unjust or inappropriate in this case.
   b. ☐ Other rebutting factors *(specify):*
7. Obligor must pay child support as follows beginning *(date):*
   a. BASIC CHILD SUPPORT

Child's name	Monthly amount	Payable to *(name)*

      Total: $ payable ☐ on the first of the month   ☐ other *(specify):*
   b. ☐ In addition obligor must pay the following:
      ☐ $ per month for child care costs to *(name):*   on *(date):*
      ☐ $ per month for health care costs not deducted from gross income
                 to *(name):*   on *(date):*
      ☐ $ per month for special educational or other needs of the children
                 to *(name):*   on *(date):*
      ☐ other *(specify):*

   c. **Total monthly child support** payable by obligor will be: $
      payable ☐ on the first of the month   ☐ other *(specify):*

Form Adopted for Mandatory Use
Judicial Council of California
FL-350 [Rev. July 1, 2003]

**STIPULATION TO ESTABLISH OR MODIFY
CHILD SUPPORT AND ORDER**

Family Code, § 4065
www.courtinfo.ca.gov

8. a. Health insurance will be maintained by *(specify name):*

   b. ☐ A health insurance coverage assignment will issue if available through employment or other group plan or otherwise available at reasonable cost. Both parents are ordered to cooperate in the presentation, collection, and reimbursement of any medical claims.

   c. Any health expenses not paid by insurance will be shared: Mother   %   Father   %

9. a. An Order/Notice to Withhold Child Support (form FL-195) will be issued.

   b. ☐ We agree that service of the earnings assignment be stayed because we have made the following alternative arrangements to ensure payment *(specify):*

10. ☐ Travel expenses for visitation will be shared: Mother   %   Father   %

11. ☐ We agree that we will promptly inform each other of any change of residence or employment, including the employer's name, address, and telephone number.

12. ☐ Other *(specify):*

13. We agree that we are fully informed of our rights under the California child support guidelines.

14. We make this agreement freely without coercion or duress.

15. The right to support

   a. ☐ has not been assigned to any county and no application for public assistance is pending.

   b. ☐ has been assigned or an application for public assistance is pending in *(county name):*

If you checked b., an attorney for the local child support agency must sign below, joining in this agreement.

Date:

_____   ▶ _____

        (TYPE OR PRINT NAME)   (SIGNATURE OF ATTORNEY FOR LOCAL CHILD SUPPORT AGENCY)

Notice: If the amount agreed to is less than the guideline amount, no change of circumstances need be shown to obtain a change in the support order to a higher amount. If the order is above the guideline, a change of circumstances will be required to modify this order. This form must be signed by the court to be effective.

Date:

_____   ▶ _____

Date: (TYPE OR PRINT NAME)   (SIGNATURE OF PETITIONER)

_____   ▶ _____

Date: (TYPE OR PRINT NAME)   (SIGNATURE OF RESPONDENT)

_____   ▶ _____

Date: (TYPE OR PRINT NAME)   (SIGNATURE OF ATTORNEY FOR PETITIONER)

_____   ▶ _____

        (TYPE OR PRINT NAME)   (SIGNATURE OF ATTORNEY FOR RESPONDENT)

THE COURT ORDERS

16. a. ☐ The guideline child support amount in item 4 is rebutted by the factors stated in item 6.

   b. Items 7 through 12 are ordered. All child support payments must continue until further order of the court, or until the child marries, dies, is emancipated, or reaches age 18. The duty of support continues as to an unmarried child who has attained the age of 18 years, is a full-time high school student, and resides with a parent, until the time the child completes the 12th grade or attains the age of 19 years, whichever first occurs. Except as modified by this stipulation, all provisions of any previous orders made in this action will remain in effect.

Date:

_____

                             JUDGE OF THE SUPERIOR COURT

NOTICE: Any party required to pay child support must pay interest on overdue amounts at the "legal" rate, which is currently 10 percent per year. This can be a large added amount.

ATTORNEY OR PARTY WITHOUT ATTORNEY *(Name, State Bar number, and address):*	COURT PERSONNEL: *STAMP DATE RECEIVED HERE*
TELEPHONE NO.: FAX NO. *(Optional):*	**DO NOT FILE**

TELEPHONE NO.:

FAX NO. *(Optional):*

E-MAIL ADDRESS *(Optional):*

ATTORNEY FOR *(Name):*

DO NOT FILE

SUPERIOR COURT OF CALIFORNIA, COUNTY OF

STREET ADDRESS:

MAILING ADDRESS:

CITY AND ZIP CODE:

BRANCH NAME:

PETITIONER/PLAINTIFF:

RESPONDENT/DEFENDANT:

OTHER PARENT:

CHILD SUPPORT CASE REGISTRY FORM	CASE NUMBER:
☐ Mother ☐ First form completed ☐ Father ☐ Change to previous information	

THIS FORM WILL NOT BE PLACED IN THE COURT FILE. IT WILL BE MAINTAINED IN A CONFIDENTIAL FILE WITH THE STATE OF CALIFORNIA.

Notice: Pages 1 and 2 of this form must be completed and delivered to the court along with the court order for support. Pages 3 and 4 are instructional only and do not need to be delivered to the court. If you did not file the court order, you must complete this form and deliver it to the court within 10 days of the date on which you received a copy of the support order. Any later change to the information on this form must be delivered to the court on another form within 10 days of the change. It is important that you keep the court informed in writing of any changes of your address and telephone number.

1. Support order information *(this information is on the court order you are filing or have received).*

    a. Date order filed:

    b. ☐ Initial child support or family support order   ☐ Modification

    c. Total monthly base current child or family support amount ordered for children listed below, plus any monthly amount ordered payable on past-due support:

    <u>Child Support:</u>   <u>Family Support:</u>   <u>Spousal Support:</u>

    (1) ☐ Current base child support: $ ☐ Reserved order   ☐ $0 (zero) order   ☐ Current base family support: $ ☐ Reserved order   ☐ $0 (zero) order   ☐ Current spousal support: $ ☐ Reserved order   ☐ $0 (zero) order

    (2) ☐ Additional monthly support: $ ☐ Additional monthly support: $

    (3) ☐ Total past-due support: $ ☐ Total past-due support: $ ☐ Total past-due support: $

    (4) ☐ Payment on past-due support: $ ☐ Payment on past-due support: $ ☐ Payment on past-due support: $

    (5) Wage withholding was ☐ ordered   ☐ ordered but stayed until *(date):*

2. Person required to pay child or family support *(name):*

    Relationship to child *(specify):*

3. Person or agency to receive child or family support payments *(name):*

    Relationship to child *(if applicable):*

TYPE OR PRINT IN INK

Form Adopted for Mandatory Use
Judicial Council of California
FL-191 [Rev. July 1, 2005]

CHILD SUPPORT CASE REGISTRY FORM

Family Code, § 4014
www.courtinfo.ca.gov

4. The child support order is for the following children:

Child's name	Date of birth	Social security number
a.		
b.		
c.		

☐ Additional children are listed on a page attached to this document.

You are required to complete the following information about yourself. You are not required to provide information about the other person, but you are encouraged to provide as much as you can. This form is confidential and will not be filed in the court file. It will be maintained in a confidential file with the State of California.

5. Father's name:

   a. Date of birth:

   b. Social security number:

   c. Street address:

      City, state, zip code:

   d. Mailing address:

      City, state, zip code:

   e. Driver's license number:

      State:

   f. Telephone number:

   g. ☐ Employed ☐ Not employed ☐ Self-employed

      Employer's name:

      Street address:

      City, state, zip code:

      Telephone number:

6. Mother's name:

   a. Date of birth:

   b. Social security number:

   c. Street address:

      City, state, zip code:

   d. Mailing address:

      City, state, zip code:

   e. Driver's license number:

      State:

   f. Telephone number:

   g. ☐ Employed ☐ Not employed ☐ Self-employed

      Employer's name:

      Street address:

      City, state, zip code:

      Telephone number:

7. ☐ A restraining order, protective order, or nondisclosure order due to domestic violence is in effect.

   a. The order protects: ☐ Father ☐ Mother ☐ Children

   b. From: ☐ Father ☐ Mother

   c. The restraining order expires on (date):

I declare under penalty of perjury under the laws of the State of California that the foregoing is true and correct.

Date:

▶

_____   _____
(TYPE OR PRINT NAME)   (SIGNATURE OF PERSON COMPLETING THIS FORM)

INFORMATION SHEET FOR CHILD SUPPORT CASE REGISTRY FORM
(Do NOT deliver this Information Sheet to the court clerk.)

Please follow these instructions to complete the *Child Support Case Registry Form* (form FL-191) if you do not have an attorney to represent you. Your attorney, if you have one, should complete this form.

Both parents must complete a *Child Support Case Registry Form.* The information on this form will be included in a national database that, among other things, is used to locate absent parents. When you file a court order, you must deliver a completed form to the court clerk along with your court order. If you did not file a court order, you must deliver a completed form to the court clerk **WITHIN 10 DAYS** of the date you received a copy of your court order. If any of the information you provide on this form changes, you must complete a new form and deliver it to the court clerk within 10 days of the change. The address of the court clerk is the same as the one shown for the superior court on your order. This form is confidential and will not be filed in the court file. It will be maintained in a confidential file with the State of California.

INSTRUCTIONS FOR COMPLETING THE *CHILD SUPPORT CASE REGISTRY FORM* (TYPE OR PRINT IN INK):

If the top section of the form has already been filled out, skip down to number 1 below. If the top section of the form is blank, you must provide this information.

Page 1, first box, top of form, left side: Print your name, address, telephone number, fax number, and e-mail address, if any, in this box. Attorneys must include their State Bar identification numbers.

Page 1, second box, top of form, left side: Print the name of the county and the court's address in this box. Use the same address for the court that is on the court order you are filing or have received.

Page 1, third box, top of form, left side: Print the names of the petitioner/plaintiff, respondent/defendant, and other parent in this box. Use the same names listed on the court order you are filing or have received.

Page 1, fourth box, top of form, left side: Check the box indicating whether you are the mother or the father. If you are the attorney for the mother, check the box for mother. If you are the attorney for the father, check the box for father. Also, if this is the first time you have filled out this form, check the box by "First form completed." If you have filled out form FL-191 before, and you are changing any of the information, check the box by "Change to previous information."

Page 1, first box, right side: Leave this box blank for the court's use in stamping the date of receipt.

Page 1, second box, right side: Print the court case number in this box. This number is also shown on the court papers.

Instructions for numbered paragraphs:

1. a. Enter the date the court order was filed. This date is shown in the "COURT PERSONNEL: STAMP DATE RECEIVED HERE" box on page 1 at the top of the order on the right side. If the order has not been filed, leave this item blank for the court clerk to fill in.

   b. If the court order you filed or received is the first child or family support order for this case, check the box by "Initial child support or family support order." If this is a change to your order, check the box by "Modification."

   c. Information regarding the amount and type of support ordered and wage withholding is on the court order you are filing or have received.

   (1) If your order provides for any type of current support, check all boxes that describe that support. For example, if your order provides for both child and spousal support, check both of those boxes. If there is an amount, put it in the blank provided. If the order says the amount is reserved, check the "Reserved order" box. If the order says the amount is zero, check the "$0 (zero) order" box. Do not include child care, special needs, uninsured medical expenses, or travel for visitation here These amounts will go in (2). Do NOT complete the Child Support Case Registry form if you receive spousal support only.

   (2) If your order provides for a set monthly amount to be paid as additional support for such needs as child care, special needs, uninsured medical expenses or travel for visitation check the box in Item 2 and enter the monthly amount. For example, if your order provides for base child support and in addition the paying parent is required to pay $300 per month, check the box in item 2 underneath the "Child Support" column and enter $300. Do NOT check this box if your order provides only for a payment of a percentage, such as 50% of the childcare.

(3) If your order determined the amount of past due support, check the box in Item 3 that states the type of past due support and enter the amount. For example, if the court determined that there was $5000 in past due child support and $1000 in past due spousal support, you would check the box in item 3 in the "Child Support" column and enter $5000 and you would also check the box in item 3 in the "Spousal Support" column and enter $1000.

(4) If your order provides for a specific dollar amount to be paid towards any past due support, check the box in Item 4 that states the type of past due support and enter the amount. For example, the court ordered $350 per month to be paid on the past due child support, you would check the box in Item 4 in the "Child Support" column and enter $350.

(5) Check the "ordered" box if wage withholding was ordered with no conditions. Check the box "ordered but stayed until" if wage withholding was ordered but is not to be deducted until a later date. If the court delayed the effective date of the wage withholding, enter the specific date. Check only one box in this item.

2. a. Write the name of the person who is supposed to pay child or family support.
   b. Write the relationship of that person to the child.

3. a. Write the name of the person or agency supposed to receive child or family support payments.
   b. Write the relationship of that person to the child.

4. List the full name, date of birth, and social security number for each child included in the support order. If there are more than five children included in the support order, check the box below item 4e and list the remaining children with dates of birth and social security numbers on another sheet of paper. Attach the other sheet to this form.

The local child support agency is required, under section 466(a)(13) of the Social Security Act, to place in the records pertaining to child support the social security number of any individual who is subject to a divorce decree, support order, or paternity determination or acknowledgment. This information is mandatory and will be kept on file at the local child support agency.

Top of page 2, box on left side: Print the names of the petitioner/plaintiff, respondent/defendant, and other parent in this box. Use the same names listed on page 1.

Top of page 2, box on right side: Print your court case number in this box. Use the same case number as on page 1, second box, right side.

You are required to complete information about yourself. If you know information about the other person, you may also fill in what you know about him or her.

5. If you are the father in this case, list your full name in this space. See instructions for a–g under item 6 below.

6. If you are the mother in this case, list your full name in this space.

   a. List your date of birth.
   b. Write your social security number.
   c. List the street address, city, state, and zip code where you live.
   d. List the street address, city, state, and zip code where you want your mail sent, if different from the address where you live.
   e. Write your driver's license number and the state where it was issued.
   f. List the telephone number where you live.
   g. Indicate whether you are employed, not employed, self-employed, or by checking the appropriate box. If you are employed, write the name, street address, city, state, zip code, and telephone number where you work.

7. If there is a restraining order, protective order, or nondisclosure order, check this box.

   a. Check the box beside each person who is protected by the restraining order.
   b. Check the box beside the parent who is restrained.
   c. Write the date the restraining order expires. See the restraining order, protective order, or nondisclosure order for this date.

If you are in fear of domestic violence, you may want to ask the court for a restraining order, protective order, or nondisclosure order.

You must type or print your name, fill in the date, and sign the *Child Support Case Registry Form* under penalty of perjury. When you sign under penalty of perjury, you are stating that the information you have provided is true and correct.

NOTICE OF RIGHTS AND RESPONSIBILITIES

Health-Care Costs and Reimbursement Procedures

IF YOU HAVE A CHILD SUPPORT ORDER THAT INCLUDES A PROVISION FOR THE REIMBURSEMENT OF A PORTION OF THE CHILD'S OR CHILDREN'S HEALTH-CARE COSTS AND THOSE COSTS ARE NOT PAID BY INSURANCE, THE LAW SAYS:

1. Notice. You must give the other parent an itemized statement of the charges that have been billed for any health-care costs not paid by insurance. You must give this statement to the other parent within a reasonable time, but no more than 30 days after those costs were given to you.

2. Proof of full payment. If you have already paid all of the uninsured costs, you must (1) give the other parent proof that you paid them and (2) ask for reimbursement for the other parent's court-ordered share of those costs.

3. Proof of partial payment. If you have paid only your share of the uninsured costs, you must (1) give the other parent proof that you paid your share, (2) ask that the other parent pay his or her share of the costs directly to the health-care provider, and (3) give the other parent the information necessary for that parent to be able to pay the bill.

4. Payment by notified parent. If you receive notice from a parent that an uninsured health-care cost has been incurred, you must pay your share of that cost within the time the court orders; or if the court has not specified a period of time, you must make payment (1) within 30 days from the time you were given notice of the amount due, (2) according to any payment schedule set by the health-care provider, (3) according to a schedule agreed to in writing by you and the other parent, or (4) according to a schedule adopted by the court.

5. Disputed charges. If you dispute a charge, you may file a motion in court to resolve the dispute, but only if you pay that charge before filing your motion.

If you claim that the other party has failed to reimburse you for a payment, or the other party has failed to make a payment to the provider after proper notice has been given, you may file a motion in court to resolve the dispute. The court will presume that if uninsured costs have been paid, those costs were reasonable. The court may award attorney fees and costs against a party who has been unreasonable.

6. Court-ordered insurance coverage. If a parent provides health-care insurance as ordered by the court, that insurance must be used at all times to the extent that it is available for health-care costs.

a. **Burden to prove.** The party claiming that the coverage is inadequate to meet the child's needs has the burden of proving that to the court.

b. **Cost of additional coverage.** If a parent purchases health-care insurance in addition to that ordered by the court, that parent must pay all the costs of the additional coverage. In addition, if a parent uses alternative coverage that costs more than the coverage provided by court order, that parent must pay the difference.

7. Preferred health providers. If the court-ordered coverage designates a preferred health-care provider, that provider must be used at all times consistent with the terms of the health insurance policy. When any party uses a health-care provider other than the preferred provider, any health-care costs that would have been paid by the preferred health provider if that provider had been used must be the sole responsibility of the party incurring those costs.

Form Approved for Optional Use
Judicial Council of California
FL-192 [Rev. July 1, 2007]

NOTICE OF RIGHTS AND RESPONSIBILITIES
Health-Care Costs and Reimbursement Procedures

Family Code, §§ 4062, 4063
www.courtinfo.ca.gov

INFORMATION SHEET ON CHANGING A CHILD SUPPORT ORDER

General Information

The court has just made a child support order in your case. This order will remain the same unless a party to the action requests that the support be changed (modified). An order for child support can be modified only by filing a motion to change child support and serving each party involved in your case. If both parents and the local child support agency (if it is involved) agree on a new child support amount, you can complete, have all parties sign, and file with the court a *Stipulation to Establish or Modify Child Support and Order* (form FL-350) or *Stipulation and Order (Governmental)* (form FL-625).

When a Child Support Order May Be Modified

The court takes several things into account when ordering the payment of child support. First, the number of children is considered. Next, the net incomes of both parents are determined, along with the percentage of time each parent has physical custody of the children. The court considers both parties' tax filing status and may consider hardships, such as a child of another relationship. An existing order for child support may be modified when the net income of one of the parents changes significantly, the parenting schedule changes significantly, or a new child is born.

Examples

- You have been ordered to pay $500 per month in child support. You lose your job. You will continue to owe $500 per month, plus 10 percent interest on any unpaid support, unless you file a motion to modify your child support to a lower amount and the court orders a reduction.
- You are currently receiving $300 per month in child support from the other parent, whose net income has just increased substantially. You will continue to receive $300 per month unless you file a motion to modify your child support to a higher amount and the court orders an increase.
- You are paying child support based upon having physical custody of your children 30 percent of the time. After several months it turns out that you actually have physical custody of the children 50 percent of the time. You may file a motion to modify child support to a lower amount.

How to Change a Child Support Order

To change a child support order, you must file papers with the court. *Remember:* You must follow the order you have now.

What forms do I need?

If you are asking to change a child support order open with the local child support agency, you must fill out one of these forms:
- FL-680, *Notice of Motion (Governmental)* **or** FL-683 *Order to Show Cause (Governmental)* **and**
- FL-684, *Request for Order and Supporting Declaration (Governmental)*

If you are asking to change a child support order that is **not** open with the local child support agency, you must fill out one of these forms:
- FL-301, *Notice of Motion* **or** FL-300, *Order to Show Cause* **and**
- FL-310, *Application for Order and Supporting Declaration* **or**
- FL-390, *Notice of Motion and Motion for Simplified Modification of Order for Child, Spousal, or Family Support*

You must also fill out one of these forms:
- FL-150, *Income and Expense Declaration* **or** FL-155, *Financial Statement (Simplified)*

What if I am not sure which forms to fill out?

Talk to the family law facilitator at your court.

After you fill out the forms, file them with the court clerk and ask for a hearing date. Write the hearing date on the form.
The clerk will ask you to pay a filing fee. If you cannot afford the fee, fill out these forms, too:
- Form FW-001, *Application for Waiver of Court Fees and Costs*
- Form FW-003, *Order on Application for Waiver of Court Fees and Costs*

You must serve the other parent. If the local child support agency is involved, serve it too.
This means someone 18 or over—**not you**—must serve the other parent copies of your filed court forms at least **16 court days** before the hearing. Add **5 calendar days** if you serve by mail within California (see Code of Civil Procedure section 1005 for other situations). **Court days** are weekdays when the court is open for business (Monday through Friday except court holidays). **Calendar days** include all days of the month, including weekends and holidays. To determine court and calendar days, go to *www.courtinfo.ca.gov/selfhelp/courtcalendars/*.

The server must also serve blank copies of these forms:
- FL-320, *Responsive Declaration to Order to Show Cause or Notice of Motion* **and** FL-150, *Income and Expense Declaration*, **or**
- FL-155, *Financial Statement (Simplified)*
Then the server fills out and signs a *Proof of Service* (form FL-330 or FL-335). Take this form to the clerk and file it.

Go to your hearing and ask the judge to change the support. Bring your tax returns from the last two years and your last two months' pay stubs. The judge will look at your information, listen to both parents, and make an order. After the hearing, fill out:
- FL-340, *Findings and Order After Hearing* **and**
- FL-342, *Child Support Information and Order Attachment*

Need help?

Contact the family law facilitator in your county or call your county's bar association and ask for an experienced family lawyer.

NOTICE OF RIGHTS AND RESPONSIBILITES
Health-Care Costs and Reimbursement Procedures

☐ **ORDER/NOTICE TO WITHHOLD INCOME FOR CHILD SUPPORT**
☐ **NOTICE OF AN ORDER TO WITHHOLD INCOME FOR CHILD SUPPORT**

☐ **Original**   ☐ **Amended**   ☐ **Termination**   Date: _____

State/Tribe/Territory _____

City/Co./Dist./Reservation _____

☐ **Non-governmental entity or Individual** _____

Case Number _____

_____   RE : _____
_____ Employer's/Withholder's   Name   Employee's/Obligor's Name (Last, First, MI)

_____   _____
_____ Employer's/Withholders   Address   Employee's/Obligoes Social Security Number

_____   _____
                                                          Employee's/Obligors Case Idenfifier

_____   _____
Employers/Withholder's Federal EIN Number (if known)   Obligee's Name (Last, First, MI)

ORDER INFORMATION: _This_ document is based on the support or withholding order from_____.
You are required by law to deduct these amounts from the employee's/obligor's income until further notice.

$_____ Per_____ current child support
$_____ Per_____ past-due child support - Arrears greater than 12 weeks? ☐ yes ☐ no
$_____ Per_____ current Gash medical support
$_____ Per_____ past-due cash medical support
$_____ Per_____ spousal support
$_____ Per_____ past-due spousal support
$_____ Per_____ other (specify)_____

for a total of _____ per_____to be forwarded to the payee below.
You do not have to vary your pay cycle to be in compliance with the support order. If your pay cycle does not match the ordered payment cycle, withhold one of the following amounts:

$_____per weekly pay period. $_____per semimonthly pay period (twice a month).
$_____per biweekly pay period (every two weeks).$_____ per monthly pay period.

REMITTANCE INFORMATION. When remitting payment, provide the pay date/date of withholding and the case identifier. If the employee's/obligor's principal place of employment is in California, begin withholding no later than the first pay period occurring 10 days after the date of this order. Send payment within 10 working days of the pay date/date of withholding. The total withheld amount, including your fee, may not exceed _____% of the employee's/obligor's aggregate disposable weekly earnings.

If the employee's/obligor's principal place of employment is not _____ , for limitations on withholding, applicable time requirements, and any allowable employer fees, follow the laws and procedures of the employee's/obligor's principal place of employment (see #3 and #9, ADDITIONAL INFORMATION TO EMPLOYERS AND OTHER WITHHOLDERS).

Make check payable to:_____Send check to: _____ . If remitting
payment by EFT/EDI, call _____ before first submission. Use this FIPS code: _____ :
Bank routing number: _____ Bank account number:_____.

If this is an Order/Notice to Withhold: **If this is a Notice of an Order to Withhold:**

Print Name _____   Print Name _____
Title of Issuing Official_____   Title (if appropriate)_____
Signature and Date _____   Signature and Date _____

☐ IV-D Agency ☐ Court   ☐ Attorney ☐ Individual ☐ Private Entity
☐ Attorney with authority under state law to issue order/notice.

NOTE: Non-IV-D Attorneys, individuals, and non-governmental entities must submit a Notice of an Order to Withhold and include a copy of the income withholding order unless, under a state's law, an attorney in that state may issue an income withholding order. In that case, the attorney may submit an Order/Notice to Withhold and include a copy of the state law

IMPORTANT: The person completing this form Is advised that the Information on this form may be shared with the obligor authorizing the attorney to Issue an Income withholding order/notice.

OMB 0970-0154

ADDITIONAL INFORMATION TO EMPLOYERS AND OTHER WITHHOLDERS

☐ If checked, you are required to provide a copy of this form to your employee/obligor. If your employee works in a state that is different from the state that issued this order, a copy must be provided to your ampioyee/obligor even if the box is not checked.

1. **Priority:** Withholding under this Order or Notice has priority over any other legal process under state law (or tribal law, if applicable) against the same income. If there are federal tax levies in effect, please notify the contact person listed below. (See 10 below.)

2. **Combining Payments:** You may combine withheld amounts from more than one employee's/obligor's income in a single payment to each agency/party requesting withholding. You must, however, separately identify the portion of the single payment that is attributable to each employee/obligor.

3. **Reporting the Paydate/Date of Withholding:** You must report the paydate/date of withholding when sending the payment. The paydate/date of withholding is the date on which the amount was withheld from the employee's wages. You must comply with the law of the state of employee's/obligors principal place of employment with respect to the time periods within which you must implement the withholding and forward the support payments.

4. **Employse/Obligor with Multiple Support Withholdings:** If there is more than one Order or Notice against this employee/obligor and you are unable to honor all support Orders or Notices due to federal, state, or tribal withholding limits, you must follow the state or tribal law/procedure of the employee's/obligor's principal place of employment. You must honor all Orders or Notices to the greatest extent possible. (See 9 below.)

5. **Termination Notification:** You must promptly notify the Child Support Enforcement (IV-D) Agency and/or the contact person listed below when the employee/obligor no longer works for you. Please provide the information requested and return a complete copy of this Order or Notice to the Child Support Enforcement (IV-D) Agency and/or the contact person listed below. (See 10 below.)
    THE EMPLOYEE/OBLIGOR NO LONGER WORKS FOR:_____
    EMPLOYEE'S/OBLIGOR'S NAME:_____ CASE IDENTIFIER:_____
    DATE OF SEPARATION FROM EMPLOYMENT:_____
    LAST KNOWN HOME ADDRESS:_____
    NEW EMPLOYER/ADDRESS:_____

6. **Lump Sum Payments:** You may be required to report and withhold from lump sum payments such as bonuses, commissions, or severance pay. If you have any questions about lump sum payments, contact the Child Support Enforcement (IV-D) Agency,

7. **Liability** If you have any doubts about the validity of the Order or Notice, contact the agency or person listed below under 10. If you fail to withhold income as the Order or Notice directs, you are liable for both the accumulated amount you should have withheld from the employee's/obligors income and any other penalties set by state or tribal law/procedure.

    _____
    _____

8. **Anti-discrimination:** You are subject to a fine determined under state or tribal law for discharging an employee/obligor from employment, refusing to employ, or taking disciplinary action against any employee/obligor because of a child support withholding.

    _____
    _____

9. **Withholding Limits:** For state orders, you may not withhold more than the lesser of 1) the amounts allowed by the Federal Consumer Credit Protection Act (15 U.S.C. § 1673(b)); or 2) the amounts allowed by the state of the employee's/obligor's principal place of employment, The federal limit applies to the aggregate disposable weekly earnings (ADWE). ADWE is the net income left after making mandatory deductions such as: state, federal, local taxes, Social Security taxes, statutory pension contributions, and Medicare taxes. The Federal CCPA limit is 50% of the ADWE for child support and alimony, which is increased by 1) 10% if the employee does not support a second family; andlor 2) 5% if arrears greater than 12 weeks.
    For tribal orders, you may not withhold more than the amounts allowed under the law of the issuing tribe. For tribal employers who receive a state order, you may not withhold more than the amounts allowed under the law of the state that issued the order.

    Child(ren)'s Names and Additional Information: _____
    _____
    _____

10. If you or your employee/obligor have any questions, contact _____ by telephone at
    _____ by Fax at _____or by internet at _____

ATTORNEY OR PARTY WITHOUT ATTORNEY *(Name, State Bar number, and address):*

FOR COURT USE ONLY

TELEPHONE NO.:　　　　　　　FAX NO. *(Optional):*

E-MAIL ADDRESS *(Optional):*

ATTORNEY FOR *(Name):*

SUPERIOR COURT OF CALIFORNIA, COUNTY OF

STREET ADDRESS:

MAILING ADDRESS:

CITY AND ZIP CODE:

BRANCH NAME:

PETITIONER/PLAINTIFF:

RESPONDENT/DEFENDANT:

OTHER PARENT:

EARNINGS ASSIGNMENT ORDER FOR SPOUSAL OR PARTNER SUPPORT ☐ **Modification**	CASE NUMBER:

TO THE PAYOR: This is a court order. You must withhold a portion of the earnings of *(specify obligor's name and birthdate):*

and pay as directed below. *(An explanation of this order is printed on page 2 of this form.)*

THE COURT ORDERS

1. You must pay part of the earnings of the employee or other person who has been ordered to pay support, as follows:

    a. ☐ $　　　　　　per month current **spousal or partner support**

    b. ☐ $　　　　　　per month **spousal or partner support arrearages**

    c. **Total deductions per month:**　$

2. ☐　The payments ordered under item 1a must be paid to *(name, address):*

3. ☐　The payments ordered under item 1b must be paid to *(name, address):*

4. The payments ordered under item 1 must continue until further written notice from the payee or the court.

5. ☐　This order modifies an existing order. **The amount you must withhold may have changed.** The existing order continues in effect until this modification is effective.

6. This order affects all earnings that are payable beginning as soon as possible but not later than 10 days after you receive it.

7. You must give the obligor a copy of this order and the blank *Request for Hearing Regarding Earnings Assignment* (form FL-450) within 10 days.

8. ☐　Other *(specify):*

9. For the purposes of this order, spousal or partner support arrearages are set at: $　　　　　　as of *(date):*

Date:

_____
JUDICIAL OFFICER

Form Adopted for Mandatory Use
Judicial Council of California
FL-435 [Rev. January 1, 2005]

**EARNINGS ASSIGNMENT ORDER FOR SPOUSAL
OR PARTNER SUPPORT**
(Family Law)

Family Code, §§ 299(d), 5208;
Code of Civil Procedure, § 706.031;
15 U.S.C. §§ 1672–1673
www.courtinfo.ca.gov

1. DEFINITION OF IMPORTANT WORDS IN THE EARNINGS ASSIGNMENT ORDER

a. **Earnings:**

(1) Wages, salary, bonuses, vacation pay, retirement pay, and commissions paid by an employer;

(2) Payments for services of independent contractors;

(3) Dividends, interest, rents, royalties, and residuals;

(4) Patent rights and mineral or other natural resource rights;

(5) Any payments due as a result of written or oral contracts for services or sales, regardless of title;

(6) Payments due for workers' compensation temporary benefits, or payments from a disability or health insurance policy or program; and

(7) Any other payments or credits due, regardless of source.

b. **Earnings assignment order:** a court order issued in every court case in which one person is ordered to pay for the support of another person. This order has priority over any other orders such as garnishments or earnings withholding orders.

Earnings should not be withheld for any other order until the amounts necessary to satisfy this order have been withheld in full. However, an *Order/Notice to Withhold Income for Child Support* for child support or family support has priority over this order for spousal or partner support.

c. **Obligor:** any person ordered by a court to pay support. The obligor is named before item 1 in the order.

d. **Obligee:** the person or governmental agency to whom the support is to be paid.

e. **Payor:** the person or entity, including an employer, that pays earnings to an obligor.

2. INFORMATION FOR ALL PAYORS.

Withhold money from the earnings payable to the obligor as soon as possible but no later than 10 days after you receive the *Earnings Assignment Order for Spousal or Partner Support.* Send the withheld money to the payee(s) named in items 2 and 3 of the order within 10 days of the pay date. You may deduct $1 from the obligor's earnings for each payment you make.

When sending the withheld earnings to the payee, state the date on which the earnings were withheld. You may combine amounts withheld for two or more obligors in a single payment to each payee, and identify what portion of that payment is for each obligor.

You will be liable for any amount you fail to withhold and can be cited for contempt of court.

3. SPECIAL INSTRUCTIONS FOR PAYORS WHO ARE EMPLOYERS

a. State and federal laws limit the amount you can withhold and pay as directed by this order. This limitation applies only to earnings defined above in item 1a(1) and are usually half the obligor's disposable earnings.

Disposable earnings are different from gross pay or take-home pay. Disposable earnings are earnings left after subtracting the money that state or federal law requires an employer to withhold. Generally these required deductions are (1) federal income tax, (2) social

security, (3) state income tax, (4) state disability insurance, and (5) payments to public employees' retirement systems.

After the obligor's disposable earnings are known, withhold the amount required by the order, **but never withhold more than 50 percent of the disposable earnings unless the court order specifies a higher percentage.** Federal law prohibits withholding more than 65 percent of disposable earnings of an employee in any case.

If the obligor has more than one assignment for support, add together the amounts of support due for all the assignments. **If 50 percent of the obligor's net disposable earnings will not pay in full all of the assignments for support,** prorate it first among all of the current support assignments in the same proportion that each assignment bears to the total current support owed. Apply any remainder to the current support. Prorate any arrearage assignments in the same proportion that each assignment bears to the total arrearage owed.

This office or person's name appears in the upper left-hand corner of the order.

If you have any questions, please contact the office or person who sent this form to you.

b. If the employee's pay period differs from the period specified in the order, prorate the amount ordered withheld so that part of it is withheld from each of the obligor's paychecks.

c. If the obligor stops working for you, notify the office that sent you this form, no later than the date of the next payment, by first-class mail. Give the obligor's last known address and, if known, the name and address of any new employer.

d. California law prohibits you from firing, refusing to hire, or taking any disciplinary action against any employee ordered to pay support through an earnings assignment. Such action can lead to a $500 civil penalty per employee.

4. INFORMATION FOR ALL OBLIGORS.

You should have received a *Request for Hearing Regarding Earnings Assignment* (form FL-450) with this *Earnings Assignment Order for Spousal or Partner Support.* If not, you may get one from either the court clerk or the family law facilitator. If you want the court to stop or modify your earnings assignment, you must file (by hand delivery or mail) an original copy of the form with the court clerk within 10 days of the date you received this order. Keep a copy of the form for your records. If you think your support order is wrong, you can ask for a modification of the order or, in some cases, you can have the order set aside and have a new order issued. You can talk to an attorney or get information from the family law facilitator about this.

5. SPECIAL INFORMATION FOR THE OBLIGOR WHO IS AN EMPLOYEE.

State law requires you to notify the payees named in items 2 and 3 of the order if you change your employment. You must provide the name and address of your new employer.

ATTORNEY OR PARTY WITHOUT ATTORNEY *(Name, State Bar number, and address):*

FOR COURT USE ONLY

TELEPHONE NO.:
FAX NO. *(Optional):*
E-MAIL ADDRESS *(Optional):*
ATTORNEY FOR *(Name):*

SUPERIOR COURT OF CALIFORNIA, COUNTY OF

STREET ADDRESS:
MAILING ADDRESS:
CITY AND ZIP CODE:
BRANCH NAME:

PETITIONER/PLAINTIFF:

RESPONDENT/DEFENDANT:

OTHER PARENT:

**REQUEST FOR HEARING REGARDING
EARNINGS ASSIGNMENT**

CASE NUMBER:

NOTICE: Complete and file this form with the court clerk to request a hearing *only* if you object to the *Order/Notice to Withhold Income for Child Support* (form FL-195/OMB0970-0154) or *Earnings Assignment Order for Spousal or Partner Support* (form FL-435). This form may not be used to modify your current child support amount. (See page 2 of form FL-192, *Information Sheet on Changing a Child Support Order.*) Page 3 of this form is instructional only and does not need to be delivered to the court.

1. A hearing on this application will be held as follows *(see instructions for getting a hearing date on page 3):*

   a. |Date: Time: ☐ Dept.:   ☐ Div.:   ☐ Room:

   b. The address of the court is: ☐ same as noted above   ☐ other *(specify):*

2. ☐ I request that service of the *Earnings Assignment Order for Spousal or Partner Support* (form FL-435) or *Order/Notice to Withhold Income for Child Support* (form FL-195/OMB0970-0154) be quashed (set aside) because

   a. ☐ I am not the obligor named in the earnings assignment.

   b. ☐ There is good cause to recall the earnings assignment because **all** of the following conditions exist:

      (1) Recalling the earnings assignment would be in the best interest of the children for whom I am ordered to pay support *(state reasons):*

      (2) I have paid court-ordered support fully and on time for the last 12 months without either an earnings assignment or another mandatory collection process.

      (3) I do not owe any arrearage (back support).

      (4) Service of the earnings assignment would cause extraordinary hardship for me, as follows *(state reasons; you must prove these reasons at any hearing on this application by clear and convincing evidence):*

   c. ☐ The other parent and I have a written agreement that allows the support order to be paid by an alternative method. A copy of the agreement is attached. **(NOTE: If the support obligation is paid to the local child support agency, this agreement must be signed by a representative of that agency.)**

Form Adopted for Mandatory Use
Judicial Council of California
FL-450 [Rev. January 1, 2005]
REQUEST FOR HEARING REGARDING EARNINGS ASSIGNMENT
(Family Law—Governmental—UIFSA)
Family Code, § 5246
www.courtinfo.ca.gov

3. ☐ I request that the earnings assignment be modified because

    a. ☐ the total amount of arrearages claimed as owing is incorrect. *(Check one or more of the following reasons.)*

        (1) ☐ I did not receive credit for all of the payments I have made. *(Check (a), (b), or both.)*

            (a) ☐ I have attached my statement of the payment history, which includes a monthly breakdown of amounts ordered and amounts paid.

            (b) ☐ I made the following payments that were not credited *(for each payment, specify the date, the amount, and the name of the person or agency paid):*

        (2) ☐ Child support was terminated *(specify name of child, child's date of birth, date of termination, and reason support was terminated):*

        (3) ☐ Other *(specify):*

    b. ☐ the monthly payment specified in the earnings assignment is more than half of my total net income each month from all sources.

    c. ☐ the monthly arrearage payment stated in the earnings assignment creates an undue hardship because *(describe the hardship and state the amount you are able to pay on your arrearage):*

(NOTE: If you want to change the amount of money being deducted for arrearage because it creates a hardship, please attach a completed *Financial Statement (Simplified)* (form FL-155) or *Income and Expense Declaration* (form FL-150).)

I declare under penalty of perjury under the laws of the State of California that the foregoing is true and correct.

Date:

▶

_____   _____
(TYPE OR PRINT NAME OF PERSON REQUESTING HEARING)   (SIGNATURE OF PERSON REQUESTING HEARING)

CLERK'S CERTIFICATE OF MAILING

I certify that I am not a party to this action and that a true copy of the *Request for Hearing Regarding Earnings Assignment* (form FL-450) was mailed, with postage fully prepaid, in a sealed envelope addressed as shown below, and that the request was mailed at *(place):*   on *(date):*

Date:

Clerk, by _____ , Deputy

REQUEST FOR HEARING REGARDING EARNINGS ASSIGNMENT
(Family Law—Governmental—UIFSA)

INFORMATION SHEET AND INSTRUCTIONS
FOR REQUEST FOR HEARING REGARDING EARNINGS ASSIGNMENT
(Do *not* deliver this information sheet to the court clerk.)

Please follow these instructions to complete the *Request for Hearing Regarding Earnings Assignment* (form FL-450) if you do not have an attorney representing you. Your attorney, if you have one, should complete this form. You must file the completed *Request for Hearing* form and its attachments with the court clerk **within 10 days** after the date your employer gave you a copy of *Earnings Assignment Order for Spousal or Partner Support* (form FL-435) or an *Order/Notice to Withhold Income for Child Support* (form FL-195/OMB0970-0154). The address of the court clerk is the same as the one shown for the superior court on the earnings assignment order. You may have to pay a filing fee. If you cannot afford to pay the filing fee, the court may waive it, but you will have to fill out some forms first. For more information about the filing fee and waiver of the filing fee, contact the court clerk or the family law facilitator in your county.

(TYPE OR PRINT IN INK)

Front page, first box, top of form, left side: Print your name, address, and telephone number in this box if they are not already there.

Item 1. **a–b.** You must contact the court clerk's office and ask that a hearing date be set for this motion. The court clerk will give you the information you need to complete this section.

Item 2. Check this box if you want the court to stop the local child support agency or the other parent from collecting any support from your earnings. If you check this box, you must check the box for either a, b, or c beneath it.

    a. Check this box if you are not the person required to pay support in the earnings assignment.

    b. Check this box if you believe that there is "good cause" to recall the earnings assignment. **Note:** The court must find that **all** of the conditions listed in item 2b exist in order for good cause to apply.

    c. Check this box if you and the other parent have a written agreement that allows you to pay the support another way. **You must attach a copy of the agreement,** which must be signed by both the other parent and a representative of the local child support agency if payments are made to a county office.

Item 3. Check this box if you want to change the earnings assignment. If you check this box, you must check the box for either a, b, or c beneath it.

    a. Check this box if the total arrearages listed in item 9 on the earnings assignment order are wrong. If you check this box, you must check one or more of (1), (2), and (3). You must attach the original of your statement of arrearages. Keep one copy for yourself.

        (1) Check this box if you believe the amount of arrearages listed on the earnings assignment order does not give you credit for all the payments you have made. If you check this box, you must check one or both of the boxes beneath it.

            (a) Check this box if you are attaching your own statement of arrearages. This statement must include a monthly listing of what you were ordered to pay and what you actually paid.

            (b) Check this box if you wish to list any payments that you believe were not included in the arrearages amount. For each payment you must list the date you paid it, the amount paid, and the person or agency (such as the local child support agency) to whom you made the payment. Bring to the hearing proof of any payment that is in dispute.

        (2) Check this box if the child support for any of the children in the case has been terminated (ended). If you check this box, you must list the following information for each child:
            • The name and birthdate of each child.
            • The date the child support order was terminated.
            • The reason child support was terminated.

        (3) Check this box if there is another reason you believe the amount of arrearages is incorrect. You must explain the reasons in detail.

    b. Check this box if the total monthly payment shown in item 1 of the earnings assignment order is more than half of your monthly net income.

    c. Check this box if the total monthly payment shown in item 1 of the earnings assignment order causes you a serious hardship. You must write the reasons for the hardship in this space.

You must date this *Request for Hearing* form, print your name, and sign the form under penalty of perjury. You must also complete the certificate of mailing at the bottom of page 2 of the form by printing the name and address of the other parties in brackets and providing a stamped envelope addressed to each of the parties. When you sign this *Request for Hearing* form, you are stating that the information you have provided is true and correct. After you file the request, the court clerk will notify you by mail of the date, time, and location of the hearing.

You must file your request within 10 days of receiving the *Earnings Assignment Order for Spousal or Partner Support* or the *Order/Notice to Withhold Income for Child Support* from your employer. You may file your request in person at the clerk's office or mail it to the clerk. In either event, it must be received by the clerk within the 10-day period.

If you need additional assistance with this form, contact an attorney or the family law facilitator in your county. Your family law facilitator can help you, for free, with any questions you have about the above information. For more information on finding a lawyer or family law facilitator, see the California Courts Online Self-Help Center at *www.courtinfo.ca.gov/selfhelp/*.

NOTICE: Use form FL-450 to request a hearing only if you object to the *Order/Notice to Withhold Income for Child Support* (form FL-195/OMB0970-0154) or *Earnings Assignment Order for Spousal or Partner Support* (form FL-435). This form will *not* modify your current support amount. (See page 2 of form FL-192, *Information Sheet on Changing a Child Support Order*.)

ATTORNEY OR PARTY WITHOUT ATTORNEY *(Name, State Bar number, and address):*

FOR COURT USE ONLY

TELEPHONE NO.: FAX NO. *(Optional):*

E-MAIL ADDRESS *(Optional):*

ATTORNEY FOR *(Name):*

SUPERIOR COURT OF CALIFORNIA, COUNTY OF

STREET ADDRESS:

MAILING ADDRESS:

CITY AND ZIP CODE:

BRANCH NAME:

PETITIONER:

RESPONDENT:

DECLARATION FOR DEFAULT OR UNCONTESTED	CASE NUMBER:
☐ **DISSOLUTION** ☐ **LEGAL SEPARATION**	

(NOTE: Items 1 through 16 apply to both dissolution and legal separation proceedings.)

1. I declare that if I appeared in court and were sworn, I would testify to the truth of the facts in this declaration.

2. I agree that my case will be proven by this declaration and that I will not appear before the court unless I am ordered by the court to do so.

3. All the information in the ☐ *Petition* ☐ *Response* is true and correct.

4. **Default or uncontested** *(Check a or b.)*

   a. ☐ The default of the respondent was entered or is being requested, and I am not seeking any relief not requested in the petition. **OR**

   b. ☐ The parties have agreed that the matter may proceed as an uncontested matter without notice, and the agreement is attached or is incorporated in the attached settlement agreement or stipulated judgment.

5. **Settlement agreement** *(Check a or b.)*

   a. ☐ The parties have entered into ☐ **an agreement** ☐ **a stipulated judgment** regarding their property their marriage or domestic partnership rights, including support, the original of which is or has been submitted to the court. I request that the court approve the agreement. **OR**

   b. ☐ **There is no agreement or stipulated judgment,** and the following statements are true *(check at least one, including item (2) if a community estate exists):*

      (1) ☐ There are no community or quasi-community assets or community debts to be disposed of by the court.

      (2) ☐ The community and quasi-community assets and debts are listed on the attached **completed** current *Property Declaration* (form FL-160), which includes an estimate of the value of the assets and debts that I propose to be distributed to each party. The division in the proposed *Judgment (Family Law)* (form FL-180) is a fair and equal division of the property and debts, or if there is a negative estate, the debts are assigned fairly and equitably.

6. **Declaration of disclosure** *(Check a, b, or c.)*

   a. ☐ Both the petitioner and respondent have filed, or are filing concurrently, a *Declaration Regarding Service of Declaration of Disclosure* (form FL-141) and an *Income and Expense Declaration* (form FL-150).

   b. ☐ This matter is proceeding by default. I am the petitioner in this action and have filed a proof of service of the preliminary *Declaration of Disclosure* (form FL-140) with the court. I hereby waive receipt of the final *Declaration of Disclosure* (form FL-140) from the respondent.

   c. ☐ This matter is proceeding as an uncontested action. Service of the final *Declaration of Disclosure* (form FL-140) is mutually waived by both parties. A waiver provision executed by both parties under penalty of perjury is contained in the settlement agreement or proposed judgment or another, separate stipulation.

7. ☐ **Child custody** should be ordered as set forth in the proposed *Judgment (Family Law)* (form FL-180).

8. ☐ **Child visitation** should be ordered as set forth in the proposed *Judgment (Family Law)* (form FL-180).

9. **Spousal, partner, and family support** *(If a support order or attorney fees are requested, submit a completed* Income and Expense Declaration *(form FL-150) unless a current form is on file. Include your best estimate of the other party's income. Check at least one of the following.)*

   a. ☐ I knowingly give up forever any right to receive spousal or partner support.

   b. ☐ I ask the court to reserve jurisdiction to award spousal or partner support in the future to *(name):*

   c. ☐ Spousal support should be ordered as set forth in the proposed *Judgment (Family Law)* (form FL-180).

   d. ☐ Family support should be ordered as set forth in the proposed *Judgment (Family Law)* (form FL-180).

Form Adopted for Mandatory Use
Judicial Council of California
FL-170 [Rev. January 1, 2007]

**DECLARATION FOR DEFAULT OR UNCONTESTED
DISSOLUTION or LEGAL SEPARATION**
(Family Law)

Family Code, § 2336
www.courtinfo.ca.gov

PETITIONER:	CASE NUMBER:
RESPONDENT:	

10. ☐ **Child support** should be ordered as set forth in the proposed *Judgment (Family Law)* (form FL-180).

11. a. I ☐ am receiving ☐ am not receiving ☐ intend to apply for public assistance for the child or children listed in the proposed order.

b. To the best of my knowledge, the other party ☐ is ☐ is not receiving public assistance.

12. ☐ The petitioner ☐ respondent is presently receiving public assistance, and all support should be made payable to the local child support agency at the address set forth in the proposed judgment. A representative of the local child support agency has signed the proposed judgment.

13. If there are minor children, check and complete item a and item b or c:

a. ☐ My gross (before taxes) monthly income is *(specify):* $

b. ☐ The estimated gross monthly income of the other party is *(specify):* $

c. ☐ I have no knowledge of the estimated monthly income of the other party for the following reasons *(specify):*

d. ☐ I request that this order be based on the ☐ petitioner's ☐ respondent's earning ability. The facts in support of my estimate of earning ability are *(specify):*

☐ Continued on Attachment 13d.

14. ☐ **Parentage** of the children of the petitioner and respondent born prior to their marriage or domestic partnership should be ordered as set forth in the proposed *Judgment (Family Law)* (form FL-180). A declaration regarding parentage is attached.

15. ☐ **Attorney fees** should be ordered as set forth in the proposed *Judgment (Family Law)* (form FL-180).

16. ☐ The petitioner ☐ respondent requests restoration of his or her former name as set forth in the proposed *Judgment (Family Law)* (form FL-180).

17. There are irreconcilable differences that have led to the irremediable breakdown of the marriage or domestic partnership, and there is no possibility of saving the marriage or domestic partnership through counseling or other means.

18. This declaration may be reviewed by a commissioner sitting as a temporary judge, who may determine whether to grant this request or require my appearance under Family Code section 2336.

STATEMENTS IN THIS BOX APPLY ONLY TO DISSOLUTIONS—Items 19 through 21

19. If this is a dissolution of marriage or of a domestic partnership created in another state, the petitioner and/or the respondent has been a resident of this county for at least three months and of the state of California for at least six months continuously and immediately preceding the date of the filing of the petition for dissolution of marriage or domestic partnership.

20. I ask that the court grant the request for a judgment for dissolution of marriage or domestic partnership based upon irreconcilable differences and that the court make the orders set forth in the proposed *Judgment (Family Law)* (form FL-180) submitted with this declaration.

21. ☐ This declaration is for the termination of **marital or domestic partner status only.** I ask the court to reserve jurisdiction over all issues whose determination is not requested in this declaration.

THIS STATEMENT APPLIES ONLY TO LEGAL SEPARATIONS

22. I ask that the court grant the request for a judgment for legal separation based upon irreconcilable differences and that the court make the orders set forth in the proposed *Judgment (Family Law)* (form FL-180) submitted with this declaration.

I understand that a judgment of legal separation does not terminate a marriage or domestic partnership and that I am still married or a partner in a domestic partnership.

23. ☐ Other *(specify):*

Date:

I declare under penalty of perjury under the laws of the State of California that the foregoing is true and correct.

▶

_____
(TYPE OR PRINT NAME)

_____
(SIGNATURE OF DECLARANT)

ATTORNEY OR PARTY WITHOUT ATTORNEY *(Name, State Bar number, and address):*

FOR COURT USE ONLY

TELEPHONE NO.:   FAX NO. *(Optional):*
E-MAIL ADDRESS *(Optional):*
ATTORNEY FOR *(Name):*

SUPERIOR COURT OF CALIFORNIA, COUNTY OF

STREET ADDRESS:
MAILING ADDRESS:
CITY AND ZIP CODE:
BRANCH NAME:

PETITIONER:

RESPONDENT:

NOTICE OF ENTRY OF JUDGMENT

CASE NUMBER:

You are notified that the following judgment was entered on *(date):*

1. ☐ Dissolution
2. ☐ Dissolution—status only
3. ☐ Dissolution—reserving jurisdiction over termination of marital status or domestic partnership
4. ☐ Legal separation
5. ☐ Nullity
6. ☐ Parent-child relationship
7. ☐ Judgment on reserved issues
8. ☐ Other *(specify):*

Date:

Clerk, by _____ , Deputy

—NOTICE TO ATTORNEY OF RECORD OR PARTY WITHOUT ATTORNEY—

Under the provisions of Code of Civil Procedure section 1952, if no appeal is filed the court may order the exhibits destroyed or otherwise disposed of after 60 days from the expiration of the appeal time.

STATEMENT IN THIS BOX APPLIES ONLY TO JUDGMENT OF DISSOLUTION

Effective date of termination of marital or domestic partnership status *(specify):*

WARNING: Neither party may remarry or enter into a new domestic partnership until the effective date of the termination of marital or domestic partnership status, as shown in this box.

CLERK'S CERTIFICATE OF MAILING

I certify that I am not a party to this cause and that a true copy of the *Notice of Entry of Judgment* was mailed first class, postage fully prepaid, in a sealed envelope addressed as shown below, and that the notice was mailed

at *(place):* _____ , California,   on *(date):*

Date:

Clerk, by _____ , Deputy

┌─ Name and address of petitioner or petitioner's attorney ─┐   ┌─ Name and address of respondent or respondent's attorney ─┐

Page 1 of 1

Form Adopted for Mandatory Use
Judicial Council of California
FL-190 [Rev. January 1, 2005]

NOTICE OF ENTRY OF JUDGMENT
(Family Law—Uniform Parentage—Custody and Support)

Family Code, §§ 2338, 7636,7637
www.courtinfo.ca.gov

Exhibit A
Nolo Supplementary Family Arbitration Rules

Nolo Press Occidental • www.nolocouples.com

1. Scope and application

Any dispute subject to arbitration pursuant to a premarital, postmarital, living together, marital settlement agreement, couples contract or relationship agreement that refers to these rules will be governed by the arbitration rules named in the agreement or otherwise selected by the parties, except that interim and post-judgment matters shall be governed by the following supplementary rules:

2. Interim relief and interim measures

(a) In the case of an arbitration where arbitrators have not yet been appointed, or where the arbitrators are unavailable, a party may seek interim remedies directly from a court as provided in subsection (c) of this section. Enforcement shall be granted as provided by the laws of the state in which the interim relief is sought.

(b) In all other cases, including cases of modification of interim relief obtained directly from a court prior to commencement of the arbitration or under subsection (a) of this section, a party shall seek interim measures as described in subsection (d) of this section from the arbitrators. A party has no right to seek interim relief from a court, except that a party to an arbitration governed by this Article may request from the court enforcement of the arbitrators' order granting interim measures and review or modification of any interim measures governing child support or child custody.

(c) In connection with an agreement to arbitrate or a pending arbitration, the court may grant under subsection (a) of this section any temporary or *pendente lite* orders a court is permitted by state law to make during the pendency of a family law proceeding, including but not limited to:

(1) A temporary restraining order or preliminary injunction;

(2) An order for temporary child custody and visitation while the arbitration is pending or until a judgment may be entered on the arbitration award;

(3) An order for temporary support of any party or child of the parties while the arbitration is pending or until a judgment may be entered on the arbitration award;

(4) An order for temporary possession and control of real or personal property of the parties;

(5) An order for the immediate sale of any asset of the parties;

(6) An order for payment of debts and obligations of the parties;

(7) Any other order necessary to ensure preservation or availability of assets or documents, the destruction or absence of which would likely prejudice the conduct or effectiveness of the arbitration.

(d) The arbitrators may, at a party's request, order any party to take any interim measures of protection that the arbitrators consider necessary in respect to the subject matter of the dispute, including interim measures analogous to interim relief specified in subsection (c) of this section. The arbitrators may require any party to provide appropriate security in connection with interim measures.

(e) In considering a request for interim relief or enforcement of interim relief, any finding of fact of the arbitrators in the proceeding shall be binding on the court, including any finding regarding the probable validity of the claim that is the subject of the interim relief sought or granted, except that the court may review any findings of fact or modify any interim measures governing child support or child custody.

(f) Where the arbitrators have not ruled on an objection to their jurisdiction, the findings of the arbitrators shall not be binding on the court until the court has made an independent finding as to the arbitrators' jurisdiction. If the court rules that the arbitrators do not have jurisdiction, the application for interim relief shall be denied.

(g) Availability of interim relief or interim measures under this section may be limited by the parties' prior written agreement, except for relief whose purpose is to provide immediate, emergency relief or protection, or relief directly related to the welfare of a child.

(h) Arbitrators who have cause to suspect that any child is abused or neglected shall report the case of that child to the appropriate child protection authorities of the county where the child resides or, if the child resides out-of-state, of the county where the arbitration is conducted.

(i) A party seeking interim measures, or any other proceeding before the arbitrators, shall proceed in accordance with the agreement to arbitrate. If the agreement to arbitrate does not provide for a method of seeking interim measures, or for other proceedings before the arbitrators, the party shall request interim measures or a hearing by notifying the arbitrators and all other parties of the request. The arbitrators shall notify the parties of the date, time, and place of the hearing.

3. Post-judgment modification and other relief

(a) In the case of any dispute which may arise after the conclusion of the original arbitration proceedings or after a court has entered a judgment between the parties, requests for modification or set-aside of any matter shall be subject to arbitration to the extent and in the same manner and to the same extent as the arbitration of a prejudgment dispute between the parties.

(b) Where arbitrators have not yet been appointed, or where the arbitrators are unavailable, a party may seek post-judgment modification relief directly from a court as provided in subsection (d) of this section. Enforcement shall be granted as provided by the law applicable to the type of post-judgment relief sought. A party may not seek directly from a court a set-aside of a judgment based on an arbitration award. The arbitrators shall have exclusive jurisdiction over such matters, except that a party to an arbitration governed by this Article may request from the court enforcement of the arbitrator's order granting such post-judgment measures.

(c) In all other cases a party shall seek post-judgment measures as described in subsection (e) of this section from the arbitrators. A party has no right to seek post-judgment relief from a court, except that a party to an arbitration governed by this Article may request from the court enforcement of the arbitrators' order granting post-judgment measures and review or modification of any post-judgment measures governing child support or child custody.

(d) In connection with an agreement to arbitrate or a pending arbitration, the court may grant under subsection (b) of this section any orders a court is permitted by state law to make upon a showing of changed circumstances after entry of judgment in a family law proceeding, including but not limited to:

(1) A restraining order or injunction;

(2) An order for modification of child custody and visitation;

(3) An order for modification of support of any party or child of the parties after judgment;

(4) Any other order necessary to ensure preservation or availability of assets or documents, the destruction or absence of which would likely prejudice the conduct or effectiveness of the arbitration.

(e) The arbitrators may, at a party's request, make any post-judgment orders the arbitrators consider necessary in respect to the subject matter of the dispute, including post-judgment measures analogous to post-judgment relief specified in subsection (d) of this section. The arbitrators may require any party to provide appropriate security in connection with post-judgment measures.

(f) In considering a request for post-judgment relief or enforcement of post-judgment relief, any finding of fact of the arbitrators in the proceeding shall be binding on the court, including any finding regarding the probable validity of the claim that is the subject of the post-judgment relief sought or granted, except that the court may review any findings of fact or modify any post-judgment measures governing child support or child custody.

(g) Where the arbitrators have not ruled on an objection to their jurisdiction, the findings of the arbitrators shall not be binding on the court until the court has made an independent finding as to the arbitrators' jurisdiction. If the court rules that the arbitrators do not have jurisdiction, the application for post-judgment relief shall be denied.

(h) Availability of post-judgment relief or post-judgment measures under this section may be limited by the parties' prior written agreement, except for relief whose purpose is to provide immediate, emergency relief or protection, or relief directly related to the welfare of a child.

(i) Arbitrators who have cause to suspect that any child is abused or neglected shall report the case of that child to the appropriate child protection authorities of the county where the child resides or, if the child resides out-of-state, of the county where the arbitration is conducted.

(j) A party seeking post-judgment measures, or any other proceeding before the arbitrators, shall proceed in accordance with the agreement to arbitrate. If the agreement to arbitrate does not provide for a method of seeking post-judgment measures, or for other proceedings before the arbitrators, the party shall request post-judgment measures or a hearing by notifying the arbitrators and all other parties of the request. The arbitrators shall notify the parties of the date, time, and place of the hearing.

More tools to make your job easier

Divorce Services Near You

Professionals who will help you do your own divorce

Legal Document Assistants, Mediators, Counselors, Accountants, Financial Planners, Attorneys

✳

for the most up-to-date list, see
Nolo's Internet Directory at
www.nolodivorce.com/dir

Divorce Services Near You

Professionals who will help you do your own divorce

Legal Document Assistants, Mediators, Counselors, Accountants, Financial Planners, Attorneys

Look for your telephone area code. Cities in each area code are in alphabetical order.

---

(18) Affordable Legal Document Assistance   LDA # 003

Commitment To Service Since 1989

1026 McHenry   Modesto   (209) 571-2400

---

(34) Divorce Centers of California   LDA # 05

Visit us at www.divorcecenters.com

1261 Lincoln Ave. #201   San Jose   (408) 295-6955

---

(28) Delta Typing Service   LDA # 02   12-03-09

𝒞 Since 1978 - Also Other Documents - FAX (209) 948-4762

3232 N. El Dorado St.   Stockton   (209) 948-2583

---

(11) Michael S. Thompson, CPA,CVA,CFFA

All financial issues: valuation & division of assets, support, tax planning, etc.

2858 Stevens Creek Blvd. #207   San Jose   (408) 247-5253

---

(12) Hamid Naraghi, Divorce Helpline

12+ years family law experience; let me help you resolve your divorce issues

515 So. Flower St., 36th Floor   Los Angeles   (800) 359-7004

---

(2) Fishel & Fishel, Attorneys at Law

Quick, Creative and Effective Solutions for your Legal Problem

110 Blue Ridge Drive, Suite 200   Martinez   (925) 229-4000

---

(1) Legal Remedy Network

Low cost paralegal service - 15 yrs experience - Reliable & Efficient

1620 Centinela Avenue, #205   Inglewood   (310) 417-4048

---

(25) California Divorce Council   LDA # 003

www.divorcecouncilsf.com

2525 Van Ness Ave. #209   San Francisco   (415) 441-5157

---

(35) Divorce Center of Los Angeles   LDA # 0019   12-30-09

𝒞 THE INTELLIGENT ALTERNATIVE   (800) 491-4491 www.divorcesos.com

11400 W. Olympic, Suite #200   Los Angeles   (310) 312-0161

---

(11) Bill Woodcock, Divorce Helpline

11+ years family law experience; let me help you resolve your divorce issues

1 Embarcadero Ctr, #500   San Francisco   (800) 359-7004

---

(17) Divorce Resource, Inc.   LDA # X204   06-16-08

Mediation and Legal Document Preparation. Mediator on Divorce Court T.V.

3002 Midvale Ave. #210   Los Angeles   (310) 441-7555

---

(10) GENEVIEVE'S CORPORATION   LDA # 38-00017   06-30-08

𝒞 Help@FastEasyDivorce.com * (650) 347-6750 * 24/7 Home Service

582 Market Street, Suite #1004   San Francisco   (415) 822-2222

---

(6) PH PARALEGAL SERVICES

Legal Document Specialist, Personal Service, Free Phone Consultation

13904 Fiji Way, #233   Marina Del Rey   (310) 822-8326

---

(9) Divorce With Dignity   LDA # 39   02-28-08

𝒞 An easy, low cost solution for preparing your legal documents.

1138-A Ballena Blvd. #2   Alameda   (800) 459-5556

---

(16) Attorney Assisted

www.AttorneyAssistedLaw.com   Mon-Fri 9 am-7 pm & most Saturdays

18411 Crenshaw Blvd. #330   Torrance   (310) 327-1598

---

(32) DIVORCE HELP   LDA # 07   12-26-09

𝒞 Reg. & Bonded in Alameda & Contra Costa Counties - 30 Years Experience

600 San Pablo Ave. #207   Albany   (510) 526-5651

---

(2) Pamela Britton White Mediation Service   LDA # 294   03-17-08

Helping Families Resolve Conflict Since 1986. Call for a FREE orientation.

850 Colorado Blvd., Suite 102   Los Angeles   (323) 340-1596

---

(5) Leininger Divorce Planning Services

Helping divorcing couples with financial goals, concerns & settlement options

3160 Castro Valley Blvd.   Castro Valley   (510) 728-3578

---

(8) Earle Law Offices, A Professional Corp.

Anthony F. Earle, Attorney At Law

19925 Stevens Creek Blvd.   Cupertino   (408) 786-1060

---

(13) Judicial Self-Help Center   LDA # 042   08-11-08

𝒞 Support Legal Access . . . It's Your Right! * JSHCLegal@aol.com

925 West Winton Ave., Suite E   Hayward   (510) 264-5300

---

(5) Legal Document Services   LDA # 77   11-29-09

𝒞 Divorce, mediation, eviction, notary & process server

20432 Silverado Ave., Ste. 5b   Cupertino   (408) 973-9004

---

(6) Legal Document Services   LDA # 28   03-25-08

𝒞 Affordable self-help alternative to high legal costs

390 Jane Court   Hayward   (510) 886-5906

Divorce Services Near You

Look for your telephone area code
Cities in each area code are in alphabetical order
Also see www.nolodivorce.com/dir

view latest list at www.nolodivorce.com/dir

---

(2) Divorce Centers of California

Divorce-Specialty, LDA and Lawyer Available; DivorceCenters@gmail.com

1501 N. Broadway, #201   **Walnut Creek**   (925) 937-6320

---

(21) Divorce Centers of California

Reasonable, settlement-oriented staff. Certified Specialist Family Law

2020 Main St., Suite 950   **Irvine**   (949) 756-8544

---

(12) Hamid Naraghi, Divorce Helpline

12+ years family law experience; let me help you resolve your divorce issues

19800 McArthur Blvd., #300   **Irvine**   (800) 359-7004

---

(5) Legal Assistance Center   LDA # 133   07-31-08

Affordable Legal Services - Divorce - Bankruptcy - Immigration

24401 Ridge Route, Ste. A104   **Laguna Hills**   (949) 716-0175

---

(19) Legal-Eaze Form Preparation   LDA # 008   11-30-09

C   Divorce * Bankruptcy * Adoptions * Guardianship * Wills * Trust * Evictions

5005 La Mart Drive #201   **Riverside**   (951) 788-1266

---

(5) Just Document Preparation   LDA # 062   12-06-09

C   Since 1996   www.JustDocPrep.com

7710 Limonite Ave. Suite N   **Riverside**   (951) 685-5444

---

(6) Due Process

Fixed Price Legal Centers, serving San Diego, Imperial & Riverside Counties

10391-A Friars Road   **San Diego**   (800) 993-1998

---

(5)   Indicates the number of years the person has been listed in our directory (not total years in business)

LDA#   Legal Document Assistants (LDAs) are not attorneys but can provide self-help services at your specific direction. LDAs must register in their counties unless working under the supervision of an attorney or a non-profit organization. The LDA numbers shown are for the county where the office is located. Professionals who are not LDAs do not need an LDA number.

C   Member of CALDA (California Association of Legal Document Assistants), an organization that promotes high standards in education, ethics and business practices. You can also find a member near you at their website, **www.calda.org**.

Look for your telephone area code. Cities in each area code are in alphabetical order.

A list of divorce services near you
also see latest list at www.nolodivorce.com/dir

Professionals who will help you do your own divorce

Legal Document Assistants, Mediators, Counselors,
Accountants, Financial Planners, Attorneys

A list of divorce services near you

Professionals who will help you do your own divorce
Legal Document Assistants, Mediators, Counselors, Accountants, Financial Planners, Attorneys

Free CD updates for 60 days
We guarantee that your Bonus CD is current or we will make it current for free if you include a copy of your sales receipt when you send the registration coupon below. It's okay to copy the coupon if you don't want to cut your book.

✂ Copy coupon if you want to save listings on previous page